P9-CEN-819

Diana Hacker

RULES FOR WRITERS

A Brief Handbook

Third Edition

Bedford Books of St. Martin's Press   Boston

For Bedford Books

President and Publisher: Charles H. Christensen
General Manager and Associate Publisher: Joan E. Feinberg
Managing Editor: Elizabeth M. Schaaf
Development Editor: Beth Castrodale
Editorial Assistant: Verity Winship
Production Editor: Michelle McSweeney
Copyeditor: Barbara G. Flanagan
Text design and typography: Claire Seng-Niemoeller
Cover design: Hannus Design Associates

For information write: St. Martin's Press, Inc.
175 Fifth Avenue, New York, NY 10010
Editorial Offices: Bedford Books *of* St. Martin's Press
75 Arlington Street, Boston, MA 02116

ISBN: 0–312–11966–6

Preface for Instructors

A decade ago, Bedford Books published the first edition of *Rules for Writers*, a brief handbook that later evolved into the longer *Bedford Handbook for Writers*. When Bedford recently proposed that we revive *Rules for Writers*, I was delighted, for the book is an old favorite of mine. It grew directly out of my classroom experience at Prince George's Community College, and I look forward to using it again in my classes at Prince George's. The brevity of *Rules for Writers* appeals to my students; so does its price.

When revising the book, I hoped to do more than bring back an old favorite. Today's computer-oriented students expect to get quick answers to their questions, so I have designed a system of graphic access through icons. I predict that the simplicity and familiarity of these icons will draw even unmotivated students into the book. And because there are only nine icons, each accompanied by a short title, *Rules for Writers* looks manageable — not too daunting.

Here are the book's principal features, beginning with the icons.

Graphic access through icons.   To help today's visually oriented students find the information they need, icons, like those on the toolbars of computer programs, are keyed to each part of *Rules for Writers*. The icons appear in six places: on the cover, in the brief menu inside the front cover, in the detailed menu inside the back cover, in the table of contents, on the part openers, and on the tabs on each left-hand page.

In most circumstances, the brief menu inside the front cover is the fastest way into the book. Designed for student use, it is as simple as possible, containing just the nine icons and sixty sections, with no subsections listed. By consulting this menu, students can usually locate the icon and the section number for the information they need. Then they can simply flip pages in search of the appropriate tabs. The tabs on the left-hand pages display the icons, and those on the right-hand pages give the section numbers.

At times students may want to use other reference features of *Rules for Writers*: the detailed menu inside the back cover, the index, the Glossary of Usage, or one of the book's directories to documentation models. "How to Use This Book" (pages xii–xix) describes these reference features and includes several tutorials that give students "hands on" experience using the book.

Comprehensive coverage and compact format. To make *Rules for Writers* brief, I have limited myself within each section to the essentials: straightforward rules backed up by concise explanations, realistic examples, and brief comments on examples. In its coverage, however, the book is complete. It is a guide to the full range of conventions of grammar, punctuation, mechanics, and usage as well as to the writing process, paragraphs, style, argument, research papers, business letters, résumés, and memos. The "Research Guide" includes the most recent versions of both the MLA and APA systems of parenthetical citations.

An emphasis on rules. As its title suggests, *Rules for Writers* focuses on rules rather than on grammatical abstractions. Though abstract section headings such as "parallelism" and "agreement" are understandable to instructors, they are not always clear to students. Rules such as "Balance parallel ideas" and "Make subjects and verbs agree" are clearer because they both identify the problem and tell students what to do about it.

Handbooks are by their very nature prescriptive, but that does not mean they must be unbending. Like other modern handbooks, *Rules for Writers* alerts students to levels of formality, rhetorical options, and current standards of usage. It distinguishes between rules intended as rhetorical advice and those that are more strictly matters of right and wrong.

A problem-solving approach to errors. Where relevant, *Rules for Writers* attends to the linguistic and social causes of errors and to the effects of errors on readers. The examples of errors in the text are realistic, most having been drawn from student papers and local newspapers. The text treats these errors as problems to be solved, often in light of rhetorical considerations, not as violations of a moral code. Instead of preaching at students, it shows them why problems occur, how to recognize them, and how to solve them.

Hand-edited sentences. Most examples appear as they would in a rough draft, with handwritten revisions made in color over typeset faulty sentences. Unlike the usual technique of printing separate incorrect and corrected versions of a sentence, hand-edited sentences highlight the difference between the two versions and suggest how extensive a change is required. Further, hand-edited sentences mimic the process of revision as it should appear in the students' own drafts.

Clear, uncluttered page design. Because the two-color page design highlights rules and hand-edited examples, *Rules for Writers* is easy to skim for quick answers to questions. Readers who want more help will find it in concise explanations following rules and in brief comments pegged to examples.

Extensive coverage of ESL problems. Three sections focus exclusively on common problems facing speakers of English as a second language. Section 29 discusses ESL problems with verbs; section 30 explains when to use the articles *a*, *an*, and *the*; and section 31 alerts ESL students to a variety of other potential trouble spots. ESL boxes throughout the book alert students to possible ESL problems; a quick-reference chart of these boxes appears at the back of the book.

Special attention to dialect differences. Section 27, "Choose standard English verb forms," helps students with such matters as omitted *-s* and *-ed* endings and omitted verbs, problems often caused by dialect differences. Section 17d, on nonstandard English, contains cross-references to practical advice that appears elsewhere in the book.

Straightforward advice on composing and revising. Instead of philosophizing about the writing process, *Rules for Writers* shows students, through a multiplicity of examples on a variety of topics, how to find a process that will work for them. The emphasis, throughout, is on flexibility.

"The Writing Process" includes three student essays, each accompanied by a draft or an outtake from a stage of the writing process.

Nine short sections on the research paper.   For easy reference, the "Research Guide" is broken up into nine short sections. The section on using the library emphasizes computerized library resources, including the Internet. The MLA and APA sections are up to date, and each documentation style is illustrated with a model research paper.

Other sections focus on matters most troublesome to students: choosing and narrowing a topic, crafting a thesis, citing sources, integrating quotations, and avoiding plagiarism at both the note-taking and the drafting stages.

Two sections on argument.   Using a process approach, section 46 shows students how to construct an argument that will have some hope of persuading readers who do not already agree with their views. The logical fallacies and common mistakes in inductive and deductive reasoning are in section 47.

A section on document design.   In both the business and the academic worlds, writers are becoming increasingly interested in document design — the use of visual cues to help readers. Section 4a, "Principles of document design," provides guidelines on selecting format options and using headings, displayed lists, and other visuals to make documents more effective. Section 4b includes both MLA and APA guidelines for preparing academic manuscripts. Section 4c gives advice on business letters, résumés, and memos.

Extensive exercises, some with answers.   At least one exercise set accompanies nearly every section of the book. Most sets begin with five lettered sentences that have answers in the back of the book so students can test their understanding independently. The sets continue with five or ten numbered sentences, the answers for which appear only in the instructor's edition so instructors may use the exercises in class or assign them as homework.

A user-friendly index. The index of *Rules for Writers* helps students find what they are looking for even if they don't know grammatical terminology. When facing a choice between *was* and *were*, for example, some students may not know to look up "Subject-verb agreement." To help such students, *Rules for Writers* includes index entries for "*was* versus *were*" and "*were* versus *was*." Similar user-friendly entries appear throughout the index.

A wide array of ancillaries. In addition to the instructor's edition, *Rules for Writers* is available with the following ancillary:

Developmental Exercises to Accompany Rules for Writers, by Wanda Van Goor and Diana Hacker

The publisher is also making available most of the resources accompanying *The Bedford Handbook for Writers*. These supplements can easily be used with *Rules for Writers* because its central section numbers (8–45) correspond with those in *The Bedford Handbook*. All of the ancillaries are free of charge to instructors, and some are available for student purchase as well.

PRACTICAL RESOURCES FOR INSTRUCTORS
Diagnostic Resources to Accompany The Bedford Handbook for Writers (with ESL versions)

Transparencies to Accompany The Bedford Handbook for Writers

PROFESSIONAL RESOURCES FOR INSTRUCTORS
Background Readings for Instructors Using The Bedford Handbook for Writers

The Bedford Guide for Writing Tutors

RESOURCES FOR STUDENTS
Supplemental Exercises for The Bedford Handbook for Writers (with Answer Key)

Resources for Research and Documentation across the Curriculum to Accompany The Bedford Handbook for Writers

Research Workbook for The Bedford Handbook for Writers

Preparing for the CLAST with The Bedford Handbook for Writers

Preparing for the TASP with The Bedford Handbook for Writers

SOFTWARE

Grammar Hotline for The Bedford Handbook for Writers (IBM and Mac versions)

Exercise Tutor for The Bedford Handbook for Writers (IBM and Mac versions)

MicroGrade: A Teacher's Gradebook (IBM and Mac versions)

Acknowledgments

I would like to thank the following reviewers for contributing useful insights based on their varied experiences in the classroom: Deborah Chappel, Arkansas State University; Sharon Emmons, Portland Community College; Joanne Ferreira, State University of New York, New Paltz; Margaret Fox, Oregon State University; Marjorie Ginsberg, William Paterson College; Fred Kemp, Texas Tech University; Judith Kohl, Dutchess Community College; Bill Lamb, Johnson County Community College; Marilyn McHugh, Ulster County Community College; Michael Robertson, Trenton State College; Ken Smith, Indiana University, South Bend; Laurel Smith, Vincennes University; Eileen Ward, College of Du Page; and Anita Wilkins, Cabrillo College.

Writing a handbook is truly a collaborative effort. Barbara Flanagan, Lloyd Shaw, William Peirce, Susan Roth, and Ruth Thomas helped me update the research paper chapters; William Peirce assisted with the chapter on argument.

I am indebted to the students whose essays appear in this edition — Gary Laporte, Karen Shaw, Marie Visosky, Tom Weitzel, and Diane Williford — not only for permission to use their work but for permission to adapt it for pedagogical purposes as well. My thanks also go to the following students for permission to use their paragraphs: Connie Hailey, Willam G. Hill, Patricia Klein, Linda Lavelle, Julie Reardon, Margaret Stack, and John Clyde Thatcher.

Several talented editors have made invaluable contributions to the book. Developmental editor Beth Castrodale has been a first-rate coach: insightful, tactful, and good humored. And she proved to have artistic talents as well; three of the book's icons came from her sketchpad. Copyeditor Barbara Flanagan has once again brought grace and consistency to the final manuscript, no small task in a handbook. I am also grateful to Andy Christensen for handling permissions and to Verity Winship and Kim Chabot for fielding a variety of problems too numerous to mention.

Book editor Michelle McSweeney has taken an active interest in all aspects of the book — from its design to its grammar — while guiding it expertly through production. Managing editor Elizabeth Schaaf orchestrated production of the book with unflappable calm. DeNee Reiton Skipper has handled the page make-up with expertise, and award-winning designer Claire Seng-Niemoeller once again deserves credit for designing the clean, uncluttered pages that highlight the book's hand-edited sentences.

Special thanks are due to publishers Chuck Christensen and Joan Feinberg. Ten years ago Chuck took a chance on an unknown community college professor with an inexplicable urge to write a handbook. I am deeply grateful to him for giving me this opportunity. In retrospect, I suppose Chuck knew that almost anyone could learn to write a handbook under the guidance of Joan Feinberg. Certainly a better teacher-editor could not have been found. Joan has consistently set a standard of excellence, and over the years she has nudged me toward it, always with intelligence, grace, and good humor. It would be impossible to overstate my gratitude.

Finally, a note of thanks goes to my mother, Georgiana Tarvin, and to Joseph and Marian Hacker, Robert Hacker, Greg Tarvin, Betty Renshaw, Bill Fry, Bill Mullinix, Joyce Magnotto, Christine McMahon, Anne King, Wanda Van Goor, Melinda Kramer, Joyce McDonald, Tom Henderson, the Dougherty family, and Robbie and Austin Nichols for their support and encouragement; and to the many students over the years who have taught me that errors, a natural by-product of the writing process, are simply problems waiting to be solved.

Diana Hacker

Prince George's Community College

How to Use This Book

Though it is small enough to hold in your hand, *Rules for Writers* will answer most of the questions you are likely to ask as you plan, draft, and revise a piece of writing: How do I choose and narrow a topic? What can I do if I get stuck? How do I know when to begin a new paragraph? Should I write *none was* or *none were*? When does a comma belong before *and*? What is the difference between *accept* and *except*? How do I cite a source with two authors?

How to find information with an instructor's help

When you are revising an essay that has been marked by your instructor, tracking down information is simple. If your instructor marks problems with a number such as *16* or a number and letter such as *12e*, you can turn directly to the appropriate section of the handbook. Just flip through the colored tabs on the upper corners of the pages until you find the number in question. The number *16*, for example, leads you to the rule "Tighten wordy sentences," and *12e* takes you to the subrule "Repair dangling modifiers." If your instructor uses an abbreviation such as *w* or *dm* instead of a number, consult the list of abbreviations and symbols on the page right before the back end-papers. There you will find the name of the problems (*wordy; dangling modifier*) and the number of the section to consult.

How to find information on your own

With a little practice, you will be able to find information in this book without an instructor's help — usually by tracking the icons that appear on the cover and inside the front cover. At times, you may want to consult the detailed menu inside the back cover, the index, the Glossary of Usage, or one of the directories to the documentation models.

The icons.   Because the icons are right on the cover, it won't take you long to become familiar with the organization of *Rules for Writers*. These icons also appear on a brief menu inside the front cover. Usually this menu is the fastest way into the book.

Let's say that you are having problems with run-on sentences. Your first step is to find the appropriate icon on the menu inside the front cover — in this case the checkmark for "Grammar." Next, find the appropriate numbered rule: "20 Revise run-on sentences." Finally, use the tabs on the upper right-hand corners of the pages to find section 20. The running head next to the tab ("Run-on sentences") will tell you that you are just where you want to be.

At times you can work straight from the icons on the cover. These icons appear on every left-hand page of the book and on the solid-color part openers. To look up correct uses of the semicolon, for example, you can find the traffic light icon (for "Punctuation") on the left-hand pages, and then, just by flipping, you can locate the appropriate running head ("The semicolon") on the right-hand pages.

The back endpapers.   The detailed menu appears inside the back cover. When the numbered section you're looking for is broken up into quite a few lettered subsections, try consulting this menu. For instance, if you have a question about the proper use of commas for items in a series, this menu will lead you quickly to section 32c.

The index.   If you aren't sure which topic to choose from one of the menus, consult the index at the back of the book. For example, you may not realize that the issue of *is* versus *are* is a matter of subject-verb agreement (section 21). In that case, simply look up "*is* versus *are*" in the index and you will be directed to the exact pages you need.

The Glossary of Usage.   When in doubt about the correct use of a particular word (such as *affect* and *effect*, *among* and *between*, or *hopefully*), consult the Glossary of Usage at the back of the book. This glossary explains the difference between commonly confused words; it also lists colloquialisms and jargon that are inappropriate in formal written English.

Directories to documentation models.   When you are documenting a research paper with either the MLA or the APA style, you can find appropriate documentation models by consulting the MLA or APA directory. The MLA directory is easy to find: Just look for the first of the pages marked with a vertical band of red. The APA directory appears on the first of the pages marked with a vertical band of gray.

How to use this book for self-study

In a composition class, most of your time should be spent writing. Therefore it is unlikely that you will want to study all of the chapters in this book in detail. Instead you should focus on the problems that tend to crop up in your own writing. Your instructor (or your college's writing center) will be glad to help you design an individualized program of self-study.

Rules for Writers has been designed so that you can learn from it on your own. By providing answers to some exercise sentences, it allows you to test your understanding of the material. Most exercise sets begin with five sentences lettered a–e and conclude with five or ten numbered sentences. Answers to the lettered sentences appear in an appendix at the end of the book.

Diana Hacker

Tutorials

The following tutorials will give you practice using the book's menus, index, Glossary of Usage, and MLA directory. Answers to all tutorials appear on pages xvii–xix.

TUTORIAL 1 Using the menus

Each of the following "rules" violates the principle it expresses. Using the brief menu inside the front cover or the more detailed menu inside the back cover, find the section in *Rules for Writers* that explains the principle. Then fix the problem. Examples:

> *Tutors in*
> ~~In~~ the writing center, ~~they~~ say that vague pronoun reference is
> ^
> unacceptable. **23**

> *come*
> Be alert for irregular verbs that have ~~came~~ to you in the wrong
>
> form. **27a**

1. A verb have to agree with its subject.
2. Each pronoun should agree with their antecedent.
3. About sentence fragments. You should avoid them.
4. Its important to use apostrophe's correctly.

5. In my opinion, I think a writer should not get in the habit of making use of too many unnecessary words that are not needed to put the message across.
6. Discriminate careful between adjectives and adverbs.
7. If your sentence begins with a long introductory word group use a comma to separate the word group from the rest of the sentence.
8. Don't write a run-on sentence, you must connect independent clauses with a comma and a coordinating conjunction or with a semicolon.
9. For clarity, a writer must be careful not to shift your point of view.
10. Do not capitalize a word just to make it look Important.

TUTORIAL 2   Using the index

Assume that you have written the following sentences and want to know the answers to the questions in brackets. Use the index at the back of the book to locate the information you need, and edit the sentences if necessary.

1. Anyone taking the school bus to the volleyball game must bring in a permission slip signed by their parents. [Does the pronoun *Anyone* agree with *their*? If not, what is the best way to fix the problem?]
2. We had intended to go surfing but spent most of our vacation lying on the beach. [Should I use *lying* or *laying*?]
3. We only looked at two houses before buying the house of our dreams. [Is *only* in the right place?]
4. In Saudi Arabia it is considered ill mannered for you to accept a gift. [Is it okay to use *you* to mean "anyone in general"?]
5. In Canada, Joanne picked up several bottles of maple syrup for her sister and me. [Should I write *for her sister and I*?]

TUTORIAL 3   Using the menus or the index

Imagine that you are in the following situations. Using either the menus or the index, find the information you need.

1. You are Ray Farley, a community college student who has been out of high school for ten years. You recall learning to punctuate items in a series by putting a comma between all items except the last two. In your college readings, however, you have noticed that most writers use a comma between all items. You're curious about the current rule. Which section of *Rules for Writers* will you consult?
2. You are Maria Sanchez, an honors student working in your university's writing center. Mike Lee, who speaks English as a second

language, has come to you for help. He is working on a rough draft that contains a number of problems involving the use of articles (*a, an,* and *the*). You know how to use articles, but you aren't able to explain the rather complicated rules on their correct use. Which section of *Rules for Writers* will you and Mike Lee consult?

3. You are John Pell, engaged to marry Jane Dalton. In a note to Jane's parents, you have written "Thank you for giving Jane and myself such a generous contribution toward our honeymoon trip to Hawaii." You wonder if you should write "Jane and I" or "Jane and me" instead. Upon consulting *Rules for Writers,* what do you learn?

4. You are Selena Young, an intern supervisor at a housing agency. Two of your interns, Jake Gilliam and Susan Green, have writing problems involving -*s* endings on verbs. Gilliam tends to drop -*s* endings; Green tends to add them where they don't belong. You suspect that both problems stem from nonstandard dialects spoken at home.

   Susan and Jake are in danger of losing their jobs because your boss thinks that anyone who writes "the tenant refuse" or "the landlords agrees" is beyond hope. You disagree. Susan and Jake are more intelligent than your boss supposes, and they have asked for your help. Where in *Rules for Writers* can they find the rules they need?

5. You are Joe Thompson, a first-year college student. Your girlfriend, Samantha, who has completed two years of college, seems to enjoy correcting your English. Just yesterday she corrected your sentence "I felt badly about her death" to "I felt bad about her death." You're sure you've heard many educated persons, including professors, say "I felt badly." Upon consulting *Rules for Writers,* what do you discover?

TUTORIAL 4   Using the Glossary of Usage

Consult the Glossary of Usage to see if the italicized words are used correctly. Then edit any sentences containing incorrect usage. Example:

an

The pediatrician gave my daughter ~~a~~ injection for her allergy.

1. Changing attitudes *toward* alcohol have *effected* the beer industry.
2. It is *mankind's* nature to think wisely and act foolishly.
3. This afternoon I plan to *lie* out in the sun and work on my tan.
4. Everyone in our office is *enthused* about this project.
5. Most sleds are pulled by no *less* than two dogs and no more than ten.

TUTORIAL 5   Using the directory to MLA documentation models

Assume that you have written a short research paper on the debate over the use of marijuana for medical purposes. You have cited the following sources in your paper, using MLA documentation, and you are ready to type your list of works cited. Turn to the first page marked with a vertical band of red and use the MLA directory to locate the appropriate models. Then write a correct entry for each source and arrange the entries in a properly formatted list of works cited. *Note:* Do not number the entries in a list of works cited.

A journal article by Gregg A. Bilz entitled "The Medical Use of Marijuana: The Politics of Medicine." The article appears on pages 117 to 135 of the *Hamline Journal of Public Law and Policy*, which is paginated by issue. The volume number is 13, the issue number is 1, and the year is 1992.

An unsigned magazine article entitled "Cross-Eyed and Painless." The article appears on page 89 of the July 6, 1991, issue of *The Economist*.

A book by Jack E. Henningfield and Nancy Almand Ator entitled *Barbiturates: Sleeping Potion or Intoxicant?* The book was published in Philadelphia in 1986 by Chelsea House Publishers.

A newspaper article by Michael Isikoff entitled "U.S. Provided Marijuana for Some AIDS Patients." The article appears on page A3 of the March 24, 1991, issue of the *Washington Post*.

A journal article by Gabriel Nahas and Colette Latour entitled "The Human Toxicity of Marijuana." The article appears on pages 495 to 497 of the *Medical Journal of Australia*, which is paginated by volume. The volume number is 156, and the year is 1992.

Answers to Tutorial 1

1. A verb has to agree with its subject. (21)
2. Each pronoun should agree with its antecedent. (22)
3. Avoid sentence fragments. (19)
4. It's important to use apostrophes correctly. (36)
5. Get rid of unnecessary words. (16)
6. Discriminate carefully between adjectives and adverbs. (26)
7. If your sentence begins with a long introductory word group, use a comma to separate the word group from the rest of the sentence. (32b)

8. Don't write a run-on sentence; you must connect independent clauses with a comma and a coordinating conjunction or with a semicolon. (20, also 32a and 34a)
9. For clarity, a writer must be careful to shift his or her [*not* their] point of view. *Or* For clarity, writers should be careful not to shift their point of view. (13a)
10. Do not capitalize a word just to make it look important. (45)

Answers to Tutorial 2

1. The index entry "*anyone*" mentions that the word is singular, so you might not need to look further to realize that the plural *their* is incorrect. The second page reference leads you to section 22, which suggests nonsexist strategies for revision, such as *Students taking the school bus to the volleyball game must bring in a permission slip signed by their parents* or *Anyone taking the school bus to the volleyball game must bring in a permission slip signed by his or her parents.*
2. The index entry "*lay, lie*" takes you to section 27b and to the Glossary of Usage, where you will learn that *lying* (meaning "reclining or resting on a surface") is correct.
3. Look up "*only*" and you will be directed to section 12a, which explains that limiting modifiers such as *only* should be placed before the words they modify. The sentence should read *We looked at only two houses before buying the house of our dreams.*
4. Looking up "*you*, inappropriate use of" leads you to section 23d and the Glossary of Usage, which explain that *you* should not be used to mean "anyone in general." You can revise the sentence by using *a person* or *one* instead of *you*, or you can restructure the sentence completely: *In Saudi Arabia, accepting a gift is considered ill mannered.*
5. The index entries "*I* versus *me*" and "*me* versus *I*" take you to section 24, which explains why *me* is correct.

Answers to Tutorial 3

1. Section 32c tells you that although usage varies, most experts advise using a comma between all items in a series — to prevent possible misreadings or ambiguities. To find this section, Ray Farley would probably use the menu system.
2. Maria Sanchez and Mike Lee would consult section 30, on articles. This section is easy to locate on the main menu.
3. Section 24 explains why "Jane and me" is correct. To find section 24, John Pell could use the menu system if he knew to look under "Problems with pronouns." Otherwise, he could look up "*I* versus

me" in the index. Pell could also look up "*myself*" in the index or he could consult the Glossary of Usage, where a cross-reference would direct him to section 24.

4. Selena Young's employees could turn to sections 21 and 27c for help. Young could use the menu system to find these sections if she knew to look under "Subject-verb agreement" or "Standard English verb forms." If she wasn't sure about the grammatical terminology, she could look up "-*s*, as verb ending" or "Verbs, -*s* forms of" in the index.

5. Section 26b explains why "I felt bad about her death" is correct. To find section 26b, Joe Thompson could use the menu system if he knew that *bad* versus *badly* is a choice between an adjective and an adverb. Otherwise he could look up "*bad, badly*" in the index or the Glossary of Usage.

Answers to Tutorial 4

1. Changing attitudes toward alcohol have *affected* the beer industry.
2. It is *human* nature to think wisely and act foolishly.
3. Correct.
4. Everyone in our office is *enthusiastic* about this project.
5. Most sleds are pulled by no *fewer* than two dogs and no more than ten.

Answers to Tutorial 5

Bilz, Gregg A. "The Medical Use of Marijuana: The Politics of Medicine." *Hamline Journal of Public Law and Policy* 13.1 (1992): 117-35.

"Cross-Eyed and Painless." *Economist* 6 July 1991: 89.

Henningfield, Jack E., and Nancy Almand Ator. *Barbiturates: Sleeping Potion or Intoxicant?* Philadelphia: Chelsea House, 1986.

Isikoff, Michael. "U.S. Provided Marijuana for Some AIDS Patients." *Washington Post* 24 Mar. 1991: A3.

Nahas, Gabriel, and Colette Latour. "The Human Toxicity of Marijuana." *Medical Journal of Australia* 156 (1992): 495-97.

Contents

Paragraphs   65

Clarity   91

Grammar   **149**

Punctuation 243

Mechanics   289

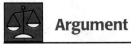

Argument   313

Research Guide 331

The Basics 421

The Writing
Process

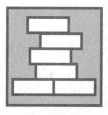

Since it's not possible to think about everything all at once, most experienced writers handle a piece of writing in stages. Roughly speaking, those stages are planning, drafting, and revising. You should generally move from planning to drafting to revising, but be prepared to circle back to earlier stages whenever the need arises.

1

Generate ideas and sketch a plan.

Before attempting a first draft, spend some time generating ideas. Mull over your subject while listening to music or driving to work, jot down inspirations on scratch paper, and explore your insights with anyone willing to listen. At this stage you should be collecting information and experimenting with ways of focusing and organizing it to best reach your readers.

1a Assess the writing situation.

Begin by taking a look at the writing situation in which you find yourself. The key elements of the writing situation include your subject, the sources of information available to you, your purpose, your audience, and constraints such as length, document design, and deadlines.

It is unlikely that you will make final decisions about all of these matters until later in the writing process — after a first draft, for example. Nevertheless, you can save yourself time by thinking about as many of them as possible in advance. For a quick checklist, see pages 10–11.

Subject

Frequently your subject will be given to you. In a psychology class, for example, you might be asked to explain Bruno Bettelheim's Freudian analysis of fairy tales. Or in a course on the history of filmmaking, you might be assigned an essay on the political impact of D. W. Griffith's silent film *The Birth of a*

Nation. In the business world, your assignment might be to draft a quarterly sales report or craft a diplomatic letter to a customer who has complained about your firm's computer software.

Sometimes you will be free to choose your own subject. Then you will be wise to select a subject that you already know something about or one that you can reasonably investigate in the time you have. Students in composition classes have written successfully on all of the subjects listed here, most of which were later narrowed into topics suitable for essays of 500–750 words. By browsing through the lists, perhaps you can pick up some ideas of your own.

Education: computers in the classroom, an inspiring teacher, sex education in junior high school, magnet schools, a learning disability such as dyslexia, programmed instruction, parochial schools, teacher certification, a local program to combat adult illiteracy, creative means of funding a college education

Careers and the workplace: working in an emergency room, the image versus the reality of a job such as lifeguarding, a police officer's workday, advantages of flextime for workers and employers, company-sponsored day care, mandatory drug testing by employers, sex or racial discrimination on the job, the psychological effects of unemployment, the rewards of a part-time job such as camp counseling

Families: an experience with adoption, a portrait of a family member who has aged well, the challenges facing single parents, living with an alcoholic, a portrait of an ideal parent, growing up in a large family, the problems of split custody, an experience with child abuse, the depiction of male-female relationships in a popular TV series, expectations versus the reality of marriage, overcoming sibling rivalry, the advantages or disadvantages of being a twin

Health: a vegetarian diet, weight loss through hypnotism, benefits of acupuncture, a fitness program for the elderly, reasons not to smoke, the rights of smokers or nonsmokers, overcoming an addiction, Prozac as a treatment for depression, the side effects of a particular treatment for cancer, life as a diabetic, the benefits of an aerobic exercise such as swimming, caring for a person with AIDS

Sports and hobbies: an unusual sport such as free-fall parachuting or bungee jumping, surviving a wilderness program, bodybuilding, a sport from another culture, the philosophy of karate, the language of sports announcers, pros and cons of banning boxing, coaching a Little League team, cutting the costs of an expensive sport such as skiing, a portrait of a favorite sports figure, sports for the handicapped, the discipline required for a sport such as gymnastics, the rewards of a hobby such as woodworking

The arts: working behind the scenes at a theater, censorship of rock and roll lyrics, photography as an art form, the Japanese tea ceremony, the influence of African art on Picasso, the appeal of a local art museum, a portrait of a favorite musician or artist, performing as a musician, a high school for the arts, the colorization of black-and-white films, science fiction as a serious form of literature, a humorous description of romance novels or hard-boiled detective thrillers

Social justice: an experience with racism or sexism, affirmative action, reverse discrimination, making public transportation accessible for the physically handicapped, an experience as a juror, a local program to aid the homeless, discrimination against homosexuals, pros and cons of a national drinking age of twenty-one

Death and dying: working on a suicide hotline, the death of a loved one, a brush with death, caring for terminally ill patients, the Buddhist view of death, explaining death to a child, passive euthanasia, death with dignity, an out-of-body experience

Violence and crime: an experience with a gun, a wartime experience, violence on television news programs, visiting a friend in prison, alternative sentencing for first offenders, victims' rights, a successful program to eliminate violence in a public high school, domestic violence and the courts

Nature and ecology: safety of nuclear power plants, solar energy, wind energy, air pollution in our national parks, forest fires on the California coast, communication among dolphins, organic gardening, backpacking in the Rockies, marine ecology, an experimental farming technique, cleaning up Boston Harbor, the preservation of beaches in Delaware

Many of these subjects are too broad. Part of your challenge as a writer will be whittling broad subjects down to manageable topics. If you are limited to a few pages, for example, you could not possibly do justice to a subject as broad as "sports for the handicapped." You would be wise to restrict your paper to a topic more manageable in the space allowed —

perhaps a description of the Saturday morning athletic program your college offers for handicapped children.

Sources of information

Where will your facts, details, and examples come from? Can
your topic be illustrated by personal experience, or will you
need to search out relevant information through direct observation, interviews, questionnaires, or reading?

PERSONAL EXPERIENCE   You can develop many topics
wholly through personal experience, depending of course on
your own life experiences. The students who wrote about lifeguarding, learning disabilities, weight loss through hypnotism,
and free-fall parachuting all spoke with the voice of experience, as did those who wrote about flextime, coaching a Little
League team, and company-sponsored day care. When narrowing their subjects, those students chose to limit themselves
to information they had at hand. For example, instead of writing about company-sponsored day care in general — a subject
that would have required a great deal of research — one student limited her discussion to the successful day care center at
the company for which she worked.

DIRECT OBSERVATION   Direct observation is an excellent
means of collecting information about a wide range of subjects, such as parent-child relationships on the television program *The Simpsons*, the language of sports announcers, or the
appeal of a local art museum. For such subjects, do not rely on
your memory alone; your information will be fresher and
more detailed if you actively collect it, with a notebook or tape
recorder in hand. As writer Stuart Chase advises young journalists assigned to report on their city's water system, "You will
write a better article if you heave yourself out of a comfortable
chair and go down in tunnel 3 and get soaked."

INTERVIEWS AND QUESTIONNAIRES   Interviews and questionnaires can supply you with detailed and interesting information on a variety of subjects. A nursing student interested in the
care of terminally ill patients might interview nurses at a hos-
pice; a political science major might speak with a local judge to
learn about alternative sentencing for first offenders; a future

teacher might conduct a survey on the classroom use of computers in local schools. It is a good idea to tape interviews to preserve any lively quotations that you might want to weave into your essay. Keep questionnaires simple and specify a deadline to ensure that you get a reasonable number of responses.

   READING   Reading will be your primary source of information for many college assignments, which will generally be of two kinds: analytical assignments that call for a close reading of one book, essay, or literary work or research assignments that send you to the library to consult a variety of sources on a particular topic. For analytical essays, you can usually assume that your reader is familiar with the work and has a copy of it at hand. You select details from the work not to inform readers but to support an interpretation. When you quote from the work, page references are often sufficient. For research papers, however, you cannot assume that your reader is familiar with your sources or has them close at hand. This means that you must formally document all quoted and summarized or paraphrased material (see 53). When in doubt about the need for formal documentation, consult your instructor.

Purpose

Your purpose will often be dictated by the specific writing situation that faces you. Perhaps you have been asked to take minutes for a club meeting, to draft a letter requesting payment from a client, or to describe the results of a biology experiment. Even though your overall purpose is fairly obvious in such situations, a close look at that purpose can help you make a variety of necessary decisions. How detailed should the minutes be? Is your purpose to summarize the meeting or to establish a careful record of discussion in case future controversies arise? How firmly should your letter request payment? Do you need the money at all costs, or do you hope to get it without risking loss of the client's business? How technical is the biology report expected to be?

   In many writing situations, part of your challenge will be discovering a purpose. Consider, for example, the topic of magnet schools — schools that draw students from different neighborhoods because of features such as advanced science classes or late-afternoon day care. Your purpose could be to inform parents of the options available in your county. Or you might argue that the county's magnet schools are not promoting racial integration as had been planned. Or you might propose that the board of education create a magnet high school for the arts on your college campus.

Although no precise guidelines will lead you to a purpose, you can begin by asking yourself which one or more of the following aims you hope to accomplish.

PURPOSES FOR WRITING

to inform	to evaluate
to persuade	to recommend
to call readers to action	to request
to change attitudes	to propose
to analyze	to provoke thought
to argue	to express feelings
to theorize	to entertain
to summarize	to give aesthetic pleasure

It is surprising how often writers misjudge their own purposes: informing, for example, when they should be recommending; summarizing when they should be analyzing; or expressing feelings about problems instead of proposing solutions. Before beginning any writing task, therefore, pause to ask, "Why am I communicating with my readers?" And this question will lead you to another important question: "Just who are those readers?"

Audience

Audience analysis can often lead you to an effective strategy for reaching your readers. One writer, whose purpose was to persuade teenagers not to smoke, jotted down the following observations about her audience:

dislike lectures, especially from older people
have little sense of their own mortality
are concerned about physical appearance and image
want to be socially accepted
have limited budgets

This analysis led the writer to focus more on the social aspects of smoking (she pointed out, for instance, that kissing a smoker is like licking an ashtray) than on the health risks. Her audience analysis also warned her against adopting a preachy tone that her readers might find offensive. Instead of lecturing to her audience, she decided to draw examples from her own experience as a hooked smoker: burning holes in her best sweater, driving in zero-degree weather late at night in search of an open tavern to buy cigarettes, rummaging through ashtrays for stale butts, and so on. The result was an essay that reached its readers instead of alienating them.

The following checklist will help you decide how to approach your audience.

AUDIENCE CHECKLIST

How well informed are your readers about the subject?

What do you want them to learn about the subject?

How interested and attentive are they likely to be?

Will they resist any of your ideas?

What is your relationship to them: Employee to supervisor? Citizen to citizen? Expert to novice? Scholar to scholar?

How much time are they willing to spend reading?

How sophisticated are they as readers? Do they have large vocabularies? Can they follow long and complex sentences?

Of course, in some writing situations the audience will not be neatly defined for you. Nevertheless, many of the choices that you make as you write will tell readers who you think they are (novices or experts, for example), so it is best to be consistent — even if this means creating an audience that is in some sense a fiction.

Writers in the business world often find themselves writing for multiple audiences. A letter to a client, for instance, might be distributed to sales representatives as well. Readers of a report may include persons with and without technical expertise or readers who want details and those who prefer a quick overview. To satisfy the demands of multiple audiences, business writers have developed a variety of strategies: attaching cover letters to more detailed reports, adding boldface headings, placing summaries in the left margin, and so on.

In the academic world, considerations of audience can be more complex than they seem at first. Your professor will read your essay, of course, but most professors play multiple roles while reading. Their first and most obvious roles are as coach and judge; less obvious is their role as an intelligent and objective reader, the kind of person who might reasonably be informed, convinced, entertained, or called to action by what you have to say.

Some professors create writing assignments that specify an audience, such as a hypothetical supervisor, readers of a local newspaper, or fellow academics in a particular field of study. Other professors expect you to imagine an audience appropriate to your purpose and your subject. Still others prefer that you write for a general audience of educated readers — nonspecialists who can be expected to read with an intelligent, critical eye. When in doubt about an appropriate audience for a particular assignment, check with your professor.

Length, document design, and deadlines

Writers seldom have complete control over length, document design, and deadlines. Journalists usually write within strict word limits set by their editors, businesspeople routinely aim for conciseness, and most college assignments specify an approximate length.

Certain document designs may also be required by your writing situation. Specific formats are used in the business world for documents such as letters, memos, reports, budget analyses, and personnel records. In the academic world, you may need to learn precise conventions for lab reports, critiques, research papers, and so on. For most undergraduate essays, a standard essay format is acceptable (see 4b).

In some writing situations, you will be free to create your own document design, complete with headings, displayed lists, and perhaps even visuals, such as charts and graphs. Quite sophisticated results are now possible on computers, and both writers and readers are becoming increasingly interested in designs that improve readability. For a discussion of the principles of document design, see 4a.

A final constraint is the deadline. The deadline tells you what is possible and helps you plan your time. For complex writing projects, such as research papers, you'll need to manage your time quite carefully. By working backward from the deadline, you can create a schedule of target dates for completing various parts of the process. See page 332 for an example.

Checklist for assessing the writing situation

At the beginning of the writing process, you may not be able to answer all of the questions on this checklist. That's fine. Just be prepared to think about them later.

NOTE: It is not necessary to think about the elements of a writing situation in the exact order listed in this chart.

SUBJECT

—Has a subject (or a range of possible subjects) been given to you, or are you free to choose your own?

—Is your subject worth writing about? Can you think of any readers who might be interested in reading about it?

—How broadly can you cover the subject? Do you need to narrow it to a more specific topic (because of length restrictions, for instance)?

—How detailed should your coverage be?

SOURCES OF INFORMATION

—Where will your information come from: Personal experience? Direct observation? Interviews? Questionnaires? Reading?

—If your information comes from reading, what sort of documentation is required?

PURPOSE

—Why are you writing: To inform readers? To persuade them? To entertain them? To call them to action? Some combination of these?

AUDIENCE

—How well informed are your readers about the subject?

—What do you want them to learn about the subject?

—How interested and attentive are they likely to be?

—Will they resist any of your ideas?

—What is your relationship to them: Employee to supervisor? Citizen to citizen? Expert to novice? Scholar to scholar?

—How much time are they willing to spend reading?

Checklist (continued)

—How sophisticated are they as readers? Do they have large vocabularies? Can they follow long and complex sentences?

LENGTH

—Are you working with any length specifications? If not, what length seems appropriate, given your subject, your purpose, and your audience?

DOCUMENT DESIGN

—Must you use a particular design for your document? If so, do you have guidelines or examples that you can consult?

DEADLINE

—What is your deadline? How much time will you need to allow for the various stages of writing, including typing and proofreading the final draft?

EXERCISE 1–1

Choose one of the subject areas mentioned on pages 3–4 and add at least five subjects to those already on the list. If other members of your class have also done this exercise, pool the results.

EXERCISE 1–2

Narrow five of the following subjects into topics that would be manageable for an essay of two to five pages.

1. Working behind the scenes at a theater
2. A sport from another culture
3. Violence between parents and children
4. The advantages or disadvantages of being a twin
5. An experience with adoption
6. Benefits of acupuncture
7. Computers in the classroom
8. Parochial schools
9. Performing as a musician
10. An experience with racism or sexism

EXERCISE 1–3

Which of the following subjects might be illustrated wholly by personal experience? For the others, suggest possible sources of information: direct observation, interviews, questionnaires, or reading.

1. The problems of split custody
2. Working in an emergency room
3. Backpacking in the Rockies
4. The influence of African art on Picasso
5. Violence on television news programs
6. The discipline required for a sport such as gymnastics
7. Photography as an art form
8. Affirmative action
9. A local program to aid the homeless
10. Visiting a friend in prison

EXERCISE 1–4

Suggest a purpose and audience for five of the following subjects.

1. A vegetarian diet
2. Cutting the costs of an expensive sport such as skiing
3. The challenges facing single parents
4. Advantages of flextime for workers and employers
5. Growing up in a large family
6. Pros and cons of a national drinking age of twenty-one
7. Science fiction as a serious form of literature
8. Free-fall parachuting or bungee jumping
9. A police officer's workday
10. Working on a suicide hotline

1b Experiment with ways to explore your subject.

Instead of just plunging into a first draft, experiment with one or more techniques for exploring your subject, perhaps one of these:

listing	keeping a journal
clustering or branching	talking
asking questions	planning on a word processor
freewriting	

For writing based on reading, note taking is also a useful technique (see 51).

Whatever technique you turn to, the goal is the same: to generate a wealth of ideas. At this early stage of the writing process, you should aim for quantity, not necessarily quality, of ideas. If an idea proves to be off the point, trivial, or too far-fetched, you can always throw it out later.

Listing

You might begin by simply listing ideas, putting them down in the order in which they occur to you — a technique sometimes known as "brainstorming." Here, for example, is a list one student writer jotted down:

> Lifeguarding — an ideal summer job?
>
>> my love of swimming and lying in the sun
>>
>> hired by Powdermill Village, an apartment complex
>>
>> first, though, there was a test
>>
>> two weeks of training — grueling physical punishment plus book work
>>
>> I passed. The work was over — or so I thought.
>>
>> greeted by manager; handed a broom, hose, disinfectant
>>
>> scrubbing bathrooms, cleaning the pool, clearing the deck of dirt and leaves
>>
>> little kids breaking every pool rule in the book — running on deck, hanging on buoyed ropes, trying to drown each other
>>
>> spent most of my time blowing the whistle
>>
>> working the evening shift no better — adults smuggling in gin and tonics, sexual advances from married men
>>
>> by end of day, a headache and broom-handled hands

The ideas appear here in the order in which they first occurred to the writer. Later she felt free to rearrange them, to cluster them under general categories, to delete some, and to add others. In other words, she treated her initial list as a source of ideas and a springboard to new ideas, not as an outline.

Clustering or branching

Unlike listing, the techniques of clustering and branching highlight relations among ideas. To cluster ideas, write your topic in the center of a sheet of paper, draw a circle around it, and surround that with related ideas connected to it with lines. If some of the satellite ideas lead to more specific clusters, write them down as well. The writer of the following diagram was exploring ideas for an essay on home uses for computers.

To use the branching technique, put the main idea at the top of a page and then list major supporting ideas beneath it, leaving plenty of space between ideas. To the right of each major idea, branch out to minor ideas, drawing lines to indicate the connections. If minor ideas lead to even more specific ideas, continue branching. Here, for example, is a branching diagram for an essay describing an innovative magnet high school called "School without Walls."

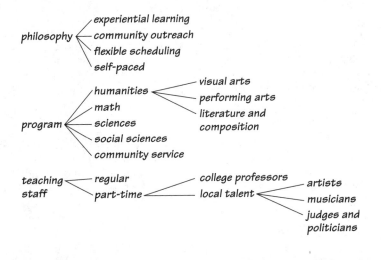

Asking questions

By asking relevant questions, you can generate many ideas — and you can make sure that you have adequately surveyed your subject. When gathering material for a story, journalists routinely ask themselves Who? What? When? Where? Why? and How? In addition to helping journalists get started, these questions ensure that they will not overlook an important fact: the date of a prospective summit meeting, for example, or the exact location of a neighborhood burglary.

Whenever you are writing about events, whether current or historical, the journalist's questions are one way to get started. One student, whose subject was the negative reaction in 1915 to D. W. Griffith's silent film *The Birth of a Nation,* began exploring her topic with this set of questions:

> *Who* objected to the film?
>
> *What* were the objections?
>
> *When* were protests first voiced?
>
> *Where* were protests most strongly expressed?
>
> *Why* did protesters object to the film?
>
> *How* did protesters make their views known?

In the academic world, scholars often generate ideas with questions related to a specific discipline: one set of questions for analyzing short stories, another for evaluating experiments in social psychology, still another for reporting field experiences in anthropology. If you are writing in a particular discipline, try to discover the questions that scholars typically explore. These are frequently presented in textbooks as checklists.

Freewriting

In its purest form, freewriting is simply nonstop writing. You set aside ten minutes or so and write whatever comes to you, without pausing to think about word choice, spelling, or even meaning. If you get stuck, you can write about being stuck, but you should keep your pencil moving. The point is to loosen up, relax, and see what happens. Even if nothing much happens, you have lost only ten minutes. It's more likely, though, that something interesting will emerge on paper — perhaps an eloquent sentence, an honest expression of feeling, or a line of thought worth exploring.

Keeping a journal

A journal is a collection of personal, exploratory writings. An entry in a journal can be any length — from a single sentence to several pages — and it is likely to be informal and experimental.

In a journal, meant for your eyes only, you can take risks. In one entry, for example, you might do some freewriting or focused freewriting. In another, you might pose a series of interesting questions, whether or not you have the answers. In still another, you might play around with language for the sheer fun of it: writing "purple prose," for instance, or parodying the style of a favorite author or songwriter.

Keeping a journal can be an enriching experience in its own right, since it allows you to explore issues of concern to you without worrying about what someone else thinks. A journal can also serve as a sourcebook of ideas to draw on in future essays; on rare occasions, in fact, a journal entry may emerge as a polished essay of interest to readers other than yourself. Some writers find that they do their best work when writing for themselves, deliberately ignoring the constraints of a formal writing situation.

Talking

The early stages of the writing process need not be lonely. Many writers begin a writing project by brainstorming ideas in a group, debating a point with friends, or engaging in conversation with a professor. Others turn to themselves for company — by talking nonstop into a tape recorder.

Talking can be a good way to get to know your audience. If you're planning to write a narrative, for instance, you can test its dramatic effect on a group of friends. Or if you hope to advance a certain argument, you can try it out on listeners who hold a different view.

As you have no doubt discovered, conversation can deepen and refine your ideas before you even begin to set them down on paper. Our first thoughts are not necessarily our wisest thoughts; by talking and listening to others we can all stretch our potential as thinkers and as writers.

Planning on a word processor

You can list or "brainstorm" ideas as easily on a word processor as with pencil and paper, especially if you are a fast typist.

Later you can delete ideas, add others, and rearrange the order, all with a few keystrokes.

If you like to begin a writing task by asking yourself questions, consider keeping sets of questions on file in your computer. A college student, for example, might use one set of questions for writing about literature, another for science reports, another for case studies in sociology or psychology, and so on. In some disciplines, software is available with sets of questions developed by experts in the field. Check with a professor or with your school's writing center to learn about such software.

Although the computer can be a useful tool for planning, its advantages over pencil and paper should not be overstated. Many writers find that they plan just as easily with pencil and paper; they turn to the computer primarily for drafting and revising.

EXERCISE 1–5

Generate a list of at least fifteen items for one of the subjects listed on pages 3–4.

EXERCISE 1–6

Using the technique of clustering or branching, explore one of the subjects listed on pages 3–4.

1c Settle on a tentative focus.

As you explore your subject, you will begin to see possible ways to focus your material. At this point, try to settle on a tentative central idea.

For many types of writing, your central idea can be asserted in one sentence, a generalization preparing readers for the supporting details that will follow. Such a sentence, which will ordinarily appear in the opening paragraph of your finished essay, is called a *thesis*. A successful thesis — like the following, all taken from articles in *Smithsonian* — points both the writer and the reader in a definite direction.

> Much maligned and the subject of unwarranted fears, most bats are harmless and highly beneficial.

> Geometric forms known as fractals may have a profound effect on how we view the world, not only in art and film but in many branches of science and technology, from astronomy to economics to predicting the weather.

> Aside from his more famous identities as colonel of the Rough Riders and President of the United States, Theodore Roosevelt was a lifelong professional man of letters.

The thesis sentence usually contains a key word or controlling idea that limits its focus. The preceding sentences, for example, prepare for essays that focus on the *beneficial* aspects of bats, the *effect* of fractals on how we view the world, and Roosevelt's identity as a writer, or *man of letters*.

It's a good idea to formulate a thesis early in the writing process, perhaps by jotting it on scratch paper, by putting it at the head of a rough outline, or by attempting to write an introductory paragraph that includes the thesis. Your tentative thesis will probably be less graceful than the thesis you include in the final version of your essay. Here, for example, is one student's early effort:

> Although they both play percussion instruments, drummers and percussionists are very different.

The thesis that appeared in the final draft of the student's paper was more polished:

> Two types of musicians play percussion instruments — drummers and percussionists — and they are as different as Quiet Riot and the New York Philharmonic.

Don't worry too soon about the exact wording of your thesis, however, because your main point may change as your drafts evolve. (See 2a and 3b.)

For some types of writing, it may be difficult or impossible to express the central idea in a thesis sentence; or it may be unwise or unnecessary to put a thesis sentence in the paper itself. A personal narrative, for example, may have a focus too subtle to be distilled in a single sentence, and such a sentence might ruin the story. Strictly informative writing, like that found in many business memos, may be difficult to summarize in a thesis. In such instances, do not try to force the central idea into a thesis sentence. Instead, think in terms of an overriding purpose, which may or may not be stated directly in the paper itself.

1d Sketch a tentative plan.

Once you have generated some ideas and formulated a tentative thesis, you may want to sketch an informal outline. Informal outlines can take many forms. Perhaps the most common is simply the thesis followed by a list of major supporting ideas.

Hawaii is losing its cultural identity.

— pure-blooded Hawaiians increasingly rare

— native language diluted

— native Hawaiians forced off ancestral lands

— little emphasis on native culture in schools

— customs exaggerated and distorted by tourism

Clustering or branching diagrams, often used to generate ideas, can also serve as rough outlines (see pages 13 and 14). And if you began by jotting down a list of ideas (see page 13), you may be able to turn the list into a rough outline by crossing out some ideas, adding others, and rearranging the ideas in a logical order.

When to use a formal outline

Early in the writing process, rough outlines have certain advantages over their more formal counterparts: They can be produced more quickly, they are more obviously tentative, and they can be revised more easily should the need arise. However, a formal outline may be useful later in the writing process, after you have written a rough draft, especially if your subject matter is complex.

The following formal outline brought order to a complex subject, methods for disposing of nuclear waste. Notice that the student's thesis is an important part of the outline. Everything else in the outline supports it, either directly or indirectly.

Thesis: Although various methods for disposing of nuclear waste have been proposed, each has serious drawbacks.

I. Antarctic ice sheet disposal is problematic for scientific and legal reasons.
   A. Our understanding of the behavior of ice sheets is too limited.
   B. An international treaty prohibits disposal in Antarctica.

II. Space disposal is unthinkable.
   A. The risk of an accident and resulting worldwide disaster is great.
   B. The cost is prohibitive.
   C. The method would be unpopular at home and abroad.

III. Seabed disposal is unwise because we do not know enough about the procedure or its impact.
   A. Scientists have not yet solved technical difficulties.
   B. We do not fully understand the impact of such disposal on the ocean's ecology.

IV. Deep underground disposal endangers public safety and creates political problems.
   A. Geologists disagree about the safest disposal sites, and no sites are completely safe.
   B. There is much political pressure against the plan from citizens who do not want their states to become nuclear dumps.

In constructing a formal outline, keep the following guidelines in mind.

1. Put the thesis at the top.
2. Make items at the same level of generality as parallel as possible (see 9).
3. Use sentences unless phrases are clear.
4. Use the conventional system of numbers and letters for the levels of generality.

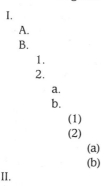

   I.
     A.
     B.
       1.
       2.
         a.
         b.
           (1)
           (2)
             (a)
             (b)
   II.

5. Always use at least two subdivisions for a category, since nothing can be divided into fewer than two parts.
6. Limit the number of major sections in the outline; if the list of roman numerals begins to look like a laundry list, find

some way of clustering the items into a few major categories with more subcategories.

7. Be flexible; in other words, be prepared to change your outline as your drafts evolve.

2

Rough out an initial draft.

As you rough out an initial draft, keep your planning materials—lists, diagrams, outlines, and so on—close at hand. In addition to helping you get started, such notes and blueprints will encourage you to keep moving. Writing tends to flow better when it is drafted relatively quickly, without many starts and stops.

For most kinds of writing, an introduction announces a main idea, several body paragraphs develop it, and a conclusion drives it home. You can begin drafting, however, at any point.

2a For most types of writing, draft an introduction that includes a thesis.

For most writing tasks, your introduction will be a paragraph of 50 to 150 words. Perhaps the most common strategy is to open the paragraph with a few sentences that engage the reader and to conclude it with a statement of the essay's main point. The sentence stating the main point is called a *thesis*. (See 1c.) In each of the following examples, the thesis has been italicized.

> To the Australian aborigines, the Dreamtime was the time of creation. It was then that the creatures of the earth, including man, came into being. There are many legends about that mystical period, but unfortunately, the koala does not fare too well in any of them. *Slow-witted though it is in life, the koala is generally depicted in myth and folklore as a trickster and a thief.*
> —Roger Caras, "What's a Koala?"

> When I was sixteen, I married and moved to a small town to live. My new husband nervously showed me the house he had rented. It was after dark when we arrived there, and I remember wondering why he seemed so apprehensive about my reaction to the house. I thought the place seemed shabby but potentially cozy and quite livable inside. The morning sun revealed the reason for his anxiety by exposing the squalor outdoors. Up to that point, my contact with any reality but that of my own middle-class childhood had come from books. *The next four years in a small Iowa town taught me that reading about poverty is a lot different from living with it.*   —Julie Reardon, student

Ideally, the sentences leading to the thesis should hook the reader, perhaps with one of the following:

a startling statistic or unusual fact

a vivid example

a description

a paradoxical statement

a quotation or bit of dialogue

a question

an analogy

a joke or an anecdote

Such hooks are particularly important when you cannot assume your reader's interest in the subject. Hooks are less necessary in scholarly essays and other writing aimed at readers with a professional interest in the subject.

Although the thesis frequently appears at the end of the introduction, it can just as easily appear at the beginning. Much work-related writing, in which a straightforward approach is most effective, commonly begins with the thesis.

> *Flextime scheduling, which has proved its effectiveness at the Library of Congress, should be introduced on a trial basis at the main branch of the Montgomery County Public Library.* By offering flexible work hours, the library can boost employee morale, cut down on absenteeism, and expand its hours of operation.
>   —David Warren, student

In narrative and descriptive writing, it is not always necessary to have an explicitly stated thesis. (See 1c.) However, an introduction without a thesis should clearly suggest the purpose and direction of the essay to follow.

Characteristics of an effective thesis

An effective thesis should be a generalization, not a fact; it should be limited, not too broad; and it should be sharply focused, not too vague.

Because a thesis must prepare readers for facts and details, it cannot itself be a fact. It must always be a generalization demanding proof or further development.

> **TOO FACTUAL** The first polygraph was developed by Dr. John A. Larson in 1921.
>
> **REVISED** Because the polygraph has not been proved reliable, even under the most controlled conditions, its use by private employers should be banned.

Although a thesis must be a generalization, it must not be *too* general. You will need to narrow the focus of any thesis that you cannot adequately develop in the space allowed. Unless you were writing a book or a very long research paper, the following thesis would be too broad.

> **TOO BROAD** Many drugs are now being used successfully to treat mental illnesses.

You would need to restrict the thesis, perhaps like this:

> **REVISED** Despite its risks and side effects, lithium is an effective treatment for depression.

Finally, a thesis should be sharply focused, not too vague. Beware of any thesis containing a fuzzy, hard-to-define word such as *interesting*, *good*, or *disgusting*.

> **TOO VAGUE** Many of the songs played on station WXQP are disgusting.

The word *disgusting* is needlessly vague. To sharpen the focus of this thesis, the writer should be more specific.

> **REVISED** Of the songs played on station WXQP, all too many depict sex crudely, sanction the beating or rape of women, or foster gang violence.

In the process of making a too-vague thesis more precise, you may find yourself outlining the major sections of your paper, as in the preceding example. This technique, known as *blueprinting*, helps readers know exactly what to expect as they read on. It also helps you, the writer, control the shape of your essay.

2b Fill out the body.

Before drafting the body of an essay, take a careful look at your introduction, focusing especially on your thesis sentence. What does the thesis promise readers? Try to keep this focus in mind.

It's a good idea to have a plan in mind as well. If your thesis sentence outlines a plan (see 2a) or if you have sketched a preliminary outline, try to block out your paragraphs accordingly. If you do not have a plan, you would be wise to pause for a moment and sketch one (see 1d). Of course it is also possible to begin without a plan—assuming you are prepared to treat your first attempt as a "discovery draft" that will almost certainly be tossed (or radically rewritten) once you discover what you really want to say.

2c Attempt a conclusion.

The conclusion should echo the main idea, without dully repeating it. Often the concluding paragraph can be relatively short. By the end of the essay, readers should already understand your main point; your conclusion simply drives it home and perhaps suggests its significance.

In addition to echoing your main idea, a conclusion might summarize the essay's key points, pose a question for future study, offer advice, or propose a course of action. To end an essay detailing the social skills required of a bartender, one writer concludes with some advice:

> If someone were to approach me one day looking for the secret to running a good bar, I suppose I would offer the following advice: Get your customers to pour out their ideas at a greater rate than you pour out the liquor. You will both win in the end. —Kathleen Lewis, student

To make the conclusion memorable, consider including a detail, example, or image from the introduction to bring readers full circle; a quotation or bit of dialog; an anecdote; or a humorous, witty, or ironic comment. To end a narrative describing a cash register holdup, one student uses an anecdote that includes some dialogue:

> It took me a long time to get over that incident. Countless times I found myself gasping as someone "pointed" a dollar bill at me. On one such occasion, a jovial little man buying a toy gun for his son came up to me and said in a Humphrey Bogart impression, "Give me all your money, Sweetheart." I didn't laugh. Instead, my heart skipped a beat, for I had heard those words before.
> —Diana Crawford, student

Whatever concluding strategy you choose, avoid introducing wholly new ideas at the end of an essay. Also avoid apologies and other limp, indeterminate endings. The essay should end crisply, preferably on a positive note.

3

Make global revisions first; then revise sentences.

For experienced writers, revising is rarely a one-step process. The larger elements of writing generally receive attention first—the focus, organization, paragraphing, content, and overall strategy. Improvements in sentence structure, word choice, grammar, punctuation, and mechanics come later.

3a Make global revisions: Think big.

Global revisions address the larger elements of writing. Usually they affect chunks of text longer than a sentence, and frequently they can be quite dramatic. Whole paragraphs might be dropped, others added. Material once stretched over two or three paragraphs might be condensed into one. Entire sections might be rearranged. Even the content may change dramatically, for the process of revising stimulates thought.

Many of us resist global revisions because we find it difficult to distance ourselves from a draft. We tend to review our work from our own, not from our audience's, perspective.

To distance yourself from a draft, put it aside for a while, preferably overnight or even longer. When you return to it, try to play the role of your audience as you read. If possible, enlist the help of reviewers — persons willing to play the role of audience for you. Ask your reviewers to focus on the larger issues of writing, not on the fine points. The following checklist may help them get started.

Checklist for global revision

PURPOSE AND AUDIENCE

— Does the draft accomplish its purpose — to inform readers, to persuade them, to entertain them, to call them to action (or some combination of these)?

— Is the draft appropriate for its audience? Does it take into consideration the audience's knowledge of the subject, level of interest in the subject, and possible attitudes toward the subject? Is the reading level appropriate?

FOCUS

— Do the introduction and conclusion focus clearly on the main point?

— Are any ideas obviously off the point?

ORGANIZATION AND PARAGRAPHING

— Can readers follow the overall structure?

— Are ideas ordered effectively?

— Does the paragraphing make sense?

— Are any paragraphs too long or too short for easy reading?

CONTENT

— Is the supporting material persuasive?

— Which ideas need further development?

— Are the parts proportioned sensibly? Do major ideas receive enough attention?

— Where might material be deleted?

Making global revisions on a word processor

The word processor is an excellent tool for revision because it allows you to make changes quickly and easily. Let's assume that you have typed and saved your rough draft on a computer equipped with word processing software. You have printed a copy of the draft, reviewed it for global revisions, and indicated on it where you need to add, delete, and move chunks of text.

Once you have called up the text onto the computer screen, you move the cursor to the place where you want to add, delete, or move text. Most word processing programs allow you to add text simply by typing it in and to delete text by hitting a delete key. Moving blocks of text usually requires several computer commands and is relatively simple.

Because the computer saves time, it encourages you to experiment with global revisions. Should you combine two paragraphs? Would your conclusion make a good introduction? Might several paragraphs be rearranged for greater impact? Will boldface headings improve readability? With little risk, you can explore the possibilities. When a revision misfires, it is easy to restore your original draft.

3b Revise and edit sentences.

Most of the rest of this book offers advice on revising sentences for clarity and on editing them for grammar, punctuation, and mechanics. The process of revising and editing sentences should ordinarily occur right on the pages of a draft.

deciding
Finally ~~we decided~~ that perhaps our dream
                    ^
needed ~~some~~ prompting, ~~and~~ we visited a fertility
                         ^
doctor and began the expensive, time-consuming
                              ^ *some*
round of procedures that held out ~~the~~ promise of
our dream's fulfillment. Our efforts, however, were ^
~~fulfilling our dream. All this was~~ to no avail/.
As ^   ^
~~and as~~ we approached the sixth year of our mar-
     ^   *could no longer*
riage, we ~~had reached the point where we couldn't~~
          ^
even discuss our childlessness without becoming

very depressed. We questioned why this had

```
happened to us?.    Why had we been singled out
      such a
for this major disappointment?
```

The original paragraph was flawed by wordiness and an excessive reliance on structures connected with *and*. Such problems can be addressed through any number of acceptable revisions. The first sentence, for example, could have been changed like this:

```
Finally we decided that perhaps our dream needed
                        After visiting
some prompting,.  and we visited a fertility doc-
      we
tor, and began the expensive, time-consuming round
                        promised hope
of procedures that held out the promise of ful-

filling our dream.
```

Though some writers might argue about the effectiveness of these improvements compared with the previous revision, most would agree that both revisions are better than the original.

Some of the paragraph's improvements involve less choice and are less open to debate. For example, the hyphen in *time-consuming* is necessary, and the question mark in the next to last sentence must be changed to a period.

As it details the various rules for revising and editing sentences, this handbook suggests when an improvement is simply one among several possibilities and when it is more strictly a matter of right and wrong.

Making sentence-level revisions on a word processor

Some writers handle sentence-level revisions directly at the computer, but most prefer to print out a hard copy of the draft, mark it up, and then return to the computer. Once you've indicated changes on the hard copy, you can enter them into the computer in a matter of minutes.

Software can provide help with sentence-level revisions. Many word processing programs have spelling checkers that will catch most but not all spelling errors, and some have thesauruses to help with word choice. Other programs, called *text analyzers* or *style checkers*, will flag a variety of possible problems: wordiness, jargon, weak verbs, long sentences, and so on. Be aware, however, that a text analyzer can only point out *possible* problems. It can tell you that a sentence is long, for example, but you must decide whether your long sentence is effective.

3c Proofread the final manuscript.

After revising and editing, you are ready to prepare the final manuscript. (See 4b for guidelines.) At this point, make sure to allow yourself enough time for proofreading—the final and most important step in manuscript preparation.

Proofreading is a special kind of reading: a slow and methodical search for misspellings, typographical mistakes, and omitted words or word endings. Such errors can be difficult to spot in your own work because you may read what you intended to write, not what is actually on the page. To fight this tendency, try proofreading out loud, articulating each word as it is actually written. You might also try proofreading your sentences in reverse order, a strategy that takes your attention away from the meanings you intended and forces you to think about small surface features instead.

Although proofreading may be dull, it is crucial. Errors strewn throughout an essay are distracting and annoying. If the writer doesn't care about this piece of writing, thinks the reader, why should I? A carefully proofread essay, on the other hand, sends a positive message: It shows that you value your writing and respect your readers.

WRITING ASSIGNMENTS AND MODEL ESSAYS

Expository student essay: Explaining an insight

Gary Laporte, who wrote "Televised Sports—A Win or a Loss?" (pages 34–36), was responding to the following assignment.

> **ASSIGNMENT: EXPLAINING AN INSIGHT**
> When you explain an insight on a topic, you offer readers a fresh or interesting way of looking at it. In other words, you give them a way of understanding something that they may have understood differently before.

You might challenge a conventional view that has not been validated by your own experience: the view, for example, that growing up in a small town is idyllic or that work as a flight attendant is glamorous. You might explain an insight about a group with which you are familiar: Harley-Davidson bikers, farmers, the physically challenged, people from another culture. You might give readers a new way of looking at some aspect of the media: maybe by poking fun at the language of sports announcers, revealing stereotypes in a television series, explaining why *Star Trek* has had such lasting appeal, or showing that the history of rap music is more complex than most people think. Or you might give readers an insight into one of your special interests, such as photography, mountain climbing, or one of the martial arts.

Your insight should appear in a thesis sentence early in the essay, most likely at the end of the introductory paragraph (see pages 21–24 of *Rules for Writers*). For this assignment, your information should come from personal knowledge, interviews, or direct observation. Aim for an essay from 500 to 1,000 words long — from two to four typed pages, double-spaced.

Laporte thought about the assignment for several days, but he was unable to come up with a subject. He was still pondering the question when he watched a basketball play-off game on television. Besides interviewing the stars of each team, the sportscaster spoke with a ten-year-old fan whose ambition was to become a famous athlete. Why famous? thought Laporte. Why not a *good* athlete? Don't people who see games on TV understand that winning depends on good play and teamwork, not on competing with one another for fame and the camera's attention?

Laporte decided that television sports might make a good essay subject since he knew something about it. He jotted down ideas during breaks in the game and came up with the following list:

Cooperation should be focus, not competition

TV creates stars — cameras follow them, commentators interview them

TV doesn't show whole game, only most dramatic shots, slow-motion replays

More people admire sports stars than admire the president of U.S.

Sports stars make more money than president, also do commercials for money

Money becomes purpose of sport

Sports should represent American values — teamwork, shared enthusiasm — easier to see in live games where spectators participate

Cheering, choosing what to watch, buying beer & hot dogs, catching fly balls

Later, Laporte reread his list and concluded that his focus should be the effect of television on both athletes and spectators. With this focus in mind, he formulated a tentative thesis and sketched a rough outline.

Although it is convenient, TV creates a distance between the sport and its fans and between the athletes and the team.

— television's convenience to fans
  — no need to travel and spend money
  — ability to see more games

— television's damage to sports
  — creates distance between the sport and fans
  — creates distance between the athletes and the team

Working from his list and outline, Laporte wrote a rough draft. He wrote quickly, focusing more on his ideas than on grammar, punctuation, and spelling. Pages 32 and 33 show Laporte's global and sentence-level revisions of his first page. Laporte's final draft appears on pages 34–36.

EXAMPLE OF GLOBAL REVISIONS

Sports on TV--A Win or a Loss?

Team sports are as much a part of Americain life as Mom and apple pie, and they have a good tendency to bring people together. They encourage team members to cooperate with one another, they also create shared enthusiasm among fans. Thanks to television, this togetherness now seems available to nearly all of us at the flick of a switch. We do not have to buy tickets, and travel to a stadium, to see the World Series or the Super Bowl, these games are on television. We can enjoy the game in the comfort of our own living room. ~~After Thanksgiving or Christmas dinner, the whole family may gather around the TV set to watch football together.~~ It would appear that television has done us a great service. But is this really the case? *Although television does make sports more accessible, it also creates a distance between the sport and the fans and between athletes and the teams they play for.*

The advantage of television is that it provides sports fans with greater convenience.

[insert]

We can see more games than if we had to attend each one in person, and we can follow a greater variety of sports.

EXAMPLE OF SENTENCE-LEVEL REVISIONS

Televised
Sports ~~on TV~~--A Win or a Loss?

Team sports~~,~~ ~~are~~ as much a part of American
tend
life as Mom and apple pie. ~~and they have a good~~
us
~~tendency~~ to bring ~~people~~ together. They encourage
and
team members to cooperate with one another, they ~~also~~

create shared enthusiasm among fans. ~~Thanks to~~
Because of
television, this togetherness now seems available ~~to~~
twist of a dial.
~~nearly all of us~~ at the ~~flick of a switch. It would~~

~~appear that television has done us a great service.~~

But is this really the case? Although television
makes
~~does make~~ sports more accessible, it also creates a

distance between the sport and the fans and between
their
athletes and ~~the~~ teams. ~~they play for.~~

The advantage of television is that it provides

sports fans with greater convenience. We do not

have to buy tickets / and travel to a stadium / to see
but
the World Series or the Super Bowl / ~~these games are~~
any
~~on television.~~ We can enjoy ~~the~~ game in the comfort
rooms.
of our own living ~~room.~~ We can see more games than

if we had to attend each one in person, and we can
a   *variety*
follow greater ~~varieties~~ of sports.

LAPORTE'S FINAL DRAFT

Televised Sports--A Win or a Loss?

Team sports, as much a part of American life as Mom and apple pie, tend to bring us together. They encourage team members to cooperate with one another, and they create shared enthusiasm among fans. Because of television, this togetherness now seems available at the twist of a dial. But is this really the case? Although television makes sports more accessible, it also creates a distance between the sport and the fans and between athletes and their teams.

The advantage of television is that it provides sports fans with greater convenience. We do not have to buy tickets and travel to a stadium to see the World Series or the Super Bowl but can enjoy any game in the comfort of our own living rooms. We can see more games than if we had to attend each one in person, and we can follow a greater variety of sports.

The price paid for this convenience, however, is high. Television changes the role of the fans who watch the game, making their participation more passive and distant. As television spectators, we see only what the camera shows. Yes, we do get a clearer look at important plays, and if we miss a detail, the commentator's explanation or the instant replay will fill us in. But we have no choice about what to watch. We cannot decide to follow the wide receiver rather than the quarterback or to watch a batter warming up rather than a commercial. Moreover, we miss all the sights, sounds, and smells that link live viewers with the players and with one another. When a fly ball comes over the fence, we cannot try to catch it. The roar of cheers after a touchdown is less exciting from the living room sofa than from the bleachers. We may feel silly cheering at all, since there is no chance those tiny figures on the screen will hear us.

The distance television has created between viewers and players does little more than reduce excitement and perhaps cheapen the experience of watching a game, but the unwholesome gap television creates between athletes and their teams threatens the foundation of team sports. Teamwork has always been paramount in team sports; the goals of the group have always overshadowed personal ambition. Television cameras, however, find it more dramatic to focus on individuals rather than on something as intangible as teamwork. In addition, the economics of television advertising and of team sports as big business create a situation in which players compete with one another for astronomical salaries and the chance to endorse products on television commercials.

Not surprisingly, the competition fostered by television causes players to try to make themselves look good, sometimes at the expense of the team. For example, a basketball player might take--and miss--a difficult shot instead of passing the ball to a teammate left unguarded closer to the basket. Or a star hockey player might work behind the scenes to keep a promising rookie from replacing him.

Team sports are a major part of American life, all the more so since television has brought them into our homes. The challenge for sports fans is to support their favorite teams in ways that encourage the best values represented by sports. One way to do this is to attend more live games rather than watch games on television. Attendance at live games may give the teams, the players, and the television networks the message that teamwork, not individual achievement and financial success, is what matters most about sports.

Descriptive student essay: Profiling a person or a place

Diane Williford, who wrote "Grandpa" (pages 38–40), was responding to the following assignment.

> **ASSIGNMENT: PROFILING A PERSON OR A PLACE**
>
> A profile describes a person or a place—not just in general, but with a particular focus. You might focus on a person's interesting job, hobby, or lifestyle. You might write about someone who has made a major contribution to his or her community, church, place of employment, or organization; someone who has overcome a problem such as anorexia or a learning disability; or someone who played a significant role in your growing up. You could profile someone you do not admire: an abusive parent, for example, or a childhood friend who joined a violent gang.
>
> If you'd rather profile a place, consider taking readers into an unfamiliar or exotic world—a scuba diving expedition, a spelunking adventure, a boat trip through the Everglades. Encourage readers to visit a favorite museum, historic district, or park (or discourage them from visiting a place you found disappointing). Introduce readers to a foreign country or an ethnic neighborhood with which you are familiar.
>
> Unless you have a good reason for omitting it, include a thesis sentence in your introductory paragraph, probably at its end (see pages 21–24 of *Rules for Writers*). For this assignment, your information should come from personal knowledge, interviews, or direct observation. Aim for an essay from 500 to 1,000 words long—two to four typed pages, double-spaced.

Through the process of freewriting, Diane Williford discovered the person she wanted to write about: her grandfather.

WILLIFORD'S FREEWRITING

Someone who played a significant role in my growing up.

Mother--no.

Father--no.

Grandmother: Taught me to be independent, to fight, to be a good mother (children always come first). No emotions, no time for children. Making money to take care of the family.

Grandfather: Always gave me time, never tried to influence me, taught me to think for myself, spoiled me.

I was raised by my grandmother in a small town in Virginia. She didn't believe in spoiling children, she believed children should be seen only when necessary, heard not at all, and given only the basics--food and clothes, a roof, a good spanking. My grandmother wasn't the type to talk much to children unless she wanted to show you something. If you didn't do it right the first time, she made you start over again until you got it right, and the only right was her right.

Grandpa was the quiet one, he was a big black man--strong and proud. Since he and grandmother had divorced before I came along, I didn't see him except on weekends. But he always made them special. I can't say if he was as smart as my grandmother was, she owned her own business, he worked for a living. But he always tried to answer my questions and he had time to listen to me.

A lot of what I know about my grandfather's past, I learned from other people. I know he fled from North Carolina in the middle of the night with his family, because he had married a near-white woman and the police and Klan were always stopping him and harassing him. I know he once shot a man dead who kept robbing his house. I know he broke a bone in his leg and never reported it to his job because jobs were scarce and he was scared he would lose it and not be able to take care of his family.

Of the two grandparents, I guess I remember my
grandfather most fondly. He's old now and lives in a
nursing home. He's still special, he's still my
grandpa.

In addition to doing freewriting, Diane Williford recalled
memories of her grandfather by telling her sons about him and
by placing a long-distance phone call to Grandpa himself.

When she sat down to write a rough draft, Williford found
that the words came quite easily. The draft expressed pretty
much what she wanted to say, but Williford saw room for
improvements. She revised the introduction, completely rewrote
the conclusion, and deleted a weak paragraph in the middle of
the essay. Then she polished sentences to make them tighter
and more emphatic and corrected a few problems with grammar
and punctuation. Here is her final draft.

WILLIFORD'S FINAL DRAFT

Grandpa

I don't have a lot of fantastic memories of
childhood. There were no spectacular family adventures, no unique family projects that taught some sort
of moral lesson, no out-of-the-ordinary holidays. We
ate family meals together, but most of the time the
children and adults lived in different worlds. The
kids went to school, did homework, and played; the
adults worked. I was lucky, though. When I wanted a
little of both worlds, I could always turn to Grandpa.

I remember vividly the weekends at his house.
Sitting on his lap, going to wrestling matches, walking
down the street or through a park--these were things I
did with Grandpa. I wasn't just a kid to him: I was his
granddaughter, and I was special. He was special too.

Thomas D. Williford was a giant of a man. He stood
six feet two inches and weighed over 250 pounds. He
moved with purpose and carried himself with respect.

Tom was a proud man, a good man, and all who knew him
said so. Even if you didn't know him, you would notice
his inner strength, his patience, his self-esteem.

Grandpa wasn't a scholar. In fact, he didn't even
make it through grade school. He was born at the turn
of the century, and educating black men wasn't a neces-
sity then. He went to work when he was sixteen, and
for the next forty years he worked in a coal factory.
Then he worked in a steel mill for another twenty
years. He stopped working only because the steel mill
closed and he was too old to find another job.

When I was with Grandpa, I could be a child and
yet see things through grown-up eyes. "You see that
tree, Cookie," he would say. "That tree was here
before those houses. God put that tree there; man
put the houses. Which is more beautiful?" If I
climbed a tree, he didn't say, "Get down." He said,
"Climb it right so you won't fall."

"You appreciate what you work for," he used to
say. He taught that lesson well. He never let me
win any game; he taught me to win by learning to
lose. If he couldn't answer a question, he was honest about it, but he would also say, "Why don't you
find out and let me know too." He listened to me and
he heard my feelings, not just my words.

There was a tougher side to Grandpa, and I suppose this, too, made him special. There was the
black man who fled with his near-white wife and children from North Carolina to avoid harassment and
threats from the Ku Klux Klan. There was the quiet
man whose home was robbed three times by the same
drunk, who reported it three times to the police with
no results, and who finally waited for the man to do

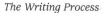
it a fourth time--and shot him dead as he climbed through the bedroom window in the middle of the night. And there was the man who fractured his leg at work, never reported it because he couldn't afford not to work, and years later still endures the pain of the ill-mended fracture.

Grandpa is almost ninety-five and now resides in a nursing home in Windsor, North Carolina. The leg he fractured forty years ago is too weak to carry his weight. His eyes are going bad. But to me he's still the big, strong man who used to take his grand-child in his arms and rock her, the man who taught a small child to see all the things around her with open eyes, the man who taught a child to try until she wins and becomes the best. He's still special and, thanks to him, so am I.

Narrative student essay: Re-creating an experience

Marie Visosky, who wrote "Orphaned at Five" (pages 42–44), was responding to the following assignment.

ASSIGNMENT: RE-CREATING AN EXPERIENCE

A narrative essay re-creates an experience for a central purpose: usually to reveal an insight about the action or people involved. You might write about an experience in which you encountered people from a culture different from your own. You might write about a turning point in your life — perhaps a time when you were forced suddenly to grow up, a time when you faced a diffi-cult challenge, or a time when you reassessed your values. You might describe an experience in which you learned to do some-thing new: coaching a Little League team, designing stage sets for a play, forming a musical group. Or you might recount an adven-ture that tested you in some way. If you have experienced work in an emergency room, on an ambulance or fire truck, or as a police officer, you might describe in vivid detail one day or eve-ning at work to give readers an inside view of this stressful job.

A narrative should have a central focus, but it is not always necessary to express the focus in a thesis sentence early in the essay (see pages 21–22 of *Rules for Writers*); at times you will want to get right to the action. A narrative should of course be based on personal experience. Aim for an essay from 500 to 1,000 words long—two to four typed pages, double-spaced.

When Marie Visosky read the narrative writing assignment, she knew immediately what she would write about. On a Thanksgiving Day when she was only five years old, she learned that both of her parents had been killed in an automobile crash. Although the memories were painful, Visosky wanted to show what the experience was like for a child too young to understand what was happening to her.

Because Visosky knew so much about her topic and because organizing the essay chronologically was easy, her first draft didn't need much global revision. She condensed the introduction and made a few cuts to tighten the narrative. Once she had completed her second draft, she turned her attention to revising and editing sentences for greater effectiveness. Here are the sentence-level changes Visosky made in the first four paragraphs of her third draft.

VISOSKY'S SENTENCE-LEVEL REVISIONS

Celery sticks ~~made great~~ *served as slugger* bats; olives were ^*substituted for baseballs*^
~~just the right size ball~~ to be smashed across the
^
kitchen. Cousins Sonny and Guido were pitcher and

catcher, and my sister Dorrie was a combination of

infield and outfield. I came up to bat for the first

time just as Gramps called for us to come into the

living room.

~~There was a~~ *A* policeman ~~standing~~ *stood* in the doorway.
^ ^
Nonnie and Aunt Sandy were crying. All morning we

had been told to stop touching the Thanksgiving
we would be punished.
dinner or ~~we'd get into a lot of trouble.~~ Who
^
expected to go to jail because of olives!

Gramps pulled Dorrie and me onto his lap and
hugged us close. "Your momma and daddy were going to
get Uncle Vince and a truck hit their car. God took
them to heaven." He started to cry. I wished he
would let us down. His sweater ~~was prickly,~~ and his
mouth was purple from wine.

(edits above the line: "prickly smelled of tobacco," inserted with carets)

Dorrie and I went home with Aunt Sandy. My
stomach was hurting and making noises, ~~Everybody~~ was
crying so I was afraid to say I was hungry.

(edits above the line: "tiger" and "but everybody" inserted with carets)

VISOSKY'S FINAL DRAFT

Orphaned at Five

Celery sticks served as slugger bats; olives substituted for baseballs to be smashed across the kitchen.
Cousins Sonny and Guido were pitcher and catcher, and my
sister Dorrie was a combination of infield and outfield.
I came up to bat for the first time just as Gramps
called for us to come into the living room.

A policeman stood in the doorway. Nonnie and Aunt
Sandy were crying. All morning we had been told to stop
touching the Thanksgiving dinner or we would be punished. Who expected to go to jail because of olives!

Gramps pulled Dorrie and me onto his lap and
hugged us close. "Your momma and daddy were going to
get Uncle Vince and a truck hit their car. God took
them to heaven." He started to cry. I wished he
would let us down. His prickly sweater smelled of
tobacco, and his mouth was purple from wine.

Dorrie and I went home with Aunt Sandy. My stomach was hurting and making tiger noises, but everybody
was crying so I was afraid to say I was hungry.

In the morning we went to a dark room where Mother and Daddy were lying in coffins. It smelled so sweet in that room, and the red-glassed candles burning everywhere made it sticky hot. Mother wore a lacy pink dress. A pink satin blanket covered her feet. Daddy looked so white, as if he wore makeup like Mother. Folded newspapers were hidden inside his trouser legs.

At night we all knelt down on the blue carpet and prayed a long, long time with Father Minnorra from Our Lady of the Angels Church. My knees were sore and I shifted my weight from one leg to the other. Aunt Sandy touched my shoulder and said, "Marie, stop that rocking. Kneel up."

The morning of the funeral was very bright. The curtains were opened in the coffin room. Aunt Sandy held my hand. She wore a black hat with a big black feather. Her eyes had big red circles around them, and her mouth was bright red. She reminded me of the clown in my circus coloring book.

Aunt Sandy kissed Daddy and lifted me to do the same. I touched his cheek. His skin was stiff. I kissed his forehead. We moved to Mother. Aunt Sandy lifted me again. I kissed Mother, then stood on the kneeler. I moved down and lifted the pink satin cover. Mother's shoes were pink. I moved back toward her head. Touching, touching as I went. Her hair was soft. Her lips were not soft. I pressed her mouth. It was tight. I pushed my fingers into her mouth. I saw and felt cotton. Aunt Sandy pulled me away.

A man in striped pants pulled down the backs of the coffins. Nonnie was crying. Gramps was blowing his nose. Someone took Dorrie and me to a big car. We sat on two little pull-down seats behind the driver.

At the cemetery everyone was crying and praying.
Aunt Sandy fainted when the two men with ropes lowered the coffins into the graves. Father Minnorra
gave Dorrie and me each a white flower. Mine was
turning brown and its petals were falling. I gave
the flower to Gramps so I could put my cold hands in
my coat pockets.

4

Choose an appropriate document design.

The term *document* is broad enough to describe anything you
might write in an English class, in other classes across the curriculum, in the business world, and in everyday life. How you
design a document (format it on the page) can affect how it is
received.

Instructors have certain expectations about how a college
paper should look (see 4b). Employers too expect documents
such as business letters and memos to be formatted in standard ways (see 4c). Although formatting documents is often a
matter of following conventions, there is some room for cre-
ativity — as current interest in document design attests (see 4a).

4a Become familiar with the principles of document design.

Well-designed documents — such as memos, résumés, manuals, and reports — have always been important in the business
world, where writers must compete for the attention of readers. By using lists, headings, and a variety of visual cues, business and technical writers make documents accessible to all
segments of an audience: readers who want a quick overview,
those who are scanning for specific information, those who
need in-depth coverage of a topic, and so on.

Document design is becoming increasingly important in
the academic world as well. The information explosion has

placed unprecedented demands on instructors' and students' time, so professional articles and student essays must be as accessible as possible. Fortunately, today's computers and printers provide academic writers with design strategies that were once prohibitively expensive. With access to software, a student can enhance an essay with boldface headings, formally displayed lists, and even graphs, charts, and other visuals.

Good document design promotes readability, but what this means depends on your purpose and audience and perhaps on other elements of your writing situation, such as your subject and any length restrictions. (See the checklist on pages 10–11.) All of your design choices — word processing options and use of headings, displayed lists, and other visuals — should be made in light of your specific writing situation.

Format options

Most typewriters and word processors present you with several format options. Before you begin typing, you should make sure that your margins, line spacing, and justification are set appropriately. If a number of fonts (typeface styles and sizes) are available, you should also determine which is most appropriate for your purposes.

MARGINS, LINE SPACING, AND JUSTIFICATION For documents written on 8 1/2" × 11" paper, you should leave a margin of between one and one and a half inches on all sides of the page. These margins prevent the text from looking too crowded, and they allow room for annotations, such as an instructor's comments or an editor's suggestions.

Most manuscripts-in-progress are double-spaced to allow room for editing. Final copy is often double-spaced as well, since single-spacing is less inviting to read. But at times the advantages of double-spacing are offset by other considerations. In a business memo, for example, you may single-space to fit the memo on one easily scanned page. And in a technical report, you might single-space to save paper, for both ecological and financial reasons.

Word processors usually give you a choice between a justified and an unjustified (ragged) right margin. When the text is justified, all of the words line up against the right margin, as they do on a typeset page like the one you are now reading. Unfortunately, text that has been justified on a word processor can be hard to read. The problem is that extra space is added between words in some lines, creating "rivers" of white that can be quite distracting. In addition, right-justified margins may create a need for excessive hyphenation at the ends of lines. Unless you have the technology to create the real look of a typeset page, you should turn off the justification feature.

FONTS   If you have a choice of fonts, you should select a normal size (10 to 12 points) and a style that is not too offbeat. Although unusual styles of type, such as those that look hand-written, may seem attractive, they slow readers down. We all read more efficiently when a text meets our usual expectations.

CAUTION: Never write or type a college essay or any other document in all capital letters. Research shows that readers experience much frustration when they are forced to read more than a few words in a row printed in all capital letters.

Headings

There is little need for headings in short essays, especially if the writer uses paragraphing and clear topic sentences to guide readers. In more complex documents, however, such as research papers, grant proposals, and business reports, headings can be a useful visual cue for readers.

Headings help readers see at a glance the organization of a document. If more than one level of heading is used, the headings also indicate the hierarchy of ideas — as they do throughout this book.

Headings serve a number of functions, depending on the needs of different readers. When readers are simply looking up information, headings will help them find it quickly. When readers are scanning, hoping to pick up the gist of things, headings will guide them. Even when readers are committed enough to read every word, headings can help. Efficient readers preview a document before they begin reading; when previewing and while reading, they are guided by any visual cues the writer provides.

CAUTION: Avoid using more headings (or more levels of headings) than you really need. Excessive use of headings can make a text choppy.

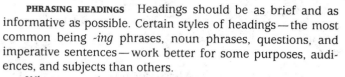

PHRASING HEADINGS Headings should be as brief and as informative as possible. Certain styles of headings—the most common being *-ing* phrases, noun phrases, questions, and imperative sentences—work better for some purposes, audiences, and subjects than others.

Whatever style you choose, use it consistently for headings on the same level. In other words, headings on the same level of organization should be written in parallel structure (see 9), as in the following examples. The first set of headings appeared in a report written for an environmental think tank, the second in a history textbook, the third in a mutual fund brochure, and the fourth in a garden designer's newsletter.

-ING HEADINGS
Safeguarding the earth's atmosphere

Charting the path to sustainable energy

Conserving global forests

Triggering the technological revolution

Strengthening international institutions

NOUN PHRASE HEADINGS
The economics of slavery

The sociology of slavery

Psychological effects of slavery

QUESTIONS AS HEADINGS
How do I buy shares?

How do I redeem shares?

What is the history of the fund's performance?

What are the tax consequences of investing in the fund?

IMPERATIVE SENTENCES AS HEADINGS
Fertilize roses in the fall.

Feed them again in the spring.

Prune roses when dormant and after flowering.

Spray roses during their growing season.

PLACING AND HIGHLIGHTING HEADINGS Headings on the same level of organization should be positioned and highlighted in a consistent way. For example, you might center your first-level headings and print them in boldface; then you might place the second-level headings flush left (against the left margin) and underline them, like this:

First-level heading

Second-level heading

Headings are usually centered or placed flush left, but at times you might decide to indent them five spaces from the left margin, like a paragraph indent. Or in a business document, you might place headings in a column to the left of the text.

To highlight headings, consider using boldface, italics, all capital letters, color, larger or smaller typeface than the text, a different font, or some combination of these:

boldface

italics

underlining

ALL CAPITAL LETTERS

color

larger typeface

smaller typeface

different font

On the whole, it is best to use restraint. Excessive highlighting results in a page that looks too busy, and it defeats its own purpose, since readers have trouble sorting out which headings are more important than others.

Important headings can be highlighted by using a fair amount of white space around them. Less important headings can be downplayed by using less white space or even by running them in with the text (as with the small all-capitals heading on page 49 of this section).

Displayed lists

Lists are easy to read or scan when they are displayed rather than run into your text. You might reasonably choose to display the following kinds of lists:

    — steps in a process

    — materials needed for a project

— parts of an object

— advice or recommendations

— items to be discussed

— criteria for evaluation (as in checklists)

Displayed lists should usually be introduced with an independent clause followed by a colon (see 35a and the above list). Periods are not used after items in a list unless the items are sentences.

Lists are most readable when they are presented in parallel grammatical form (see 9). In the sample list, for instance, the items are all noun phrases. As with headings, some kinds of lists might be more appropriately presented as *-ing* phrases, as imperative sentences, or as questions.

To draw the reader's eye to a list, consider using bullets (circles or squares) or dashes if there is no need to number the items. If there is some reason to number the items, use an arabic number followed by a period for each item.

Although displayed lists can be a useful visual cue, they should not be overdone. Too many of them will give a document a choppy, cluttered look. And lists that are very long (sometimes called "laundry lists") should be avoided as well. Readers can hold only so many ideas in their short-term memory, so if a list grows too long, you should find some way of making it more concise or clustering similar items.

Visuals

Visuals such as charts, graphs, tables, diagrams, maps, and photographs convey information concisely and vividly. In a student essay not intended for publication, you can use another person's visuals as long as you credit the borrowing (see 53). And with access to computer graphics, you can create your own visuals to enhance an essay or a report.

This section suggests when charts, graphs, tables, and diagrams might be appropriate for your purposes. It also discusses where you might place such visuals.

USING CHARTS, GRAPHS, TABLES, AND DIAGRAMS   In documents that help readers follow a process or make a decision, flow charts can be useful; for an example, see page 153 of this book. Pie charts are appropriate for indicating ratios or apportionment, as in the following example.

PIE CHART

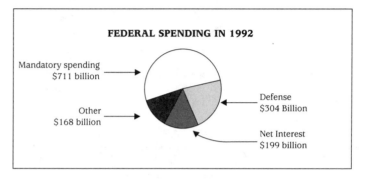

FEDERAL SPENDING IN 1992

Mandatory spending
$711 billion

Other
$168 billion

Defense
$304 Billion

Net Interest
$199 billion

Line graphs and bar graphs illustrate disparities in numerical data. Line graphs are appropriate when you want to illuminate trends over a period of time, such as trends in sales, in unemployment, or in population growth. Bar graphs can be used for the same purpose. In addition, bar graphs are useful for highlighting comparisons, such as vote totals for rival political candidates or the number of refugees entering the United States during different time periods.

LINE GRAPH

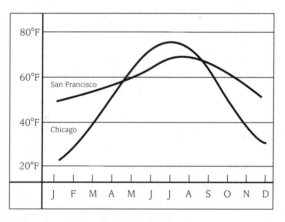

80°F

60°F

San Francisco

40°F

Chicago

20°F

J F M A M J J A S O N D

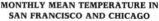

**MONTHLY MEAN TEMPERATURE IN
SAN FRANCISCO AND CHICAGO**

BAR GRAPH

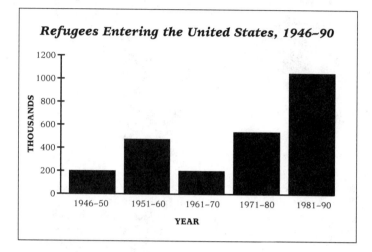

Refugees Entering the United States, 1946–90

Tables are not as visually interesting as line graphs or charts, but they allow for inclusion of specific numerical data, such as exact percentages. The following table presents the responses of students and faculty to one question on a campus-wide questionnaire.

TABLE

Is American education based too much on European history and values?

	PERCENT		
	NO	UNDECIDED	YES
Nonwhite students	21	25	54
White students	55	29	16
Nonwhite faculty	15	20	65
White faculty	57	27	16

Diagrams are useful — and sometimes indispensable — in scientific and technical writing. It is more concise, for example, to use the following diagram than it would be to explain the chemical formula in words.

DIAGRAM

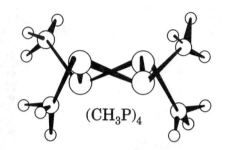

$(CH_3P)_4$

PLACING VISUALS   A visual may be placed in the text of a document, near a discussion to which it relates, or it can be put in an appendix, labeled, and referred to in the text. In much college writing, the convention is to place visuals in an appendix; when in doubt, check with your professor.

Placing visuals in the text of a document can be tricky. Usually you will want the visual to appear close to the sentences that relate to it, but page breaks won't always allow this placement. At times you may need to insert the visual at a later point and tell readers where it can be found or, with the help of software, you may be able to make the text flow around the visual.

In newsletters and in business and technical documents, page layout is both an art and a science. The best way to learn how to lay out pages is to work with colleagues who have had experience solving the many problems that can arise.

4b For academic essays, use standard manuscript formats.

If your instructor provides formal guidelines for formatting an essay — or a more specialized document such as a lab report, a case study, or a research paper — you should of course follow them. Otherwise, use the manuscript format that is standard for the discipline in which you are writing.

This section describes two manuscript formats: MLA, used in English and the humanities, and APA, used in the social sciences. For manuscript formats used in other disciplines, consult a specialized style manual; a list of such style manuals appears in 56d.

NOTE: The guidelines in this section apply to academic manuscripts both with and without documentation. If you are writing a paper that uses sources, you should also consult the documentation guidelines in 55 and 56.

MLA manuscript guidelines (English and the humanities)

In most English and humanities classes, you will be asked to use the MLA (Modern Language Association) manuscript format. The following guidelines are consistent with advice in the *MLA Handbook for Writers of Research Papers*, 4th ed. (New York: MLA, 1995).

To see how an MLA essay is formatted, take a look at these models:

—An MLA essay based on personal experience (pages 54–55)

—An MLA research paper (pages 384–97)

MATERIALS Use 8 1/2" × 11", 20-pound white paper. If the paper emerges from the printer in a continuous sheet, separate the pages, remove the feeder strips from the sides of the paper, and assemble the pages in order. Secure the pages with a paper clip. Unless your instructor suggests otherwise, do not staple the pages together or use any sort of binder.

TITLE AND IDENTIFICATION Essays written for English and humanities classes do not require a title page unless your instructor requests one. Unless you are told otherwise, against the left margin about one inch from the top of the page, place your name, the instructor's name, the course name and number, and the date on separate lines; double-space between lines. Double-space again and center the title of the paper in the width of the page. Capitalize the first and last words of the title and all other words except articles, prepositions, and coordinating conjunctions (see 45c). Double-space after the title and begin typing the text of the paper. (See the essay on pages 54–55.)

If you use a title page, follow the model on page 384.

MARGINS, SPACING, AND INDENTATION Leave margins of at least one inch but no more than an inch and a half on all sides of the page.

Double-space between lines and indent the first line of each paragraph one-half inch (or five spaces) from the left margin.

MLA ESSAY FORMAT

↕ 1/2 "
Weitzel 1

↕ 1"

Tom Weitzel

Dr. Fry

English 101

16 October 1995

1/2 "
indent ←→

Double-
spacing
throughout

Title,
centered

Who Goes to the Races?

A favorite pastime of mine is observing people,
and my favorite place to observe is at the horse races.
After many encounters with the racing crowd, I have discovered that there are four distinct groups at the
track: the once-a-year bunch, the professionals, the
clubhouse set, and the unemployed.

The largest group at the track consists of those
who show up once a year. They know little about horses
or betting and rely strictly on race track gimmick

1"
←→

sheets and newspaper predictions for selecting possible
winners. If that doesn't work, they use intuition,
lucky numbers, favorite colors, or appealing names.
They bet larger amounts as the day goes along, gambling
on every race, including long-shot bets on exactas and
daily doubles. The vast majority go home broke and
frustrated.

1"
←→

More subtle and quiet are the professionals. They
follow the horses from track to track and live in
campers and motor homes. Many are married couples, some
are retired, and all are easily spotted with their lunch
sacks, water jugs, and binoculars. Since most know one
another, they section themselves off in a particular
area of the stadium. All rely on the racing form and on
personal knowledge of each horse, jockey, and track in
making the proper bet. They bet only on the smart races,

↕ 1"

MLA ESSAY FORMAT (*continued*)

1/2 "
Weitzel 2

1"

rarely on the favorites. Never do they bet on exactas
or daily doubles. More often than not they either break
even or go home winners.

Isolated from the others is the clubhouse set.
Found either at the cocktail lounge or in the restau-
rant, usually involved in business transactions, these
racing fans rarely see a race in person and do their
betting via the waiter. It's difficult to tell whether
they go home sad, happy, or in between. They keep their
emotions to themselves.

The most interesting members of the racetrack population are the unemployed. They will be found not in
the clubhouse, but right down at the rail next to the
finish line. Here one can discover the real emotion of
the racetrack--the screaming, the cursing, and the pushing. The unemployed are not in it for the sport.
Betting is not a game for them, but a battle for survival. If they lose, they must borrow enough money to
carry them until the next check comes in, and then, of
course, they head right back to the track. This particular group arrives at the track beaten and leaves
beaten.

I have probably lost more money than I have won
at the track, but observing these four interesting
groups of people makes it all worthwhile.

1"

1"

For a quotation longer than four typed lines of prose or three lines of verse, indent each line one inch (or ten spaces) from the left margin. Double-space between the body of the paper and the quotation, and double-space the lines of the quotation. Quotation marks are not needed when a quotation is set off from the text by indenting. See page 394 for an example; see also 37b.

PAGINATION   Put your last name followed by the page number in the upper right corner of each page, one-half inch below the top edge. (If you have a separate title page, the title page is uncounted and unnumbered.) Use arabic numerals (1, 2, 3, and so on). Do not put a period after the number and do not enclose the number in parentheses.

PUNCTUATION AND TYPING   In typing the paper, leave one space after words, commas, colons, and semicolons and between dots in ellipses. Leave two spaces after periods, question marks, and exclamation points unless your instructor prefers one space. To form a dash, type two hyphens with no space between them; do not put a space on either side of the dash.

HEADINGS   The Modern Language Association neither encourages nor discourages use of headings and currently provides no guidelines for their use. If you would like to use headings in a long essay or research paper, check first with your instructor. Although headings are not used as frequently in English and the humanities as in other disciplines, the trend seems to be changing.

VISUALS   The Modern Language Association classifies visuals as tables and figures (figures include graphs, charts, maps, photographs, and drawings). Label each table with an arabic numeral (Table 1, Table 2, etc.) and provide a clear caption that identifies the subject; the label and caption should appear on separate lines above the table. For figures, a label and a caption are usually placed below the figure, and they need not appear on separate lines. The word "Figure" may be abbreviated to "Fig."

In professional articles, visuals should be placed in the text, as close as possible to the sentences that relate to them.

For student essays, some instructors may prefer that you put visuals at the end of your essay.

DOCUMENTATION If your essay draws on secondary sources, consult the MLA documentation guidelines and the sample research paper in 55.

STUDENT ESSAY WITHOUT DOCUMENTATION The student essay on pages 54–55 illustrates MLA manuscript format. Because the essay is not based on written sources, it doesn't illustrate MLA documentation style. For a sample research paper that uses MLA documentation, see 55.

APA manuscript guidelines (the social sciences)

In most social science classes, such as psychology, sociology, anthropology, and business, you will be asked to use the APA (American Psychological Association) manuscript format. The following guidelines are based on the *Publication Manual of the American Psychological Association*, 4th ed. (Washington, D.C.: APA, 1994).

To see how an APA paper is formatted, take a look at the research paper on pages 408–17.

MATERIALS AND TYPEFACE Use 8 1/2" × 11" white paper of at least 20-pound weight. For a paper typed on a word processor, make sure that the print quality meets your instructor's standards. Avoid a typeface that is unusual or hard to read.

TITLE PAGE Begin a college paper with a title page. Type the page number, flush right (against the right margin), about one-half inch from the top of the page. Before the page number type a short title, consisting of the first two or three words of your title.

The APA manual does not provide guidelines for the placement of certain information necessary for college papers, but most instructors will want you to supply a title page similar to the one on page 408.

MARGINS, SPACING, AND INDENTATION Use margins of at least one inch on all sides of the page. If you are working on a word processor, do not justify the right margin.

Double-space throughout the paper, and indent the first line of each paragraph five spaces from the left margin.

For quotations longer than forty words, indent each line five spaces from the left margin. Double-space between the body of the paper and the quotation, and double-space between lines in the quotation. Quotation marks are not needed when a quotation is indented. (See 37b.)

PAGE NUMBERS AND SHORT TITLE   In the upper right-hand corner of each page, about one-half inch from the top of the page, type the page number, preceded by the short title that you typed on the title page. Number all pages, including the title page.

PUNCTUATION AND TYPING   Although the APA guidelines call for one space after all punctuation, most college professors allow (or even prefer) two spaces at the end of a sentence. Use one space after all other punctuation.

To form a dash, type two hyphens with no space between them. Do not put a space on either side of the dash.

ABSTRACT   If your instructor requires one, include an abstract right after the title page. An abstract is a 75-to-100-word paragraph that provides readers with a quick overview of your essay. It should express your thesis (or central idea) and your key points; it should also briefly suggest any implications or applications of the research you discuss in the paper.

HEADINGS   Although headings are not necessary, their use is encouraged in the social sciences. For most undergraduate papers, use no more than one or two levels of headings. Major headings should be centered, with the first letter of important words capitalized; minor words—articles, short prepositions, and coordinating conjunctions—are not capitalized unless they are the first word. Subheadings should be typed flush left (against the left margin) and underlined; the rules on capitalization are the same as for major headings. (For an example of an APA paper that uses major headings, see pages 408–17.)

VISUALS   The American Psychological Association classifies visuals as tables and figures (figures include graphs, charts, drawings, and photographs). Use visuals for important, directly relevant information that would be needlessly hard to follow if presented wholly in written form.

Keep visuals as simple as possible and label them clearly: Table 1, Figure 3, and so on. Each visual should include a caption that concisely describes its subject; in the bar graph on page 51, for example, the caption "Refugees Entering the United States, 1946–90" describes the data included in the graph. Always discuss a visual in the text of your paper, drawing the reader's attention to its most significant features.

According to the APA manual, tables and figures in student manuscripts are often placed in the text of the paper. It is a good idea, however, to ask your instructor for guidelines.

DOCUMENTATION If your essay draws on any secondary sources, consult the APA documentation guidelines and the sample APA research paper in 56d.

4c For business documents, use standard business formats.

This section provides guidelines for preparing business letters, résumés, and memos. For a more detailed discussion of these and other business documents — proposals, reports, executive summaries, and so on — consult a business writing textbook or take a look at examples currently being written at the organization for which you are writing.

Business letters

In writing a business letter, be direct, clear, and courteous, but do not hesitate to be firm if necessary. State your purpose or request at the beginning of the letter and include only pertinent information in the body. By being as direct and concise as possible, you show that you value your reader's time.

A sample business letter appears on page 60. This letter is typed in what is known as "block" style. The return address at the top and the close and signature at the bottom are lined up just to the right of the center of the width of the page. The inside address, the salutation, and the body of the letter are flush left (against the left margin). The paragraphs are not indented.

BUSINESS LETTER IN BLOCK FORM

Return   ⌐ 121 Knox Road, #6
address   College Park, MD 20740
                   ⌐ March 4, 1996

Linda Hennessee, Managing Editor
<u>World Discovery</u>   Inside
1650 K Street, NW   address
Washington, DC 20036

Dear Ms. Hennessee: ——— Salutation

I am applying for the summer editorial internship you
listed with the Career Development Center at the University of Maryland. I am currently a junior at the University of Maryland, with a double major in English and
Latin American Studies.

Over the past three years I have gained considerable
experience in newspaper and magazine journalism, as you
will see on my enclosed résumé. I am familiar with
the basic procedures of editing and photographic development, but my primary interests lie in feature writing
and landscape photography. My professional goal is to   ——— Body
work as a photojournalist with an international focus,
preferably for a major magazine. I cannot imagine a better introduction to that career than a summer at <u>World
Discovery</u>.

I am available for an interview almost any time and can
be reached at 301-555-2651. I will be in Virginia from
April 4 to April 12; if you want to contact me there the
number is 703-555-2006.

I look forward to hearing from you.

                Close ——— Sincerely,

           Signature ——— *Jeffrey Richardson*

                      Jeffrey Richardson

Enc.

If you choose to indent your paragraphs, you are using "semi-block" style, which is considered less formal. If you choose to move all elements of the letter flush left, you are using the most formal style, "full block." This style is usually preferred when the letter is typed on letterhead stationery that gives the return address of the writer or the writer's company.

When writing to a woman, use the abbreviation *Ms.* in the salutation unless you know that the woman prefers another form of address. If you are not writing to a particular person, you can use the salutation *Dear Sir or Madam* or you can address the company itself—*Dear Solar Technology.*

Below the signature, flush left, you may include the abbreviation *Enc.* to indicate that something is being enclosed with the letter or the abbreviation *cc* followed by a colon and the name of someone who is receiving a copy of the letter.

Résumés

An effective résumé presents relevant information in a clear and concise form. The trick is to present yourself in the best possible light without going on at length and wasting your reader's time.

A sample résumé appears on page 62. Notice that the writer has used headings and bullets to make his résumé easy to scan and to draw attention to important information. Notice too that he presents his work experience and his educational history in reverse chronological order—to highlight his most recent accomplishments.

When you send your résumé, you should include a letter that tells what position you seek and where you learned about it (see page 60). The letter should also summarize your education and past experience, relating them to the job you are applying for. End the letter with a suggestion for a meeting, and tell your prospective employer when you will be available.

Memos

Business memos (short for *memorandums*) are a form of communication used within a company or organization. Usually brief and to the point, a memo reports information, makes a request, or recommends an action. The format of a memo, which varies from company to company, is designed for easy distribution, quick reading, and efficient filing.

RÉSUMÉ

Jeffrey Richardson
121 Knox Road, #6
College Park, MD 20740
301-555-2651

OBJECTIVE: To obtain an editorial internship with a magazine.

SKILLS

- Ability to write analytical stories, features, and
  interviews on deadline and under pressure.
- Strong background in photography: use of various types of
  cameras; darkroom procedures; landscape photography.
- Knowledge of copyediting and proofreading procedures.
- Languages: Spanish, French (reading).

WORK EXPERIENCE

The Diamondback (circulation 20,000), University of Maryland,
College Park, Maryland, January 1993-present.
    Edit photos for daily student newspaper.

Globe (circulation 80,000), Fairfax, Virginia, summers
1993-95.
    Worked as intern on assignments from staff editors of this
    surburban Washington, DC, weekly paper: wrote stories about
    local issues and personalities; interviewed political
    candidates; performed editorial tasks (editing, proofreading,
    caption writing); coedited and took photographs for
    special supplement "The Landscapes of Northern Virginia:
    A Photoessay" (1995).

ADDITIONAL EXPERIENCE

Fairfax County Adult Education Program, summer 1994.
    Tutored Latino students in English as a Second Language.

EDUCATION

University of Maryland, College Park, Maryland.
    Bachelor of Arts expected June 1997, English and Latin
    American Studies

Activities: Photographers' Workshop, Spanish Club.

References available upon request.

BUSINESS MEMO

Commonwealth Press

MEMORANDUM

To: Production, Promotion, and Editorial Assistants

cc: Stephen Chapman

From: Helen Brown

Date: February 28, 1996

Subject: New computers for staff

We will receive the new personal computers next week for
the assistants in production, promotion, and editorial. In
preparation, I would like you to take part in a training
program and to rearrange your work areas to accommodate the
new equipment.

Training Program

A computer consultant will teach in-house workshops on how to use
our spreadsheet program. If you have already tried the program,
be prepared to discuss any problems you have encountered.

Workshops for our three departments will be held in the training room at the following times:

       • Production: Monday, March 11, 10:00 a.m. to 2:00 p.m.
       • Promotion: Wednesday, March 13, 10:00 a.m. to 2:00 p.m.
       • Editorial: Friday, March 15, 10:00 a.m. to 2:00 p.m.

Lunch will be provided in the cafeteria. If you cannot attend,
please let me know by March 4.

Allocation and Setup

To give everyone access to a computer, we will set up the new
computers as follows: two in the assistants' workspace in
production; two in the area outside the conference room for the
promotion assistants; and two in the library for the editorial
assistants.

Assistants in all three departments should see me before the
end of the week to discuss preparation of the spaces to
accommodate the new equipment.

Most memos display the name of the recipient, the name of the sender, the date, and the subject on separate lines at the top of the page. Many companies have preprinted forms for memos, and some word processors allow you to call up a memo "template" that prints standard memo lines — "To," "From," "Date," and "Subject" — at the top of the page.

Because readers of memos are busy people, you cannot assume that they will read your memo word for word. Therefore the subject line should describe the subject as clearly and concisely as possible, and the introductory paragraph should get right to the point. In addition, the body of the memo should be well organized and easy to scan. To promote scanning, use headings where possible and display any items that deserve special attention by setting them off from the text. A sample memo with headings and a displayed list appears on page 63.

Paragraphs

Except for special-purpose paragraphs, such as introductions and conclusions (see 2a and 2c), paragraphs are clusters of information supporting an essay's main point (or advancing a story's action). Aim for paragraphs that are clearly focused, well developed, organized, coherent, and neither too long nor too short for easy reading.

5

Focus on a main point.

A paragraph should be unified around a main point. The point should be clear to readers, and all sentences in the paragraph must relate to it.

5a State the main point in a topic sentence.

As readers move into a paragraph, they need to know where they are — in relation to the whole essay — and what to expect in the sentences to come. A good topic sentence, a one sentence summary of the paragraph's main point, acts as a signpost pointing in two directions: backward toward the thesis of the essay and forward toward the body of the paragraph.

Like a thesis statement (see 1c), a topic sentence is more general than the material supporting it. Usually the topic sentence comes first, as in the following paragraph. (The topic sentence is italicized.)

> *Nearly all living creatures manage some form of communication.* The dance patterns of bees in their hive help to point the way to distant flower fields or announce successful foraging. Male stickleback fish regularly swim upside-down to indicate outrage in a courtship contest. Male deer and lemurs mark territorial ownership by rubbing their own body secretions on boundary stones or trees. Everyone has seen a frightened dog put his tail between his legs and run in panic. We, too, use ges-

tures, expressions, postures, and movement to give our words point. [Italics added.] — Olivia Vlahos, *Human Beginnings*

Sometimes the topic sentence is introduced by a transitional sentence linking it to earlier material. In the following paragraph, the topic sentence (italicized) has been delayed to allow for a transition.

> But flowers are not the only source of spectacle in the wilderness. *An opportunity for late color is provided by the berries of wildflowers, shrubs, and trees.* Baneberry presents its tiny white flowers in spring but in late summer bursts forth with clusters of red berries. Bunchberry, a ground-cover plant, puts out red berries in the fall, and the red berries of wintergreen last from autumn well into winter. In California, the bright red, fist-sized clusters of Christmas berries can be seen growing beside highways for up to six months of the year. [Italics added.]
> — James Crockett et al., *Wildflower Gardening*

Occasionally the topic sentence may be withheld until the end of the paragraph — but only if the earlier sentences hang together so well that the reader perceives their direction, if not their exact point.

Although it is generally wise to use topic sentences, at times they are unnecessary. A topic sentence may not be needed if a paragraph continues developing an idea clearly introduced in a previous paragraph, if the details of the paragraph unmistakably suggest its main point, or if the paragraph appears in a narrative of events where generalizations might interrupt the flow of the story.

5b Do not stray from the point.

Sentences that do not support the topic sentence destroy the unity of a paragraph. If the paragraph is otherwise well focused, such offending sentences can simply be deleted or perhaps moved elsewhere. In the following paragraph describing the inadequate facilities in a high school, the information about the word processing instructor (in italics) is clearly off the point.

> As the result of tax cuts, the educational facilities of Lincoln High School have reached an all-time low. Some of the books date back to 1985 and have long since shed their covers. The

lack of lab equipment makes it necessary for four to five students to work at one table, with most watching rather than performing experiments. The few computers in working order must share one dot matrix printer. *Also, the word processing instructor left to have a baby at the beginning of the semester, and most of the students don't like the substitute.* As for the furniture, many of the upright chairs have become recliners, and the desk legs are so unbalanced that they play seesaw on the floor.

Sometimes the cure for a disunified paragraph is not as simple as deleting or moving material. Writers often wander into uncharted territory because they cannot think of enough evidence to support a topic sentence. Feeling that it is too soon to break into a new paragraph, they move on to new ideas for which they have not prepared the reader. When this happens, the writer is faced with a choice: Either find more evidence to support the topic sentence or adjust the topic sentence to mesh with the evidence that is available.

EXERCISE 5–1

Underline the topic sentence in the following paragraph and eliminate any material that does not clarify or develop the central idea.

A recent plan of the mayor's threatens to destroy one of the oldest and most successfully integrated neighborhoods in our city, replacing it with luxury condominiums and a shopping mall. This neighborhood, Thompson's Fields, was settled by a mixture of immigrants from Ireland, Italy, Poland, and Austria in the early part of the twentieth century. Over the years black and Hispanic families have also moved in and have become part of the community. When the mayor designated a five-block area along the neighborhood's main street as the location for a redevelopment program, the community decided to take the mayor to court. The mayor has hired the best urban planners and architects in the country to design and build three large skyscrapers along with parking facilities for the area. One woman has even moved to the city from California to work on the project. If the court accepts the case, the lawyer for the residents will be Ann Tyson, who grew up in Thompson's Fields. The residents have seen a great deal of change over the years, but they refuse to stand by while their homes are razed for some gentrification project that they will never enjoy.

6

Develop the main point.

Topic sentences are generalizations in need of support, so once you have written a topic sentence, ask yourself, "How do I know that this is true?" Your answer will suggest how to develop the paragraph.

6a Flesh out skimpy paragraphs.

Though an occasional short paragraph is fine, particularly if it functions as a transition or emphasizes a point, a series of brief paragraphs suggests inadequate development. How much development is enough? That varies, depending on the writer's purpose and audience.

For example, when she wrote a paragraph attempting to convince readers that it is impossible to lose fat quickly, health columnist Jane Brody knew that she would have to present a great deal of evidence because many dieters want to believe the opposite. She did *not* write:

> When you think about it, it's impossible to lose — as many diets suggest—10 pounds of *fat* in ten days, even on a total fast. Even a moderately active person cannot lose so much weight so fast. A less active person hasn't a prayer.

This three-sentence paragraph is too skimpy to be convincing. But the paragraph that Brody wrote contains enough evidence to convince even skeptical readers:

> When you think about it, it's impossible to lose — as many diets suggest — 10 pounds of *fat* in ten days, even on a total fast. A pound of body fat represents 3,500 calories. To lose 1 pound of fat, you must expend 3,500 more calories than you consume. Let's say you weigh 170 pounds and, as a moderately active person, you burn 2,500 calories a day. If your diet contains only 1,500 calories, you'd have an energy deficit of 1,000 calories a day. In a week's time that would add up to a 7,000-calorie deficit, or 2 pounds of real fat. In ten days, the accumulated deficit would represent nearly 3 pounds of lost body fat. Even if

you ate nothing at all for ten days and maintained your usual level of activity, your caloric deficit would add up to 25,000 calories. . . . At 3,500 calories per pound of fat, that's still only 7 pounds of lost fat.   — Jane Brody, *Jane Brody's Nutrition Book*

6b Choose a suitable pattern of development.

Although paragraphs may be patterned in an almost infinite number of ways, certain patterns of development occur frequently, either alone or in combination: examples and illustrations, narration, description, process, comparison and contrast, analogy, cause and effect, classification and division, and definition. There is nothing magical about these methods of development. They simply reflect some of the ways in which we think.

Examples and illustrations

Examples, perhaps the most common pattern of development, are appropriate whenever the reader might be tempted to ask, "For example?" Though examples are just selected instances, not a complete catalog, they are enough to suggest the truth of many topic sentences, as in the following paragraph.

> Normally my parents abided scrupulously by "The Budget," but several times a year Dad would dip into his battered, black strongbox and splurge on some irrational, totally satisfying luxury. Once he bought over a hundred comic books at a flea market, doled out to us thereafter at the tantalizing rate of two a week. He always got a whole flat of pansies, Mom's favorite flower, for us to give her on Mother's Day. One day a boy stopped at our house selling fifty-cent raffle tickets on a sailboat and Dad bought every ticket the boy had left — three books' worth.   — Connie Hailey, student

Illustrations are extended examples, frequently presented in story form. Because they require several sentences apiece, they are used more sparingly than examples. When well selected, however, they can be a vivid and effective means of developing a point. The writer of the following paragraph uses illustrations to demonstrate that Harriet Tubman, famous conductor on the underground railway for escaping slaves, was a genius at knowing how and when to retreat.

Part of Harriet Tubman's strategy of conducting was, as in all battle-field operations, the knowledge of how and when to retreat. Numerous allusions have been made to her moves when she suspected that she was in danger. When she feared the party was closely pursued, she would take it for a time on a train southward bound. No one seeing Negroes going in this direction would for an instant suppose them to be fugitives. Once on her return she was at a railway station. She saw some men reading a poster and she heard one of them reading it aloud. It was a description of her, offering a reward for her capture. She took a southbound train to avert suspicion. At another time when Harriet heard men talking about her, she pretended to read a book which she carried. One man remarked, "This cannot be the woman. The one we want can't read or write." Harriet devoutly hoped the book was right side up.

—Earl Conrad, *Harriet Tubman*

Narration

A paragraph of narration tells a story or part of a story. Narrative paragraphs are usually arranged in chronological order, but they may also contain flashbacks, interruptions that take the story back to an earlier time. The following paragraph, from Jane Goodall's *In the Shadow of Man,* recounts one of the author's experiences in the African wild.

One evening when I was wading in the shallows of the lake to pass a rocky outcrop, I suddenly stopped dead as I saw the sinuous black body of a snake in the water. It was all of six feet long, and from the slight hood and the dark stripes at the back of the neck I knew it to be a Storm's water cobra—a deadly reptile for the bite of which there was, at that time, no serum. As I stared at it an incoming wave gently deposited part of its body on one of my feet. I remained motionless, not even breathing, until the wave rolled back into the lake, drawing the snake with it. Then I leaped out of the water as fast as I could, my heart hammering.   —Jane Goodall, *In the Shadow of Man*

Description

A descriptive paragraph sketches a portrait of a person, place, or thing by using concrete and specific details that appeal to one or more of our senses—sight, sound, smell, taste, and touch. Consider, for example, the following description of the grasshopper invasions that devastated the midwestern land-scape in the late 1860s.

> They came like dive bombers out of the west. They came by the millions with the rustle of their wings roaring overhead. They came in waves, like the rolls of the sea, descending with a terrifying speed, breaking now and again like a mighty surf. They came with the force of a williwaw and they formed a huge, ominous, dark brown cloud that eclipsed the sun. They dipped and touched earth, hitting objects and people like hail-stones. But they were not hail. These were live demons. They popped, snapped, crackled, and roared. They were dark brown, an inch or longer in length, plump in the middle and tapered at the ends. They had transparent wings, slender legs, and two black eyes that flashed with a fierce intelligence.
>
> —Eugene Boe, "Pioneers to Eternity"

Process

A process paragraph is patterned in time order, usually chronologically. A writer may choose this pattern either to describe a process or to show readers how to perform a process. The following paragraph describes what happens when water freezes.

> In school we learned that with few exceptions the solid phase of matter is more dense than the liquid phase. Water, alone among common substances, violates this rule. As water begins to cool, it contracts and becomes more dense, in a per-fectly typical way. But about four degrees above the freezing point, something remarkable happens. It ceases to contract and begins expanding, becoming less dense. At the freezing point the expansion is abrupt and drastic. As water turns to ice, it adds about one-eleventh to its liquid volume.
>
> —Chet Raymo, "Curious Stuff, Water and Ice"

Here is a paragraph that shows readers how to perform a process — that of opening an oyster.

> An oyster has an irregular shape. The valves are rough and their lips hard to find. Crooked and wrinkled, the hairline crack between the valves can't be widened with the blade of a knife; the point must enter first. Furthermore, a big Chincoteague doesn't fit the left hand. One must hold the animal slanting against the edge of the kitchen sink and poke around, seeking the slot by touch as much as by sight. It takes painful practice. When the knifepoint finds a purchase, push carefully and

quickly before the oyster realizes what's afoot and gets a firmer grip on itself. Push in the wrong place—it's easy to mistake a growth line for the groove—and the knife takes on a life of its own. It can skid and open up your hand. This delicate work requires patient agility to find the groove, push the knife in, then slit the muscle and open the critter without losing too much juice. (Restaurants serve oysters on their flat shell. It's better to throw that one away and lay the delicacies on a bed of crushed ice in the roundest half-shell which holds its delicious liquor. Sprinkle each one with lemon juice—a healthy oyster will wriggle the slightest bit at this to prove it's alive—lift the dishlike shell to the lips, and drink the oyster down. It's a delicious, addicting experience.)

— Philip Kopper, "How to Open an Oyster"

Comparison and contrast

To compare two subjects is to draw attention to their similarities, although the word *compare* also has a broader meaning that includes a consideration of differences. To contrast is to focus only on differences.

Whether a comparison-and-contrast paragraph stresses similarities or differences, it may be patterned in one of two ways. The two subjects may be presented one at a time, block style, as in the following paragraph of contrast.

So Grant and Lee were in complete contrast, representing two diametrically opposed elements in American life. Grant was the modern man emerging; beyond him, ready to come on the stage, was the great age of steel and machinery, of crowded cities and a restless burgeoning vitality. Lee might have ridden down from the old age of chivalry, lance in hand, silken banner fluttering over his head. Each man was the perfect champion of his cause, drawing both his strengths and weaknesses from the people he led.

— Bruce Catton, "Grant and Lee: A Study in Contrasts"

Or a paragraph may proceed point by point, treating the two subjects together, one aspect at a time. The following paragraph uses the point-by-point method to contrast the writer's academic experiences in an American high school and an Irish convent.

Strangely enough, instead of being academically inferior to my American high school, the Irish convent was superior. In my class at home, *Love Story* was considered pretty heavy reading,

so imagine my surprise at finding Irish students who could re-
cite passages from *War and Peace.* In high school we complained
about having to study *Romeo and Juliet* in one semester, whereas
in Ireland we simultaneously studied *Macbeth* and Dickens's *Hard
Times,* in addition to writing a composition a day in English class.
In high school, I didn't even begin algebra until the ninth grade,
while at the convent seventh graders (or their Irish equivalent)
were doing calculus and trigonometry.

— Margaret Stack, student

Analogy

Analogies draw comparisons between items that appear to
have little in common. Writers turn to analogies for a variety of
reasons: to make the unfamiliar seem familiar, to provide a
concrete understanding of an abstract topic, to argue a point,
or to provoke fresh thoughts or changed feelings about a subject. In the following paragraph, physician Lewis Thomas
draws an analogy between the behavior of ants and that of
humans. Thomas's analogy helps us to understand the social
behavior of ants and forces us to question the superiority of
our own human societies.

Ants are so much like human beings as to be an embarrass-
ment. They farm fungi, raise aphids as livestock, launch armies
into wars, use chemical sprays to alarm and confuse enemies,
capture slaves. The families of weaver ants engage in child labor,
holding their larvae like shuttles to spin out the thread that sews
the leaves together for their fungus gardens. They exchange
information ceaselessly. They do everything but watch television.

— Lewis Thomas, "On Societies as Organisms"

Cause and effect

A paragraph may move from cause to effects or from an effect
to its causes. The topic sentence in the following paragraph
mentions an effect; the rest of the paragraph lists several
causes.

The fantastic water clarity of the Mount Gambier sinkholes
results from several factors. The holes are fed from aquifers
holding rainwater that fell decades — even centuries — ago, and
that has been filtered through miles of limestone. The high level
of calcium that limestone adds causes the silty detritus from
dead plants and animals to cling together and settle quickly to

the bottom. Abundant bottom vegetation in the shallow sink-holes also helps bind the silt. And the rapid turnover of water prohibits stagnation.

— Hillary Hauser, "Exploring a Sunken Realm in Australia"

Classification and division

Classification is the grouping of items into categories according to some consistent principle. The following paragraph classifies species of electric fish.

> Scientists sort electric fishes into three categories. The first comprises the strongly electric species like the marine electric rays or the freshwater African electric catfish and South American electric eel. Known since the dawn of history, these deliver a punch strong enough to stun a human. In recent years, biologists have focused on a second category: weakly electric fish in the South American and African rivers that use tiny voltages for communication and navigation. The third group contains sharks, non-electric rays, and catfish, which do not emit a field but possess sensors that enable them to detect the minute amounts of electricity that leak out of other organisms.

— Anne Rudloe and Jack Rudloe, "Electric Warfare: The Fish That Kill with Thunderbolts"

Division takes one item and divides it into parts. As with classification, division should be made according to some consistent principle. The following paragraph describes the parts of a lemon and their uses.

> Absolutely every part of a lemon is useful in some way, from its seeds to its outermost peel. Lemon-pip oil, unsaturated and aromatic, is important in the soap industry and in special diets. The pulp left over from squeezed lemons is evaporated and concentrated into "citrus molasses" which is sold as a base for making vinegar and as an ingredient in bland syrups and alcohol. The remains of the "rag" or pulp is also sold as cattle feed. Most of the pectin used to thicken and solidify jams, jellies, and marmalades comes from the white pith of citrus fruits. Among these, lemon and lime pectin has the highest "jelly grade" or capacity to thicken liquids. It is widely used in medicines taken to combat diarrhea. The flavedo, or outer yellow layer of lemon peel, is invaluable for its intense taste and scent. (The word *zest,* which originally meant "skin or peel," then specifically "citrus peel," is now in common use as signifying "lively enjoyment.")

— Margaret Visser, *Much Depends on Dinner*

Definition

A definition puts a word or concept into a general class and then provides enough details to distinguish it from others in the same class. In the following paragraph, the writer defines envy as a special kind of desire.

> Envy is so integral and so painful a part of what animates human behavior in market societies that many people have forgotten the full meaning of the word, simplifying it into one of the synonyms of desire. It is that, which may be why it flourishes in market societies: democracies of desire, they might be called, with money for ballots, stuffing permitted. But envy is more or less than desire. It begins with the almost frantic sense of emptiness inside oneself, as if the pump of one's heart were sucking on air. One has to be blind to perceive the emptiness, of course, but that's just what envy is, a selective blindness. *Invidia,* Latin for envy, translates as "nonsight," and Dante had the envious plodding along under cloaks of lead, their eyes sewn shut with leaden wire. What they are blind to is what they have, God-given and humanly nurtured, in themselves.
>
> — Nelson W. Aldrich, Jr., *Old Money*

6c Consider possible ways of arranging information.

In addition to choosing a pattern of development (or a combination of patterns), you may need to make decisions about arrangement. If you are using examples, for instance, you'll need to decide how to order the examples. Or if you are contrasting two items point by point, you'll need to decide which points to discuss first, second, and so on. Often considerations of purpose and audience will help you make these choices.

Three common ways of arranging information are treated in this section: time order, spatial order, and order of climax. Other possible arrangements include order of complexity (from simple to complex), order of familiarity (from most familiar to least familiar), and order of audience appeal (from "safe" ideas to those that may challenge the audience's views).

Order of time

Time order, usually chronological, is appropriate for a variety of purposes such as narrating a personal experience, telling an anecdote, describing an experiment, or explaining a process. The following paragraph, arranged in chronological order, appears in *Blue Highways,* an account of the author's travels on the back roads of America.

> Orion Saddle Road, after I was committed to it, narrowed to a single rutted lane affording no place to turn around; if I met somebody, one of us would have to back down. The higher I went, the more that idea unnerved me — the road was bad enough driving forward. The compass swung from point to point, and within five minutes it had touched each of the three hundred sixty degrees. The clutch started pushing back, and ruts and craters and rocks threw the steering wheel into nasty jerks that wrenched to the spine. I understood why, the day before, I'd thought there could be no road over the Chiricahuas; there wasn't. No wonder desperadoes hid in this inaccessibility.
> — William Least Heat Moon

Time order need not be chronological. For example, you might decide to arrange events in the order in which they were revealed to you, not in the order in which they happened. Or you might choose to begin with a dramatic moment and then flash back to the events that led up to it.

Order of space

For descriptions of a location or a scene, a spatial arrangement will seem natural. Imagine yourself holding a video camera and you'll begin to see the possibilities. Might you pan the scene from afar and then zoom to a close-up? Would you rather sweep the camera from side to side — or from top to bottom? Or should you try for a more impressionistic effect, focusing the camera on first one and then another significant feature of the scene?

The writer of the following paragraph describes the contents of a long, narrow pool hall by taking us from the front to the back.

> The pool tables were in a line side by side from the front to the back of the long, narrow building. The first one was the biggest, and the best snooker players used it. Beyond it were the other tables used by lesser players, except for the last one. This was the bank's pool table, used only by the best players in the county.
> — William G. Hill, student

Order of climax

When ideas are presented in the order of climax, they build toward a conclusion. Consider the following paragraph describing the effects on workers of long-term blue-collar employment. All of the examples have an emotional impact, but the final one — even though it might at first seem trivial — is the most powerful. It shows us just how degrading blue-collar work can become.

> I met people who taught me about human behavior. I saw people take amphetamines to keep up with ever-rising production rates. I saw good friends, and even relatives, physically attack each other over job assignments that would mean a few cents' difference. I observed women cheating on their husbands and men cheating on their wives. I watched women hand over their entire paycheck to a bookie. I saw pregnant women, their feet too swollen for shoes, come to work in slippers. I saw women with colds stuff pieces of tissue up their nostrils so they wouldn't have to keep stopping to blow their nose.
> — Linda Lavelle, student

Because the order of climax saves the most dramatic examples for the end, it is appropriate only when readers are likely to persist until the end. In much business writing, for example, you cannot assume that readers will read more than the first couple of sentences of a paragraph. In such cases, you will be wise to open with your most powerful examples, even at the risk of allowing the paragraph to fizzle at the end.

6d If necessary, adjust paragraph length.

Most readers feel comfortable reading paragraphs that range between 100 and 200 words. Shorter paragraphs force too much starting and stopping, and longer ones strain the reader's attention span. There are exceptions to this guideline, however. Paragraphs longer than 200 words frequently appear in scholarly writing, where they suggest seriousness and depth. Paragraphs shorter than 100 words occur in newspapers because of narrow columns; in informal essays to quicken the pace; and in business letters, where readers routinely skim for main ideas.

In an essay, the first and last paragraphs will ordinarily be the introduction and conclusion. These special-purpose paragraphs are likely to be shorter than the paragraphs in the body of the essay. Typically, the body paragraphs will mimic the essay's organization: one paragraph per point in short essays, a group of paragraphs per point in longer ones. Some ideas require more development than others, however, so it is best to be flexible. If an idea stretches to a length unreasonable for a paragraph, you should divide it, even if you have presented comparable points in the essay in single paragraphs.

Paragraph breaks are not always made for strictly logical reasons. Writers use them for the following reasons as well.

REASONS FOR BEGINNING A NEW PARAGRAPH

— to mark off the introduction and the conclusion
— to signal a shift to a new idea
— to indicate an important shift in time or place
— to emphasize a point (by placing it at the beginning or the end, not in the middle, of a paragraph)
— to highlight a contrast
— to signal a change of speakers (in dialogue)
— to provide readers with a needed pause
— to break up text that looks too dense

Beware of using too many short, choppy paragraphs, however. Readers want to see how your ideas connect, and they become irritated when you break their momentum by forcing them to pause every few sentences. Here are some reasons you might have for combining some of the paragraphs in a rough draft.

REASONS FOR COMBINING PARAGRAPHS

— to clarify the essay's organization
— to connect closely related ideas
— to maintain momentum
— to bind together text that looks too choppy

7

Improve coherence.

When sentences and paragraphs flow from one to another without noticeable bumps, gaps, or shifts, they are said to be coherent. Coherence can be improved by strengthening the various ties between old information and new: in other words, between sentences that have been read and those that are about to be read. A number of techniques for strengthening those ties are detailed in this section.

7a Link ideas clearly.

In the first draft of a paragraph or essay, writers do not always link their ideas as clearly as possible. To check a draft for clear connections among ideas, try to look at it from the point of view of a reader. Think in terms of the reader's expectations.

What readers look for in a paragraph

As you know, readers usually expect to learn a paragraph's main point in a topic sentence early in the paragraph. Then, as they move into the body of the paragraph, they expect to encounter specific details, facts, or examples that support the topic sentence — either directly or indirectly. Consider the following example, in which all of the sentences following the topic sentence directly support it.

> A passenger list of the early years of the Orient Express would read like a *Who's Who of the World,* from art to politics. Sarah Bernhardt and her Italian counterpart Eleonora Duse used the train to thrill the stages of Europe. For musicians there were Toscanini and Mahler. Dancers Nijinsky and Pavlova were there, while lesser performers like Harry Houdini and the girls of the Ziegfeld Follies also rode the rails. Violinists were allowed to practice on the train, and occasionally one might see trapeze artists hanging like bats from the baggage racks.
> — Barnaby Conrad III, "Train of Kings"

If a sentence does not directly support the topic sentence, readers expect it to support another sentence in the paragraph and therefore to support the topic sentence indirectly. Composition scholar Francis Christensen has invented a useful system for numbering the sentences in a paragraph to depict the hierarchic connections among sentences that readers look for. The topic sentence, being most general, receives the number 1, and any sentences that directly support it receive the number 2. Sentences that support level 2 sentences receive the number 3, and so on. Here, for example, is Christensen's numbering system as applied to a paragraph by columnist Ellen Goodman.

1. In the years since Kitty Genovese's murder, social scientists have learned a great deal about bystander behavior.

   2. They've learned that the willingness to intervene depends on a number of subtle factors beyond fear.

      3. It turns out that people are less likely to help if they are in a crowd of bystanders than if they are the only one.

         4. Their sense of responsibility is diffused.

         4. If the others aren't helping, they begin to reinterpret what they are seeing.

      3. People are also more passive in urban neighborhoods or crowded city spots where they suffer from "excessive overload" or simply turn off.

      3. They rarely get involved if they believe that the victim knows the assailant.

         4. This is especially true if the crime being witnessed is . . . a rape or attempted rape.

Because the sentences in this paragraph are arranged in a clear hierarchy, readers can easily follow the writer's train of thought.

To check one of your own paragraphs for clear connections among ideas, look to see if the hierarchic chain has been broken at any point. The topic sentence should announce the main idea, and the rest of the sentences should support it either directly or indirectly. When a sentence supports the topic sentence indirectly, it must support an earlier sentence that is clearly linked (directly or indirectly) to the topic sentence. If you can't find such a sentence, you'll need to add one or rethink the entire chain of ideas.

What readers look for in an essay

Like the sentences within paragraphs, the paragraphs within an essay should be arranged in a clear hierarchy. Readers expect to learn the essay's main point in the first paragraph, often in a thesis statement (see 1c). And by scanning the topic sentence of each paragraph in the body of the essay, readers hope to understand how each paragraph connects with what has come before. As a rule, a topic sentence should tell readers whether the information they are about to read supports the thesis statement directly or supports a key idea in the essay, which in turn supports the thesis.

Consider the following thesis statement and topic sentences, taken from an essay by student Thu Hong Nguyen. Each of Nguyen's topic sentences supports the thesis statement directly.

THESIS STATEMENT IN OPENING PARAGRAPH
From the moment she is mature enough to understand commands, to the day she is married off, to the time when she bears her own children, a Vietnamese woman tries to establish a good name as a diligent daughter, a submissive wife, and an altruistic mother.

TOPIC SENTENCE IN FIRST BODY PARAGRAPH
In order to be approved of by everyone, a Vietnamese daughter must work diligently to help her parents.

TOPIC SENTENCE IN SECOND BODY PARAGRAPH
Once she enters an arranged marriage, a good Vietnamese woman must submit to her husband.

TOPIC SENTENCE IN THIRD BODY PARAGRAPH
Finally, to be recognized favorably, a Vietnamese woman must sacrifice herself for the benefit of the children it is her duty to bear.

Topic sentences do not always have to interlock with the thesis quite so tightly as in Nguyen's essay. Nevertheless, by scanning the opening sentence or two of each paragraph, readers should have at least a rough sense of the connections of ideas within the whole essay.

7b Repeat key words.

Repetition of key words is an important technique for gaining coherence, because if too much information seems new, a paragraph will be hard to read. To prevent repetitions from becoming dull, you can use variations of a key word (*hike, hiker, hiking*), pronouns referring to the word (*hikers . . . they*), or synonyms (*walk, trek, wander, tramp, climb*).

In the following paragraph describing plots among indentured servants in seventeenth-century America, the well-known historian Richard Hofstadter binds sentences together by repeating the key word *plots* and echoing it with variations (all in italics).

> *Plots* hatched by several servants to run away together occurred mostly in the plantation colonies, and the few recorded servant *uprisings* were entirely limited to those colonies. Virginia had been forced from its very earliest years to take stringent steps against *mutinous plots,* and severe punishments for *such behavior* were recorded. Most servant *plots* occurred in the seventeenth century: a contemplated *uprising* was nipped in the bud in York County in 1661; apparently led by some left-wing offshoots of the *Great Rebellion,* servants *plotted* an *insurrection* in Gloucester County in 1663, and four leaders were condemned and executed; some discontented servants apparently joined *Bacon's Rebellion* in the 1670s. In the 1680s the planters became newly apprehensive of discontent among the servants "owing to their great necessities and want of clothes," and it was feared that they would *rise up* and *plunder* the storehouses and ships; in 1682 there were plant-cutting *riots* in which servants and laborers, as well as some planters, took part. [Italics added.]
>
> — Richard Hofstadter, *America at 1750*

7c Use parallel structures for parallel ideas.

Parallel grammatical structures are frequently used within sentences to underscore the similarity of ideas (see 9). They may also be used to bind together a series of sentences expressing similar information. In the following passage describing folk beliefs, anthropologist Margaret Mead presents similar information in parallel grammatical form.

Actually, almost every day, even in the most sophisticated home, something is likely to happen that evokes the memory of some old folk belief. The salt spills. A knife falls to the floor. Your nose tickles. Then perhaps, with a slightly embarrassed smile, the person who spilled the salt tosses a pinch over his left shoulder. Or someone recites the old rhyme, "Knife falls, gentleman calls." Or as you rub your nose you think, That means a letter. I wonder who's writing?

—Margaret Mead, "New Superstitions for Old"

A less skilled writer might have varied the structure, perhaps like this: *The salt gets spilled. Mother drops a knife on the floor. Your nose begins to tickle.* But these sentences are less effective; Mead's parallel structures help tie the paragraph together.

7d Maintain consistency.

Coherence suffers whenever a draft shifts confusingly from one point of view to another or from one verb tense to another. (See 13.) In addition, coherence can suffer when new information is introduced with the subject of each sentence. As a rule, a sentence's subject should echo a subject or object in the previous sentence.

The following rough-draft paragraph is needlessly hard to read because so few of the sentences' subjects are tied to earlier subjects or objects. The subjects appear in italics.

One goes about trapping in this manner. At the very outset *one* acquires a "trapping" state of mind. A *library* of books must be read, and preferably *someone* with experience should educate the novice. *Preparing* for the first expedition takes several steps. The *purchase* of traps is first. A *pair* of rubber gloves, waterproof *boots*, and the grubbiest *clothes* capable of withstanding human use come next to outfit the trapper for his adventure. The *decision* has to be made on just what kind of animals to seek, what sort of bait to use, and where to place the traps. Finally, the *trapper* needs a heavy stick, in case it is necessary to club the animal and drown him. [Italics added.]

Although the writer repeats a number of key words, such as *trapping*, the paragraph seems disconnected because new information is introduced with the subject of each sentence.

To improve the paragraph, the writer used the first-person pronoun as the subject of every sentence. The revision is much easier to read.

I went about trapping in this manner. To acquire a "trapping" state of mind, I read a library of books and talked at length with an experienced trapper, my father. Then I purchased the traps and outfitted myself by collecting a pair of rubber gloves, waterproof boots, and the grubbiest clothes capable of withstanding human use. Next I decided just what kinds of animals to seek, what sort of bait to use, and where to place my traps. Finally, I found a heavy stick, in case it would be necessary to club the animal and drown it. [Italics added.]

—John Clyde Thatcher, student

Notice that Thatcher combined some of his original sentences. By doing so, he was able to avoid excessive repetitions of the pronoun *I*. Notice, too, that he varied his sentence openings (most sentences do not begin with *I*) so that readers are not likely to find the repetitions tiresome.

7e Provide transitions.

Certain words and phrases signal connections between ideas, connections that might otherwise be missed. Included in the following list are coordinating conjunctions, such as *and, but,* and *or*; subordinating conjunctions, such as *although* and *if*; conjunctive adverbs, such as *however* and *therefore*; and transitional phrases, such as *in addition* and *for example*.

TO SHOW ADDITION
and, also, besides, further, furthermore, in addition, moreover, next, too, first, second

TO GIVE EXAMPLES
for example, for instance, to illustrate, in fact, specifically

TO COMPARE
also, in the same manner, similarly, likewise

TO CONTRAST
but, however, on the other hand, in contrast, nevertheless, still, even though, on the contrary, yet, although

TO SUMMARIZE OR CONCLUDE
in other words, in short, in summary, in conclusion, to sum up, that is, therefore

TO SHOW TIME
after, as, before, next, during, later, finally, meanwhile, then, when, while, immediately

TO SHOW PLACE OR DIRECTION
above, below, beyond, farther on, nearby, opposite, close, to the left

TO INDICATE LOGICAL RELATIONSHIP
if, so, therefore, consequently, thus, as a result, for this reason, since

Skilled writers use transitional expressions with care, making sure, for example, not to use *consequently* when *also* would be more precise. They are also careful to select transitions with an appropriate tone, perhaps preferring *so* to *thus* in an informal piece, *in summary* to *in short* for a scholarly essay.

In the following paragraph, taken from an argument that dinosaurs had the " 'right-sized' brains for reptiles of their body size," biologist Stephen Jay Gould uses transitions (italicized) with skill.

> I don't wish to deny that the flattened, minuscule head of the large bodied "Stegosaurus" houses little brain from our subjective, top-heavy perspective, *but* I do wish to assert that we should not expect more of the beast. *First of all,* large animals have relatively smaller brains than related, small animals. The correlation of brain size with body size among kindred animals (all reptiles, all mammals, *for example*) is remarkably regular. *As* we move from small to large animals, from mice to elephants *or* small lizards to Komodo dragons, brain size increases, *but* not so fast as body size. *In other words,* bodies grow faster than brains, *and* large animals have low ratios of brain weight to body weight. *In fact,* brains grow only about two-thirds as fast as bodies. *Since* we have no reason to believe that large animals are consistently stupider than their smaller relatives, we must conclude that large animals require relatively less brain to do as well as smaller animals. *If* we do not recognize this relationship, we are likely to underestimate the mental power of very large animals, dinosaurs in particular. [Italics added.]
> — Stephen Jay Gould, "Were Dinosaurs Dumb?"

EXERCISE 7–1

Use Francis Christensen's numerical system (see 7a) to indicate the relations among sentences in the following paragraph.

Once children have learned to read, they go beyond their textbooks and explore the popular books written just for them. In order to see how these books portray men and women, I decided to visit the St. Peter Public Library. One book I found, *The Very Worst Thing,* tells of the adventures of a little boy on his first day in a new school. He arrives at school wearing the new sweater his mother has knit for him and is greeted by his teacher, Miss Pruce, and his male principal. At recess, the girls jump rope and toss a ball back and forth while the boys choose football teams and establish a tree house club. For show-and-tell that day, Henry, his new friend, brings a snake and some mice; Alice shows her foreign dolls; and Elizabeth demonstrates how to make fudge with Rice Krispies. In another book, *Come Back, Amelia Bedelia,* Amelia is fired from her job of baking for Mrs. Rogers, so she tries to find work as a beautician, a seamstress, a file clerk, and an office girl for a doctor. After trying all of these jobs unsuccessfully, she goes back to Mrs. Rogers and gets back her old job by making cream puffs. The rest of the books I looked at contained similar sex-role stereotypes—boys wear jeans and T-shirts, set up lemonade stands, and play broomball, while girls wear dresses, play dress-up, and jump rope. Men are businessmen, soldiers, veterinarians, and truck drivers. Women are housewives, teachers, and witches who make love potions for girls wanting husbands.   —Patricia Klein, student

EXERCISE 7–2

If you were to divide the paragraph in Exercise 7–1 into two paragraphs, at what point would you make the break? Why?

EXERCISE 7–3

Looking again at the paragraph in Exercise 7–1, find examples of the following techniques for gaining coherence: repetition of key words, parallel structures, and transitions.

THE STAND-ALONE PARAGRAPH

Most paragraphs appear with other paragraphs in an essay, a report, a letter, a memo, or some other kind of document. The exception is the stand-alone paragraph, which is meant to be read by itself. Stand-alone paragraphs are assigned in many English classes; you will also use them for essay exams and other short writing assignments in the academic world. In the business world, you will use them for brief reports, evaluations, proposals, and so on.

A stand-alone paragraph is a miniature essay. Like an essay, it has a clear beginning, a middle, and an end. But because it is so much shorter than an essay, it must get to the point faster. Usually, a stand-alone paragraph begins with a topic sentence that expresses its main point, as in the following one-paragraph profile of a person. (The topic sentence is italicized.)

> *Paul Norman has loved airplanes all his life.* Even when he was a little boy, he wanted to be a pilot. He used to draw airplanes on all his schoolwork. He also folded paper airplanes and designed new folding techniques so the planes would fly in certain ways. In high school and college, he studied subjects that would help him become a pilot. He took every geography and math course his high school offered, and in college he took physics and aerodynamics as well as advanced math. Unfortunately, Paul's vision was not acute enough for him to qualify as a professional or a military pilot, so he tried another way of working with planes. He went back to school and earned a master's degree in business administration; now he is the manager of a major airport in Houston. From child to adult, Paul has not changed his major interest — airplanes.

Because the stand-alone paragraph appears by itself, it needs a conclusion. Usually the concluding sentence sums up the paragraph's main point, as in the example just given.

EXERCISE 7–4

Write a stand-alone paragraph modeled on one of the patterns discussed in section 6b. Some possible topics — most of which you'll need to narrow — are listed here.

Examples or illustrations: sexism in a comic strip, ways to include protein in a vegetarian diet, the benefits of a particular summer job, community services provided by your college, violence on the six o'clock news, educational software for children

Narration: the active lifestyle of a grandparent, life with an alcoholic, working in an emergency room, the benefits (or problems) of intercultural dating, growing up in a large family, the rewards of working in a nursing home, an experience that taught you a lesson, a turning point in your life

Description: your childhood home, an ethnic neighborhood, a rock concert, a favorite painting in an art gallery, a garden, a classic car, a hideous building or monument, a style of dress, a family heirloom (such as a crazy quilt or a collection of Christmas tree ornaments), a favorite park or retreat

Process: how to repair something, how to develop a successful job interview style, how to meet someone of the opposite sex, how to practice safe scuba diving, how to build a set for a play, how to survive in the wilderness, how to train a dog, how to quit smoking, how to make bread

Comparison and contrast: two neighborhoods, teachers, political candidates, colleges, products; country living versus city living; the stereotype of a job versus the reality; a change in attitude toward your family's religion or ethnic background

Analogy: between a family reunion and a circus, between training for a rigorous sport and boot camp, between settling an argument and being a courtroom judge, between a dogfight and a boxing match, between raising a child and tending a garden

Cause and effect: the effects of water pollution on a particular area, the effects of divorce on a child, the effects of an illegal drug, why a particular film or television show is popular, why an area of the country has high unemployment, why early training is essential for success as a ballet dancer, violinist, or athlete

Classification: types of clothing worn on your college campus, types of people who go to college mixers, types of dieters, types of television weather reports, types of rock bands, types of teachers

Definition: a computer addict, an ideal parent or teacher, an authoritarian personality, an intellectual, sexism, anorexia nervosa, a typical heroine in a Harlequin romance, a typical blind date

Clarity

8

Coordinate equal ideas; subordinate minor ideas.

When combining two or more ideas in one sentence, use coordination to create equal emphasis and use subordination to create unequal emphasis.

Coordination

Coordination draws attention equally to two or more ideas. To coordinate single words or phrases, join them with a coordinating conjunction or with a pair of correlative conjunctions (see 57g). To coordinate independent clauses — word groups that could stand alone as a sentence — join them with a comma and a coordinating conjunction or with a semicolon:

, and	, but	, or	, nor
, for	, so	, yet	;

The semicolon is often accompanied by a conjunctive adverb such as *moreover, furthermore, therefore,* or *however* or by a transitional phrase such as *for example, in other words,* or *as a matter of fact.* (See page 264 for a more complete list.)

Assume, for example, that you want to draw equal attention to the following two ideas.

Grandma lost her sight. Her hearing sharpened.

To coordinate these ideas, you can join them with a comma and the coordinating conjunction *but* or with a semicolon and the conjunctive adverb *however.*

Grandma lost her sight, but her hearing sharpened.

Grandma lost her sight; however, her hearing sharpened.

It is important to choose a coordinating conjunction or conjunctive adverb appropriate to your meaning. In the preceding example, the two ideas contrast with one another, calling for *but* or *however.*

Subordination

To give unequal emphasis to two or more ideas, express the major idea in an independent clause and place any minor ideas in subordinate clauses or phrases. (See 59.) Subordinate clauses, which cannot stand alone, typically begin with one of the following words.

after	before	though	where	who
although	if	unless	whether	whom
as	since	until	which	whose
because	that	when	while	

Deciding which idea to emphasize is not simply a matter of right and wrong. Consider the two ideas about Grandma's sight and hearing.

> Grandma lost her sight. Her hearing sharpened.

If your purpose is to stress your grandmother's acute hearing rather than her blindness, subordinate the idea concerning her blindness.

> *As Grandma lost her sight,* her hearing sharpened.

To focus on your grandmother's blindness, subordinate the idea concerning her hearing.

> *Though her hearing sharpened,* Grandma gradually lost her sight.

8a Combine choppy sentences.

Short sentences demand attention, so they should be used primarily for emphasis. Too many short sentences, one after the other, create a choppy style.

If an idea is too minor to deserve its own sentence, try combining it with a sentence close by. Put any minor ideas in subordinate structures such as phrases or subordinate clauses.

CHOPPY The huts vary in height. They measure from ten to fifteen feet in diameter. They contain no modern conveniences.

IMPROVED The huts, which vary in height and measure from ten to fifteen feet in diameter, contain no modern conveniences.

Three sentences have become one, with minor ideas expressed in a subordinate clause beginning with *which*.

▶ Agnes~~, was~~ another student I worked with~~. She~~ was a hyperactive child.

A minor idea is now expressed in an appositive phrase describing Agnes.

▶ ~~Sister Consilio was~~ *E*nveloped in a black robe with only her face
   and hands visible~~. She~~ was an imposing figure.
   Sister Consilio

A minor idea is now expressed in a participial phrase beginning with *Enveloped*.

▶ My sister owes much of her recovery to a bodybuilding program~~.~~
   that she
   ~~She~~ began ~~the program~~ three years ago.

A minor idea is now expressed in an adjective clause beginning with *that*.

▶ *When my*
   ~~My~~ son asked his great-grandmother if she had been a slave~~. She~~
   she
   became very angry.

A minor idea is now expressed in an adverb clause beginning with *When*.

Although subordination is ordinarily the most effective technique for combining short, choppy sentences, coordination is appropriate when the ideas are equal in importance.

▶ The hospital decides when patients will sleep and wake~~. It~~
   and
   dictates what and when they will eat~~. It~~ tells them when they
   may be with family and friends.

Equivalent ideas are expressed in a coordinate series.

ESL NOTE: When combining or restructuring sentences, do not repeat the subject of the sentence; also do not repeat an object or an adverb in an adjective clause. See 31b and 31c.

▶ The apartment that we moved into ~~it~~ needed many repairs.

▶ Kim climbed into the tree house that the boys were playing

in. ~~it.~~
  ∧

8b Avoid ineffective coordination.

Coordinate structures are appropriate only when you intend to draw the reader's attention equally to two or more ideas: *Gregory Krakower praises loudly, and he criticizes softly.* If one idea is more important than another — or if a coordinating conjunction does not clearly signal the relation between the ideas — you should subordinate the lesser idea.

▶ We keep our use of insecticides, herbicides, and fungicides to a
             because
  minimum/~~and~~ we are concerned about the environment.
       ∧

The revision puts the less important idea in an adverb clause beginning with *because*. The subordinating conjunction *because* signals the connection between the ideas more clearly than the coordinating conjunction *and*.

        noticing
▶ My uncle, ~~noticed~~ my frightened look/ ~~and~~ told me that
    ∧   ∧

Grandma had to feel my face because she was blind.

The less important idea has become a participial phrase modifying the noun *uncle*.

  After four hours,
▶ ~~Four hours went by, and~~ a rescue truck finally arrived, but by
  ∧

that time we had been evacuated in a helicopter.

Three independent clauses were excessive. The least important idea has become a prepositional phrase.

EXERCISE 8–1

Combine or restructure the following sentences by subordinating minor ideas or by coordinating ideas of equal importance. You must decide which ideas are minor because the sentences are given out of context. Revisions of lettered sentences appear in the back of the book. Example:

> The crew team finally returned to shore, ~~and~~ *where they* had a party on the beach ~~and celebrated~~ *to celebrate* the start of the season.

a. My grandfather has dramatic mood swings, and he was diagnosed as manic-depressive.

b. The losing team was made up of superstars. These superstars acted as isolated individuals on the court.

c. Thurmont means "gateway to the mountains." It is minutes from the Blue Ridge Mountains. It's also minutes from the historic town of Catoctin.

d. The aides help the younger children with reading and math. These are the children's weakest subjects.

e. My first sky dive was from an altitude of 12,500 feet, and it was the most frightening experience of my life.

1. Bay Street is located in the heart of downtown Nassau. It houses the Straw Market.

2. I noticed that the sky was glowing orange and red. I bent down to crawl into the bunker.

3. Our waitress was costumed in a kimono. She had painted her face white. She had arranged her hair in an upswept lacquered beehive.

4. Cocaine is an addictive drug and it can seriously harm you both physically and mentally, if death doesn't get you first.

5. These particles are known as "stealth liposomes," and they can hide in the body for a long time without detection.

6. At the airport I was met by my host mother, Madame Nicole Kimmel. She was a very excitable woman who knew absolutely no English.

7. He walked up to the pitcher's mound. He dug his toe into the ground. He swung his arm around backward and forward. Then he threw the ball and struck the batter out.

8. The Chesapeake and Ohio Canal is a 184-mile waterway constructed in the 1800s. It was a major source of transportation for goods during the Civil War era.

9. The lift chairs were going around very fast. They were bumping the skiers into their seats.
10. The first football card set was released by the Goudey Gum Company in 1933. The set featured only three football players. They were Red Grange, Bronko Nagurski, and Knute Rockne.

8c Do not subordinate major ideas.

If a sentence buries its major idea in a subordinate construction, readers may not give the idea enough attention. Express the major idea in an independent clause and subordinate any minor ideas.

▶ Lanie, who now walks with the help of braces/. had polio as
   had polio as a child,
   a child.

The writer wanted to focus on Lanie's ability to walk, but the original sentence buried this information in an adjective clause. The revision puts the major idea in an independent clause and tucks the less important idea into an adjective clause (*who had polio as a child*).

▶ *As*
   I was driving home from my new job, heading down Ranchitos
   Road, when my car suddenly overheated.

The writer wanted to emphasize that the car was overheating, not the fact of driving home. The revision expresses the major idea in an independent clause, the less important idea in an adverb clause (*As I was driving home from my new job*).

8d Do not subordinate excessively.

In attempting to avoid short, choppy sentences, writers sometimes go to the opposite extreme, putting more subordinate ideas into a sentence than its structure can bear. If a sentence collapses of its own weight, occasionally it can be restructured. More often, however, such sentences must be divided.

▶ Our job is to stay between the stacker and the tie machine

watching to see if the newspapers jam, ~~in which case~~ we pull
                                    If they do,

the bundles off and stack them on a skid, because otherwise

they would back up in the stacker.

EXERCISE 8–2

In each of the following sentences, the idea that the writer wished to emphasize is buried in a subordinate construction. Restructure each sentence so that the independent clause expresses the major idea and lesser ideas are subordinated. Revisions of lettered sentences appear in the back of the book. Example:

> *Though*
> Catherine has weathered many hardships, ~~though~~ she has
> ^
> rarely become discouraged. [*Emphasize that Catherine has*
>
> *rarely become discouraged.*]

a. We experienced a routine morning at the clinic until an infant in cardiac arrest arrived by ambulance. [*Emphasize the arrival of the infant.*]
b. My 1969 Camaro, which is no longer street legal, is an original SS396. [*Emphasize the fact that the car is no longer street legal.*]
c. I presented the idea of job sharing to my supervisors, who to my surprise were delighted with the idea. [*Emphasize the supervisors' response to the idea.*]
d. Although native Hawaiians try to preserve their ancestors' sacred customs, outsiders have forced changes on them. [*Emphasize the Hawaiians' attempt to preserve their customs.*]
e. Sophia's country kitchen, which overlooks a field where horses and cattle graze among old tombstones, was formerly a lean-to porch. [*Emphasize that the kitchen overlooks the field.*]

1. My grandfather, who raised his daughters the old-fashioned way, was born eighty-six years ago in Puerto Rico. [*Emphasize how the grandfather raised his daughters.*]
2. I was losing consciousness when my will to live kicked in. [*Emphasize the will to live.*]

3. Louis's team worked with the foreign mission by building new churches and restoring those damaged by hurricanes. [*Emphasize the building and restoring.*]

4. The rotor hit, gouging a hole about an eighth of an inch deep in my helmet. [*Emphasize the fact that the rotor gouged a hole in the helmet.*]

5. Although Sarah felt that we lacked decent transportation, our family owned a Jeep, a pickup truck, and a sports car. [*Emphasize Sarah's feeling that the family lacked decent transportation.*]

9

Balance parallel ideas.

If two or more ideas are parallel, they are easier to grasp when expressed in parallel grammatical form. Single words should be balanced with single words, phrases with phrases, clauses with clauses.

A kiss can be a comma, a question mark, or an exclamation point.
— Mistinguett

This novel is not to be tossed lightly aside, but to be hurled with great force.
— Dorothy Parker

In matters of principle, stand like a rock; in matters of taste, swim with the current.
— Thomas Jefferson

Writers often use parallelism to create emphasis. (See 14c.)

9a Balance parallel ideas in a series.

Readers expect items in a series to appear in parallel grammatical form. When one or more of the items violates readers' expectations, a sentence will be needlessly awkward.

▶ Abused children commonly exhibit one or more of the

following symptoms: withdrawal, rebelliousness,
                                    depression.
restlessness, and ~~they are depressed.~~
                  ^

The revision presents all of the items as nouns.

▶ Esperanza is responsible for stocking merchandise, writing
                                 selling
orders for delivery, and ~~sales of~~ computers.
                          ^

The revision uses *-ing* forms for all items in the series.

▶ After assuring us that he was sober, Sam drove down the
                                        went through
middle of the road, ran one red light, and two stop signs.
                                         ^

The revision adds a verb to make the three items parallel: *drove
. . . , ran . . . , went through. . . .*

NOTE: In headings and lists, aim for as much parallelism as the content allows. See 4a.

9b Balance parallel ideas presented as pairs.

When pairing ideas, underscore their connection by expressing them in similar grammatical form. Paired ideas are usually
connected in one of these ways:

— with a coordinating conjunction such as *and, but,* or *or*

— with a pair of correlative conjunctions such as *either . . .
or* or *not only . . . but also*

— with a word introducing a comparison, usually *than*
or *as*

Parallel ideas linked with coordinating conjunctions

Coordinating conjunctions (*and, but, or, nor, for, so,* and *yet*)
link ideas of equal importance. When those ideas are closely
parallel in content, they should be expressed in parallel grammatical form.

▶ At Lincoln High School, vandalism can result in suspension
        expulsion
or even ~~being expelled~~ from school.
        ∧

The revision balances the nouns *expulsion* and *suspension*.

▶ Many states are reducing property taxes for homeowners and
    extending
~~extend~~ financial aid in the form of tax credits to renters.
∧

The revision balances the verb *reducing* with the verb *extending*.

Parallel ideas linked with correlative conjunctions

Correlative conjunctions come in pairs: *either . . . or, neither . . . nor, not only . . . but also, both . . . and, whether . . . or.* Make sure that the grammatical structure following the second half of the pair is the same as that following the first half.

▶ The shutters were not only too long but also ~~were~~ too wide.

The words *too long* follow *not only*, so *too wide* should follow *but also*. Repeating *were* creates an unbalanced effect.

                                            to
▶ I was advised either to change my flight or take the train.
                                            ∧

To change my flight, which follows *either*, should be balanced with *to take the train*, which follows *or*.

Comparisons linked with than *or* as

In comparisons linked with *than* or *as*, the elements being compared should be expressed in parallel grammatical structure.

                        to ground
▶ It is easier to speak in abstractions than ~~grounding~~ one's
                        ∧

thoughts in reality.

                                            receiving
▶ He couldn't persuade me that giving is as much a joy as ~~to receive.~~
                                            ∧

To speak in abstractions is balanced with *to ground one's thoughts in reality*. *Giving* is balanced with *receiving*.

NOTE: Comparisons should also be logical and complete. See 10c.

9c Repeat function words to clarify parallels.

Function words such as prepositions (*by, to*) and subordinating conjunctions (*that, because*) signal the grammatical nature of the word groups to follow. Although they can sometimes be omitted, include them whenever they signal parallel structures that might otherwise be missed by readers.

▶ Many smokers try switching to a brand they find distasteful
　　　　　　　　to
or a low tar and nicotine cigarette.
　　　∧

In the original sentence the prepositional phrase was too complex for easy reading. The repetition of the preposition *to* prevents readers from losing their way.

EXERCISE 9–1

Edit the following sentences to correct faulty parallelism. Revisions of lettered sentences appear in the back of the book. Example:

We began the search by calling the Department of Social
　　　　　　　　　requesting
Services and ~~requested~~ a list of licensed day care centers in
　　　　　　∧
our area.

a. The system has capabilities such as communicating with other computers, processing records, and mathematical functions.
b. The personnel officer told me that I would answer the phone, welcome visitors, distribute mail, and some typing.
c. Nolan helped by cutting the grass, trimming shrubs, mulching flowerbeds, and leaf cleanup.
d. How ideal it seems to raise a family here in Winnebago instead of the air-polluted suburbs.
e. Michiko told the judge that she had been pulled out of a line of fast-moving traffic and of her perfect driving record.

1. The summer of our engagement, we saw a few plays, attended family outings, and a few parties.
2. At the arts and crafts table, the children make potholders, key rings, weave baskets, paint, and assemble model cars.
3. The examiners observed us to see if we could stomach the grotesque accidents and how to cope with them.

4. During basic training, I was not only told what to do but also what to think.

5. Activities on Wednesday afternoons include fishing trips, dance lessons, and computers.

6. Bill finds it harder to be fair to himself than being fair to others.

7. More plants fail from improper watering than any other cause.

8. Your adviser familiarizes you with the school and how to select classes appropriate for your curriculum.

9. To administer the poison, the tribe's sorcerers put it in their victims' food, throw it into their huts, or it can be dropped into their mouths or nostrils while they sleep.

10. The babysitter was expected to feed two children, entertain them, take phone messages, and some cleaning in the kitchen.

10

Add needed words.

Do not omit words necessary for grammatical or logical completeness. Readers need to see at a glance how the parts of a sentence are connected.

> **ESL NOTE:** Languages sometimes differ in the need for certain words. In particular, be alert for missing verbs, articles, subjects, or expletives. See 29e, 30, and 31a.

10a Add words needed to complete compound structures.

In compound structures, words are often omitted for economy: *Tom is a man who means what he says and [who] says what he means.* Such omissions are perfectly acceptable as long as the omitted words are common to both parts of the compound structure.

If the shorter version is not grammatical or idiomatic because an omitted word is not common to both parts of the compound structure, the word must be put back in.

>   *accepted*
> I never have and never will accept a bribe.
>   ^
>
> *Have . . . accept* is not grammatically correct.

>   *in*
> Many of these tribes still believe and live by ancient laws.
>   ^
>
> *Believe . . . by* is not idiomatic in English.

10b Add the word *that* if there is any danger of misreading without it.

If there is no danger of misreading, the word *that* may be omitted when it introduces a subordinate clause. *The value of a principle is the number of things [that] it will explain.* Occasionally, however, a sentence might be misread without *that*.

>   *that*
> Looking out the family room window, Sarah saw her favorite
>   ^
> tree, which she had climbed so often as a child, was gone.
>
> Sarah didn't see the tree; she saw that the tree was gone.

10c Add words needed to make comparisons logical and complete.

Comparisons should be made between items that are alike. To compare unlike items is illogical and distracting.

>   *those in*
> Henry preferred the hotels in Pittsburgh to Philadelphia.
>   ^
>
> Hotels must be compared with hotels.

> Some say that Ella Fitzgerald's renditions of Cole Porter's songs
>   *singer's*
> are better than any other ~~singer~~.
>   ^
>
> Ella Fitzgerald's renditions cannot be logically compared to a singer. The revision uses the possessive form *singer's*, with the word *renditions* being implied.

Sometimes the word *other* must be inserted to make a comparison logical.

other
▶ Chicago is larger than any city in Illinois.
                         ^

Since Chicago is not larger than itself, the original comparison was not logical.

Sometimes the word *as* must be inserted to make a comparison grammatically complete.

as
▶ Ben is as talented, if not more talented than, the other actors.
          ^

The construction *as talented* is not complete without a second *as*: *as talented as . . . the other actors*.

Finally, comparisons should be complete enough to ensure clarity. The reader should understand what is being compared.

INCOMPLETE   Brand X is less salty.

COMPLETE   Brand X is less salty than Brand Y.

Also, there should be no ambiguity. In the following sentence, two interpretations are possible.

AMBIGUOUS   Ken helped me more than my roommate.

CLEAR   Ken helped me more than *he helped* my roommate.

CLEAR   Ken helped me more than my roommate *did*.

10d Add the articles *a, an,* and *the* where necessary for grammatical completeness.

Articles are sometimes omitted in recipes and other instructions that are meant to be followed while they are being read. Such omissions are inappropriate, however, in nearly all other forms of writing, whether formal or informal.

                  a   *an*
▶ Blood can be drawn only by doctor or by authorized person
            the ^   ^
who has been trained in procedure.
                     ^

ESL NOTE: Articles can cause special problems for speakers of English as a second language. See 30.

EXERCISE 10–1

Add any words needed for grammatical or logical completeness in the following sentences. Revisions of lettered sentences appear in the back of the book. Example:

> *that*
> The officer at the desk feared the prisoner in the interrogation
> ∧
>
> room would escape.

a. Dip paintbrush into paint remover and spread thick coat on small section of door.
b. Christopher has an attention span longer than his sister.
c. SETI (the Search for Extraterrestrial Intelligence) has and will continue to excite interest among space buffs.
d. Samantha got along better with the chimpanzees than Albert.
e. We were glad to see Yellowstone National Park was recovering from the devastating forest fire.

1. Their starting salaries are higher than other professionals with more seniority.
2. In my opinion, her dependence on tranquilizers is no healthier than the alcoholic or the addict.
3. Jupiter is larger than any planet in our solar system.
4. Darryl was both gratified and apprehensive about his scholarship to UCLA.
5. It was obvious that the students liked the new teacher more than the principal.

11

Untangle mixed constructions.

A mixed construction contains parts that do not sensibly fit together. The mismatch may be a matter of grammar or of logic.

11a Untangle the grammatical structure.

Once you head into a sentence, your choices are limited by the range of grammatical patterns in English. (See 58 and 59.) You cannot begin with one grammatical plan and switch without warning to another.

> **MIXED**   For most drivers who have a blood alcohol content of .05 percent double their risk of causing an accident.

> **REVISED**   For most drivers who have a blood alcohol content of .05 percent, the risk of causing an accident is doubled.

> **REVISED**   Most drivers who have a blood alcohol content of .05 percent double their risk of causing an accident.

The writer began with a long prepositional phrase that was destined to be a modifier but then tried to press it into service as the subject of the sentence. This cannot be done. If the sentence is to begin with the prepositional phrase, the writer must finish the sentence with a subject and verb (*risk . . . is doubled*). The writer who wishes to stay with the original verb (*double*) must head into the sentence another way: *Most drivers. . . .*

> *Being*
> ▶ ~~When an employee is~~ promoted without warning can be
>   ^
>   alarming.

The adverb clause *When an employee is promoted without warning* cannot serve as the subject of the sentence. The revision replaces the adverb clause with a gerund phrase, a word group that can function as the subject. (See 59b and 59c.)

> ▶ Although I feel that Mr. Dawe is an excellent calculus instructor,
>
>   ~~but~~ a few minor changes in his method would benefit both him
>
>   and the class.

The *although* clause is subordinate, so it cannot be linked to an independent clause with the coordinating conjunction *but*.

Occasionally a mixed construction is so tangled that it defies grammatical analysis. When this happens, back away from the sentence, rethink what you want to say, and then say it again as clearly as you can.

> **MIXED**   In the whole-word method children learn to recognize entire words rather than by the phonics method in which they learn to sound out letters and groups of letters.

> **REVISED**   The whole-word method teaches children to recognize entire words; the phonics method teaches them to sound out letters and groups of letters.

ESL NOTE: English does not allow double subjects; nor does it allow an object or adverb to be repeated in an adjective clause. See 31b and 31c.

▶ The squirrel that came down our chimney ~~it~~ did much

damage.

▶ Hearing screams, Serena ran over to the pool that her

daughter was swimming in. ~~it~~.
                          ^

11b Straighten out the logical connections.

The subject and the predicate should make sense together; when they don't, the error is known as *faulty predication.*

                  Tiffany
▶ We decided that ~~Tiffany's welfare~~ would not be safe living with
                  ^
her mother.

Tiffany, not her welfare, may not be safe.

                       double personal exemption for the
▶ Under the revised plan, the elderly/~~who now receive a double~~
                                      ^
~~personal exemption,~~ will be abolished.

The exemption, not the elderly, will be abolished.

An appositive and the noun to which it refers should be logically equivalent. When they are not, the error is known as *faulty apposition.*

▶ ~~The tax accountant,~~ *Tax accounting,* a very lucrative field, requires intelligence,

patience, and attention to detail.

The tax accountant is a person, not a field.

11c Avoid *is when, is where,* and *reason . . . is because* constructions.

In formal English many readers object to *is when, is where,* and *reason . . . is because* constructions on either grammatical or logical grounds.

▶ Anorexia nervosa is ~~where people~~ *a disorder suffered by people who* diet to the point of starvation

because they believe they are too fat.

Anorexia nervosa is a disorder, not a place.

▶ ~~The reason~~ I missed the exam ~~is~~ because my motorcycle

broke down.

The writer might have changed *because* to *that* (*The reason I missed the exam is that my motorcycle broke down*), but the revision above is more concise.

EXERCISE 11–1

Edit the following sentences to untangle mixed constructions. Revisions of lettered sentences appear in the back of the book. Example:

~~By~~ *L* loosening the soil around your jade plant will help the air

and nutrients penetrate to the roots.

a. My instant reaction was filled with anger and disappointment.
b. I brought a problem into the house that my mother wasn't sure how to handle it.

c. It is through the misery of others that has made old Harvey rich.

d. A cloverleaf is when traffic on limited-access freeways can change direction.

e. Bowman established the format in which future football card companies would emulate for years to come.

1. Depending on the number and strength of drinks, the amount of time that has passed since the last drink, and one's body weight determines the concentration of alcohol in the blood.

2. By pushing the button for the insert mode opens the computer's memory.

3. The reason the Eskimos were forced to eat their dogs was because the caribou, on which they depended for food, migrated out of reach.

4. The shelter George stayed in required the men to leave at nine in the morning, in which they had to take their belongings with them.

5. Using surgical gloves is a precaution now worn by dentists to prevent contact with the patients' blood and saliva.

12

Repair misplaced and dangling modifiers.

Modifiers, whether they are single words, phrases, or clauses, should point clearly to the words they modify. As a rule, related words should be kept together.

12a Put limiting modifiers such as *only* in front of the words they modify.

Limiting modifiers such as *only, even, almost, nearly,* and *just* should appear in front of a verb only if they modify the verb: *At first, I couldn't even touch my toes, much less grasp them.* If they limit the meaning of some other word in the sentence, they should be placed in front of that word.

> Lasers ~~only~~ destroy the target, leaving the surrounding healthy
>   *only*
> ^
>
> tissue intact.

> *even*
> ▶ Our team didn't ~~even~~ score once.
>   ^

Only limits the meaning of *the target*, not *destroy*. *Even* modifies *once*, not *score*.

The limiting modifier *not* is frequently misplaced, suggesting a meaning the writer did not intend.

> *Not all*
> ▶ ~~All~~ wicker is ~~not~~ antique.
>   ^

The original version means that no wicker is antique. The revision makes the writer's intended meaning clear.

12b Place phrases and clauses so that readers can see at a glance what they modify.

Although phrases and clauses can appear at some distance from the words they modify, make sure your meaning is clear. When phrases or clauses are oddly placed, absurd misreadings can result.

MISPLACED The king returned to the clinic where he had undergone heart surgery in a limousine sent by the White House.

REVISED Traveling in a limousine sent by the White House, the king returned to the clinic where he had undergone heart surgery.

The heart surgery did not occur in a limousine. The revision prevents this absurd misreading.

> *On the walls*
> ▶ ~~There~~ are many pictures of comedians who have performed at
>   ^
>
> Gavin's. ~~on the walls~~.
>   ^

The comedians weren't performing on the walls; the pictures were on the walls.

> *150-pound,*
> ▶ The robber was described as a six-foot-tall man with a heavy
>   ^
>
> mustache. ~~weighing 150 pounds~~.
>   ^

The robber, not the mustache, weighed 150 pounds.

Occasionally the placement of a modifier leads to an ambiguity, in which case two revisions will be possible, depending on the writer's intended meaning.

AMBIGUOUS   The exchange students we met for coffee occasionally questioned us about our latest slang.

CLEAR   The exchange students we occasionally met for coffee questioned us about our latest slang.

CLEAR   The exchange students we met for coffee questioned us occasionally about our latest slang.

In the original version, it was not clear whether the meeting or the questioning happened occasionally. The revisions eliminate the ambiguity.

12c Move awkwardly placed modifiers.

As a rule, a sentence should flow from subject to verb to object, without lengthy detours along the way. When a long adverbial element separates a subject from its verb, a verb from its object, or a helping verb from its main verb, the result is usually awkward.

> *After*
> ▶ ~~Our son, after~~ doctors told him that he would never walk again,
> *our son* ^
> began an intensive program of rehabilitation.
> ^
> There is no reason to separate the subject *Our son* from the verb *began* with a long adverb clause.

12d Do not split infinitives needlessly.

An infinitive consists of *to* plus a verb: *to think, to breathe, to dance*. When a modifier appears between *to* and the verb, an infinitive is said to be "split": *to carefully balance*. If a split infinitive is obviously awkward, it should be revised.

> *If possible, the*
> ▶ ~~The~~ patient should try to/~~if possible,~~ avoid going up and
> ^
> down stairs.

Usage varies when a split infinitive is less awkward than the preceding one. To be on the safe side, however, you should not split such infinitives, especially in formal writing.

▶ The presidential candidate decided to ~~formally~~ launch his
        formally.
campaign⁄
      ^

When a split infinitive is more natural and less awkward than alternative phrasing, most readers find it acceptable: *We decided to actually enforce the law* is a perfectly natural construction in English. *We decided actually to enforce the law* is not.

EXERCISE 12–1

Edit the following sentences to correct misplaced or awkwardly placed modifiers. Revisions of lettered sentences appear in the back of the book. Example:

        in a telephone survey
Answering extensive questions can be annoying▪ ~~in a telephone~~
                        ^   ^

~~survey.~~

a. He only wanted to buy three roses, not a dozen.
b. Within the next few years, orthodontists will be using the technique Kurtz developed as standard practice.
c. Celia received a flier about a workshop on making a kimono from a Japanese nun.
d. Jurors are encouraged to carefully and thoroughly sift through the evidence.
e. Each state would set a program into motion of recycling all re-usable products.

1. The orderly confessed that he had given a lethal injection to the patient after ten hours of grilling by the police.
2. Several recent studies have encouraged heart patients to more carefully watch their cholesterol levels.
3. He promised never to remarry at her deathbed.
4. The recordings were all done at the studio of the late Jimi Hendrix named Electric Ladyland.
5. The old Marlboro ads depicted a man on a horse smoking a cigarette.

12e Repair dangling modifiers.

A dangling modifier fails to refer logically to any word in the sentence. Dangling modifiers are usually introductory word groups (such as verbal phrases) that suggest but do not name an actor. When a sentence opens with such a modifier, readers expect the subject of the following clause to name the actor. If it doesn't, the modifier dangles.

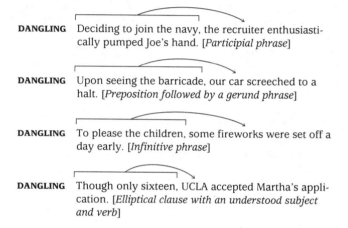

DANGLING   Deciding to join the navy, the recruiter enthusiastically pumped Joe's hand. [*Participial phrase*]

DANGLING   Upon seeing the barricade, our car screeched to a halt. [*Preposition followed by a gerund phrase*]

DANGLING   To please the children, some fireworks were set off a day early. [*Infinitive phrase*]

DANGLING   Though only sixteen, UCLA accepted Martha's application. [*Elliptical clause with an understood subject and verb*]

These dangling modifiers falsely suggest that the recruiter decided to join the navy, that the car saw the barricade, that the fireworks intended to please the children, and that UCLA is only sixteen years old.

To repair a dangling modifier, you can revise the sentence in one of two ways:

1. Name the actor immediately following the introductory modifier, or
2. turn the modifier into a word group that names the actor.

▶ Upon entering the doctor's office, a skeleton. ~~caught my attention.~~ *I noticed*
   As I entered

▶ ~~Upon entering~~ the doctor's office, a skeleton caught my attention.

A dangling modifier cannot be repaired simply by moving it: *A skeleton caught my attention upon entering the doctor's office.* The sentence still suggests — absurdly — that the skeleton entered the doctor's office.

When the driver opened
▶ ~~Opening~~ the window to let out a huge bumblebee, the car
  ^

accidentally swerved into the lane of oncoming cars.

The car didn't open the window; the driver did.

women have often been denied
▶ After completing seminary training, ~~women's~~ access to the
  ^

pulpit. ~~has often been denied.~~
^
The women (not their access to the pulpit) complete the training.

To check for dangling modifiers, use the flow chart below.

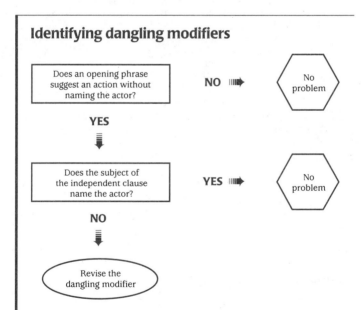

Identifying dangling modifiers

Does an opening phrase suggest an action without naming the actor?

NO ⇒ No problem

YES

Does the subject of the independent clause name the actor?

YES ⇒ No problem

NO

Revise the dangling modifier

If you find a dangling modifier, revise the sentence in one of two ways:

1. Change the subject of the independent clause so that it names the actor implied by the modifier.
2. Turn the modifier into a word group that includes the actor.

EXERCISE 12–2

Edit the following sentences to correct dangling modifiers. Most sentences can be revised in more than one way. Revisions of lettered sentences appear in the back of the book. Example:

> *a student must complete*
> To acquire a degree in almost any field, two science courses.
> ^   ^
>
> ~~must be completed.~~

a. Reaching the heart, a bypass was performed on the severely blocked arteries.
b. Nestled in the cockpit, the pounding of the engine was muffled only slightly by my helmet.
c. While dining at night, the lights along the Baja coastline created a romantic atmosphere perfect for our first anniversary.
d. While still a beginner at tennis, the coaches recruited my sister to train for the Olympics.
e. After returning to Jamaica, Marcus Garvey's "Back to Africa" movement slowly died.

1. Exhausted from battling the tide and the undertow, a welcome respite appeared in the swimmer's view—the beach!
2. When investigating burglaries and thefts, it was easy for me to sympathize with the victims because I had been a victim myself.
3. As a child growing up in Nigeria, my mother taught me to treat all elders with respect.
4. At the age of twelve, my social studies teacher entered me in a public speaking contest.
5. Although too expensive for her budget, Juanita bought the lavender skirt.

13

Eliminate distracting shifts.

13a Make the point of view consistent.

The point of view of a piece of writing is the perspective from which it is written: first person (*I* or *we*), second person (*you*), or third person (*he/she/it/one* or *they*). The *I* (or *we*) point of view, which emphasizes the writer, is a good choice for informal letters and writing based primarily on personal experience. The *you* point of view, which emphasizes the reader, works well for giving advice or explaining how to do something. The third-person point of view, which emphasizes the subject, is appropriate in formal academic and professional writing.

Writers who are having difficulty settling on an appropriate point of view sometimes shift confusingly from one to another. The solution is to choose a suitable perspective and then stay with it.

▶ One week our class met in a junkyard to practice rescuing a

victim trapped in a wrecked car. We learned to dismantle the
                                      We   *our*
car with the essential tools. ~~You~~ were graded on ~~your~~ speed
      our   ^   ^
and ~~your~~ skill in extricating the victim.
      ^

The writer should have stayed with the *we* point of view. *You* is inappropriate because the writer is not addressing readers directly. *You* should not be used in a vague sense meaning "anyone." (See 23d.)

                    You
▶ ~~Everyone~~ should purchase a lift ticket unless you plan to spend
      ^

most of your time walking or crawling up a steep hill.

Here *you* is an appropriate choice because the writer is giving advice directly to readers.

            Police officers are
▶ ~~A police officer is~~ often criticized for always being there when
      ^

they aren't needed and never being there when they are.

Although the writer might have changed *they* to *he or she* (to match the singular *officer*), the revision in the plural is more concise. (See also 17f and 22a.)

13b Maintain consistent verb tenses.

Consistent verb tenses clearly establish the time of the actions being described. When a passage begins in one tense and then shifts without warning and for no reason to another, readers are distracted and confused.

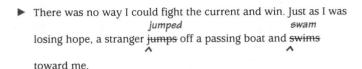
▶ There was no way I could fight the current and win. Just as I was
               jumped   *swam*

losing hope, a stranger ~~jumps~~ off a passing boat and ~~swims~~
                              ^   ^

toward me.

Writers often encounter difficulty with verb tenses when
writing about literature. The literary convention is to describe
fictional events consistently in the present tense.

▶ The scarlet letter is a punishment sternly placed upon Hester's
                                         is

breast by the community, and yet it ~~was~~ an extremely fanciful
                                       ^

and imaginative product of Hester's own needlework.

13c   Make verbs consistent in mood and voice.

Unnecessary shifts in the mood of a verb can be as distracting
as needless shifts in tense. There are three moods in English:
the *indicative,* used for facts, opinions, and questions; the
imperative, used for orders or advice; and the *subjunctive,* used
in certain contexts to express wishes or conditions contrary to
fact (see 28b).
    The following passage shifts confusingly from the indica-
tive to the imperative mood.

▶ The officers advised us against allowing anyone into our homes
                          They also suggested that we

without proper identification. ~~Also,~~ alert neighbors to vacation
                                  ^

schedules.

    Since the writer's purpose was to report the officers' advice, the
    revision puts both sentences in the indicative.

A verb may be in either the active voice (with the subject
doing the action) or the passive voice (with the subject receiving the action). (See 28c.) If a writer shifts without warning
from one to the other, readers may be left wondering why.

▶ When the tickets are ready, the travel agent notifies the
      lists each ticket
client**/**, ~~Each ticket is then listed~~ on a daily register form**,** and
files ^
a copy of the itinerary**.** ~~is filed~~.
^   ^

The passage began in the active voice (*agent notifies*) and then
switched to the passive (*ticket is listed, copy is filed*). Because the
active voice is clearer and more direct, the writer put all the verbs
in the active voice.

13d Avoid sudden shifts from indirect to direct questions or quotations.

An indirect question reports a question without asking it: *We
asked whether we could take a swim.* A direct question asks
directly: *Can we take a swim?* Sudden shifts from indirect to
direct questions are awkward.

▶ I wonder whether the sister knew of the murder and, if so, ~~did~~
      whether she reported
~~she report~~ it to the police.
^

The revision poses both questions indirectly. The writer could
also ask both questions directly: *Did the sister know of the murder
and, if so, did she report it to the police?*

An indirect quotation reports someone's words without
quoting word for word: *Annabelle said that she is a Virgo.* A
direct quotation presents the exact words of a speaker or
writer, set off with quotation marks: *Annabelle said, "I am a
Virgo."* Unannounced shifts from indirect to direct quotations
are distracting and confusing, especially when the writer fails
to insert the necessary quotation marks, as in the following
example.

                        asked me not to
▶ Mother said that she would be late for dinner and ~~please do not~~
                           came   ^
leave for choir practice until Dad ~~comes~~ home.
                               ^

The revision reports all of the mother's words. The writer could
also quote directly: *Mother said, "I will be late for dinner. Please do
not leave for choir practice until Dad comes home."*

EXERCISE 13–1

Edit the following sentences to eliminate distracting shifts. Revisions of lettered sentences appear in the back of the book. Example:

> *they*
> For most people, quitting smoking is not easy once ~~you~~ are
>   ^
> hooked.

a. The young man who burglarized our house was sentenced to probation for one year, a small price to pay for robbing someone of their personal possessions as well as of their trust in other human beings.

b. After the count of three, Mikah and I placed the injured woman on the scoop stretcher. Then her vital signs were taken by me.

c. A minister often has a hard time because they have to please so many different people.

d. We drove for eight hours until we reached the South Dakota Badlands. You could hardly believe the eeriness of the landscape at dusk.

e. The question is whether ferrets bred in captivity have the instinct to prey on prairie dogs or is this a learned skill.

1. The polygraph examiner will ask if you have ever stolen goods on the job, if you have ever taken drugs, and have you ever killed or threatened to kill anyone.

2. A single parent often has only their ingenuity to rely on.

3. As I was pulling in the decoys, you could see and hear the geese heading back to the bay.

4. Rescue workers put water on her face and lifted her head gently onto a pillow. Finally, she opens her eyes.

5. With a little self-discipline and a desire to improve oneself, you too can enjoy the benefits of running.

14

Emphasize your point.

Within each sentence, emphasize your point by expressing it in the subject and verb, the words that receive the most attention from readers. As a rule, choose an active verb and pair it with a subject that names the person or thing doing the action.

Within longer stretches of prose, you can draw attention to ideas deserving special emphasis by using a variety of techniques, usually involving some element of surprise.

14a Prefer active verbs.

Active verbs express meaning more emphatically and vigorously than their weaker counterparts—forms of the verb *be* or verbs in the passive voice. Forms of the verb *be* (*be, am, is, are, was, were, being, been*) lack vigor because they convey no action. Verbs in the passive voice lack strength because their subjects receive the action instead of doing it (see 28c and 58c).

Although the forms of *be* and passive verbs have legitimate uses, if an active verb can carry your meaning, use it.

> **BE VERB**   A surge of power *was* responsible for the destruction of the coolant pumps.
>
> **PASSIVE**   The coolant pumps *were destroyed* by a surge of power.
>
> **ACTIVE**   A surge of power *destroyed* the coolant pumps.

Even among active verbs, some are more active—and therefore more vigorous and colorful—than others. Carefully selected verbs can energize a piece of writing.

> ▶ The goalie crouched low, ~~reached~~ out his stick, and ~~sent~~ the *swept* ^ *hooked* ^
>
> rebound away from the mouth of the net.

When to replace be verbs

Not every *be* verb needs replacing. The forms of *be* (*be, am, is, are, was, were, being, been*) work well when you want to link a subject to a noun that clearly renames it or to an adjective that describes it: *History is a bucket of ashes. Scoundrels are always sociable.* And when used as helping verbs before present participles (*is flying, are disappearing*) to express ongoing action, *be* verbs are fine: *Derrick was plowing the field when his wife went into labor.* (See 28a.)

If using a *be* verb makes a sentence needlessly wordy, however, consider replacing it. Often a phrase following the verb will contain a word (such as *destruction*) that suggests a more vigorous, active alternative (*destroyed*).

▶ Burying nuclear waste in Antarctica would ~~be in violation of~~ an
violate

international treaty.

Violate is less wordy and more vigorous than *be in violation of.*

▶ Escaping into the world of drugs, I ~~was rebellious about~~ every
rebelled against

rule set down by my parents.

Rebelled against is more active than *was rebellious about.*

When to replace passive verbs

In the active voice, the subject of the sentence does the action; in the passive, the subject receives the action.

ACTIVE   Hernando *caught* the fly ball.

PASSIVE   The fly ball *was caught* by Hernando.

In passive sentences, the actor (in this case *Hernando*) frequently disappears from the sentence: *The fly ball was caught.*

In most cases, you will want to emphasize the actor, so you should use the active voice. To replace a passive verb with an active alternative, make the actor the subject of the sentence.

▶ ~~The transformer was struck by a bolt of lightning,~~ plunging us
A bolt of lightning struck the transformer,

into darkness.

The active verb (*struck*) makes the point more forcefully than the passive verb (*was struck*).

The passive voice is appropriate when you wish to emphasize the receiver of the action or to minimize the importance of the actor. For example, in the sentence about the fly ball, you would choose the active voice if you wanted to emphasize the actor, Hernando: *Hernando caught the fly ball.* But you would choose the passive voice if you wanted to emphasize the ball and the catch: *The fly ball was caught by Hernando.* (See 28c.)

14b As a rule, choose a subject that names the person or thing doing the action.

In weak, unemphatic prose, both the actor and the action may be buried in sentence elements other than the subject and the verb. In the following sentence, for example, the actor and the action both appear in prepositional phrases, word groups that do not receive much attention from readers.

| WEAK | Exposure to Dr. Martinez's excellent teaching had the effect of inspiring me to major in education. |
| EMPHATIC | Dr. Martinez's excellent teaching inspired me to major in education. |

Consider the subjects and verbs of the two versions — *exposure had* versus *teaching inspired.* Clearly the latter expresses the writer's point more emphatically.

Cocaine used
► ~~The use of cocaine~~ by pregnant women can ~~be a~~ cause ~~of~~ severe
brain damage in infants.

In the original version, the subject and verb — *use can be* — express the point blandly. *Cocaine can cause* alerts readers to the dangers of cocaine more emphatically than *use can be.*

EXERCISE 14–1

Revise any weak, unemphatic sentences by replacing *be* verbs or passive verbs with active alternatives and, if necessary, by naming in the subject the person or thing doing the action. Some sentences are emphatic; do not change them. Revisions of lettered sentences appear in the back of the book. Example:

The ranger doused the campfire before giving us
~~The campfire was doused by the ranger before we were given~~
a ticket for unauthorized use of a campsite.

a. Her letter was in acknowledgment of the students' participation in the literacy program.

b. The entire operation is managed by Ahmed, the producer.

c. Finally the chute caught air and popped open with a jolt at about 2,000 feet.

d. There were fighting players on both sides of the rink.

e. At the crack of rocket and mortar blasts, I jumped from the top bunk and landed on my buddy below, who was crawling on the floor looking for his boots.

1. Just as the police were closing in, two shots were fired by the terrorists from the roof of the hotel.

2. Julia was successful in her first attempt to pass the bar exam.

3. The bomb bay doors rumbled open and freezing air whipped through the plane.

4. C.B.'s are used to find parts, equipment, food, lodging, and anything else that is needed by truckers.

5. There were fireworks exploding all around us.

14c Experiment with techniques for gaining special emphasis.

By experimenting with certain techniques, usually involving some element of surprise, you can draw attention to ideas that deserve special emphasis. Use such techniques sparingly, however, or they will lose their punch. The writer who tries to emphasize everything ends up emphasizing nothing.

Using sentence endings for emphasis

You can highlight an idea simply by withholding it until the end of a sentence. The technique works something like a punch line. In the following example, the sentence's meaning is not revealed until its very last word.

> The only completely consistent people are dead.
>
> — Aldous Huxley

Using parallel structure for emphasis

Parallel grammatical structure draws special attention to paired ideas or to items in a series. (See 9.) When parallel ideas are paired, the emphasis falls on words that underscore comparisons or contrasts, especially when they occur at the end of a phrase or clause.

> We must *stop talking* about the *American dream* and *start listening* to the *dreams of Americans*. —Reubin Askew

Using punctuation for emphasis

Obviously the exclamation point can add emphasis, but you should not overuse it. As a rule, the exclamation point is more appropriate in dialogue than in ordinary prose.

> I oozed a glob of white paint onto my palette, whipped some medium into it, loaded my brush, and announced to the class, "Move over, Michelangelo. Here I come!"
> —Carolyn Goff, student

A dash or a colon may be used to draw attention to word groups worth special attention. (See 35a, 35b, and 39a.)

> The middle of the road is where the white line is—and that's the worst place to drive. —Robert Frost

> I turned to see what the anemometer read: The needle had pegged out at 106 knots. —Jonathan Shilk, student

15

Provide some variety.

When a rough draft is filled with too many same-sounding sentences, try injecting some variety—as long as you can do so without sacrificing clarity or ease of reading.

15a Vary your sentence openings.

Most sentences in English begin with the subject, move to the verb, and continue along to the object, with modifiers tucked in along the way or put at the end. For the most part, such sentences are fine. Put too many of them in a row, however, and they become monotonous.

Adverbial modifiers, being easily movable, can often be inserted ahead of the subject. Such modifiers might be single words, phrases, or clauses.

> *Eventually a*
> ▶ Ⱥ few drops of sap ~~eventually~~ began to trickle into the metal
>
> pail.

Like most adverbs, *eventually* does not need to appear close to the verb it modifies (*began*).

> *Just as the sun was coming up, a*
> ▶ Ⱥ pair of black ducks flew over the blind. ~~just as the sun was~~
>
> ~~coming up.~~

The adverb clause, which modifies the verb *flew,* is as clear at the beginning of the sentence as it is at the end.

Adjectives and participial phrases can frequently be moved to the beginning of a sentence without loss of clarity.

> *Dejected and withdrawn,*
> ▶ Edward /~~dejected and withdrawn,~~ nearly gave up his search
>
> for a job.

>   *A*   *John and I*
> ▶ ~~John and I,~~ anticipating a peaceful evening, sat down at the
>
> campfire to brew a cup of coffee.

CAUTION: When beginning a sentence with an adjective or a participial phrase, make sure that the subject of the sentence names the person or thing described in the introductory phrase. If it doesn't, the phrase will dangle. (See 12e.)

15b Use a variety of sentence structures.

A writer should not rely too heavily on simple sentences and compound sentences, for the effect tends to be both monotonous and choppy. (See 8a and 8b.) Too many complex or compound-complex sentences, however, can be equally mo-

notonous. If your style tends to one or the other extreme, try
to achieve a better mix of sentence types.

For a discussion of sentence types, see 60a.

15c Try inverting sentences occasionally.

A sentence is inverted if it does not follow the normal subject-verb-
object pattern. (See 58.) Many inversions sound artificial and should
be avoided except in the most formal contexts. But if an inversion
sounds natural, it can provide a welcome touch of variety.

> *Opposite the produce section is a*
> ▶ A̶ refrigerated case of mouth-watering cheeses; i̶s̶ o̶p̶p̶o̶s̶i̶t̶e̶ t̶h̶e̶
>   ⌃   ⌃
>
>   p̶r̶o̶d̶u̶c̶e̶ s̶e̶c̶t̶i̶o̶n̶; a friendly attendant will cut off just the amount
>
>   you want.

> *Set at the top two corners of the stage were huge*
> ▶ H̶u̶g̶e̶ lavender hearts outlined in bright white lights. w̶e̶r̶e̶ s̶e̶t̶
>   ⌃   ⌃
>
>   a̶t̶ t̶h̶e̶ t̶o̶p̶ t̶w̶o̶ c̶o̶r̶n̶e̶r̶s̶ o̶f̶ t̶h̶e̶ s̶t̶a̶g̶e̶.

EXERCISE 15–1

Edit the following paragraph to increase variety in sentence structure.

I have spent thirty years of my life on a tobacco farm, and I cannot
understand why people smoke. The whole process of raising tobacco
involves deadly chemicals. The ground is treated for mold and chemically fertilized before the tobacco seed is ever planted. The seed is
planted and begins to grow, and then the bed is treated with weed
killer. The plant is then transferred to the field. It is sprayed with poison to kill worms about two months later. Then the time for harvest
approaches, and the plant is sprayed once more with a chemical to
retard the growth of suckers. The tobacco is harvested and hung in a
barn to dry. These barns are havens for birds. The birds defecate all
over the leaves. After drying, these leaves are divided by color, and
no feces are removed. They are then sold to the tobacco companies.
I do not know what the tobacco companies do after they receive the
tobacco. I do not need to know. They cannot remove what I know is
in the leaf and on the leaf. I don't want any of it to pass through my
mouth.

16

Tighten wordy sentences.

Long sentences are not necessarily wordy, nor are short sentences always concise. A sentence is wordy if it can be tightened without loss of meaning.

16a Eliminate redundancies.

Redundancies such as *cooperate together, close proximity, basic essentials,* and *true fact* are a common source of wordiness. There is no need to say the same thing twice.

▶ Black slaves were ~~called or~~ stereotyped as lazy even though they

were the main labor force of the South.

      works
▶ Daniel ~~is now employed~~ at a private rehabilitation center
    ^
~~working~~ as a registered physical therapist.

Modifiers are redundant when their meanings are suggested by other words in the sentence.

▶ Sylvia ~~very hurriedly~~ scribbled her name, address, and phone

number on the back of a greasy napkin.

▶ Joel was determined ~~in his mind~~ to lose weight.

The words *scribbled* and *determined* already contain the notions suggested by the modifiers *very hurriedly* and *in his mind.*

16b Avoid unnecessary repetition of words.

Though words may be repeated deliberately, for effect, repetitions will seem awkward if they are clearly unnecessary. When a more concise version is possible, choose it.

▶ Our fifth patient, in room six, is ~~a~~ mentally ill. ~~patient.~~

         grow

▶ The best teachers help each student to ~~become a better student~~

both academically and emotionally.

16c Cut empty or inflated phrases.

An empty phrase can be cut with little or no loss of meaning. Common examples are introductory word groups that apologize or hedge: *in my opinion, I think that, it seems that, one must admit that,* and so on.

        O

▶ ~~In my opinion,~~ ~~O~~ur current policy in Central America is

misguided on several counts.

▶ ~~It seems that~~ *Lonesome Dove* is one of Larry McMurtry's

most ambitious novels.

Readers understand without being told that they are hearing the writer's opinion or educated guess.

Inflated phrases can be reduced to a word or two without loss of meaning.

INFLATED	CONCISE
along the lines of	like
as a matter of fact	in fact
at all times	always
at the present time	now, currently
at this point in time	now, currently
because of the fact that	because
by means of	by
by virtue of the fact that	because
due to the fact that	because
for the purpose of	for
for the reason that	because
have the ability to	be able to
in light of the fact that	because
in the nature of	like
in order to	to

INFLATED	CONCISE
in spite of the fact that	although, though
in the event that	if
in the final analysis	finally
in the neighborhood of	about
until such time as	until

▶ We will file the appropriate papers ~~in the event that~~ *if* we are

unable to meet the deadline.

16d Simplify the structure.

If the structure of a sentence is needlessly indirect, try simplifying it. Look for opportunities to strengthen the verb.

▶ The financial analyst claimed that because of volatile market

conditions she could not ~~make an~~ estimate ~~of~~ the company's

future profits.

The verb *estimate* is more direct than *make an estimate of.*

The colorless verbs *is, are, was,* and *were* frequently generate excess words.

▶ The secretary ~~is responsible for monitoring and balancing~~ *monitors and balances* the

budgets for travel, contract services, and personnel.

Actions originally appearing in subordinate structures have become verbs replacing *is.*

The expletive constructions *there is* and *there are* (or *there was* and *there were*) can also generate excess words. The same is true of expletive constructions beginning with *it.* (See 58c.)

▶ ~~There is~~ *A*nother module ~~that~~ tells the story of Charles Darwin

and introduces the theory of evolution.

> *H   must*
> ~~It is important that~~ ⟨hikers remain inside the park boundaries.
>   ^

Expletive constructions do have legitimate uses, however. For example, they are appropriate when a writer has a good reason for delaying the subject. (See 58c.)

Finally, verbs in the passive voice may be needlessly indirect. When the active voice expresses your meaning as well, use it. (See 14a and 28c.)

> *our coaches have recruited*
> All too often, athletes with marginal academic skills. ~~have been~~
>   ^   ^
> ~~recruited by our coaches.~~

16e Reduce clauses to phrases, phrases to single words.

Word groups functioning as modifiers can often be made more compact. Look for any opportunities to reduce clauses to phrases or phrases to single words.

> We took a side trip to Monticello, ~~which was~~ the home of
> Thomas Jefferson.

> *silk*
> For her birthday we gave Jess a stylish vest. ~~made of silk.~~
>   ^ ^

EXERCISE 16–1

Edit the following sentences for wordiness. Revisions of lettered sentences appear in the back of the book. Example:

> *even though*
> The Wilsons moved into the house ~~in spite of the fact that~~
>   ^
> the back door was only ten yards from the train tracks.

a. The drawing room in the west wing is the room that is said to be haunted.
b. Dr. Santini has seen problems like yours countless numbers of times.
c. In my opinion, Bloom's race for the governorship is a futile exercise.

d. If there are any new fares, then they must be reported by message to our transportation offices in Chicago, Peoria, and Springfield.
e. In the heart of Beijing lies the Forbidden City, which is an imperial palace built in very ancient times during the Ming dynasty.

1. Seeing the barrels, the driver immediately slammed on his brakes.
2. The thing data sets are used for is communicating with other computers.
3. The town of New Harmony, located in Indiana, was founded as a utopian community.
4. Martin Luther King, Jr., was a man who set a high standard for future leaders to meet.
5. The price of driving while drunk or while intoxicated can be extremely high.

17

Choose appropriate language.

Language is appropriate when it suits your subject, engages your audience, and blends naturally with your own voice.

17a Stay away from jargon.

Jargon is specialized language used among members of a trade, profession, or group. Use jargon only when readers will be familiar with it; even then, use it only when plain English will not do as well.

> **JARGON**   For years the indigenous body politic of South Africa attempted to negotiate legal enfranchisement without result.

> **REVISED** For years the indigenous people of South Africa negotiated in vain for the right to vote.

Broadly defined, jargon includes puffed-up language designed more to impress readers than to inform them. The following are common examples from business, government, higher education, and the military, with plain English translations in parentheses.

ameliorate (improve)	indicator (sign)
commence (begin)	optimal (best, most favorable)
components (parts)	parameters (boundaries, limits)
endeavor (try)	peruse (read, look over)
exit (leave)	prior to (before)
facilitate (help)	utilize (use)
factor (consideration, cause)	viable (workable)
impact on (affect)	

Sentences filled with jargon are hard to read, and they are often wordy as well.

▶ All ~~employees functioning in the capacity of~~ work-study
must prove that they are currently enrolled.
students ~~are required to give evidence of current enrollment.~~
                    ^

                    begin   *improving*
▶ Mayor Summers will ~~commence~~ his term of office by ~~ameliorating~~
                        ^ *poor neighborhoods.*   ^
living conditions in ~~economically deprived zones.~~
                        ^

17b Avoid pretentious language and most euphemisms.

Hoping to sound profound or poetic, some writers embroider their thoughts with large words and flowery phrases, language that in fact sounds pretentious. Pretentious language is so ornate and often so wordy that it obscures the thought that lies beneath.

                    parents become old,
▶ When our ~~progenitors reach their silver-haired and golden years,~~
            ^ *bury*   *old-age*
we frequently ~~ensepulcher~~ them in homes ~~for senescent beings~~
                ^   *dead.*   ^
as if they were already ~~among the deceased.~~
                        ^

Euphemisms, nice-sounding words or phrases substituted for words thought to sound harsh or ugly, are sometimes appropriate. It is customary, for example, to say that a couple is "sleeping together" or that someone has "passed away." Most euphemisms, however, are needlessly evasive or even deceitful. Like pretentious language, they obscure the intended meaning.

EUPHEMISM	PLAIN ENGLISH
adult entertainment	pornography
preowned automobile	used car
economically deprived	poor
selected out	fired
negative savings	debts
strategic withdrawal	retreat or defeat
revenue enhancers	taxes
chemical dependency	drug addiction
nuclear engagement	nuclear war
correctional facility	prison

EXERCISE 17–1

Edit the following sentences to eliminate jargon, pretentious or flowery language, and euphemisms. You may need to make substantial changes in some sentences. Revisions of lettered sentences appear in the back of the book. Example:

> After two weeks in the legal department, Sue has ~~worked into~~ *mastered*
> the routine*,* ~~of the office,~~ and her ~~functional and self-~~ *office* *performance has*
> ~~management skills have~~ exceeded all expectations.

a. It is a widespread but unproven hypothesis that the parameters of significant personal change for persons in midlife are extremely narrow.

b. The former proprietor of the previously owned car assured Kyle that the mileage had not been adjusted backward.

c. In 1985 I purchased a residential property in need of substantial upgrading.

d. When Sal was selected out from his high-paying factory job, he learned what it was like to be economically depressed.

e. Passengers should endeavor to finalize the customs declaration form prior to exiting the aircraft.

1. Because factory orders and profits have trended downward, we will not be enhancing our staffing over the course of the next fiscal year.

2. As I approached the edifice of confinement where my brother was incarcerated, several inmates loudly vocalized a number of lewd remarks.

3. The nurse announced that there had been a negative patient-care outcome due to a therapeutic misadventure on the part of the surgeon.

4. When we returned from our evening perambulation, we shrank back in horror as we surmised that our domestic dwelling was being swallowed up in hellish flames.

5. The bottom line is that the company is experiencing a negative cash flow.

17c Avoid obsolete, archaic, and invented words.

Obsolete words are words found in the writing of the past that have dropped out of use entirely. Archaic words are old words that are still used, but only in special contexts such as literature or advertising. Although dictionaries list obsolete words such as *recomfort* and *reechy* and archaic words such as *anon* and *betwixt,* these words are not appropriate for current use.

Invented words (also called *neologisms*) are words too recently created to be part of standard English. Many invented words fade out of use without becoming standard. *Build-down, throughput,* and *palimony* are neologisms that may not last. *Scuba, disco, sexist, software,* and *spinoff* are no longer neologisms; they have become standard English. Avoid using invented words in your writing unless they are given in the dictionary as standard or unless no other word expresses your meaning.

17d In most contexts, avoid slang, regional expressions, and nonstandard English.

Slang is an informal and sometimes private vocabulary that expresses the solidarity of a group such as teenagers, rock musicians, or football fans; it is subject to more rapid change than standard English. For example, the slang teenagers use to express approval changes every few years; *cool, groovy, neat, wicked, awesome,* and *stylin'* have replaced one another within the last three decades. Sometimes slang becomes so widespread that it is accepted as standard vocabulary. *Jazz,* for example, started out as slang but is now generally accepted to describe a style of music.

Although slang has a certain vitality, it is a code that not everyone understands, and it is very informal. Therefore, it is inappropriate in most written work.

> ► If we don't begin studying for the final, a whole semester's
>   *will be wasted.*
>   work ~~is going down the tubes.~~
>   ^

> ► The government's "filth" guidelines for food will ~~gross you out.~~ *disgust you.*
>   ^

Regional expressions are common to a group in a geographical area. *Let's talk with the bark off* (for *Let's speak frankly*) is an expression in the southern United States, for example. Regional expressions have the same limitations as slang and are therefore inappropriate in most writing.

> ► John was four blocks from the house before he remembered
>   *turn on*
>   to ~~cut~~ the headlights~~, on.~~
>   ^   ^

> ► I'm not ~~for~~ sure, but I think the dance has been postponed.

As you probably know, many people speak two varieties of English — standard English, used in academic and business situations, and a nonstandard dialect, spoken with close acquaintances who share a regional or social heritage. In written English, a dialect may be used in dialogue, to reflect actual speech, but in most other contexts it is out of place. Like slang and regionalisms, nonstandard English is a language shared by a select group. Standard English, by contrast, is accessible to all.

If you speak a nonstandard dialect, try to identify the ways in which your dialect differs from standard English. Look especially for the following features of nonstandard English, which commonly cause problems in writing.

Misuse of verb forms such as *began* and *begun* (See 27a.)

Omission of *-s* endings on verbs (See 27c.)

Omission of *-ed* endings on verbs (See 27d.)

Omission of necessary verbs (See 27e.)

Double negatives (See 26d.)

You might also scan the Glossary of Usage, which alerts you to nonstandard words and expressions such as *ain't, could of, hisself, theirselves, them* (meaning "those"), *they* (meaning "their"), *it is* (meaning "there is"), and so on.

17e Choose an appropriate level of formality.

In deciding on a level of formality, consider both your subject and your audience. Does the subject demand a dignified treatment, or is a relaxed tone more suitable? Will readers be put off if you assume too close a relationship with them, or might you alienate them by seeming too distant?

For most college and professional writing, some degree of formality is appropriate. In a philosophy paper or in a letter applying for a job, for example, it is a mistake to sound too breezy and informal.

TOO INFORMAL	I'd like to get that receptionist's job you've got in the paper.
MORE FORMAL	I would like to apply for the receptionist's position listed in the *Peoria Journal Star.*

Informal writing is appropriate for private letters, business correspondence between close associates, articles in popular magazines, and personal narratives. In such writing, formal language can seem out of place.

▶ Once a pitcher for the Cincinnati Reds, Bob shared with me the
                              began
secrets of his trade. His lesson ~~commenced~~ with his famous
      which he threw ^
curve ball, ~~implemented~~ by tucking the little finger behind the
   ^   *revealed*
ball instead of holding it straight out. Next he ~~elucidated~~ the
                                    ^
mysteries of the sucker pitch, a slow ball coming behind a fast

windup.

EXERCISE 17–2

Edit the following paragraph to eliminate slang and maintain a consistent level of formality.

The graduation speaker really blew it. He should have discussed the options and challenges facing the graduating class. Instead, he shot his mouth off at us and trashed us for being lazy and pampered. He did make some good points, however. Our profs have certainly babied us by not holding fast to deadlines, by dismissing assignments that the class ragged them about, by ignoring our tardiness, and by handing out easy C's like hotcakes. Still, we resented this speech as the final word from the college establishment. It should have been the orientation speech when we started college.

17f Avoid sexist language.

Sexist language is language that stereotypes or demeans men or women, usually women. Some sexist language reflects genuine contempt for women: referring to a woman as a "broad," for example, or calling a lawyer a "lady lawyer," or saying in an advertisement, "If our new sports car were a lady, it would get its bottom pinched."

Other forms of sexist language, while they may not suggest conscious sexism, reflect stereotypical thinking: referring to nurses as women and doctors as men, using different conventions when naming or identifying women and men, or assuming that all of one's readers are men.

> ▶ After the nursing student graduates, she must face a difficult
> *he or* ^
>
> state board examination.

> ▶ Running for city council are Andrew Steinbrenner, an attorney,
>
> and ~~Mrs.~~ Cynthia Jones, a professor of English. ~~and mother~~
> ^
> ~~of three.~~

> ▶ If you are a senior government official, your ~~wife~~ *spouse* is required to
> ^
> report any gifts *he or* she receives that are valued at more than $100.
> ^

Still other forms of sexist language result from outmoded traditions. The pronouns *he, him,* and *his,* for instance, were traditionally used to refer indefinitely to persons of either sex.

TRADITIONAL   A journalist is stimulated by *his* deadline.

Today, however, such usage is widely viewed as sexist because it excludes women and encourages sex-role stereotyping—the view that men are somehow more suited than women to be journalists, doctors, and so on.

One option, of course, is to substitute *his or her* for *his: A journalist is stimulated by his or her deadline.* This strategy is fine in small doses, but it generates needless words that become awkward when repeated throughout an essay. A better strategy, many writers have discovered, is simply to write in the plural.

REVISED   *Journalists* are stimulated by *their* deadlines.

Yet another strategy is to recast the sentence so that the problem does not arise.

REVISED   A journalist is stimulated by *a* deadline.

When sexist language occurs throughout an essay, it is sometimes possible to adjust the essay's point of view. If the essay might be appropriately rewritten from the *I,* the *we,* or the *you* point of view, the problem of sexist language will not arise. (See 13a.)

Like the pronouns *he, him,* and *his,* the nouns *man* and *men* were once used indefinitely to refer to persons of either sex. Current usage demands gender-neutral terms instead.

INAPPROPRIATE	APPROPRIATE
chairman	chairperson, moderator, chair, head
clergyman	member of the clergy, minister, pastor
congressman	member of Congress, representative, legislator
fireman	firefighter
foreman	supervisor
mailman	mail carrier, postal worker, letter carrier
mankind	people, humans
manpower	personnel
policeman	police officer
salesman	salesperson, sales associate, salesclerk
to man	to operate, to staff
weatherman	weather forecaster, meteorologist
workman	worker, laborer

Clarity

EXERCISE 17–3

Edit the following sentences to eliminate sexist language or sexist assumptions. Revisions of lettered sentences appear in the back of the book. Example:

>   *Scholarship athletes*   *their*
>   ~~A scholarship athlete~~ must be as concerned about ~~his~~ academic
>   ^   *they are*   *their*   ^
>   performance as ~~he is~~ about ~~his~~ athletic performance.
>   ^   ^

a. Mrs. Asha Purpura, who is a doctor's wife, is the defense attorney appointed by the court. Al Jones has been assigned to work with her on the case.

b. If a young graduate is careful about investments, he can accumulate a significant sum in a relatively short period.

c. An elementary school teacher should understand the concept of nurturing if she intends to be a success.

d. Because Dr. Brown and Dr. Dorothy Coombs were the senior professors in the department, they served as co-chairmen of the promotion committee.

e. If man does not stop polluting his environment, mankind will perish.

1. I have been trained to doubt an automobile mechanic, even if he has an excellent reputation.

2. After a new president is elected, he must wait several months before his inauguration.

3. In the recent gubernatorial race, Lena Weiss, a defense lawyer and mother of two, easily defeated Harvey Tower, an architect.

4. In my hometown, the lady mayor has led the fight for a fair share of federal funds for new schools.

5. As partners in a successful real estate firm, John Crockett and Sarah Cooke have been an effective sales team; he is particularly skillful at arranging attractive mortgage packages; she is a vivacious blonde who stays fit by doing aerobics daily.

18

Find the exact words.

Two reference works will help you find words to express your meaning exactly: a good dictionary and a book of synonyms and antonyms such as *Roget's International Thesaurus*.

18a Select words with appropriate connotations.

In addition to their strict dictionary meanings (or *denotations*), words have *connotations,* emotional colorings that affect how readers respond to them. The word *steel* denotes "made of or resembling commercial iron that contains carbon," but it also calls up a cluster of images associated with steel, such as the sensation of touching it. These associations give the word its connotations — cold, smooth, unbending.

If the connotation of a word does not seem appropriate for your purpose, your audience, or your subject matter, you should change the word. When a more appropriate synonym does not come quickly to mind, consult a dictionary or a thesaurus.

▶ The model was ~~skinny~~ *slender* and fashionable.
^

The connotation of the word *skinny* is too negative.

▶ As I covered the boats with marsh grass, the ~~perspiration~~ *sweat* I
^

had worked up evaporated in the wind, making the cold

morning air seem even colder.

The term *perspiration* is too dainty for the context, which suggests vigorous exercise.

EXERCISE 18–1

Use a dictionary or thesaurus to find at least four synonyms for each of the following words. Be prepared to explain any slight differences in meaning.

1. decay (verb)
2. difficult (adjective)
3. hurry (verb)
4. pleasure (noun)
5. secret (adjective)
6. talent (noun)

18b Prefer specific, concrete nouns.

Unlike general nouns, which refer to broad classes of things, specific nouns point to definite and particular items. *Film,* for example, names a general class, *science fiction film* names a narrower class, and *Jurassic Park* is more specific still. Other examples: *team, football team, Denver Broncos; music, symphony, Beethoven's Ninth; work, carpentry, cabinetmaking.*

Unlike abstract nouns, which refer to qualities and ideas (*justice, beauty, realism, dignity*), concrete nouns point to immediate, often sensory experience and to physical objects (*steeple, asphalt, lilac, stone, garlic*).

Specific, concrete nouns express meaning more vividly than general or abstract ones. Although general and abstract language is sometimes necessary to convey your meaning, ordinarily prefer specific, concrete alternatives.

▶ The senator spoke about the challenges of the future: problems *of famine, pollution, dwindling resources, and arms control.* ~~concerning the environment and world peace.~~
 ∧

Nouns such as *thing, area, aspect, factor,* and *individual* are especially dull and imprecise.

                                         rewards.
▶ A career in transportation management offers many ~~things~~.
                                                 ∧
                      experienced technician.
▶ Try pairing a trainee with an ~~individual with technical experience~~.
                                        ∧

18c Do not misuse words.

If a word is not in your active vocabulary, you may find yourself misusing it, sometimes with embarrassing consequences. When in doubt, check the dictionary.

       climbing
▶ The fans were ~~migrating~~ up the bleachers in search of seats.
       ∧

                           avail.
▶ Mrs. Johnson tried to fight but to no ~~prevail~~.
                               ∧

       permeated
▶ Drugs have so ~~diffused~~ our culture that they touch all
       ∧

segments of society.

Be especially alert for misused word forms — using a noun such as *absence, significance,* or *persistence,* for example, when your meaning requires the adjective *absent, significant,* or *persistent.*

> ► Most dieters are not ~~persistence~~ *persistent* enough to make a permanent

change in their eating habits.

EXERCISE 18–2

Edit the following sentences to correct misused words. Revisions of lettered sentences appear in the back of the book. Example:

> The training required for a ballet dancer is ~~all-absorbent.~~ *all-absorbing.*

a. Many of us are not persistence enough to make a change for the better.

b. It is sometimes difficult to hear in church because the agnostics are so terrible.

c. Liu Kwan began his career as a lawyer, but now he is a real estate mongrel.

d. When Robert Frost died at age eighty-eight, he left a legacy of poems that will make him immortal for years to come.

e. This patient is kept in isolation to prevent her from obtaining our germs.

1. Waste, misuse of government money, security and health violations, and even pilfering have become major dilemmas at the FBI.

2. Trifle, a popular English dessert, contains a ménage of ingredients that do not always appeal to American tastes.

3. Grand Isle State Park is surrounded on three sides by water.

4. Frequently I cannot do my work because the music blaring from my son's room detracts me.

5. Tom Jones is an illegal child who grows up under the care of Squire Western.

18d Use standard idioms.

Idioms are speech forms that follow no easily specified rules. The English say "Maria went *to hospital,*" an idiom strange to American ears, which are accustomed to hearing *the* in front of *hospital.* Native speakers of a language seldom have problems with idioms, but prepositions sometimes cause trouble, especially when they follow certain verbs and adjectives. When in doubt, consult a good desk dictionary.

UNIDIOMATIC	IDIOMATIC
according with	according to
abide with (a decision)	abide by (a decision)
agree to (an idea)	agree with (an idea)
angry at (a person)	angry with (a person)
capable to	capable of
comply to	comply with
desirous to	desirous of
different than	different from
intend on doing	intend to do
off of	off
plan on doing	plan to do
preferable than	preferable to
prior than	prior to
superior than	superior to
sure and	sure to
try and	try to
type of a	type of

ESL NOTE: Because idioms follow no particular rules, you must learn them individually. You may find it helpful to keep a list of idioms that you frequently encounter in conversation and in reading.

EXERCISE 18–3

Edit the following sentences to eliminate errors in the use of idiomatic expressions. If a sentence is correct, write "correct" after it. Answers to lettered sentences appear in the back of the book. Example:

> *by*
> We agreed to abide ~~with~~ the decision of the judge.
>   ^

a. Queen Anne was so angry at Sarah Churchill that she refused to see her again.

b. Prior to the Russians' launching of *Sputnik,* *-nik* was not an English suffix.

c. Try and come up with the rough outline, and Marika will fill in the details.

d. For the frightened refugees, the dangerous trek across the mountains was preferable than life in a war zone.

e. The parade moved off of the street and onto the beach.

1. Be sure and report on the danger of releasing genetically engineered bacteria into the atmosphere.

2. Why do you assume that embezzling bank assets is so different than robbing the bank?

3. Most of the class agreed to Sylvia's view that nuclear proliferation is potentially a very dangerous problem.

4. What type of a wedding are you planning?

5. Andrea intends on joining the Peace Corps after graduation.

18e Avoid worn-out expressions.

The frontiersman who first announced that he had "slept like a log" no doubt amused his companions with a fresh and unlikely comparison. Today, however, that comparison is a cliché, a saying that has lost its dazzle from overuse. No longer can it surprise.

To see just how dully predictable clichés are, put your hand over the right column below and then finish the phrases on the left.

cool as a	cucumber
beat around	the bush
blind as a	bat
busy as a	bee, beaver
crystal	clear
dead as a	doornail
out of the frying pan	into the fire
light as a	feather
like a bull	in a china shop
playing with	fire
nutty as a	fruitcake
selling like	hotcakes
starting out at the bottom	of the ladder
water over the	dam
white as a	sheet, ghost
avoid clichés like the	plague

The cure for clichés is frequently simple: Just delete them. When this won't work, try adding some element of surprise.

One student, for example, who had written that she had butterflies in her stomach, revised her cliché like this:

> If all of the action in my stomach is caused by butterflies, there must be a horde of them, with horseshoes on.

The image of butterflies wearing horseshoes is fresh and unlikely, not dully predictable like the original cliché.

18f Use figures of speech with care.

A figure of speech is an expression that uses words imaginatively (rather than literally) to make abstract ideas concrete. Most often, figures of speech compare two seemingly unlike things to reveal surprising similarities.

In a *simile,* the writer makes the comparison explicitly, usually by introducing it with *like* or *as:* "By the time cotton had to be picked, grandfather's neck was as red as the clay he plowed." In a *metaphor,* the *like* or *as* is omitted, and the comparison is implied. For example, in the Old Testament Song of Solomon, a young woman compares the man she loves to a fruit tree: "With great delight I sat in his shadow, and his fruit was sweet to my taste."

Writers sometimes use figures of speech without thinking carefully about the images they evoke. This can result in a *mixed metaphor,* the combination of two or more images that don't make sense together.

▶ Crossing Utah's salt flats in his new Corvette, my father flew
  at jet speed.
  ~~under a full head of steam.~~
  ^

▶ Our office staff decided to put all controversial issues on a back

  burner. ~~in a holding pattern.~~
        ^

EXERCISE 18–4

Edit the following sentences to replace worn-out expressions and clarify mixed figures of speech. Revisions of lettered sentences appear in the back of the book. Example:

the color drained from his face.

When he heard about the accident, ~~he turned white as a sheet.~~
                                   ^

a. Juanita told Kyle that keeping skeletons in the closet would be playing with fire.
b. The president thought that the scientists were using science as a sledgehammer to grind their political axes.
c. Ours was a long courtship; we waited ten years before finally deciding to tie the knot.
d. We ironed out the sticky spots in our relationship.
e. Sasha told us that he wasn't willing to put his neck out on a limb.

1. I could read him like a book; he had egg all over his face.
2. Tears were strolling down the child's face.
3. High school is a seething caldron of raw human emotion.
4. There are too many cooks in the broth here at corporate headquarters.
5. Once she had sunk her teeth into it, Helen burned through the assignment.

Grammar

19

Repair sentence fragments.

A sentence fragment is a word group that pretends to be a sentence. Some fragments are clauses that contain a subject and a verb but begin with a subordinating word. Others are phrases that lack a subject, a verb, or both.

Sentence fragments are quite easy to recognize when they appear out of context, like this one:

> On the old wooden stool in the corner of my grandmother's kitchen.

When they appear next to related sentences, however, they are harder to spot.

> On that morning I sat in my usual spot. On the old wooden stool in the corner of my grandmother's kitchen.

To be a sentence, a word group must consist of at least one full independent clause. An independent clause has a subject and a verb, and it either stands alone or could stand alone. To test a word group for sentence completeness, use the flow chart on page 153. For example, by using the flow chart, you can see exactly why *On the old wooden stool in the corner of my grandmother's kitchen* is a fragment: It lacks both a verb and a subject.

You can repair most fragments in one of two ways: Either pull the fragment into a nearby sentence, making sure to punctuate the new sentence correctly, or turn the fragment into a sentence. To repair the sample fragment, you would probably choose to combine it with the sentence that precedes it, like this:

> On that morning I sat in my usual spot, on the old wooden stool in the corner of my grandmother's kitchen.

ESL NOTE: Unlike some languages, English does not allow omission of subjects (except in imperative sentences); nor does it allow omission of verbs. See 31a and 29e.

19a Attach fragmented subordinate clauses or turn them into sentences.

A subordinate clause is patterned like a sentence, with both a subject and a verb, but it begins with a word that marks it as subordinate. The following words commonly introduce subordinate clauses:

after	how	that	which
although	if	though	while
as	in order that	unless	who
as if	rather than	until	whom
because	since	when	whose
before	so that	where	why
even though	than	whether	

Subordinate clauses function within sentences as adjectives, as adverbs, or as nouns. They cannot stand alone. (See 59b.)

Most fragmented clauses beg to be pulled into a sentence nearby.

▶ Jane will address the problem of limited on-campus parking/
if
I̶f̶ she is elected special student adviser.

If introduces a subordinate clause that modifies the verb *will address*. For punctuation of subordinate clauses appearing at the end of a sentence, see 33f.

▶ Although we seldom get to see wildlife in the city/, A̶t the zoo
a

we can still find some of our favorites.

Although introduces a subordinate clause that modifies the verb *can find*. For punctuation of subordinate clauses appearing at the beginning of a sentence, see 32b.

If a fragmented clause cannot be attached to a nearby sentence or if you feel that attaching it would be awkward, try rewriting it. The simplest way to turn a subordinate clause into a sentence is to delete the opening word or words that mark it as subordinate.

▶ Violence has produced a great deal of apprehension among

teachers at Dean Junior High. ~~So that~~ *S*elf-preservation, in

fact, has become their primary aim.

19b Attach fragmented phrases or turn them into sentences.

Like subordinate clauses, phrases function within sentences as adjectives, as adverbs, or as nouns. They cannot stand alone. Fragmented phrases are often prepositional or verbal phrases; sometimes they are appositives, words or word groups that rename nouns or pronouns. (See 59a, 59c, and 59d.)

Often a fragmented phrase may simply be pulled into a nearby sentence.

▶ Mary is suffering from agoraphobia*,* *a* fear of the outside world.

A fear of the outside world is an appositive renaming the noun *agoraphobia.* For punctuation of appositives, see 32e.

If a fragmented phrase cannot be pulled into a nearby sentence effectively, turn the phrase into a sentence. You may need to add a subject, a verb, or both.

▶ In the study skills workshop, we learned the value of discipline
    We also learned
and hard work. ~~Also~~ how to organize our time, take meaningful
             ^
notes, interpret assignments, pinpoint trouble spots, and seek help.

The word group beginning *Also how to organize* is a fragmented verbal phrase. The revision turns the fragment into a sentence by adding a subject and a verb.

19c Attach other fragmented word groups or turn them into sentences.

Other word groups that are commonly fragmented include parts of compound predicates, lists, and examples introduced by *such as, for example,* or similar expressions.

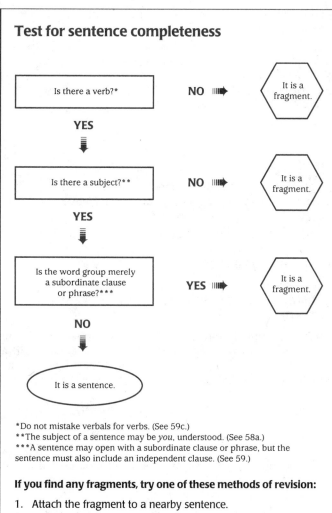

Test for sentence completeness

Is there a verb?* — **NO** ⯈ It is a fragment.

YES ⯬

Is there a subject?** — **NO** ⯈ It is a fragment.

YES ⯬

Is the word group merely a subordinate clause or phrase?*** — **YES** ⯈ It is a fragment.

NO ⯬

It is a sentence.

*Do not mistake verbals for verbs. (See 59c.)
**The subject of a sentence may be *you,* understood. (See 58a.)
***A sentence may open with a subordinate clause or phrase, but the sentence must also include an independent clause. (See 59.)

If you find any fragments, try one of these methods of revision:

1. Attach the fragment to a nearby sentence.
2. Turn the fragment into a sentence.

Parts of compound predicates

A predicate consists of a verb and its objects, complements, and modifiers (see 58b). A compound predicate includes two or more predicates joined by a coordinating conjunction such as *and, but,* or *or.* Because the parts of a compound predicate have the same subject, they should appear in the same sentence.

▶ Aspiring bodybuilders must first ascertain their strengths and

weaknesses~~//~~ **a**nd then decide what they want to achieve.

Notice that no comma appears between the parts of a compound predicate. (See 33a.)

Lists

When a list is mistakenly fragmented, it can often be attached to a nearby sentence with a colon or a dash. (See 35a and 39a.)

▶ It has been said that there are only three indigenous American

art forms~~/.~~: **m**usical comedy, jazz, and soap opera.

Examples introduced by *such as, for example,* or similar expressions

Expressions that introduce examples (or explanations) can lead to unintentional fragments. Although you may begin a sentence with some of the following words or phrases, make sure that what you have written is a sentence, not a fragment.

also	especially	in addition	namely	that is
and	for example	like	or	
but	for instance	mainly	such as	

Sometimes fragmented examples can be attached to the preceding sentence.

▶ The South has produced some of our greatest twentieth-

century writers~~/.~~ **s**uch as Flannery O'Connor, William Faulkner,

Alice Walker, Tennessee Williams, and Thomas Wolfe.

At times, however, it may be necessary to turn the fragment into a sentence.

▶ If Eric doesn't get his way, he goes into a fit of rage. For

         he lies   *opens*

  example, ~~lying~~ on the floor screaming or ~~opening~~ the cabinet

        ^   *slams*

  doors and then ~~slamming~~ them shut.

     ^

The writer corrected this fragment by adding a subject — *he* — and substituting verbs for the verbals *lying, opening,* and *slamming.*

19d Exception: Occasionally a fragment may be used deliberately, for effect.

Skilled writers occasionally use sentence fragments for the following special purposes.

FOR EMPHASIS	Following the dramatic Americanization of their children, even my parents grew more publicly confident. *Especially my mother.* —Richard Rodriguez
TO ANSWER A QUESTION	Are these new drug tests 100 percent reliable? *Not in the opinion of most experts.*
AS A TRANSITION	*And now the opposing arguments.*
EXCLAMATIONS	*Not again!*
IN ADVERTISING	*Fewer calories. Improved taste.*

Although fragments are sometimes appropriate, writers and readers do not always agree on when they are appropriate. Therefore you will find it safer to write in complete sentences.

EXERCISE 19–1

Repair any fragment by attaching it to a nearby sentence or by rewriting it as a complete sentence. If a word group is correct, write "correct" after it. Revisions of lettered sentences appear in the back of the book. Example:

                                       a

One Greek island that should not be missed is Mykonos~~.~~ ~~A~~

vacation spot for Europeans and a playpen for the rich.

a. As I stood in front of the microwave, I recalled my grandmother bending over her old black stove. And remembered what she taught me: that any food can have soul if you love the people you are cooking for.

b. After only one date with Tomás, I came to a conclusion. That with his English and my Spanish we were destined never to communicate.

c. I stepped on some frozen moss and started sliding down the face of a flat rock toward the falls. Suddenly I landed on another rock.

d. We need to stop believing myths about drinking. That strong black coffee will sober you up, for example, or that a cold shower will straighten you out.

e. As we walked up the path, we came upon the gun batteries. Large gray concrete structures covered with ivy and weeds.

1. Sitting at a sidewalk café near the Sorbonne, I could pass as a French student. As long as I kept my mouth shut.

2. Mother loved to play all our favorite games. Canasta, Monopoly, hide-and-seek, and even kick the can.

3. The horses were dressed up with hats and flowers. Some even wore sunglasses.

4. I had pushed these fears into one of those quiet places in my mind. Hoping they would stay there asleep.

5. To give my family a comfortable, secure home life. That is my most important goal.

6. If a woman from the desert tribe showed anger toward her husband, she was whipped in front of the whole village. And shunned by the rest of the women.

7. A tornado is a violent whirling wind. One that produces a funnel-shaped cloud and moves over land in a slim path of destruction.

8. With machetes, the explorers cut their way through the tall grasses to the edge of the canyon. Where they began to lay out their tapes for the survey.

9. In my three years of driving, I have never had an accident. Not one wreck, not one fender-bender, not even a little dent.

10. The pilots ejected from the burning plane, landing in the water not far from the ship. And immediately popped their flares and life vests.

20

Revise run-on sentences.

Run-on sentences are independent clauses that have not been joined correctly. An independent clause is a word group that can stand alone as a sentence. (See 60.) When two independent clauses appear in one sentence, they must be joined in one of these ways:

— with a comma and a coordinating conjunction (*and, but, or, nor, for, so, yet*)

— with a semicolon (or occasionally a colon or a dash)

There are two types of run-on sentences. When a writer puts no mark of punctuation and no coordinating conjunction between independent clauses, the result is called a fused sentence.

┌─────────────**INDEPENDENT CLAUSE**─────────────┐
FUSED   Gestures are a means of communication for everyone

┌───────── **INDEPENDENT CLAUSE** ─────────┐
they are essential for the hearing-impaired.

A far more common type of run-on sentence is the comma splice — two or more independent clauses joined by a comma without a coordinating conjunction. In some comma splices, the comma appears alone.

COMMA   Gestures are a means of communication for everyone,
SPLICE   they are essential for the hearing-impaired.

In other comma splices, the comma is accompanied by a joining word that is *not* a coordinating conjunction. There are only seven coordinating conjunctions in English: *and, but, or, nor, for, so,* and *yet.* Notice that all of these words are short — only two or three letters long.

COMMA   Gestures are a means of communication for everyone,
SPLICE   however, they are essential for the hearing-impaired.

In this example, *however* is a conjunctive adverb, not a coordinating conjunction. When a conjunctive adverb such as *however, therefore,* or *moreover* or a transitional phrase such as *in fact* or *for example* appears between independent clauses, it must be preceded by a semicolon. (See page 264 for a more complete list of these words and phrases.)

To correct a run-on sentence, you have four choices:

1. Use a comma and a coordinating conjunction (*and, but, or, nor, for, so, yet*).

but
▶ Gestures are a means of communication for everyone, they are
                                                     ∧
essential for the hearing-impaired.

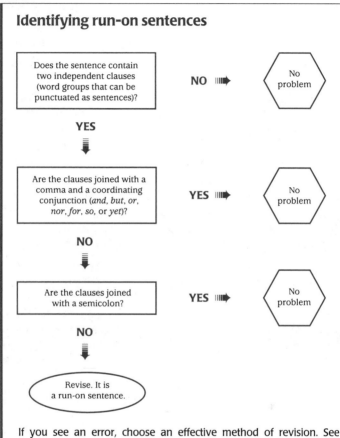

Identifying run-on sentences

Does the sentence contain two independent clauses (word groups that can be punctuated as sentences)?

NO ▶ No problem

YES ⬇

Are the clauses joined with a comma and a coordinating conjunction (*and, but, or, nor, for, so,* or *yet*)?

YES ▶ No problem

NO ⬇

Are the clauses joined with a semicolon?

YES ▶ No problem

NO ⬇

Revise. It is a run-on sentence.

If you see an error, choose an effective method of revision. See 20a–d for specific revision strategies.

2. Use a semicolon (or, if appropriate, a colon or a dash). A semicolon may be used alone; it can also be accompanied by a conjunctive adverb or transitional phrase.

▶ Gestures are a means of communication for everyone‚; they

are essential for the hearing-impaired.

▶ Gestures are a means of communication for everyone/ they *; however,*

are essential for the hearing-impaired.

3. Make the clauses into separate sentences.

▶ Gestures are a means of communication for everyone/. they *T*

are essential for the hearing-impaired.

4. Restructure the sentence, perhaps by subordinating one of the clauses.

Although gestures

▶ ~~Gestures~~ are a means of communication for everyone, they are

essential for the hearing-impaired.

One of these revision techniques will often work better than the others for a particular sentence. The fourth technique, the one requiring the most extensive revision, is frequently the most effective.

20a Consider separating the clauses with a comma and a coordinating conjunction.

There are seven coordinating conjunctions in English: *and, but, or, nor, for, so,* and *yet.* When a coordinating conjunction joins independent clauses, it is usually preceded by a comma. (See 32a.)

and

▶ The paramedic asked where I was hurt, as soon as I told him,

he cut up the leg of my favorite pair of jeans.

▶ Many government officials privately admit that the polygraph is

yet

unreliable, ~~however,~~ they continue to use it as a security measure.

However is a conjunctive adverb, not a coordinating conjunction, so it cannot be used with only a comma to join independent clauses. (See 20b.)

20b Consider separating the clauses with a semicolon (or, if appropriate, with a colon or a dash).

When the independent clauses are closely related and their relation is clear without a coordinating conjunction, a semicolon is an acceptable method of revision. (See 34a.)

▶ Tragedy depicts the individual confronted with the fact of

death/; comedy depicts the adaptability and ongoing survival

of human society.

A semicolon is required between independent clauses that have been linked with a conjunctive adverb (such as *however, therefore,* or *moreover*) or with a transitional phrase (such as *in fact* or *for example*). For a longer list, see page 264.

▶ The timber wolf looks much like a large German shepherd/;

however, the wolf has longer legs, larger feet, a wider head,

and a long, bushy tail.

If the first independent clause introduces the second or if the second clause summarizes or explains the first, a colon or a dash may be an appropriate method of revision. (See 35b and 39a.) In formal writing, the colon is usually preferred to the dash.

▶ The experience taught Juanita a lesson/: $\overset{S}{\text{she}}$ could not always

rely on her parents to bail her out of trouble.

20c Consider making the clauses into separate sentences.

▶ Why shouldn't a divorced wife receive half of her husband's

pension and other retirement benefits/? $\overset{S}{\text{she}}$ was her husband's

partner for many years.

Since one independent clause is a question and the other is a statement, they should be separate sentences.

> I gave the necessary papers to the police officer. ~~t~~hen he said
>
>   ^T^
>
> I would have to accompany him to the police station, where a
>
> counselor would talk with me and call my parents.

Because the second independent clause is quite long, a sensible revision is to use separate sentences.

20d Consider restructuring the sentence, perhaps by subordinating one of the clauses.

If one of the independent clauses is less important than the other, turn it into a subordinate clause or phrase. (For more about subordination, see 8.)

>   *who*
> Lindsey is a top competitor ~~she~~ has been riding since the age
>
> of seven.

> *When the*
> ~~The~~ new health plan was explained to the employees in my
>
> division, everyone agreed to give it a try.

> Saturday afternoon Julie came running into the house/~~she~~
>
> ~~wanted~~ to get permission to go to the park.

Minor ideas in these sentences are now expressed in subordinate clauses or phrases.

EXERCISE 20–1

Revise any run-on sentences using the method of revision suggested in brackets. Revisions of lettered sentences appear in the back of the book. Example:

> *Because*
> Orville was obsessed with his weight, he rarely ate anything
>
> sweet and delicious. [*Restructure the sentence.*]

a. The city had one public swimming pool, it stayed packed with children all summer long. [*Restructure the sentence.*]

b. The building is being renovated, therefore at times we have no heat, water, or electricity. [*Use a comma and a coordinating conjunction.*]

c. Why should we pay taxes to support public transportation, we prefer to save energy dollars by carpooling. [*Make two sentences.*]

d. Suddenly there was a loud silence, the shelling had stopped. [*Use a semicolon.*]

e. Martin looked out the window in astonishment, he had never seen snow before. [*Use a colon.*]

1. For the first time in her adult life, Lucia had time to waste, she could spend a whole day curled up with a good book. [*Use a semicolon.*]

2. Be sure to take your credit card, Disney has a way of making you want to spend money. [*Restructure the sentence.*]

3. The next time an event is canceled because of bad weather, don't blame the meteorologist, blame nature. [*Make two sentences.*]

4. While we were walking down Grover Avenue, Gary told us about his Aunt Elsinia, she was an extraordinary woman. [*Restructure the sentence.*]

5. The president of Algeria was standing next to the podium he was waiting to be introduced. [*Restructure the sentence.*]

6. On most days I had only enough money for bus fare, lunch was a luxury I could not afford. [*Use a semicolon.*]

7. There was one major reason for John's wealth, his grandfather had been a multimillionaire. [*Use a colon.*]

8. The neighborhood was ruled by gangs, what kind of environment was this for my four-year-old daughter. [*Make two sentences.*]

9. Of the many geysers in Yellowstone National Park, the most famous is Old Faithful, it sometimes reaches 150 feet in height. [*Restructure the sentence.*]

10. Wind power for the home is a supplementary source of energy, it can be combined with electricity, gas, or solar energy. [*Restructure the sentence.*]

EXERCISE 20-2

Revise any run-on sentences using a technique that you find effective. If a sentence is correct, write "correct" after it. Revisions of lettered sentences appear in the back of the book. Example:

but

I ran the three blocks as fast as I could, ~~however~~ I still missed

^

the bus.

a. The trail up Mount Finegold was declared impassable, therefore, we decided to return to our hotel a day early.
b. The duck hunter set out his decoys in the shallow bay and then settled in to wait for the first real bird to alight.
c. The instructor never talked to the class, she just assigned busy-work and sat at her desk reading the newspaper.
d. Researchers were studying the fertility of Texas land tortoises they X-rayed all the female tortoises to see how many eggs they had.
e. The suburbs seemed cold, they lacked the warmth and excitement of our Italian neighborhood.

1. Are you able to endure boredom, isolation, and potential violence, then the army may well be the adventure for you.
2. Jet funny cars are powered by jet engines, these engines are the same type that are used on fighter aircraft and helicopters.
3. If one of the dogs should happen to fall through the ice, it would be cut loose from the team and left to its fate, the sled drivers could not endanger the rest of the team for just one dog.
4. The volunteers worked hard to restore calm and search for survivors after the bombing, as a matter of fact, many of them did not sleep for the first three days of the emergency.
5. Nuclear power plants produce energy by fission, a process that generates radioactive waste.
6. After days of struggling with her dilemma, Rosa came to a decision, she would sacrifice herself for her people and her cause.
7. The Carrier Air Wing Eight, called CAG-8, is made up of ten squadrons, each has its own mission and role.
8. We didn't trust her, she had lied before.
9. I pushed open the first door with my back, turning to open the second door, I encountered a young woman in a wheelchair holding it open for me.
10. If you want to lose weight and keep it off, consider this advice, don't try to take it off faster than you put it on.

21

Make subjects and verbs agree.

In the present tense, verbs agree with their subjects in number (singular or plural) and in person (first, second, or third). The present-tense ending -s is used on a verb only if its subject is third-person singular; otherwise the verb takes no ending. Consider, for example, the present-tense forms of the verb *give:*

	SINGULAR	PLURAL
FIRST PERSON	I give	we give
SECOND PERSON	you give	you give
THIRD PERSON	he/she/it gives	they give
	Alison gives	parents give

The verb *be* varies from this pattern; unlike any other verb, it has special forms in *both* the present and the past tense.

PRESENT-TENSE FORMS OF BE		PAST-TENSE FORMS OF BE	
I am	we are	I was	we were
you are	you are	you were	you were
he/she/it is	they are	he/she/it was	they were

Speakers of standard English know by ear that *he talks, she has,* and *it doesn't* (not *he talk, she have,* and *it don't*) are the standard forms. For such speakers, problems with subject-verb agreement arise only in certain tricky situations, which are detailed in this section.

If you don't trust your ear, consult the charts on pages 170–71. See also 27c.

If you have difficulty identifying subjects and verbs, see 58a and 57c.

21a Make the verb agree with its subject, not with a word that comes between.

Word groups often come between the subject and the verb. Such word groups, usually modifying the subject, may contain a noun that at first appears to be the subject. By mentally stripping away such modifiers, you can isolate the noun that is in fact the subject.

The *tulips* in the pot on the balcony *need* watering.

▶ High levels of air pollution causes damage to the respiratory tract.

The subject is *levels,* not *pollution.* Strip away the phrase *of air pollution* to hear the correct verb: *levels cause.*

      costs
▶ A good set of golf clubs ~~cost~~ about eight hundred dollars.
                           ^

The subject is *set,* not *clubs.* Strip away the phrase *of golf clubs* to
hear the correct verb: *set costs.*

NOTE: Phrases beginning with the prepositions *as well as, in
addition to, accompanied by, together with,* and *along with* do
not make a singular subject plural.

                                        was
▶ The governor, as well as his press secretary, ~~were~~ shot.
                                              ^

To emphasize that two people were shot, the writer could use *and*
instead: *The governor and his press secretary were shot.*

21b Treat most compound subjects connected by *and* as plural.

A subject with two or more parts is said to be compound. If the
parts are connected by *and,* the subject is nearly always plural.

           ⌒
Leon and *Jan* often *jog* together.

                                      have
▶ Jill's natural ability and her desire to help others ~~has~~ led to a
                                              ^

career in the ministry.

Ability and desire is a plural subject, so its verb should be *have.*

EXCEPTIONS: When the parts of the subject form a single unit or
when they refer to the same person or thing, treat the subject
as singular.

Strawberries and cream was a last-minute addition to the menu.

Sue's friend and adviser was surprised by her decision.

When a compound subject is preceded by *each* or *every,* treat
it as singular.

Each tree, shrub, and vine needs to be sprayed.

Every car, truck, and van is required to pass inspection.

This exception does not apply when a compound subject is followed by *each: Alan and Marcia each have different ideas.*

21c With compound subjects connected by *or* or *nor* (or by *either . . . or* or *neither . . . nor*), make the verb agree with the part of the subject nearer to the verb.

A driver's *license* or credit *card is* required.

A driver's *license* or two credit *cards are* required.

▶ If a relative or neighbor ~~are~~ *is* abusing a child, notify the police

immediately.

▶ Neither the instructor nor her students ~~was~~ *were* able to find the

classroom.

The verb must be matched with the part of the subject closer to it: *neighbor is* in the first sentence, *students were* in the second.

NOTE: If one part of the subject is singular and the other is plural, put the plural one last to avoid awkwardness.

21d Treat most indefinite pronouns as singular.

Indefinite pronouns are pronouns that do not refer to specific persons or things. The following commonly used indefinite pronouns are singular:

anybody	either	everything	none	someone
anyone	everybody	neither	no one	something
each	everyone			

Many of these words appear to have plural meanings, and they are often treated as such in casual speech. In formal written English, however, they are nearly always treated as singular.

Everyone on the team *supports* the coach.

▶ Each of the furrows ~~have~~ *has* been seeded.

▶ Everybody who signed up for the ski trip ~~were~~ *was* taking lessons.

The subjects of these sentences are *each* and *everybody*. These indefinite pronouns are third-person singular, so the verbs must be *has* and *was*.

The indefinite pronouns *none* and *neither* are considered singular when used alone.

None is immune to this disease.

Neither is able to attend.

When these pronouns are followed by prepositional phrases with a plural meaning, however, usage varies. Some experts insist on treating the pronouns as singular, but many writers disagree. It is safer to treat them as singular.

None of these trades *requires* a college education.

Neither of those pejoratives *fits* Professor Brady.

A few indefinite pronouns (*all, any, some*) are singular or plural depending on the noun or pronoun they refer to.

Some of the *lemonade has* disappeared.

Some of the *rocks were* slippery.

21e Treat collective nouns as singular unless the meaning is clearly plural.

Collective nouns such as *jury, committee, audience, crowd, class, troop, family,* and *couple* name a class or a group. In American English, collective nouns are nearly always treated as singular: They emphasize the group as a unit. Occasionally, when there is some reason to draw attention to the individual members of the group, a collective noun may be treated as plural. (Also see 22b.)

SINGULAR   The *class respects* the teacher.

PLURAL   The *class are* debating among themselves.

To underscore the notion of individuality in the second sentence, many writers would add a clearly plural noun such as *members*.

PLURAL   The class *members are* debating among themselves.

meets
▶ The scout troop ~~meet~~ in our basement on Tuesdays.
^

The troop as a whole meets in the basement; there is no reason to draw attention to its individual members.

were
▶ A young couple ~~was~~ arguing loudly about politics while holding
^
hands.

The meaning is clearly plural. Only individuals can argue and hold hands.

NOTE: The phrase *the number* is treated as singular, *a number* as plural.

SINGULAR   *The number* of school-age children *is* declining.

PLURAL   *A number* of children *are* attending the wedding.

NOTE: When units of measurement are used collectively, treat them as singular; when they refer to individual persons or things, treat them as plural.

SINGULAR   *Three-fourths* of the pie *has* been eaten.

PLURAL   *One-fourth* of the drivers *were* drunk.

21f Make the verb agree with its subject even when the subject follows the verb.

Verbs ordinarily follow subjects. When this normal order is reversed, it is easy to become confused. Sentences beginning with *there is* or *there are* (or *there was* or *there were*) are inverted; the subject follows the verb.

> There *are* surprisingly few *children* in our neighborhood.

Occasionally you may decide to invert a sentence for variety or effect. When you do so, check to make sure that your subject and verb agree.

> *are*
> ▶ In the corner ~~is~~ a small aquarium and an enormous terrarium.
>
> The subject *aquarium and terrarium* is plural, so the verb must be *are*.

21g Make the verb agree with its subject, not with a subject complement.

One basic sentence pattern in English consists of a subject, a linking verb, and a subject complement: *Jack is a securities lawyer.* Because the subject complement names or describes the subject (*Jack*), it is sometimes mistaken for the subject. (See 58b on subject complements.)

> These *problems are* a way to test your skill.

> *are*
> ▶ A tent and a sleeping bag ~~is~~ the required equipment for campers.
>
> *Tent and bag* is the subject, not *equipment*.

> *is*
> ▶ A major force in today's economy ~~are~~ women — as earners,
>
> consumers, and investors.
>
> *Force* is the subject, not *women*. If the corrected version seems awkward, make *women* the subject: *Women are a major force in today's economy — as earners, consumers, and investors.*

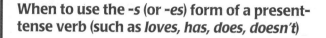

When to use the -s (or -es) form of a present-tense verb (such as *loves, has, does, doesn't*)

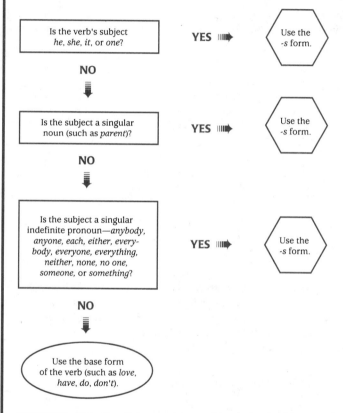

Is the verb's subject *he, she, it,* or *one*?   **YES** ⟹ Use the -s form.

NO ⬇

Is the subject a singular noun (such as *parent*)?   **YES** ⟹ Use the -s form.

NO ⬇

Is the subject a singular indefinite pronoun—*anybody, anyone, each, either, everybody, everyone, everything, neither, none, no one, someone,* or *something*?   **YES** ⟹ Use the -s form.

NO ⬇

Use the base form of the verb (such as *love, have, do, don't*).

EXCEPTION: Choosing the correct present-tense form of *be*—*am, is,* or *are*—is not quite so simple. See the chart on the next page for both the present- and the past-tense forms of *be*.

ESL CAUTION: Do not use the -s form on a verb that follows a helping verb such as *can, must,* or *should*. (See 29a.)

Subject-verb agreement chart

PRESENT-TENSE FORMS OF *LOVE* (A TYPICAL VERB)

	SINGULAR		PLURAL	
FIRST PERSON	I	love	we	love
SECOND PERSON	you	love	you	love
THIRD PERSON	he/she/it	loves	they	love

PRESENT-TENSE FORMS OF *HAVE*

	SINGULAR		PLURAL	
FIRST PERSON	I	have	we	have
SECOND PERSON	you	have	you	have
THIRD PERSON	he/she/it	has	they	have

PRESENT-TENSE FORMS OF *DO*

	SINGULAR		PLURAL	
FIRST PERSON	I	do/don't	we	do/don't
SECOND PERSON	you	do/don't	you	do/don't
THIRD PERSON	he/she/it	does/doesn't	they	do/don't

PRESENT-TENSE AND PAST-TENSE FORMS OF *BE*

	SINGULAR		PLURAL	
FIRST PERSON	I	am/was	we	are/were
SECOND PERSON	you	are/were	you	are/were
THIRD PERSON	he/she/it	is/was	they	are/were

21h *Who, which,* and *that* take verbs that agree with their antecedents.

Like most pronouns, the relative pronouns *who, which,* and *that* have antecedents, nouns or pronouns to which they refer. Relative pronouns used as subjects of subordinate clauses take verbs that agree with their antecedents.

Take a *suit that travels* well.

Problems can arise with the constructions *one of the* and *only one of the.* As a rule, treat *one of the* constructions as plural, *only one of the* constructions as singular.

▶ Our ability to use language is one of the things that set̸s us apart
from animals.

The antecedent of *that* is *things*, not *one*. Several things set us
apart from animals.

▶ Dr. Barker knew that Frank was the only one of his sons who
was
~~were~~ responsible enough to handle the estate.
  ∧
The antecedent of *who* is *one*, not *sons*. Only one son was responsible enough.

21i Words such as *athletics, economics, mathematics, physics, statistics, measles, mumps,* and *news* are usually singular, despite their plural form.

is
▶ Statistics ~~are~~ among the most difficult courses in our program.
  ∧

EXCEPTION: When they describe separate items rather than a
collective body of knowledge, words such as *athletics, mathematics, physics,* and *statistics* are plural: *The statistics on school
retention rates are impressive.*

21j Titles of works and words mentioned as words are singular.

describes
▶ *Lost Cities* ~~describe~~ the discoveries of many ancient civilizations.
  ∧
is
▶ *Controlled substances* ~~are~~ a euphemism for illegal drugs.
  ∧

EXERCISE 21–1

Underline the subject (or compound subject) and then select the verb
that agrees with it. (If you have difficulty identifying the subject, consult 58a.) Answers to lettered sentences appear in the back of the
book. Example:

<u>Someone</u> in the audience (has̲/have) volunteered to participate
in the experiment.

a. Your friendship over the years and your support on a wide variety of national issues (has/have) meant a great deal to us.

b. Two-week-old onion rings in the ashtray (is/are) not a pretty sight.

c. Each of the twenty-five actors (was/were) given a five-minute try-out, and only three of us were called back for a more intensive audition.

d. The main source of income for Trinidad (is/are) oil and pitch.

e. When Governor John White returned to Roanoke, he found that there (was/were) no signs of life or traces of the settlers he had left behind.

1. Neither the professor nor his assistants (was/were) able to solve the mystery of the eerie glow in the laboratory.

2. Quilts made by the Amish (commands/command) high prices.

3. Located at the south end of the complex (was/were) an Olympic-size pool, two basketball courts, and four tennis courts.

4. The most significant lifesaving device in automobiles (is/are) seat belts.

5. The old iron gate and the brick wall (makes/make) our courthouse appear older than its fifty years.

6. The dangers of smoking (is/are) well documented.

7. There (was/were) a Peanuts cartoon and a few Mother Goose rhymes pinned to the bulletin board.

8. When food supplies (was/were) scarce, the slaves had to make do with the less desirable parts of the animals.

9. The slaughter of pandas for their much-sought-after pelts (has/have) caused the panda population to decline dramatically.

10. Hidden under the floorboards (was/were) a bag of coins and a rusty sword.

EXERCISE 21–2

Edit the following sentences for problems with subject-verb agreement. If a sentence is correct, write "correct" after it. Answers to lettered sentences appear in the back of the book. Example:

were
Jack's first days in the infantry ~~was~~ grueling.
^

a. High concentrations of carbon monoxide results in headaches, dizziness, unconsciousness, and even death.

b. Not until my interview with Dr. Hwang were other possibilities opened to me.

c. After hearing the evidence and the closing arguments, the jury was sequestered.

d. Crystal chandeliers, polished floors, and a new oil painting has transformed Sandra's apartment.

e. Either Gertrude or Alice take the dog out for its nightly walk.

1. Small pieces of fermented bread was placed around the edge of the platter.
2. Of particular concern are penicillin and tetracycline, antibiotics used to make animals more resistant to disease.
3. The presence of certain bacteria in our bodies is one of the factors that determine our overall health.
4. Nearly everyone on the panel favor the arms control agreement.
5. Every year a number of kokanee salmon, not native to the region, is introduced into Flathead Lake.
6. Measles is a contagious childhood disease.
7. Neither Paul nor Arthur is usually here on Sundays.
8. At MGM Studios at Disney World, the wonders of moviemaking comes alive.
9. SEACON is the only one of our war games that emphasize scientific and technical issues.
10. The key program of Alcoholics Anonymous are the twelve steps to recovery.

22

Make pronouns and antecedents agree.

A pronoun is a word that substitutes for a noun. (See 57b.) Many pronouns have antecedents, nouns or pronouns to which they refer. A pronoun and its antecedent agree when they are both singular or both plural.

SINGULAR   *Dr. Sarah Simms* finished *her* rounds.

PLURAL   The *doctors* finished *their* rounds.

> **ESL NOTE:** The pronouns *he, his, she, her, it,* and *its* must agree in gender (masculine, feminine, or neuter) with their antecedents, not with the words they modify.
>
> *Jane* visited *her* [not *his*] brother in Denver.

22a Do not use plural pronouns to refer to singular antecedents.

Writers are frequently tempted to use plural pronouns to refer to two kinds of singular antecedents: indefinite pronouns and generic nouns.

Indefinite pronouns

Indefinite pronouns refer to nonspecific persons or things. Even though some of the following indefinite pronouns may seem to have plural meanings, treat them as singular in formal English.

anybody	either	neither	somebody
anyone	everybody	nobody	someone
anything	everyone	none	something
each	everything	no one	

In class *everyone* performs at *his or her* [not *their*] fitness level.

When a plural pronoun refers mistakenly to a singular indefinite pronoun, you can usually choose one of three options for revision.

1. Replace the plural pronoun with *he or she* (or *his or her*).
2. Make the antecedent plural.
3. Rewrite the sentence so that no problem of agreement exists.

▶ When someone has been drinking, ~~they are~~ *he or she is* likely to speed.

▶ When ~~someone has~~ *drivers have* been drinking, they are likely to speed.

▶ ~~When someone~~ *A driver who* has been drinking, ~~they are~~ *is* likely to speed.

Because the *he or she* construction is wordy, often the second or third revision strategy is more effective. Be aware that the traditional use of *he* (or *his*) to refer to persons of either sex is now widely considered sexist. (See 17f.)

Generic nouns

A generic noun represents a typical member of a group, such as a typical student, or any member of a group, such as any lawyer. Although generic nouns may seem to have plural meanings, they are singular.

> Every *runner* must train rigorously if *he or she wants* [not *they want*] to excel.

When a plural pronoun refers mistakenly to a generic noun, you will usually have the same three revision options as just mentioned for indefinite pronouns.

▶ A medical student must study hard if ~~they want~~ to succeed.
   he or she wants

▶ ~~A medical student~~ must study hard if they want to succeed.
   Medical students

▶ A medical student must study hard ~~if they want~~ to succeed.

22b Treat collective nouns as singular unless the meaning is clearly plural.

Collective nouns such as *jury, committee, audience, crowd, class, troop, family, team,* and *couple* name a class or a group. Ordinarily the group functions as a unit, so the noun should be treated as singular; if the members of the group function as individuals, however, the noun should be treated as plural. (See also 21e.)

AS A UNIT The *committee* granted *its* permission to build.

AS INDIVIDUALS The *committee* put *their* signatures on the document.

▶ The jury has reached ~~their~~ decision.
   its

There is no reason to draw attention to the individual members of the jury, so *jury* should be treated as singular. Notice also that the writer treated the noun as singular when choosing the verb *has,* so for consistency the pronoun must be *its.*

their
▶ The audience shouted "Bravo" and stamped ~~its~~ feet.
                                                    ^

It is difficult to see how the audience as a unit can stamp *its* feet. The meaning here is clearly plural, requiring *their*.

22c Treat most compound antecedents connected by *and* as plural.

Joanne and John moved to the mountains, where *they* built a log cabin.

22d With compound antecedents connected by *or* or *nor* (or by *either . . . or* or *neither . . . nor*), make the pronoun agree with the nearer antecedent.

Either *Bruce* or *James* should receive first prize for *his* sculpture.

Neither the *mouse* nor the *rats* could find *their* way through the maze.

NOTE: If one of the antecedents is singular and the other plural, as in the second example, put the plural one last to avoid awkwardness.

EXCEPTION: If one antecedent is male and the other female, do not follow the traditional rule. The sentence *Either Bruce or Ann should receive the blue ribbon for her sculpture* makes no sense. The best solution is to recast the sentence: *The blue ribbon for best sculpture should go to Bruce or Ann.*

EXERCISE 22–1

Edit the following sentences to eliminate problems with pronoun-antecedent agreement. Most of the sentences can be revised in more than one way, so experiment before choosing a solution. If a sentence is correct, write "correct" after it. Revisions of lettered sentences appear in the back of the book. Example:

Recruiters
▶ ~~The recruiter~~ may tell the truth, but there is much that they
  ^
choose not to tell.

a. I can be standing in front of a Xerox machine, with parts scattered around my feet, and someone will ask me to let them make a copy.

b. The sophomore class elects its president tomorrow.

c. The instructor has asked everyone to bring their own tools to carpentry class.

d. An eighteenth-century architect was also a classical scholar; they were often at the forefront of archeological research.

e. On the first day of class, Mr. Bhatti asked each individual why they wanted to stop smoking.

1. If a driver refuses to take a blood or breath test, he or she will have their licenses suspended for six months.

2. Why should we care about the timber wolf? One answer is that they have proved beneficial to humans by killing off weakened prey.

3. No one should be forced to sacrifice their prized possession — life — for someone else.

4. Seven qualified Hispanic agents applied, each hoping for a career move that would let them use their language and cultural training on more than just translations and drug deals; the job went to a non-Hispanic who was taking a crash course in Spanish.

5. If anyone notices any suspicious activity, they should report it to the police.

6. The crowd grew until they filled not only the plaza but also the surrounding streets.

7. David lent his motorcycle to someone who allowed their friend to use it.

8. By the final curtain, ninety percent of the audience had voted with their feet.

9. A good teacher is patient with his or her students, and they usually maintain an even temper.

10. A graduate student needs to be willing to take on a sizable debt unless they have wealthy families.

23

Make pronoun references clear.

Pronouns substitute for nouns; they are a kind of shorthand. In a sentence like *After Andrew intercepted the ball, he kicked it as hard as he could,* the pronouns *he* and *it* substitute for the nouns *Andrew* and *ball*. The word a pronoun refers to is called its *antecedent*.

23a Avoid ambiguous or remote pronoun reference.

Ambiguous pronoun reference occurs when a pronoun could refer to two or more possible antecedents.

> *The pitcher broke when Gloria set it*
> ▶ ~~When Gloria set the pitcher~~ on the glass-topped table~~, it broke~~.
>   ^   ^

> *"You have*
> ▶ Tom told James~~, that he had~~ won the lottery.*"*
>   ^   ^

What broke—the table or the pitcher? Who won the lottery—Tom or James? The revisions eliminate the ambiguity.

Remote pronoun reference occurs when a pronoun is too far away from its antecedent for easy reading.

> ▶ After the court ordered my ex-husband to pay child support,
>
>   he refused. Approximately eight months later, we were back
>
>   in court. This time the court ordered him to make payments
>
>   directly to the Support and Collections Unit, which would
>
>   in turn pay me. For the first six months I received regular
>   *my ex-husband*
>   payments, but then they stopped. Again ~~he~~ was summoned to
>   ^
>   appear in court; he did not respond.

The pronoun *he* was too distant from its antecedent, *ex-husband*, which appeared several sentences earlier.

23b Generally, avoid broad reference of *this, that, which,* and *it.*

For clarity, the pronouns *this, that, which,* and *it* should ordinarily refer to specific antecedents rather than to whole ideas or sentences. When a pronoun's reference is needlessly broad, either replace the pronoun with a noun or supply an antecedent to which the pronoun clearly refers.

▶ More and more often, especially in large cities, we are finding
ourselves victims of serious crimes. We learn to accept ~~this~~ *our fate*
with minor gripes and groans.

For clarity the writer substituted a noun (*fate*) for the pronoun *this,* which referred broadly to the idea expressed in the preceding sentence.

▶ Romeo and Juliet were both too young to have acquired much
a fact
wisdom, which accounts for their rash actions.

The writer added an antecedent (*fact*) that the pronoun *which* clearly refers to.

EXCEPTION: Many writers view broad reference as acceptable when the pronoun refers clearly to the sense of an entire clause.

If you pick up a starving dog and make him prosperous, he will not bite you. This is the principal difference between a dog and a man.
— Mark Twain

23c Do not use a pronoun to refer to an implied antecedent.

A pronoun must refer to a specific antecedent, not to a word that is implied but not present in the sentence.

the braids
▶ After braiding Ann's hair, Sue decorated ~~them~~ with ribbons.

The pronoun *them* referred to Ann's braids (implied by the term *braiding*), but the word *braids* did not appear in the sentence.

Modifiers, such as possessives, cannot serve as antecedents. A modifier may strongly imply the noun that the pronoun might logically refer to, but it is not itself that noun.

Euripides
▶ In ~~Euripides'~~ *Medea*, ~~he~~ describes the plight of a woman rejected
  ‸
by her husband.

The pronoun *he* cannot refer logically to the possessive modifier
Euripides'. The revision substitutes the noun *Euripides* for the pronoun *he*, thereby eliminating the problem.

23d Avoid the indefinite use of *they, it,* and *you.*

Do not use the pronoun *they* to refer indefinitely to persons
who have not been specifically mentioned. *They* should always
refer to a specific antecedent.

▶ Sometimes a list of ways to save energy is included with the
                        the gas company suggests
  gas bill. For example, ~~they suggest~~ setting a moderate
                        ‸
  temperature for the hot water heater.

The word *it* should not be used indefinitely in constructions such as "It is said on television . . ." or "In the article it
says that. . . ."

    The
▶ ~~In the~~ report ~~it~~ points out that lifting the ban on Compound 1080
  ‸
  would prove detrimental, possibly even fatal, to the bald eagle.

The pronoun *you* is appropriate when the writer is
addressing the reader directly: *Once you have kneaded the
dough, let it rise in a warm place for at least twenty-five minutes.*
Except in informal contexts, however, the indefinite *you*
(meaning "anyone in general") is inappropriate.

        one doesn't
▶ In Ethiopia ~~you don't~~ need much property to be considered
  ‸
  well-off.

If the pronoun *one* seems too stilted, the writer might recast the
sentence: *In Ethiopia a person doesn't need much property to be
considered well-off.*

23e To refer to persons, use *who, whom,* or *whose,* not *that* or *which.*

In most contexts, use *who, whom,* or *whose* to refer to persons, *that* or *which* to refer to animals or things. Although *that* is occasionally used to refer to persons, it is more polite to use a form of *who. Which* is reserved only for animals or things, so it is impolite to use it to refer to persons.

                                              whom

▶ When he heard about my seven children, four of ~~which~~ lived
                                              ^

   at home, Gill smiled and said, "I love children."

EXERCISE 23–1

Edit the following sentences to correct errors in pronoun reference. In some cases you will need to decide on an antecedent that the pronoun might logically refer to. Revisions of lettered sentences appear in the back of the book. Example:

   Following the breakup of AT&T, many other companies began
                           The competition
   to offer long-distance phone service. ~~This~~ has led to lower
                               ^

   long-distance rates.

a. The detective removed the bloodstained shawl from the body and then photographed it.
b. In Professor Jamal's class, you are lucky to earn a C.
c. Please be patient with the elderly residents which have difficulty moving through the cafeteria line.
d. The Comanche braves' lifestyle was particularly violent; they gained respect for their skill as warriors.
e. All students can secure parking permits from the campus police office; they are open from 8 A.M. until 8 P.M.

1. Many people believe that the polygraph test is highly reliable if you employ a licensed examiner.
2. Because of Paul Robeson's outspoken attitude toward fascism, he was labeled a Communist.
3. In the encyclopedia it states that male moths can smell female moths from several miles away.

4. Be sure to visit Istanbul's bazaar, where they sell everything from Persian rugs to electronic calculators.
5. If you have a sweet tooth, you can visit the confectioner's shop, where it is still made as it was a hundred years ago.

24

Distinguish between pronouns such as *I* and *me*.

The personal pronouns in the following chart change what is known as case form according to their grammatical function in a sentence. Pronouns functioning as subjects (or subject complements) appear in the *subjective* case; those functioning as objects appear in the *objective* case; and those showing ownership appear in the *possessive* case.

	SUBJECTIVE CASE	OBJECTIVE CASE	POSSESSIVE CASE
SINGULAR	I	me	my
	you	you	your
	he/she/it	him/her/it	his/her/its
PLURAL	we	us	our
	you	you	your
	they	them	their

Pronouns in the subjective and objective cases are frequently confused. Most of the rules in this section specify when to use one or the other of these cases (*I* or *me, he* or *him*, and so on). Rule 24g details a special use of pronouns and nouns in the possessive case.

24a Use the subjective case (*I, you, he, she, it, we, they*) for subjects and subject complements.

When personal pronouns are used as subjects, ordinarily your ear will tell you the correct pronoun. Problems sometimes arise, however, with compound word groups containing a pronoun, so it is not always safe to trust your ear.

> *he*
> ▶ Joel ran away because his stepfather and ~~him~~ had quarreled.
>   ^

His stepfather and he is the subject of the verb *had quarreled.* If we strip away the words *his stepfather and,* the correct pronoun becomes clear: *he had quarreled* (not *him had quarreled*).

When a pronoun is used as a subject complement (a word following a linking verb), your ear may mislead you, since the incorrect form is frequently heard in casual speech. (See subject complement, 58b.)

> *she.*
> ▶ Sandra confessed that the artist was ~~her.~~
>   ^

The pronoun *she* functions as a subject complement with the linking verb *was.* In formal, written English, subject complements must be in the subjective case. If your ear rejects *artist was she* as too stilted, try rewriting the sentence: *Sandra confessed that she was the artist.*

24b Use the objective case (*me, you, him, her, it, us, them*) for all objects.

When a personal pronoun is used as a direct object, an indirect object, or the object of a preposition, ordinarily your ear will lead you to the correct pronoun. When an object is compound, however, you may occasionally become confused.

> ▶ Janice was indignant when she realized that the salesclerk was
>   *her.*
>   insulting her mother and ~~she.~~
>   ^

Her mother and her is the direct object of the verb *was insulting.* Strip away the words *her mother and* to hear the correct pronoun: *was insulting her* (not *was insulting she*).

> *me*
> ▶ Geoffrey went with my family and ~~I~~ to King's Dominion.
>   ^

Me is an object of the preposition *with.* We would not say *Geoffrey went with I.*

When in doubt about the correct pronoun, some writers try to avoid making the choice by using a reflexive pronoun such as *myself*. Such evasions are nonstandard, even though they are used by some educated persons.

> *me*
> ▶ The Egyptian cab driver gave my husband and ~~myself~~ some
>   ∧
>
> good tips on traveling in North Africa.

My husband and me is the indirect object of the verb *gave*. For correct uses of *myself,* see the Glossary of Usage.

24c Put an appositive and the word to which it refers in the same case.

Appositives are noun phrases that rename nouns or pronouns. A pronoun used as an appositive has the same function (usually subject or object) as the word(s) the appositive renames.

> *I,*
> ▶ At the drama festival, two actors, Christina and ~~me,~~ were
>   ∧
>
> selected to do the last scene of *King Lear.*

The appositive *Christina and I* renames the subject, *actors.*

> ▶ The college interviewed only two applicants for the job,
>   *me.*
> Professor Stevens and ~~I.~~
>   ∧

The appositive *Professor Stevens and me* renames the direct object *applicants.*

24d In elliptical constructions following *than* or *as,* choose the pronoun that expresses your meaning.

In an elliptical construction, words are omitted yet understood. When an elliptical construction follows a comparison beginning with *than* or *as,* your choice of a pronoun will depend on your intended meaning. Consider, for example, the difference in meaning between these sentences:

> My husband likes football better than I.
>
> My husband likes football better than me.

Finish each sentence mentally and its meaning becomes clear: *My husband likes football better than I [do]. My husband likes football better than [he likes] me.*

▶ Even though he is sometimes ridiculed by the other boys,

                                               they.

Norman is much better off than ~~them.~~
                                        ^

They is the subject of the verb *are*, which is understood: *Norman is much better off than they [are].* If the correct English seems too formal, you can always add the verb.

                                                      her.

▶ We respected no other candidate as much as ~~she.~~
                                                         ^

This sentence means that we respected no other candidate as much as *we respected her*. *Her* is the direct object of the understood verb *respected*.

24e When deciding whether *we* or *us* should precede a noun, choose the pronoun that would be appropriate if the noun were omitted.

   We

▶ ~~Us~~ tenants would rather fight than move.
  ^

                                      us

▶ Management is short-changing ~~we~~ tenants.
                                    ^

No one would say *Us would rather fight than move* or *Management is short-changing we*.

24f Use the objective case for subjects and objects of infinitives.

An infinitive is the word *to* followed by the base form of a verb. (See 59c.) Subjects of infinitives are an exception to the rule that subjects must be in the subjective case. Whenever an infinitive has a subject, it must be in the objective case. Objects of infinitives also are in the objective case.

                            me   *him*

▶ The crowd expected Chris and ~~I~~ to defeat Tracy and ~~he~~ in the
                                    ^   ^

doubles championship.

Chris and me is the subject of the infinitive *to defeat;* Tracy and
him is the direct object of the infinitive.

24g Use the possessive case to modify a gerund.

A pronoun that modifies a gerund or a gerund phrase should
appear in the possessive case (*my, our, your, his/her/its, their*).
A gerund is a verb form ending in *-ing* that functions as a noun.
Gerunds frequently appear in phrases, in which case the whole
gerund phrase functions as a noun. (See 59c.)

> *our*
> ▶ My father always tolerated ~~us~~ talking after the lights were out.
>   ^

The possessive pronoun *our* modifies the gerund *talking*.

Nouns as well as pronouns may modify gerunds. To form
the possessive case of a noun, use an apostrophe and an *-s*
(*a victim's suffering*) or just an apostrophe (*victims' suffering*).
(See 36a.)

> *Brenda's*
> ▶ We had to pay a fifty-dollar fine for ~~Brenda~~ driving without a
>   ^
> permit.

The possessive noun *Brenda's* modifies the gerund phrase *driving
without a permit*.

Gerund phrases should not be confused with participial
phrases, which function as adjectives, not as nouns: *We saw
Brenda driving a yellow convertible.* Here *driving a yellow convertible* is a participial phrase modifying the noun *Brenda*. (See
59c.)

Sometimes the choice between the objective or the possessive case conveys a subtle difference in meaning:

We watched *them* dancing.

We watched *their* dancing.

In the first sentence the emphasis is on the people; *dancing* is
a participle modifying the pronoun *them*. In the second sentence the emphasis is on the dancing; *dancing* is a gerund, and
their is a possessive pronoun modifying the gerund.

EXERCISE 24–1

Edit the following sentences to eliminate errors in case. If a sentence is correct, write "correct" after it. Answers to lettered sentences appear in the back of the book. Example:

> Grandfather cuts down trees for neighbors much younger
>   *he.*
> than ~~him.~~
>   ^

a. My Ethiopian neighbor was puzzled by the dedication of we joggers.
b. The jury was astonished when the witness suddenly confessed that the murderer was none other than he.
c. Sue's husband is ten years older than her.
d. Everyone laughed whenever Sandra described how her brother and her had seen the Loch Ness monster and fed it sandwiches.
e. There is only a slim chance of his getting an infection from the procedure.

1. Grandfather said he would give anything to live nearer to Paulette and me.
2. A professional counselor advised the division chief that Marco, Fidelia, and myself should be allowed to apply for the opening.
3. Because of last night's fire, we are fed up with him drinking and smoking.
4. The student ethics board gave Marlo and I the opportunity to defend ourselves against the instructor's false charges.
5. During the testimony, the witness pointed directly at the defendant and announced that the thief was him.

25

Distinguish between *who* and *whom*.

The choice between *who* and *whom* (or *whoever* and *whomever*) occurs primarily in subordinate clauses and in questions. *Who* and *whoever,* subjective-case pronouns, are used for subjects and subject complements. *Whom* and *whomever,* objective-case pronouns, are used for objects. (For more about pronoun case, see 24.)

25a In subordinate clauses, use *who* and *whoever* for subjects or subject complements, *whom* and *whomever* for all objects.

When *who* and *whom* (or *whoever* and *whomever*) introduce subordinate clauses, their case is determined by their function *within the clause they introduce.* To choose the correct pronoun, you must isolate the subordinate clause and then decide how the pronoun functions within it. (See subordinate clauses, 59b.)

In the following two examples, the pronouns *who* and *whoever* function as the subjects of the clauses they introduce.

> *who*
> ▶ The prize goes to the runner ~~whom~~ collects the most points.
> ^

The subordinate clause is *who collects the most points.* The verb of the clause is *collects,* and its subject is *who.*

> *whoever*
> ▶ He tells that story to ~~whomever~~ will listen.
> ^

The writer selected the pronoun *whomever,* thinking that it was the object of the preposition *to.* However, the object of the preposition is the entire subordinate clause *whoever will listen.* The verb of the clause is *will listen,* and its subject is *whoever.*

Who occasionally functions as a subject complement in a subordinate clause. Subject complements occur with linking verbs (usually *be, am, is, are, was, were, being,* and *been*). (See 58b.)

> *who*
> ▶ The receptionist knows ~~whom~~ you are.
> ^

The subordinate clause is *who you are.* Its subject is *you,* and its subject complement is *who.*

When functioning as an object in a subordinate clause, *whom* (or *whomever*) appears out of order, before both the subject and the verb. To choose the correct pronoun, you must mentally restructure the clause.

> *whom*
> ▶ You will work with our senior industrial engineers, ~~who~~ you
> ^
> will meet later.

The subordinate clause is *whom you will meet later*. The subject of the clause is *you,* the verb is *will meet,* and *whom* is the direct object of the verb. This becomes clear if you mentally restructure the clause: *you will meet whom.*

When functioning as the object of a preposition in a subordinate clause, *whom* is often separated from its preposition.

▶ The tutor ~~who~~ *whom* I was assigned to was very supportive.

Whom is the object of the preposition *to.* In this sentence, the writer might choose to drop *whom*: *The tutor I was assigned to was very supportive.*

NOTE: Inserted expressions such as *they know, I think,* and *she says* should be ignored in determining the case of a relative pronoun.

▶ All of the show-offs, bullies, and tough guys in school want to take on a big guy ~~whom~~ *who* they know will not hurt them.

Who is the subject of *will hurt,* not the object of *know.*

25b In questions, use *who* and *whoever* for subjects, *whom* and *whomever* for all objects.

When *who* and *whom* (or *whoever* and *whomever*) are used to open questions, their case is determined by their function within the question. In the following example, *who* functions as the subject of the question.

▶ ~~Whom~~ *Who* is responsible for this dastardly deed?

When *whom* functions as the object of a verb or the object of a preposition in a question, it appears out of normal order. To choose the correct pronoun, you must mentally restructure the question.

▶ ~~Who~~ *Whom* did the committee select?

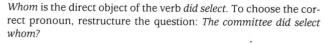
Whom is the direct object of the verb *did select.* To choose the correct pronoun, restructure the question: *The committee did select whom?*

Whom
▶ ~~Who~~ did you enter into the contract with?
   ^

Whom is the object of the preposition *with,* as is clear if you restructure the question: *You did enter into the contract with whom?*

USAGE NOTE: In spoken English, *who* is frequently used to open a question even when it functions as an object: *Who did Joe replace?* Although some readers will accept such constructions in informal written English, it is safer to use the correct form, *whom: Whom did Joe replace?*

EXERCISE 25–1

Edit the following sentences to eliminate errors in the use of *who* and *whom* (or *whoever* and *whomever*). If a sentence is correct, write "correct" after it. Answers to lettered sentences appear in the back of the book. Example:

whom
What is the name of the person ~~who~~ you are sponsoring for
                              ^
membership in the club?

a. In his first production of *Hamlet,* who did Laurence Olivier replace?
b. Who was Martin Luther King's mentor?
c. Datacall allows you to talk to whoever needs you no matter where you are in the building.
d. Some group leaders cannot handle the pressure; they give whomever makes the most noise most of their attention.
e. One of the women who Martinez hired became the most successful lawyer in the agency.

1. When medicine is scarce and expensive, physicians must give it to whomever has the best chance to survive.
2. Who was accused of receiving Mafia funds?
3. They will become business partners with whomever is willing to contribute to the company's coffers.
4. The only interstate travelers who get pulled over for speeding are the ones whom cannot afford a radar detector.
5. The elderly woman who I was asked to take care of was a clever, delightful companion.

26

Choose adjectives and adverbs with care.

Adjectives ordinarily modify nouns or pronouns; occasionally they function as subject complements following linking verbs. Adverbs modify verbs, adjectives, or other adverbs. (See 57d and 57e.)

Many adverbs are formed by adding *-ly* to adjectives (*formal, formally; smooth, smoothly*). But don't assume that all words ending in *-ly* are adverbs or that all adverbs end in *-ly*. Some adjectives end in *-ly* (*lovely, friendly*) and some adverbs don't (*always, here, there*). When in doubt, consult a dictionary.

> **ESL NOTE:** In English, adjectives are not pluralized to agree with the words they modify: *The red* [not *reds*] *roses were a wonderful surprise*.

26a Use adverbs, not adjectives, to modify verbs, adjectives, and adverbs.

When adverbs modify verbs (or verbals), they nearly always answer the question When? Where? How? Why? Under what conditions? How often? or To what degree? When adverbs modify adjectives or other adverbs, they usually qualify or intensify the meaning of the word they modify. (See 57e.)

The incorrect use of adjectives in place of adverbs to modify verbs occurs primarily in casual or nonstandard speech.

> ► The manager must see that the office runs ~~smooth~~ and ~~efficient.~~
>   *smoothly* and *efficiently*.

The incorrect use of the adjective *good* in place of the adverb *well* is especially common in casual and nonstandard speech.

well
▶ Marcia performed very ~~good~~ at her Drama Club audition.
                          ^

NOTE: The word *well* is an adjective when it means "healthy," "satisfactory," or "fortunate": *I am very well, thank you. All is well. It is just as well.*

Adjectives are sometimes used incorrectly to modify adjectives or adverbs.

really
▶ For a man eighty years old, Joe plays golf ~~real~~ well.
                                              ^

Really modifies the adverb *well.*

ESL NOTE: Placement of adjectives and adverbs can be a tricky matter for second language speakers. See 31c.

26b Use adjectives, not adverbs, as subject complements.

Adjectives ordinarily precede nouns, but they can also function as subject complements following linking verbs (see 58b). When an adjective functions as a subject complement, it describes the subject.

Justice is *blind.*

Problems can arise with verbs such as *smell, taste, look,* and *feel,* which sometimes, but not always, function as linking verbs. If the word following one of these verbs describes the subject, use an adjective; if it modifies the verb, use an adverb.

ADJECTIVE The detective looked *cautious.*

ADVERB The detective looked *cautiously* for fingerprints.

The adjective *cautious* describes the detective; the adverb *cautiously* modifies the verb *looked.*

Linking verbs suggest states of being, not actions. Notice, for example, the different meanings of *looked* in the preceding examples. To look cautious suggests the state of being cautious; to look cautiously is to perform an action in a cautious way.

▶ The lilacs in our backyard smell especially ~~sweetly~~ *sweet* this year.
                                                        ^

▶ Lori looked ~~well~~ *good* in her new raincoat.
              ^

The verbs *smell* and *looked* suggest states of being, not actions. Therefore, they should be followed by adjectives, not adverbs. (Contrast with action verbs: *We smelled the flowers. Lori looked for her raincoat.*)

26c Use comparatives and superlatives with care.

Most adjectives and adverbs have three forms: the positive, the comparative, and the superlative.

POSITIVE	COMPARATIVE	SUPERLATIVE
soft	softer	softest
fast	faster	fastest
careful	more careful	most careful
bad	worse	worst
good	better	best

Comparative versus superlative

Use the comparative to compare two things, the superlative to compare three or more.

▶ Which of these two brands of toothpaste is ~~best?~~ *better?*
                                             ^

▶ Though Shaw and Jackson are impressive, Hobbs is the ~~more~~ *most*
                                                       ^

qualified of the three candidates running for mayor.

Form of comparatives and superlatives

To form comparatives and superlatives of most one- and two-syllable adjectives, use the endings *-er* and *-est: smooth, smoother, smoothest; easy, easier, easiest.* With longer adjectives, use *more* and *most: exciting, more exciting, most exciting.*

Some one-syllable adverbs take the endings *-er* and *-est* (*fast, faster, fastest*), but longer adverbs and all of those ending in *-ly* form the comparative and superlative with *more* and *most*.

The comparative and superlative forms of the following adjectives and adverbs are irregular: *good, better, best; bad, worse, worst; badly, worse, worst.*

▶ The Kirov was the ~~talentedest~~ ballet company we had ever seen.
                    most talented

▶ Lloyd's luck couldn't have been ~~worser~~ than David's.
                                   worse

Double comparatives or superlatives

Do not use double comparatives or superlatives. When you have added *-er* or *-est* to an adjective or adverb, do not also use *more* or *most* (or *less* or *least*).

▶ Of all her family, Julia is the ~~most~~ happiest about the move.

▶ That is the most ~~inanest~~ joke I have ever heard.
                   inane

Absolute concepts

Avoid expressions such as *more straight, less perfect, very round,* and *most unique.* Either something is *unique* or it isn't. It is illogical to suggest that absolute concepts come in degrees.

▶ That is the most ~~unique~~ wedding gown I have ever seen.
                   unusual

▶ The painting would have been even more ~~priceless~~ had it been
                                          valuable

signed.

26d Avoid double negatives.

Standard English allows two negatives only if a positive meaning is intended: *The orchestra was not unhappy with its performance.* Double negatives used to emphasize negation are nonstandard.

Negative modifiers such as *never, no,* and *not* should not be paired with other negative modifiers or with negative words such as *neither, none, no one, nobody,* and *nothing.*

▶ Management is not doing ~~nothing~~ *anything* to see that the trash is

picked up.

▶ George won't ~~never~~ *ever* forget that day.

▶ I enjoy living alone because I don't have to answer to ~~nobody.~~ *anybody.*

The double negatives *not . . . nothing, won't never,* and *don't . . . nobody* are nonstandard.

The modifiers *hardly, barely,* and *scarcely* are considered negatives in standard English, so they should not be used with negatives such as *not, no one,* or *never.*

▶ Maxine is so weak she ~~can't~~ *can* hardly climb stairs.

EXERCISE 26–1

Edit the following sentences to eliminate errors in the use of adjectives and adverbs. If a sentence is correct, write "correct" after it. Answers to lettered sentences appear in the back of the book. Example:

> When I watched Carl run the 440 on Saturday, I was amazed at
> how ~~good~~ *well* he paced himself.

a. When Tina began breathing normal, we could relax.
b. All of us on the team felt badly about our performance.
c. Tim's friends cheered and clapped very loud when he made it to the bottom of the beginners' slope.
d. The vaulting box, commonly known as the horse, is the easiest of the four pieces of equipment to master.
e. Last Christmas was the most perfect day of my life.

1. When answering the phone, you should speak clearly and courteous.
2. In the early 1970s, chances for survival of the bald eagle looked real slim.

3. After checking to see how bad I had been hurt, my sister dialed 911.
4. Professor Brown's public praise of my performance on the exam made me feel a little strangely.
5. The hall closet is so filled with ski equipment that the door won't hardly close.

27

Choose standard English verb forms.

In nonstandard English, spoken by those who share a regional or cultural heritage, verb forms sometimes differ from those of standard English. In writing, use standard English verb forms unless you are quoting nonstandard speech or using nonstandard forms for literary effect. (See 17d.)

Except for the verb *be*, all verbs in English have five forms. The following chart lists the five forms and provides a sample sentence in which each might appear.

BASE FORM	Usually I (*walk, ride*).
PAST TENSE	Yesterday I (*walked, rode*).
PAST PARTICIPLE	I have (*walked, ridden*) many times before.
PRESENT PARTICIPLE	I am (*walking, riding*) right now.
-S FORM	He/she/it (*walks, rides*) regularly.

Both the past-tense and past-participle forms of regular verbs end in *-ed* (*walked, walked*). Irregular verbs form the past tense and past participle in other ways (*rode, ridden*).

The verb *be* has eight forms instead of the usual five: *be, am, is, are, was, were, being, been.*

27a Use the correct forms of irregular verbs.

For all regular verbs, the past-tense and past-participle forms are the same (ending in *-ed* or *-d*), so there is no danger of confusion. This is not true, however, for irregular verbs, such as the following.

BASE FORM	PAST TENSE	PAST PARTICIPLE
go	went	gone
fight	fought	fought
fly	flew	flown

The past-tense form, which never has a helping verb, expresses action that occurred entirely in the past. The past participle is used with a helping verb—either with *has, have,* or *had* to form one of the perfect tenses or with *be, am, is, are, was, were, being,* or *been* to form the passive voice.

PAST TENSE   Last July, we *went* to Paris.

PAST PARTICIPLE   We have *gone* to Paris twice.

When you aren't sure which verb form to choose (*went* or *gone, began* or *begun,* and so on), consult the list of common irregular verbs that begins on page 199. Choose the past-tense form if the verb in your sentence doesn't have a helping verb; choose the past-participle form if it does.

In nonstandard English speech, the past-tense and past-participle forms may differ from those of standard English, as in the following sentences.

▶ Yesterday we ~~seen~~ *saw* an unidentified flying object.

▶ The reality of the situation finally ~~sunk~~ *sank* in.

The past-tense forms *saw* and *sank* are required because there are no helping verbs.

▶ The truck was apparently ~~stole~~ *stolen* while the driver ate lunch.

▶ The teacher asked Dwain if he had ~~did~~ *done* his homework.

Because of the helping verbs, the past-participle forms are required: *was stolen, had done.*

When in doubt about the standard English forms of irregular verbs, consult the following list or look up the base form of the verb in the dictionary, which also lists any irregular forms. (If no additional forms are listed in the dictionary, the verb is regular, not irregular.)

Common irregular verbs

BASE FORM	PAST TENSE	PAST PARTICIPLE
arise	arose	arisen
awake	awoke, awaked	awaked, awoke
be	was, were	been
beat	beat	beaten, beat
become	became	become
begin	began	begun
bend	bent	bent
bite	bit	bitten, bit
blow	blew	blown
break	broke	broken
bring	brought	brought
build	built	built
burst	burst	burst
buy	bought	bought
catch	caught	caught
choose	chose	chosen
cling	clung	clung
come	came	come
cost	cost	cost
deal	dealt	dealt
dig	dug	dug
dive	dived, dove	dived
do	did	done
drag	dragged	dragged
draw	drew	drawn
dream	dreamed, dreamt	dreamed, dreamt
drink	drank	drunk
drive	drove	driven
eat	ate	eaten
fall	fell	fallen
fight	fought	fought
find	found	found
fly	flew	flown
forget	forgot	forgotten, forgot
freeze	froze	frozen
get	got	gotten, got
give	gave	given
go	went	gone
grow	grew	grown
hang (suspend)	hung	hung
hang (execute)	hanged	hanged
have	had	had
hear	heard	heard
hide	hid	hidden

BASE FORM	PAST TENSE	PAST PARTICIPLE
hurt	hurt	hurt
keep	kept	kept
know	knew	known
lay (put)	laid	laid
lead	led	led
lend	lent	lent
let (allow)	let	let
lie (recline)	lay	lain
lose	lost	lost
make	made	made
prove	proved	proved, proven
read	read	read
ride	rode	ridden
ring	rang	rung
rise (get up)	rose	risen
run	ran	run
say	said	said
see	saw	seen
send	sent	sent
set (place)	set	set
shake	shook	shaken
shoot	shot	shot
shrink	shrank	shrunk
sing	sang	sung
sink	sank	sunk
sit (be seated)	sat	sat
slay	slew	slain
sleep	slept	slept
speak	spoke	spoken
spin	spun	spun
spring	sprang	sprung
stand	stood	stood
steal	stole	stolen
sting	stung	stung
strike	struck	struck, stricken
swear	swore	sworn
swim	swam	swum
swing	swung	swung
take	took	taken
teach	taught	taught
throw	threw	thrown
wake	woke, waked	waked, woken
wear	wore	worn
wring	wrung	wrung
write	wrote	written

27b Distinguish among the forms of *lie* and *lay*.

Writers and speakers frequently confuse the various forms of *lie* (meaning "to recline or rest on a surface") and *lay* (meaning "to put or place something"). *Lie* is an intransitive verb; it does not take a direct object: *The tax forms lie on the table.* The verb *lay* is transitive; it takes a direct object: *Please lay the tax forms on the coffee table.* (See 58b.)

In addition to confusing the meaning of *lie* and *lay*, writers and speakers are often unfamiliar with the standard English forms of these verbs.

BASE FORM	PAST TENSE	PAST PARTICIPLE	PRESENT PARTICIPLE
lie	lay	lain	lying
lay	laid	laid	laying

▶ Sue was so exhausted that she ~~laid~~ down for a nap.
  lay

The past-tense form of *lie* ("to recline") is *lay*.

▶ Mary ~~lay~~ the baby on my lap.
  laid

The past-tense form of *lay* ("to place") is *laid*.

▶ My mother's letters were ~~laying~~ in the corner of the chest.
  lying

The present participle of *lie* ("to rest on a surface") is *lying*.

EXERCISE 27–1

Edit the following sentences for problems with irregular verbs. If a sentence is correct, write "correct" after it. Answers to lettered sentences appear in the back of the book. Example:

Was it you I ~~seen~~ last night at the concert?
  saw

a. Noticing that my roommate was shivering and looking pale, I rung for the nurse.
b. When I get the urge to exercise, I lay down until it passes.
c. Grandmother had drove our new jeep to the sunrise church service on Savage Mountain, so we were left with the station wagon.

d. I just heard on the news that Claudia Brandolini has broke the world record for the high jump.

e. In her junior year, Cindy run the 440-yard dash in 51.1 seconds.

1. How many times have you swore to yourself, "I'll diet tomorrow, after one more piece of cheesecake"?

2. The burglar must have gone immediately upstairs, grabbed what looked good, and took off.

3. In just a week the ground had froze, and the first winter storm had left over a foot of snow.

4. I locked my brakes, leaned the motorcycle to the left, and laid it down to keep from slamming into the fence.

5. Larry claimed that he had drank a bad soda, but Esther suspected the truth.

27c Use -s (or -es) endings on present-tense verbs that have third-person singular subjects.

All singular nouns (*child, tree*) and the pronouns *he, she,* and *it* are third-person singular; indefinite pronouns such as *everyone* and *neither* are also third-person singular. When the subject of a sentence is third-person singular, its verb takes an -s or -es ending in the present tense. (See also 21.)

	SINGULAR		PLURAL	
FIRST PERSON	I	know	we	know
SECOND PERSON	you	know	you	know
THIRD PERSON	he/she/it	knows	they	know
	child	knows	parents	know
	everyone	knows		

In nonstandard speech, the -s ending required by standard English is sometimes omitted.

▶ Ellen taught him what he ~~know~~ *knows* about the paperwork.

▶ Sulfur dioxide ~~turn~~ *turns* leaves yellow, ~~dissolve~~ *dissolves* marble, and ~~eat~~ *eats* away iron and steel.

The subjects *he* and *sulfur dioxide* are third-person singular, so the verbs must end in -s.

CAUTION: Do not add the *-s* ending to the verb if the subject is not third-person singular.

The writers of the following sentences, knowing they sometimes dropped *-s* endings from verbs, overcorrected by adding the endings where they don't belong.

▶ I prepare~~s~~ program specifications and logic diagrams.

The writer mistakenly concluded that the *-s* ending belongs on present-tense verbs used with *all* singular subjects, not just *third-person* singular subjects. The pronoun *I* is first-person singular, so its verb does not require the *-s*.

▶ The dirt floors require~~s~~ continual sweeping.

The writer mistakenly thought that the *-s* ending on the verb indicated plurality. The *-s* goes on present-tense verbs used with third-person *singular* subjects.

Has *versus* have

In the present tense, use *has* with third-person singular subjects; all other subjects require *have*.

	SINGULAR		PLURAL	
FIRST PERSON	I	have	we	have
SECOND PERSON	you	have	you	have
THIRD PERSON	he/she/it	has	they	have

In some dialects, *have* is used with all subjects. But standard English requires *has* for third-person singular subjects.

▶ This respected musician almost always ~~have~~ *has* a message to convey in his work.

▶ As for the retirement income program, it ~~have~~ *has* finally been established.

The subjects *musician* and *it* are third-person singular, so the verb should be *has* in each case.

CAUTION: Do not use *has* if the subject is not third-person singular. The writers of the following sentences were aware that they often wrote *have* when standard English requires *has*. Here they are using what appears to them to be the "correct" form, but in an inappropriate context.

> ► My business law classes ~~has~~ *have* helped me to understand more
>   about contracts.

> ► I ~~has~~ *have* much to be thankful for.
>   The subjects of these sentences—*classes* and *I*—are third-person plural and first-person singular, so standard English requires *have*.

Does *versus* do *and* doesn't *versus* don't

In the present tense, use *does* and *doesn't* with third-person singular subjects; all other subjects require *do* and *don't*.

	SINGULAR		**PLURAL**	
FIRST PERSON	I	do/don't	we	do/don't
SECOND PERSON	you	do/don't	you	do/don't
THIRD PERSON	he/she/it	does/doesn't	they	do/don't

The use of *don't* instead of the standard English *doesn't* is a feature of many dialects in the United States. Use of *do* for *does* is rarer.

> ► Grandfather really ~~don't~~ *doesn't* have a place to call home.

> ► ~~Do~~ *Does* she know the correct procedure for setting up the experiment?
>   *Grandfather* and *she* are third-person singular, so the verbs should be *doesn't* and *does*.

Am, is, *and* are; was *and* were

The verb *be* has three forms in the present tense (*am, is, are*) and two in the past tense (*was, were*). Use *am* and *was* with first-person singular subjects; use *is* and *was* with third-person singular subjects. With all other subjects, use *are* and *were*.

	SINGULAR		PLURAL	
FIRST PERSON	I	am/was	we	are/were
SECOND PERSON	you	are/were	you	are/were
THIRD PERSON	he/she/it	is/was	they	are/were

was
▶ Judy wanted to borrow Tim's notes, but she ~~were~~ too shy to
                                                ∧
ask for them.

The subject *she* is third-person singular, so the verb should be *was*.

27d Do not omit *-ed* endings on verbs.

Speakers who do not fully pronounce *-ed* endings sometimes omit them unintentionally in writing. Failure to pronounce *-ed* endings is common in many dialects and in informal speech, even in standard English. In the following frequently used words and phrases, for example, the *-ed* ending is not always fully pronounced.

advised	developed	prejudiced	stereotyped
asked	fixed	pronounced	used to
concerned	frightened	supposed to	

When a verb is regular, both the past tense and the past participle are formed by adding *-ed* to the base form of the verb. (See 27a.)

Past tense

Use an *-ed* or *-d* ending to express the past tense of regular verbs. The past tense is used when the action occurred entirely in the past.

fixed
▶ Over the weekend, Ed ~~fix~~ his brother's skateboard and tuned up
              ∧
his mother's 1955 Thunderbird.

advised
▶ Last summer my counselor ~~advise~~ me to ask my chemistry
                           ∧
instructor for help.

Past participles

Past participles are used in three ways: (1) following *have, has,* or *had* to form one of the perfect tenses; (2) following *be, am, is, are, was, were, being,* or *been* to form the passive voice; and (3) as adjectives modifying nouns or pronouns. The perfect tenses are listed on page 209, and the passive voice is discussed in 28c. For a discussion of participles functioning as adjectives, see 59c.

>   *asked*
> Robin has ~~ask~~ me to go to California with her.
>   ^
>
> *Has asked* is present perfect tense (*have* or *has* followed by a past participle).

>   *publicized*
> Though it is not a new phenomenon, domestic violence is ~~publicize~~
>   ^
> more frequently than before.
>
> *Is publicized* is a verb in the passive voice (a form of *be* followed by a past participle).

> All aerobics classes end in a cool-down period to stretch
> *tightened*
> ~~tighten~~ muscles.
> ^
> The past participle *tightened* functions as an adjective modifying the noun *muscles.*

27e Do not omit needed verbs.

Although standard English allows some linking verbs and helping verbs to be contracted, at least in informal contexts, it does not allow them to be omitted.

Linking verbs, used to link subjects to subject complements, are frequently a form of *be: be, am, is, are, was, were, being, been.* (See 58b.) Some of these forms may be contracted (*I'm, she's, we're, you're, they're*), but they should not be omitted altogether.

>   *are*
> When we out there in the evening, we often hear the
>   ^
> helicopters circling above.

is
▶ Alvin a man who can defend himself.
   ∧

Helping verbs, used with main verbs, include forms of *be, do,* and *have* or the words *can, will, shall, could, would, should, may, might,* and *must.* (See 57c.) Some helping verbs may be contracted (*he's leaving, we'll celebrate, they've been told*), but they should not be omitted altogether.

have
▶ We been in Chicago since last Thursday.
   ∧
                                    would
▶ Do you know someone who be good for the job?
                                ∧

ESL NOTE: Speakers of English as a second language sometimes have problems with omitted verbs and correct use of helping verbs. See 29e and 29a.

EXERCISE 27–2

Edit the following sentences for problems with -*s* and -*ed* verb forms and for omitted verbs. If a sentence is correct, write "correct" after it. Answers to lettered sentences appear in the back of the book. Example:

> *has*
> The psychologist ~~have~~ so many problems in her own life that
>   *doesn't*   ∧
> she ~~don't~~ know how to advise anyone else.
>   ∧

a. I love to watch Anthony as he leaps off the balance beam and lands lightly on his feet.
b. The museum visitors were not suppose to touch the exhibits.
c. Our church has all the latest technology, even a close-circuit television.
d. We often don't know whether he angry or just joking.
e. All four children plays one or two instruments.

1. The bald eagle feed mostly on carrion, such as the carcasses of deer or the bodies of dead salmon.
2. We were ask to sign a contract committing ourselves to not smoking for forty-eight hours.
3. The training for security checkpoint screeners, which takes place in an empty airplane hangar, consist of watching out-of-date videos.

4. Do he have enough energy to hold down two jobs while going to night school?
5. How would you feel if a love one had been a victim of a crime like this?

28

Use verbs in the appropriate tense, mood, and voice.

28a Choose the appropriate verb tense.

Tenses indicate the time of an action in relation to the time of the speaking or writing about that action.

The most common problem with tenses — shifting confusingly from one tense to another — is discussed in 13. Other problems with tenses are detailed in this section, after the following survey of tenses.

Survey of tenses

English has three simple tenses (past, present, and future) and three perfect tenses (present perfect, past perfect, and future perfect). In addition, there is a progressive form of each of these six tenses.

SIMPLE TENSES   The simple present tense is used primarily to describe habitual actions (*Jane walks to work*) or to refer to actions occurring at the time of speaking (*I see a cardinal in our maple tree*). It is also used to state facts or general truths and to describe fictional events in a literary work (see page 210). The present tense may even be used to express future actions that are to occur at some specified time (*The semester begins tomorrow*).

The simple past tense is used for actions completed entirely in the past (*Yesterday Jane walked to work*).

The simple future tense is used for actions that will occur in the future (*Tomorrow Jane will walk to work*) or for actions that are predictable, given certain causes (*Meat will spoil if not properly refrigerated*).

In the following chart, the simple tenses are given for the regular verb *walk,* the irregular verb *ride,* and the highly irregular verb *be.*

SIMPLE PRESENT

SINGULAR		PLURAL	
I	walk, ride, am	we	walk, ride, are
you	walk, ride, are	you	walk, ride, are
he/she/it	walks, rides, is	they	walk, ride, are

SIMPLE PAST

SINGULAR		PLURAL	
I	walked, rode, was	we	walked, rode, were
you	walked, rode, were	you	walked, rode, were
he/she/it	walked, rode, was	they	walked, rode, were

SIMPLE FUTURE

I, you, he/she/it, we, they   will walk, ride, be

PERFECT TENSES More complex time relations are indicated by the perfect tenses. A verb in one of the perfect tenses (a form of *have* plus the past participle) expresses an action that was or will be completed by the time of another action.

PRESENT PERFECT

I, you, we, they	have walked, ridden, been
he/she/it	has walked, ridden, been

PAST PERFECT

I, you, he/she/it, we, they	had walked, ridden, been

FUTURE PERFECT

I, you, he/she/it, we, they	will have walked, ridden, been

PROGRESSIVE FORMS The simple and perfect tenses already discussed have progressive forms that describe actions in progress. A progressive verb consists of a form of *be* followed by a present participle.

PRESENT PROGRESSIVE

I	am walking, riding, being
he/she/it	is walking, riding, being
you, we, they	are walking, riding, being

PAST PROGRESSIVE

I, he/she/it	was walking, riding, being
you, we, they	were walking, riding, being

FUTURE PROGRESSIVE

I, you, he/she/it, we, they   will be walking, riding, being

PRESENT PERFECT PROGRESSIVE

I, you, we, they   have been walking, riding, being
he/she/it   has been walking, riding, being

PAST PERFECT PROGRESSIVE

I, you, he/she/it, we, they   had been walking, riding, being

FUTURE PERFECT PROGRESSIVE

I, you, he/she/it, we, they   will have been walking, riding, being

---

ESL NOTE: The progressive forms are not normally used with mental activity verbs such as *believe*. See 29a.

Special uses of the present tense

Use the present tense when writing about literature, when expressing general truths, and when quoting, summarizing, or paraphrasing an author's views.

When writing about a work of literature, you may be tempted to use the past tense. The convention, however, is to describe fictional events in the present tense. (See also 13b.)

▶ In Masuji Ibuse's *Black Rain,* a child ~~reached~~ *reaches* for a pomegranate in his mother's garden, and a moment later he ~~was~~ *is* dead, killed by the blast of the atomic bomb.

Scientific principles or general truths should appear in the present tense, unless such principles have been disproved.

▶ Galileo taught that the earth ~~revolved~~ *revolves* around the sun.

Since Galileo's teaching has not been discredited, the verb should be in the present tense. The following sentence, however, is acceptable: *Ptolemy taught that the sun revolved around the earth.*

When you are quoting, summarizing, or paraphrasing the author of a nonliterary work, use present-tense verbs such as *writes, reports, asserts,* and so on. (See page 358 for a more complete list.) This convention is followed even when the author is dead.

>   *writes*
> ▶ Baron Bowan of Colwood ~~wrote~~ that a metaphysician is "one
>   ^
>
> who goes into a dark cellar at midnight without a light, looking
>
> for a black cat that is not there."

EXCEPTION: When you are documenting a paper with the APA (American Psychological Association) style of in-text citations, which include a date after the author's name, use past-tense verbs such as *reported* or *demonstrated* or present perfect verbs such as *has reported* or *has demonstrated*.

> E. Wilson (1996) reported that positive reinforcement alone was a less effective teaching technique than a mixture of positive reinforcement and constructive criticism.

The past perfect tense

The past perfect tense consists of a past participle preceded by *had* (*had worked, had gone*). (See page 209.) This tense is used for an action already completed by the time of another past action or for an action already completed at some specific past time.

> Everyone *had spoken* by the time I arrived.
>
> Everyone *had spoken* by 10:00 A.M.

Writers sometimes use the simple past tense when they should use the past perfect.

> ▶ We built our cabin high on a pine knoll, forty feet above an
>   *had been*
> abandoned quarry that ~~was~~ flooded in 1920 to create a lake.
>   ^
>
> The building of the cabin and the flooding of the quarry both occurred in the past, but the flooding was completed before the time of building.

>   *had*
> ▶ By the time we arrived at the party, the guest of honor left.
>   ^
>
> The past perfect tense is needed because the action of leaving was completed at a specific past time (by the time we arrived).

Some writers tend to overuse the past perfect tense. Do not use the past perfect if two past actions occurred at the same time.

▶ When we arrived in Paris, Pauline ~~had~~ met us at the train station.

Sequence of tenses with infinitives and participles

An infinitive is the base form of a verb preceded by *to.* (See 59c.) Use the present infinitive to show action at the same time as or later than the action of the verb in the sentence.

raise
▶ The club had hoped to ~~have raised~~ a thousand dollars by April 1.
^

The action expressed in the infinitive (*to raise*) occurred later than the action of the sentence's verb (*had hoped*).

Use the perfect form of an infinitive (*to have* followed by the past participle) for an action occurring earlier than that of the verb in the sentence.

have joined
▶ Dan would like to ~~join~~ the navy, but he did not pass the physical.
^

The liking occurs in the present; the joining would have occurred in the past.

Like the tense of an infinitive, the tense of a participle is also governed by the tense of the sentence's verb. Use the present participle (ending in *-ing*) for an action occurring at the same time as that of the sentence's verb.

Hiking the Appalachian Trail in early spring, we spotted many wildflowers.

Use the past participle (such as *given* or *helped*) or the present perfect participle (*having* plus the past participle) for an action occurring before that of the verb.

Discovered off the coast of Florida, the *Atocha* yielded many treasures.

Having worked her way through college, Melanie graduated debt-free.

28b Use the subjunctive mood in the few contexts that require it.

There are three moods in English: the *indicative,* used for facts, opinions, and questions; the *imperative,* used for orders or advice; and the *subjunctive,* used in certain contexts to express wishes, requests, or conditions contrary to fact. Of these moods, only the subjunctive causes problems for writers.

Forms of the subjunctive

In the subjunctive mood, present-tense verbs do not change form to indicate the number and person of the subject (see 21). Instead, the subjunctive uses the base form of the verb (*be, drive, employ*) with all subjects.

> It is important that you *be* [not *are*] prepared for the interview.

> We asked that she *drive* [not *drives*] more slowly.

Also, in the subjunctive mood, there is only one past-tense form of *be: were* (never *was*).

> If I *were* [not *was*] you, I'd proceed more cautiously.

Uses of the subjunctive

The subjunctive mood appears only in a few contexts: in contrary-to-fact clauses beginning with *if* or expressing a wish; in *that* clauses following verbs such as *ask, insist, recommend, request,* and *suggest;* and in certain set expressions.

IN CONTRARY-TO-FACT CLAUSES BEGINNING WITH *IF* When a subordinate clause beginning with *if* expresses a condition contrary to fact, use the subjunctive mood.

>   *were*
> ▶ If I ~~was~~ a member of Congress, I would vote for that bill.
>   ^

>   *were*
> ▶ We could be less cautious if Jake ~~was~~ more trustworthy.
>   ^

> The verbs in these sentences express conditions that do not exist: The writer is not a member of Congress, and Jake is not trustworthy.

Do not use the subjunctive mood in *if* clauses expressing conditions that exist or may exist.

If Dana *wins* the contest, she will leave for Barcelona in June.

IN CONTRARY-TO-FACT CLAUSES EXPRESSING A WISH In formal English the subjunctive is used in clauses expressing a wish or desire; in informal speech, however, the indicative is more common.

FORMAL I wish that Dr. Kurtinitis *were* my professor.

INFORMAL I wish that Dr. Kurtinitis *was* my professor.

IN *THAT* CLAUSES FOLLOWING VERBS SUCH AS *ASK, INSIST, RECOMMEND, REQUEST,* AND *SUGGEST* Because requests have not yet become reality, they are expressed in the subjunctive mood.

> Professor Moore insists that her students ~~are~~ *be* on time.

> We recommend that Lambert ~~files~~ *file* form 1050 soon.

IN CERTAIN SET EXPRESSIONS The subjunctive mood, once more widely used in English, remains in certain set expressions: *Be* that as it may, as it *were, come* rain or shine, far *be* it from me, and so on.

EXERCISE 28–1

Edit the following sentences to eliminate errors in verb tense or mood. If a sentence is correct, write "correct" after it. Answers to lettered sentences appear in the back of the book. Example:

After the path ~~was~~ *had been* plowed, we were able to walk through the park.

a. The palace of Knossos in Crete is believed to have been destroyed by fire around 1375 B.C.E.
b. Watson and Crick discovered the mechanism that controlled inheritance in all life: the workings of the DNA molecule.

c. In 1941 Hitler decided to kill the Jews. But Himmler and his SS were three years ahead of him; they had mass murder in mind since 1938.

d. Toni could be an excellent student if she wasn't so distracted by problems at home.

e. My sister Deanna was outside playing with the new puppies that were born only a few weeks earlier.

1. Our neighbor stood at the door looking so pale and ashen that we thought he just saw a ghost.

2. Ken recommended that Juan remain on the beginners' slope for at least a week.

3. As soon as my aunt applied for the position of pastor, the post was filled by an inexperienced seminary graduate who had been so hastily snatched that his mortarboard was still in midair.

4. Don Quixote, in Cervantes' novel, was an idealist ill suited for life in the real world.

5. When the doctor said "It's a girl," I was stunned. For nine months I dreamed about playing baseball with my son.

28c Use the active voice unless you have a good reason for choosing the passive.

Transitive verbs (verbs that take a direct object) appear in either the active or the passive voice. (See 58c.) In the active voice, the subject of the sentence does the action; in the passive, the subject receives the action. Although both voices are grammatically correct, the active voice is usually more effective because it is simpler, more direct, and less wordy.

ACTIVE   The committee *reached* a decision.

PASSIVE   A decision *was reached* by the committee.

To transform a sentence from the passive to the active voice, make the actor the subject of the sentence.

▶ For the opening flag ceremony, ~~a dance was choreographed by~~
                choreographed a dance
  Mr. Martins to the song "Two Hundred Years and Still a Baby."
  ^

The revision emphasizes Mr. Martins by making him the subject.

We did not take down the

▶ ~~The~~ Christmas decorations ~~were not taken down~~ until
   ^

Valentine's Day.

Very often the actor does not even appear in a passive-voice sentence. To make such a sentence active, the writer must decide on an appropriate subject — in this case, *we.*

The passive voice is appropriate if you wish to emphasize the receiver of the action or to minimize the importance of the doer.

APPROPRIATE   Many native Hawaiians *are forced* to leave their
PASSIVE   beautiful beaches to make room for hotels and
                condominiums.

APPROPRIATE   As the time for harvest approaches, the tobacco
PASSIVE   plants *are sprayed* with a chemical to retard the
                growth of suckers.

The writer of the first sentence wished to emphasize the receivers of the action, Hawaiians. The writer of the second sentence wished to focus on the tobacco plants, not on the people spraying them.

ESL NOTE: Some speakers of English as a second language tend to avoid the passive voice even when it is appropriate. For advice on transforming an active-voice sentence to the passive, see 58c.

EXERCISE 28–2

Change the following sentences from the passive to the active voice. You may need to invent an actor to be the subject in the active voice. Revisions of lettered sentences appear in the back of the book. Example:

We

~~It was~~ learned from the test that our son was reading on the
^

second-grade level.

a. Each monk's cell was painted by Fra Angelico.
b. Carbon dating is used by scientists to determine the approximate age of an object.
c. As the patient undressed, scars were seen on his back, stomach, and thighs. We suspected child abuse.
d. It was noted right away that the taxi driver had been exposed to Americans because he knew all the latest slang.
e. The holes were patched and sanded, the walls were primed, and the ceiling was painted.

1. All of my friends were invited to the party by my mother.
2. No loyalty at all was shown by the dog to his owner, who had mistreated him.
3. It can be concluded that a college education provides a significant economic advantage.
4. The land was ruthlessly stripped of timber before the settlers realized the consequences of their actions.
5. Home equity loans were explained to me by the assistant manager.

ESL Grammar

Sections 29, 30, and 31 of *Rules for Writers* have a special audience: speakers of English as a second language (ESL) who have learned English but continue to have problems in a few trouble spots.

29

Be alert to special problems with verbs.

Both native and nonnative speakers of English encounter the following problems with verbs, which are treated elsewhere in this handbook:

> problems with subject-verb agreement (21)
>
> misuse of verb forms (27)
>
> problems with tense, mood, and voice (28)

This section focuses on features of the English verb system that cause special problems for second language speakers.

29a Match helping verbs and main verbs appropriately.

Only certain combinations of helping verbs and main verbs make sense in English. The correct combinations are discussed in this section, after the following review of helping verbs and main verbs.

Review of helping verbs and main verbs

Helping verbs always appear before main verbs. (See 57c.)

       HV MV   HV   MV
We *will leave* for the picnic at noon. *Do* you *want* a ride?

Some helping verbs—*have, do,* and *be*—change form to indicate tense; others, known as modals, do not.

FORMS OF *HAVE, DO,* AND *BE*
have, has, had
do, does, did
be, am, is, are, was, were, being, been

MODALS
can, could, may, might, must, shall, should, will, would (*also* ought to)

Every main verb has five forms (except *be,* which has eight forms). The following list shows these forms for the regular verb *help* and the irregular verb *give.* (See 27a for a list of common irregular verbs.)

BASE FORM	help, give
PAST TENSE	helped, gave
PAST PARTICIPLE	helped, given
PRESENT PARTICIPLE	helping, giving
***-S* FORM**	helps, gives

Modal + base form

After the modals *can, could, may, might, must, shall, should, will,* and *would,* use the base form of the verb.

▶ My cousin will send~~s~~ us photographs from her wedding.

       speak
▶ We could ~~spoke~~ Spanish when we were young.
      ^

CAUTION: Do not use *to* in front of a main verb that follows a modal. (*Ought to* is an exception.)

▶ Gina can ~~to~~ drive us home if we miss the bus.

Do, does, or *did + base form*

After helping verbs that are a form of *do,* use the base form of the verb.

The helping verbs *do, does,* and *did* are used in three ways: (1) to express a negative meaning with the adverb *not* or *never,* (2) to ask a question, and (3) to emphasize a main verb used in a positive sense.

▶ Mariko does not wants any more dessert.

▶ Did Janice ~~bought~~ buy the gift for Katherine?

▶ We do ~~hoping~~ hope that you will come to the party.

Have, has, *or* had + *past participle (perfect tenses)*

After the helping verb *have, has,* or *had,* use the past participle to form one of the perfect tenses. (See 28a.) Past participles usually end in *-ed, -d, -en, -n,* or *-t.* (See 27a.)

▶ On cold nights many churches in the city have ~~offer~~ offered shelter to

the homeless.

▶ An-Mei has not ~~speaking~~ spoken Chinese since she was a child.

The helping verbs *have, has,* and *had* are sometimes preceded by a modal helping verb such as *will: By nightfall, we will have driven five hundred miles.* (See also perfect tenses, 28a.)

Form of be + *present participle (progressive forms)*

After the helping verb *be, am, is, are, was, were,* or *been,* use the present participle to express a continuing action. (See progressive forms, 28a.)

▶ Carlos is ~~build~~ building his house on a cliff overlooking the ocean.

▶ Uncle Roy was ~~driven~~ driving a brand new red Corvette.

The helping verb *be* must be preceded by a modal (*can, could, may, might, must, shall, should, will,* or *would*): *Edith will be going to Germany soon.* The helping verb *been* must be preceded by *have, has,* or *had*: *Andy has been studying English for five years.* (See also progressive forms, 28a.)

CAUTION: Certain verbs are not normally used in the progressive sense in English. In general, these verbs express a state of being or mental activity, not a dynamic action. Common examples are *appear, believe, belong, contain, have, hear, know, like, need, see, seem, taste, think, understand,* and *want.*

> *want*
> ▶ I ~~am wanting~~ to see August Wilson's *Fences* at Arena Stage.
>   ^

Some of these verbs, however, have special uses in which progressive forms are normal. (*We are thinking about going to the Bahamas.*) You will need to make a note of exceptions as you encounter them.

Form of be + past participle (passive voice)

When a sentence is written in the passive voice, the subject receives the action instead of doing it (*Melissa was given a special award*). (See 28c.)

To form the passive voice, use *be, am, is, are, was, were, being,* or *been* followed by a past participle (usually ending in *-ed, -d, -en, -n,* or *-t*).

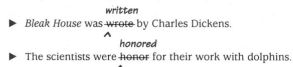

> *written*
> ▶ *Bleak House* was ~~wrote~~ by Charles Dickens.
>   ^
> *honored*
> ▶ The scientists were ~~honor~~ for their work with dolphins.
>   ^

When the helping verb is *be, being,* or *been,* it must be preceded by another helping verb. *Be* must be preceded by a modal such as *will: Senator Dixon will be defeated. Being* must be preceded by *am, is, are, was,* or *were: The child was being teased. Been* must be preceded by *have, has,* or *had: I have been invited to a party.*

CAUTION: Although they may seem to have passive meanings, verbs such as *occur, happen, sleep, die,* and *fall* may not be used to form the passive voice because they are intransitive. Only transitive verbs, those that take direct objects, may be used to form the passive voice. (See transitive and intransitive verbs, 58b.)

> ▶ The earthquake ~~was~~ occurred last Wednesday.

EXERCISE 29–1

Revise any sentences in which helping and main verbs do not match. You may need to look at the list of irregular verbs in 27a to determine the correct form of some irregular verbs. Answers to lettered sentences appear in the back of the book. Example:

> Maureen should find~~s~~ an apartment closer to campus.

a. We will making this a better country.
b. There is nothing in the world that TV has not touch on.
c. Did you understood my question?
d. A hard wind was blown while we were climbing the mountain.
e. The child's innocent world has been taking away from him.

1. Children are expose at an early age to certain aspects of adult life.
2. We've spend too much money this month, especially on things we don't really need.
3. Have you find your wallet yet?
4. I have ate Thai food only once before.
5. It would have help to know the cost before the work began.

29b In conditional sentences, choose verbs with care.

Conditional sentences state that one set of circumstances depends on whether another set of circumstances exists. Choosing verbs in such sentences can be tricky, partly because two clauses are involved: usually an *if* or a *when* or an *unless* clause and an independent clause.

Three kinds of conditional sentences are discussed in this section: factual, predictive, and speculative.

Factual

Factual conditional sentences express factual relationships. These relationships might be scientific truths, in which case the present tense is used in both clauses.

> If water *cools* to 32°F, it *freezes*.

Or they might be present or past relationships that are habitually true, in which case the same tense is used in both clauses.

> When Sue *bicycles* along the canal, her dog *runs* ahead of her.
>
> Whenever the coach *asked* for help, I *volunteered*.

Predictive

Predictive conditional sentences are used to predict the future or to express future plans or possibilities. In such a sentence, an *if* or *unless* clause contains a present-tense verb; the verb in the independent clause usually consists of the modal *will, can, may, should,* or *might* followed by the base form of the verb.

> If you *practice* regularly, your tennis game *will improve.*

> We *will lose* our remaining wetlands unless we *act* now.

Speculative

Speculative conditional sentences are used for three purposes: (1) to speculate about unlikely possibilities in the present or future, (2) to speculate about events that did not happen in the past, and (3) to speculate about conditions that are contrary to fact. Each purpose requires its own combination of verbs.

UNLIKELY POSSIBILITIES Somewhat confusingly, English uses the past tense in an *if* clause to speculate about a possible but unlikely condition in the present or future. The verb in the independent clause consists of *would, could,* or *might* plus the base form of the verb.

> If I *had* the time, I *would travel* to Senegal.

> If Stan *studied* harder, he *could master* calculus.

In the *if* clause, the past-tense form *were* is used with subjects that would normally take *was: Even if I were* [not *was*] *invited, I wouldn't go to the picnic.* (See also 28b.)

EVENTS THAT DID NOT HAPPEN English uses the past perfect tense in an *if* clause to speculate about an event that did not happen in the past or to speculate about a state of being that was unreal in the past. (See past perfect tense, 28a.) The verb in the independent clause consists of *would have, could have,* or *might have* plus the past participle.

> If I *had saved* enough money, I *would have traveled* to Senegal last year.

> If Aunt Grace *had been* alive for your graduation, she *would have been* very proud.

CONDITIONS CONTRARY TO FACT To speculate about conditions that are currently unreal or contrary to fact, English usually uses the past-tense verb *were* (never *was*) in an *if* clause. (See 28b.) The verb in the independent clause consists of *would, could,* or *might* plus the base form of the verb.

> If Grandmother *were* alive today, she *would be* very proud of you.

> I *would make* children's issues a priority if I *were* president.

EXERCISE 29–2

Edit the following conditional sentences for problems with verbs. In some cases, more than one revision is possible. Revisions of lettered sentences appear in the back of the book. Example:

> *had*
> If I ~~have~~ the money, I would meet Sid in Spain next summer.
>   ^

a. He would have won the election if he went to the inner city to campaign.
b. If Martin Luther King, Jr., was alive today, he would be appalled by the violence in our inner cities.
c. Whenever my uncle comes to visit, he brought me a present.
d. We will lose our largest client unless we would update our computer system.
e. If Verena wins a fellowship, she would go to graduate school.

1. If it would not be raining, we could go fishing.
2. If Lee had followed the doctor's orders, he had recovered from his operation by now.
3. You would have met my cousin if you came to the party last night.
4. Whenever I washed my car, it rains.
5. Our daughter would have drowned if Officer Blake didn't risk his life to save her.

29c Become familiar with verbs that may be followed by gerunds or infinitives.

A gerund is a verb form that ends in *-ing* and is used as a noun: *sleeping, dreaming.* (See 59c.) An infinitive is the base form of the verb preceded by the word *to: to sleep, to dream.* The word *to* is not a preposition in this use but an infinitive marker.

A few verbs may be followed by either a gerund or an

infinitive; others may be followed by a gerund but not by an infinitive; still others may be followed by an infinitive (either directly or with a noun or pronoun intervening) but not by a gerund.

Verb + gerund or infinitive

These commonly used verbs may be followed by a gerund or an infinitive, with little or no difference in meaning:

begin	continue	like	start
can't stand	hate	love	

I love *skiing.*   I love *to ski.*

With a few verbs, however, the choice of a gerund or infinitive changes the meaning dramatically:

forget	remember	stop	try

She stopped *speaking* to Lucia. [She no longer spoke to Lucia.]

She stopped *to speak* to Lucia. [She paused so that she could speak to Lucia.]

Verb + gerund

These verbs may be followed by a gerund but not by an infinitive:

admit	discuss	imagine	put off	risk
appreciate	enjoy	miss	quit	suggest
avoid	escape	postpone	recall	tolerate
deny	finish	practice	resist	

Bill enjoys *playing* [not *to play*] the piano.

Verb + infinitive

These verbs may be followed by an infinitive but not by a gerund:

agree	decide	manage	pretend	wait
ask	expect	mean	promise	want
beg	have	offer	refuse	wish
claim	hope	plan		

We plan *to visit* [not *visiting*] the Yucatán next week.

Verb + noun (or pronoun) + infinitive

With certain verbs in the active voice, a noun or pronoun must come between the verb and the infinitive that follows it. The noun or pronoun usually names a person who is affected by the action.

advise	command	instruct	require
allow	convince	order	tell
ask	encourage	persuade	urge
cause	have	remind	warn

The class urged *Luis to tell* the story of his escape.

A few verbs may be followed either by an infinitive directly or by an infinitive preceded by a noun or pronoun.

ask	expect	need	want	would like

We asked *to speak* to the congregation.

We asked *Rabbi Abrams to speak* to our congregation.

Verb + noun or pronoun + unmarked infinitive

An unmarked infinitive is an infinitive without *to*. A few verbs may be followed by a noun or pronoun and an unmarked (but not a marked) infinitive.

have ("cause")	let ("allow")	make ("force")

Please let *me pay* [not *to pay*] for the tickets.

EXERCISE 29–3

Form sentences by adding gerund or infinitive constructions to the following sentence openings. In some cases, more than one kind of construction may be possible. Possible sentences for lettered items appear in the back of the book. Example:

> Please remind *your sister to call me.*
> ∧

a. I enjoy
b. Will you help Samantha
c. The team hopes

d. Ricardo and his brothers miss
e. The babysitter let

1. Pollen makes
2. The club president asked
3. Next summer we plan
4. Waverly intends
5. Please stop

29d Become familiar with commonly used two-word verbs.

Many verbs in English consist of a verb followed by a preposition or adverb known as a *particle*. A two-word verb (also known as a *phrasal verb*) often expresses an idiomatic meaning that cannot be understood literally. Consider the verbs in the following sentences, for example.

> We *ran across* Professor Magnotto on the way to the bookstore.
>
> Calvin *dropped in* on his adviser this morning.
>
> Regina told me to *look* her *up* when I got to Seattle.

As you probably know, *ran across* means "encountered," *dropped in* means "paid an unexpected visit," and *look up* means "get in touch with." When you were first learning English, however, these two-word verbs must have suggested strange meanings.

Some two-word verbs are intransitive; they do not take direct objects. (See 58b.)

> This morning I *got up* at dawn.

Transitive two-word verbs (those that take direct objects) have particles that are either separable or inseparable. Separable particles may be separated from the verb by the direct object.

> Lucy *called* the wedding *off.*

When the direct object is a noun, a separable particle may also follow the verb immediately:

> At the last minute, Lucy *called off* the wedding.

Grammar

When the direct object is a pronoun, however, the particle must be separated from the verb.

Why was there no wedding? Lucy *called* it *off* [not *called off* it].

Inseparable particles must follow the verb immediately. A direct object cannot come between the verb and the particle.

The police will *look into* the matter [not *look* the matter *into*].

The following list includes common two-word verbs. If a particle can be separated from the verb by a direct object, a pronoun is shown between the verb and the particle: *ask (someone) out.* When in doubt about the meaning of a two-word verb, consult the dictionary.

COMMON TWO-WORD VERBS

ask (someone) out
break down
burn (something) down
burn down
burn (something) up
burn up
bring (something or someone) up
call (something) off
call (someone) up
clean (something) up
clean up
come across
cut (something) up
do (something) over
drop in (on someone)
drop (someone or something) off
drop out (of something)
fill (something) out
fill (something) up
get along (with someone)
get away (with something)
get up
give (something) away
give (something) back
give in
give up
go out (with someone)
go over (something)

grow up
hand (something) in
hand (something) out
hang (something) up
help out
help (someone) out
keep on (doing something)
keep up (with someone or something)
leave (something) out
look into (something)
look (something) over
look (something) up
make (something) up
pick (something) out
pick (someone) up
pick (something) up
play around
point (something) out
put (something) away
put (something) back
put (something) off
put (something) on
put (something) out
put (something) together
put up (with someone or something)
quiet down
run across (someone or something)

COMMON TWO-WORD VERBS

run into (someone or
   something)
run out (of something)
see (someone) off
shut (something) off
speak to (someone)
speak up
stay away (from someone or
   something)
stay up
take care of (someone or
   something)
take off
take (someone) off

take (something) out
take (something) over
think (something) over
throw (something) away
throw (something) out
try (something) on
try (something) out
turn (something) down
turn (something) on
turn up
wake up
wake (someone) up
wear out
wrap (something) up

EXERCISE 29-4

From the list of two-word verbs, choose ten verbs, preferably ones whose meaning you are not sure of. First look the verbs up in the dictionary; then use each verb in a sentence of your own.

29e Do not omit needed verbs.

Some languages allow the omission of the verb when the meaning is clear without it; English does not.

▶ Jim ^is^ exceptionally intelligent.

▶ Many streets in San Francisco ^are^ very steep.

▶ Nancy ^is^ in the backyard.

30

Use the articles *a, an,* and *the* appropriately.

Except for occasional difficulty in choosing between *a* and *an,* native speakers of English encounter few problems with articles. To speakers whose native language is not English, however, articles can prove troublesome, for the rules governing their use are surprisingly complex. This section summarizes those rules.

The definite article *the* and the indefinite articles *a* and *an* signal that a noun is about to appear. The noun may follow the article immediately, or modifiers may intervene (see 57a, 57d).

> *the* candidate, *the* well-qualified *candidate*
>
> *a* sunset, *a* spectacular *sunset*
>
> *an* apple, *an* appetizing *apple*

Articles are not the only words used to mark nouns. Other noun markers (sometimes called *determiners*) include possessive nouns (*Helen's*), numbers, and the following pronouns: *my, your, his, her, its, our, their, whose, this, that, these, those, all, any, each, either, every, few, many, more, most, much, neither, several, some.*

Usually an article is not used with another noun marker. Common exceptions include expressions such as *a few, the most,* and *all the.*

30a Use *a* (or *an*) with singular count nouns whose specific identity is not known to the reader.

Count nouns refer to persons, places, or things that can be counted: *one girl, two girls; one city, three cities; one apple, four apples.* Noncount nouns refer to entities or abstractions that cannot be counted: *water, steel, air, furniture, patience, knowledge.* It is important to remember that noncount nouns vary from language to language. To see what nouns English categorizes as noncount nouns, refer to the list on page 231.

If a singular count noun names something not known to the reader—perhaps because it is being mentioned for the first time, perhaps because its specific identity is unknown even to the writer—the noun should be preceded by *a* or *an* unless it has been preceded by another noun marker. *A* (or *an*) usually means "one among many" but can also mean "any one."

>   *a*
> ▶ Mary Beth and Jason arrived in ⌃limousine.
>
>   *an*
> ▶ We are looking for ⌃apartment close to the lake.

NOTE: *A* is used before a consonant sound: *a banana, a tree, a picture, a hand, a happy child. An* is used before a vowel sound: *an eggplant, an occasion, an uncle, an hour, an honorable person.* Notice that words beginning with *h* can have either a consonant sound (*hand, happy*) or a vowel sound (*hour, honorable*). (See also the Glossary of Usage.)

30b Do not use *a* (or *an*) with noncount nouns.

A (or *an*) is not used to mark noncount nouns, such as *sugar, gold, honesty,* or *jewelry.*

► Claudia asked her mother for ~~an~~ advice.

If you want to express an amount for a noncount noun, you can use *some, any,* or *more*: *some paper, any information, more pasta.* Or you can add a count noun in front of the noncount noun: *a quart of milk, a piece of furniture, a bar of soap.*

pound of

► Mother asked us to pick up a sugar at the corner store.
^

NOTE: A few noncount nouns may also be used as count nouns: *Bill loves lemonade; Bill offered me a lemonade.*

COMMONLY USED NONCOUNT NOUNS

Food and drink: bacon, beef, bread, broccoli, butter, cabbage, candy, cauliflower, celery, cereal, cheese, chicken, chocolate, coffee, corn, cream, fish, flour, fruit, ice cream, lemonade, lettuce, meat, milk, oil, pasta, rice, salt, spinach, sugar, tea, water, wine, yogurt

Nonfood substances: air, cement, coal, dirt, gasoline, gold, paper, petroleum, plastic, rain, silver, snow, soap, steel, wood, wool

Abstract nouns: advice, anger, beauty, confidence, courage, employment, fun, happiness, health, honesty, information, intelligence, knowledge, love, poverty, satisfaction, truth, wealth, wisdom

Other: biology (and other areas of study), clothing, equipment, furniture, homework, jewelry, luggage, lumber, machinery, mail, money, news, poetry, pollution, research, scenery, traffic, transportation, violence, weather, work

30c Use *the* with most nouns whose specific identity is known to the reader.

The definite article *the* is used with most nouns whose identity is known to the reader. (For exceptions, see 30d.) Usually the identity will be clear to the reader for one of the following reasons:

- The noun has been previously mentioned.
- A phrase or a clause following the noun restricts its identity.
- A superlative such as *best* or *most intelligent* makes the noun's identity specific.
- The noun describes a unique person, place, or thing.
- The context or situation makes the noun's identity clear.

▶ A truck loaded with dynamite cut in front of our van. When
   the
   truck skidded a few seconds later, we almost plowed into it.
   ^

The noun *truck* is preceded by *A* when it is first mentioned. When the noun is mentioned again, it is preceded by *the* since readers now know the specific truck being discussed.

                        the
▶ Bob warned me that gun on the top shelf of the cupboard was
                     ^
   loaded.

The phrase *on the top shelf of the cupboard* identifies the specific gun.

                        the
▶ Our petite daughter dated tallest boy in her class.
                          ^
The superlative *tallest* restricts the identity of the noun *boy*.

                                    the
▶ During an eclipse, one should not look directly at sun.
                                        ^
There is only one sun in our solar system, so its identity is clear.

                     the
▶ Please don't slam door when you leave.
                   ^
Both the speaker and the listener know which door is meant.

30d Do not use *the* with plural or noncount nouns meaning "all" or "in general"; do not use *the* with most proper nouns.

When a plural or a noncount noun means "all" or "in general," it is not marked with *the*.

▶ ~~The~~ F̲ountains are an expensive element of landscape design.

▶ In some parts of the world, ~~the~~ rice is preferred to all other

grains.

Although there are many exceptions, *the* is not used with most singular proper nouns. Do not use *the* with names of persons (Jessica Webner), names of streets, squares, parks, cities, and states (Prospect Street, Union Square, Denali National Park, Miami, Idaho), names of continents and most countries (South America, Italy), and names of bays and single lakes, mountains, and islands (Tampa Bay, Lake Geneva, Mount Everest, Crete).

Exceptions to this rule include names of large regions, deserts, and peninsulas (the East Coast, the Sahara, the Iberian Peninsula) and names of oceans, seas, gulfs, canals, and rivers (the Pacific, the Dead Sea, the Persian Gulf, the Panama Canal, the Amazon).

NOTE: *The* is used to mark plural proper nouns: the United Nations, the Finger Lakes, the Andes, the Bahamas, and so on.

EXERCISE 30–1

Articles have been omitted from the following story, adapted from *Zen Flesh, Zen Bones,* compiled by Paul Reps. Insert the articles *a, an,* and *the* where English requires them and be prepared to explain the reasons for your choices.

Moon Cannot Be Stolen

Ryokan, who was Zen master, lived simple life in little hut at foot of mountain. One evening thief visited hut only to discover there was nothing in it to steal.

Ryokan returned and caught him. "You may have come long way to visit me," he told prowler, "and you should not return empty-handed. Please take my clothes as gift." Thief was bewildered. He took Ryokan's clothes and slunk away. Ryokan sat naked, watching moon. "Poor fellow," he mused, "I wish I could give him this beautiful moon."

31

Be aware of other potential trouble spots.

31a Do not omit subjects or the expletive *there* or *it*.

English requires a subject for all sentences except imperatives, in which the subject *you* is understood (*Give to the poor*). (See 58a.) If your native language allows the omission of an explicit subject in other sentences or clauses, be especially alert to this requirement in English.

▶ *I have*
  ~~Have~~ a large collection of baseball cards.
  ^

▶ Your aunt is very energetic; *she* seems young for her age.
  ^

When the subject has been moved from its normal position before the verb, English sometimes requires an expletive (*there* or *it*) at the beginning of the sentence or clause. (See 58c.) *There* is used at the beginning of a sentence or clause that draws the reader's (or listener's) attention to the location or existence of something.

▶ *There is*
  ~~Is~~ an apple in the refrigerator.
  ^

▶ As you know, *there* are many religious sects in India.
  ^

Notice that the verb agrees with the subject that follows it: *apple is, sects are.* (See 21f.)

In one of its uses, the word *it* functions as an expletive, to call attention to a subject following the verb.

> *It is*
> ▶ ~~Is~~ healthy to eat fruit and grains.
>   ^
>   *It is*
> ▶ ~~Is~~ clear that we must change our approach.
>   ^

The subjects of these sentences are *to eat fruit and grains* (an infinitive phrase) and *that we must change our approach* (a noun clause). (See 59c and 59b.)

As you probably know, the word *it* is also used as the subject of sentences describing the weather or temperature, stating the time, indicating distance, or suggesting an environmental fact.

> *It is* raining in the valley, and *it is* snowing in the mountains.

> In July, *it is* very hot in Arizona.

> *It is* 9:15 A.M.

> *It is* three hundred miles to Chicago.

> *It gets* noisy in our dorm on weekends.

31b Do not repeat the subject of a sentence.

English does not allow a subject to be repeated in its own clause.

> ▶ The doctor ~~she~~ advised me to cut down on salt.

> The pronoun *she* repeats the subject *doctor*.

The subject of a sentence should not be repeated even if a word group intervenes between the subject and the verb.

> ▶ The car that had been stolen ~~it~~ was found.

> The pronoun *it* repeats the subject *car*.

31c Do not repeat an object or adverb in an adjective clause.

In some languages an object or an adverb is repeated later in the adjective clause in which it appears; in English such repetitions are not allowed. Adjective clauses begin with relative pronouns (*who, whom, whose, which, that*) or relative adverbs (*when, where*), and these words always serve a grammatical function within the clauses they introduce. (See 59b.) Another word in the clause cannot also serve that same grammatical function.

When a relative pronoun functions as the object of a verb or the object of a preposition, do not add another word with the same function later in the clause.

▶ The puppy ran after the car that we were riding in•it̶.
                                                  ∧

The relative pronoun *that* is the object of the preposition *in*, so the object *it* is not allowed.

Even when the relative pronoun has been omitted, do not add another word with its same function.

▶ The puppy ran after the car we were riding in•it̶.
                                            ∧

The relative pronoun *that* is understood even though it is not present in the sentence.

Like a relative pronoun, a relative adverb should not be echoed later in its clause.

▶ The place where I work t̶h̶e̶r̶e̶ is one hour from my apartment

in the city.

The adverb *there* should not echo the relative adverb *where*.

EXERCISE 31–1

In the following sentences, add needed subjects or expletives and delete any repeated subjects, objects, or adverbs. Answers to lettered sentences appear in the back of the book. Example:

Nancy is the woman whom I talked to ~~her~~ last week.

a. The roses they brought home they cost three dollars each.
b. Are two grocery stores on Elm Street.
c. The prime minister she is the most popular leader in my country.
d. Pavel hasn't heard from the cousin he wrote to her last month.
e. The king, who had served since the age of sixteen, he was an old man when he died.

1. Henri and Nicole they are good friends.
2. Is important to study the grammar of English.
3. The neighbor we trusted he was a thief.
4. I don't use the subway because am afraid.
5. Archaeologists have excavated the city where the old Persian kings are buried there.

31d Place adjectives and adverbs with care.

Adjectives modify nouns or pronouns; adverbs modify verbs, adjectives, or other adverbs (see 57d and 57e). Both native and nonnative speakers encounter problems in the use of adjectives and adverbs (see 26). For nonnative speakers, the placement of adjectives and adverbs can also be troublesome.

Placement of adjectives

No doubt you have already learned that in English adjectives usually precede the nouns they modify and that they may also appear following linking verbs. (See 26b and 58b.)

Janine wore a *new* necklace. Janine's necklace was *new*.

When adjectives pile up in front of a noun, however, you may sometimes have difficulty arranging them. English is quite particular about the order of cumulative adjectives, those not separated by commas. (See 33d.)

Janine was wearing a *beautiful antique silver* necklace. [Not *silver antique beautiful* necklace]

The chart on page 238 shows the order in which cumulative adjectives ordinarily appear in front of the noun they modify. This list is just a general guide; don't be surprised when you encounter exceptions.

Usual order of cumulative adjectives

ARTICLE OR OTHER NOUN MARKER   a, an, the, her, Joe's, two, some

EVALUATIVE WORD   attractive, dedicated, delicious, ugly, disgusting

SIZE   large, enormous, small, little

LENGTH OR SHAPE   long, short, round, square

AGE   new, old, young, antique

COLOR   yellow, blue, crimson

NATIONALITY   French, Scandinavian, Vietnamese

RELIGION   Catholic, Protestant, Jewish, Muslim

MATERIAL   silver, walnut, wool, marble

NOUN/ADJECTIVE   tree (as in *tree house*), kitchen (as in *kitchen table*)

THE NOUN MODIFIED   house, sweater, bicycle, bread, woman, priest

NOTE: Long strings of cumulative adjectives tend to be awkward. As a rule, use no more than two or three of them between the article (or other noun marker) and the noun modified. Here are several examples:

a beautiful old pine table
two enormous French urns
an exotic purple jungle flower

Susan's large round painting
some small blue medicine
  bottles

Placement of adverbs

Adverbs modifying verbs appear in various positions: at the beginning or end of the sentence, before or after the verb, or between a helping verb and its main verb.

Slowly, we drove along the rain-slick road.

Mia handled the teapot very *carefully*.

Martin *always* wins our tennis matches.

Christina is *rarely* late for our lunch dates.

My daughter has *often* spoken of you.

An adverb may not, however, be placed between a verb and its direct object.

▶ Mother wrapped ~~carefully~~ the gift. *carefully.*

The adverb *carefully* may be placed at the beginning or at the end of this sentence or before the verb. It cannot appear after the verb because the verb is followed by the direct object *gift*.

EXERCISE 31–2

Using the chart on page 238, arrange the following modifiers and nouns in their proper order. Answers to lettered items appear in the back of the book. Example:

two new French racing bicycles
new, French, two, bicycles, racing

a. woman, young, an, Vietnamese, attractive
b. dedicated, a, priest, Catholic
c. old, her, sweater, blue, wool
d. delicious, Joe's, Scandinavian, bread
e. many, cages, bird, antique, beautiful

1. round, two, marble, tables, large
2. several, yellow, tulips, tiny
3. a, sports, classic, car
4. courtyard, a, square, small, brick
5. charming, restaurants, Italian, several

31e Distinguish between present participles and past participles used as adjectives.

Both present and past participles may be used as adjectives. The present participle always ends in *-ing*. Past participles usually end in *-ed*, *-d*, *-en*, *-n*, or *-t*. (See 27a.)

PRESENT PARTICIPLES	confusing, speaking
PAST PARTICIPLES	confused, spoken

Participles used as adjectives can precede the nouns they modify; they can also follow linking verbs, in which case they will describe the subject of the sentence. (See 58b.)

It was a *depressing* movie. Jim was a *depressed* young man.

The essay was *confusing*. The student was *confused*.

A present participle should describe a person or thing causing or stimulating an experience; a past participle should describe a person or thing undergoing an experience.

The lecturer was *boring* [not *bored*].

The audience was *bored* [not *boring*].

In the first example, the lecturer is causing boredom, not experiencing it. In the second example, the audience is experiencing boredom, not causing it.

The participles that cause the most trouble for nonnative speakers are those describing mental states:

annoying / annoyed	exhausting / exhausted
boring / bored	fascinating / fascinated
confusing / confused	frightening / frightened
depressing / depressed	satisfying / satisfied
exciting / excited	surprising / surprised

When you come across these words in your writing, check to see that you have used them correctly.

EXERCISE 31–3

Edit the following sentences for proper use of present and past participles. If a sentence is correct, write "correct" after it. Answers to lettered sentences appear in the back of the book. Example:

excited
Danielle and Monica were very ~~exciting~~ to be going to a

Broadway show for the first time.

a. Having to listen to everyone's complaints was irritated.
b. The noise in the hall was distracted to me.

c. He was not pleased with his grades last semester.
d. The violence in recent movies is often disgusted.
e. I have never seen anyone as surprised as Mona when she walked through the door and we turned on the lights.

1. Megan worked on her art project for eight hours but still she was not satisfying.
2. That blackout was the most frightened experience I've ever had.
3. I couldn't concentrate on my homework because I was distracted.
4. Three weeks after his promotion, he decided that being the boss was bored.
5. The exhibit on the La Brea tar pits was fascinated.

31f Become familiar with common prepositions that show time and place.

The most frequently used prepositions in English are *at, by, for, from, in, of, on, to,* and *with.* Each of these prepositions has a variety of uses that must be learned gradually, in context.

Prepositions that indicate time and place can be difficult to master because the differences among them are subtle and idiomatic. The chart on page 242 limits itself to three troublesome prepositions that show time and place: *at, on,* and *in.*

Not every possible use is listed in the chart, so don't be surprised when you encounter exceptions and idiomatic uses that you must learn one at a time. For example, in English we ride *in* a car but *on* a bus, train, or subway. And when we fly *on* (not *in*) a plane, we are not sitting on top of the plane.

EXERCISE 31–4

In the following sentences, replace any prepositions that are not used correctly. If a sentence is correct, write "correct" after it. Answers to lettered sentences appear in the back of the book. Example:

> *at*
> The play begins ~~on~~ 7:00 P.M.
> ^

a. We spent seven days on June in the beach, and it rained every day.
b. In the 1980s, the gap between the rich and the poor in the United States became wider.
c. Usually she met with her patients on the afternoon, but in that day she stayed at home to take care of her son.

At, on, and *in* to show time and place

Showing time

AT   *at* a specific time: *at* 7:00, *at* dawn, *at* dinner

ON   *on* a specific day or date: on Tuesday, on June 4

IN   *in* a part of a 24-hour period: *in* the afternoon, *in* the daytime [but *at* night]

     in a year or month: *in* 1999, *in* July

     in a period of time: finished *in* three hours

Showing place

AT   *at* a meeting place or location: *at* home, *at* the club

     at the edge of something: sitting *at* the desk

     at the corner of something: turning *at* the intersection

     at a target: throwing the snowball *at* Lucy

ON   *on* a surface: placed *on* the table, hanging *on* the wall

     on a street: the house *on* Spring Street

IN   *in* an enclosed space: *in* the garage, *in* the envelope

     in a geographic location: *in* San Diego, *in* Texas

---

d. The clock is hanging on the wall on the dining room.
e. In Germany it is difficult for foreigners to become citizens even if they've lived at the country for a long time.

1. He sat on his bed in his room at the hotel.
2. Only the adults in the family were allowed to sit on the dining room table; the children ate in another room.
3. If the train is on time it will arrive on six o'clock at the morning.
4. She licked the stamp, stuck it in the envelope, put the envelope on her pocket, and walked to the nearest mailbox.
5. The mailbox was in the intersection of Laidlaw Avenue and Williams Street.

Punctuation

32

The comma

The comma was invented to help readers. Without it, sentence parts can collide into one another unexpectedly, causing misreadings.

> **CONFUSING**   If you cook Elmer will do the dishes.
>
> **CONFUSING**   While we were eating a rattlesnake approached our campsite.

Add commas in the logical places (after *cook* and *eating*), and suddenly all is clear. No longer is Elmer being cooked, the rattlesnake being eaten.

Various rules have evolved to prevent such misreadings and to speed readers along through complex grammatical structures. Those rules are detailed in this section.

32a   Use a comma before a coordinating conjunction joining independent clauses.

When a coordinating conjunction connects two or more independent clauses — word groups that could stand alone as separate sentences — a comma must precede it. There are seven coordinating conjunctions in English: *and, but, or, nor, for, so,* and *yet.*

A comma tells readers that one independent clause has come to a close and that another is about to begin.

▶ Nearly everyone has heard of love at first sight**,** but I fell in love

at first dance.

EXCEPTION: If the two independent clauses are short and there is no danger of misreading, the comma may be omitted.

> The plane took off and we were on our way.

CAUTION: As a rule, do *not* use a comma to separate coordinate word groups that are not independent clauses. See 33a.

▶ A good money manager controls expenses/and invests surplus

dollars to meet future needs.

The word group following *and* is not an independent clause.

32b Use a comma after an introductory clause or phrase.

The most common introductory word groups are clauses and phrases functioning as adverbs. Such word groups usually tell when, where, how, why, or under what conditions the main action of the sentence occurred. See 59a, 59b, and 59c.

A comma tells readers that the introductory clause or phrase has come to a close and that the main part of the sentence is about to begin.

▶ When Irwin was ready to eat, his cat jumped onto the table.

Without the comma, readers may have Irwin eating his cat. The comma signals that *his cat* is the subject of a new clause, not part of the introductory one.

▶ Near a small stream at the bottom of the canyon, we discovered

an abandoned shelter.

The comma tells readers that the introductory prepositional phrase has come to a close.

EXCEPTION: The comma may be omitted after a short adverb clause or phrase if there is no danger of misreading.

In no time we were at 2,800 feet.

Sentences also frequently begin with phrases describing the noun or pronoun immediately following them. The comma tells readers that they are about to learn the identity of the person or thing described; therefore, the comma is usually required even when the phrase is short. See 59c.

▶ Knowing that he couldn't outrun a car, Sy took to the fields.
      ^

▶ Excited about the move, Alice and Don began packing their
      ^
books.

The commas tell readers that they are about to hear the nouns described: *Sy* in the first sentence, *Alice and Don* in the second.

NOTE: Other introductory word groups include transitional expressions and absolute phrases. See 32f.

EXERCISE 32–1

Add or delete commas where necessary in the following sentences. If a sentence is correct, write "correct" after it. Answers to lettered sentences appear in the back of the book. Example:

Because it rained all Labor Day, our picnic was rather soggy.
                              ^

a. As he was writing up the report, Officer Sweet heard a strange noise coming from the trash dumpster.
b. The man at the next table complained loudly and the waiter stomped off in disgust.
c. Instead of eating half a cake or two dozen cookies I now grab a banana or an orange.
d. Nursing is physically, and mentally demanding, yet the pay is low.
e. Uncle Sven's dulcimers disappeared as soon as he put them up for sale but he always kept one for himself.

1. When the runaway race car hit the gas tank exploded.
2. He pushed the car beyond the toll gate and poured a bucket of water on the smoking hood.
3. Lighting the area like a second moon the helicopter circled the scene.
4. While one of the robbers tied Laureen to a chair, and gagged her with an apron, the other emptied the contents of the safe into a knapsack.
5. Many musicians of Bach's time played several instruments, but few mastered them as early or played with as much expression as Bach.

32c Use a comma between all items in a series.

When three or more items are presented in a series, those items should be separated from one another with commas.

> At Dominique's one can order fillet of rattlesnake, bison burgers, or pickled eel.

Although some writers view the comma between the last two items as optional, most experts advise using the comma because its omission can result in ambiguity.

> ▶ Uncle David willed me all of his property, houses, and
>
> warehouses.

> Did Uncle David will his property *and* houses *and* warehouses — or simply his property, consisting of houses and warehouses? If the former meaning is intended, a comma is necessary to prevent ambiguity.

32d Use a comma between coordinate adjectives not joined by *and.*

When two or more adjectives each modify a noun separately, they are coordinate.

> With the help of a therapist, Mother has become a *strong, confident, independent* woman.

Adjectives are coordinate if they can be joined with *and* (strong *and* confident *and* independent) or if they can be scrambled (an *independent, strong, confident* woman).

Adjectives that do not modify the noun separately are cumulative, and no commas are used between them.

> *Three large gray* shapes moved slowly toward us.

We cannot insert the word *and* between cumulative adjectives (three *and* large *and* gray shapes). Nor can we scramble them (*gray three large* shapes).

COORDINATE ADJECTIVES

> ▶ Roberto is a warm, gentle, affectionate father.

CUMULATIVE ADJECTIVES

▶ Ira ordered a rich/chocolate/layer cake.

EXERCISE 32–2

Add or delete commas where necessary in the following sentences. If a sentence is correct, write "correct" after it. Answers to lettered sentences appear in the back of the book. Example:

We gathered our essentials, took off for the great outdoors,

and ignored the fact that it was Friday the 13th.

a. She wore a black silk cape, a rhinestone collar, satin gloves and high tops.
b. There is no need to prune, weed, fertilize or repot your air fern.
c. City Café is noted for its spicy vegetarian dishes and its friendly efficient service.
d. Juan walked through the room with casual elegant grace.
e. My cat's pupils had constricted to small black shining dots.

1. My brother and I found a dead garter snake, picked it up and placed it on Miss Eunice's doorstep.
2. For breakfast the children ordered cornflakes, English muffins with peanut butter and cherry Cokes.
3. Patients with severe irreversible brain damage should not be put on life support machines.
4. Cyril was clad in a luminous orange rain suit and a brilliant white helmet.
5. Anne Frank and thousands like her were forced to hide in attics, cellars and secret rooms in an effort to save their lives.

32e Use commas to set off nonrestrictive elements.

Word groups describing nouns or pronouns (adjective clauses, adjective phrases, and appositives) are restrictive or nonrestrictive. A *restrictive* element defines or limits the meaning of the word it modifies and is therefore essential to the meaning of the sentence. Because it contains essential information, a restrictive element is not set off with commas.

| RESTRICTIVE | For camp the children needed clothes *that were washable.* |

If you remove a restrictive element from a sentence, the meaning changes significantly, becoming more general than you intended. The writer of the example sentence does not mean that the children needed clothes in general. The intended meaning is more limited: The children needed *washable* clothes.

A *nonrestrictive* element describes a noun or pronoun whose meaning has already been clearly defined or limited. Because it contains nonessential or parenthetical information, a nonrestrictive element is set off with commas.

| NONRESTRICTIVE | For camp the children needed sturdy shoes, *which were expensive.* |

If you remove a nonrestrictive element from a sentence, the meaning does not change dramatically. Some meaning is lost, to be sure, but the defining characteristics of the person or thing described remain the same as before. The children needed *sturdy shoes,* and these happened to be expensive.

Adjective clauses

Adjective clauses are patterned like sentences, containing subjects and verbs, but they function within sentences as modifiers of nouns or pronouns. They always follow the word they modify, usually immediately. Adjective clauses begin with a relative pronoun (*who, whom, whose, which, that*) or with a relative adverb (*where, when*).

Nonrestrictive adjective clauses are set off with commas; restrictive adjective clauses are not.

NONRESTRICTIVE CLAUSE

▶ Ed's house, which is located on thirteen acres, was completely

furnished with bats in the rafters and mice in the kitchen.

The clause *which is located on thirteen acres* does not restrict the meaning of *Ed's house,* so the information is nonessential.

RESTRICTIVE CLAUSE

▶ An office manager for a corporation/ that had government

contracts/ asked her supervisor whether she could reprimand

her co-workers for smoking.

Because the adjective clause *that had government contracts* identifies the corporation, the information is essential.

NOTE: Use *that* only with restrictive clauses. Many writers prefer to use *which* only with nonrestrictive clauses, but usage
varies.

Phrases functioning as adjectives

Prepositional or verbal phrases functioning as adjectives may
be restrictive or nonrestrictive. Nonrestrictive phrases are set
off with commas; restrictive phrases are not.

NONRESTRICTIVE PHRASE

▶ The helicopter, with its 100,000-candlepower spotlight
           ^

illuminating the area, circled above.
              ^

The *with* phrase is nonessential because its purpose is not to
specify which of two or more helicopters is being discussed.

RESTRICTIVE PHRASE

▶ One corner of the attic was filled with newspapers/ dating from

the turn of the century.

Dating from the turn of the century restricts the meaning of *newspapers,* so the comma should be omitted.

Appositives

An appositive is a noun or noun phrase that renames a nearby
noun. Nonrestrictive appositives are set off with commas;
restrictive appositives are not.

NONRESTRICTIVE APPOSITIVE

▶ Norman Mailer's first novel**,** *The Naked and the Dead***,** was a
    ʌ   ʌ
best-seller.

The term *first* restricts the meaning to one novel, so the appositive *The Naked and the Dead* is nonrestrictive.

RESTRICTIVE APPOSITIVE

▶ The song⁄ "Fire It Up⁆" was blasted out of amplifiers ten feet tall.

Once they've read *song,* readers still don't know precisely which
song the writer means. The appositive following *song* restricts its
meaning.

EXERCISE 32–3

Add or delete commas where necessary in the following sentences. If
a sentence is correct, write "correct" after it. Answers to lettered sentences appear in the back of the book. Example:

My youngest sister**,** who plays left wing on the team**,** now lives
                    ʌ   ʌ
at The Sands**,** a beach house near Los Angeles.
             ʌ

a. B. B. King and Lucille, his customized black Gibson have electrified audiences all over the world.
b. The Scott Pack which is a twenty-five-pound steel bottle of air is
   designed to be worn on a firefighter's back.
c. The woman running for the council seat in the fifth district had a
   long history of community service.
d. Shakespeare's tragedy, *King Lear,* was given a splendid performance by the actor, Laurence Olivier.
e. Douglass's first autobiography, *Narrative of the Life of Frederick
   Douglass, an American Slave,* was published in 1845.

1. I had the pleasure of talking to a woman who had just returned
   from India where she had lived for ten years.
2. The Irish students knew by heart the exploits of Cuchulain a legendary Irish warrior but they knew nothing about Freud or Marx
   or any religion but their own.
3. The gentleman waiting for a prescription is Mr. Rhee.

4. *Where the Wild Things Are,* the 1964 Caldecott Medal winner, is my nephew's favorite book.
5. Going on an archaeological dig which has always been an ambition of mine seems out of the question this year.

32f Use commas to set off transitional and parenthetical expressions, absolute phrases, and elements expressing contrast.

Transitional expressions

Transitional expressions serve as bridges between sentences or parts of sentences. They include conjunctive adverbs such as *however, therefore,* and *moreover* and transitional phrases such as *for example, as a matter of fact,* and *in other words.* (For more complete lists, see 34b.)

When a transitional expression appears between independent clauses in a compound sentence, it is preceded by a semicolon and is usually followed by a comma. (See 34b.)

▶ Minh did not understand our language; moreover, he was

unfamiliar with our customs.

When a transitional expression appears at the beginning of a sentence or in the middle of an independent clause, it is usually set off with commas.

▶ As a matter of fact, American football was established by fans

who wanted to play a more organized game of rugby.

▶ The prospective babysitter looked very promising; she was

busy, however, throughout the month of January.

EXCEPTION: If a transitional expression blends smoothly with the rest of the sentence, calling for little or no pause in reading, it does not need to be set off with a comma. Expressions such as *also, at least, certainly, consequently, indeed, of course, moreover, no doubt, perhaps, then,* and *therefore* do not always call for a pause.

> Alice's bicycle is broken; *therefore* you will need to borrow Sue's.

NOTE: The conjunctive adverb *however* always calls for a pause, but it should not be confused with *however* meaning "no matter how," which does not: *However hard Bill tried, he could not match his previous record.*

Parenthetical expressions

Expressions that are distinctly parenthetical should be set off with commas. Providing supplemental information, they interrupt the flow of a sentence or appear at the end as afterthoughts.

▶ Evolution, as far as we know, doesn't work this way.

▶ The bass weighed about twelve pounds, give or take a few

  ounces.

Absolute phrases

An absolute phrase, which modifies the whole sentence, usually consists of a noun followed by a participle or participial phrase. (See 59e.) Absolute phrases may appear at the beginning or at the end of a sentence. Wherever they appear, they should be set off with commas.

▶ Her tennis game at last perfected, Krista won the cup.

▶ Brian was forced to rely on public transportation, his car

  having been wrecked the week before.

> In the first example, the absolute phrase appears at the beginning of the sentence; in the second example, it appears at the end.

Contrasted elements

Sharp contrasts beginning with words such as *not, never,* and *unlike* are set off with commas.

▶ Celia, unlike Robert, had no loathing for dance contests.
   ^   ^

▶ Jane talks to me as an adult and friend, not as her little sister.
                                          ^

32g Use commas to set off nouns of direct address, the words *yes* and *no*, interrogative tags, and mild interjections.

▶ Forgive us, Dr. Spock, for reprimanding Jason.
             ^   ^

▶ Yes, the loan will probably be approved.
      ^

▶ The film was faithful to the book, wasn't it?
                                    ^

▶ Well, cases like these are difficult to decide.
       ^

32h Use commas with expressions such as *he said* to set off direct quotations. (See also 37f.)

▶ Naturalist Arthur Cleveland Bent remarked, "In part the
                                            ^
   peregrine declined unnoticed because it is not adorable."

▶ "Convictions are more dangerous foes of truth than lies,"
                                                          ^
   wrote philosopher Friedrich Nietzsche.

32i Use commas with dates, addresses, titles, and numbers.

Dates

In dates, the year is set off from the rest of the sentence with a pair of commas.

▶ On December 12, 1890, orders were sent out for the arrest of

Sitting Bull.

EXCEPTIONS: Commas are not needed if the date is inverted or if only the month and year are given.

The recycling plan went into effect on 15 April 1994.

January 1994 was an extremely cold month.

Addresses

The elements of an address or place name are separated by commas. A zip code, however, is not preceded by a comma.

▶ John Lennon was born in Liverpool, England, in 1940.

▶ Please send the package to Greg Tarvin at 708 Spring Street,

Washington, Illinois 61571.

Titles

If a title follows a name, separate it from the rest of the sentence with a pair of commas.

▶ Sandra Belinsky, M.D., has been appointed to the board.

Numbers

In numbers more than four digits long, use commas to separate the numbers into groups of three, starting from the right. In numbers four digits long, a comma is optional.

    3,500 [*or* 3500]
    100,000
    5,000,000

EXCEPTIONS: Do not use commas in street numbers, zip codes, telephone numbers, or years.

32j Use a comma to prevent confusion.

In certain contexts, a comma is necessary to prevent confusion. If the writer has omitted a word or phrase, for example, a comma may be needed to signal the omission.

▶ To err is human; to forgive, divine.

If two words in a row echo each other, a comma may be needed for ease of reading.

▶ All of the catastrophes that we had feared might happen,

happened.

Sometimes a comma is needed to prevent readers from grouping words in ways that do not match the writer's intention.

▶ Patients who can, walk up and down the halls several times a

day.

EXERCISE 32–4: All uses of the comma

Add or delete commas where necessary in the following sentences. If a sentence is correct, write "correct" after it. Answers to lettered sentences appear in the back of the book. Example:

"Yes, Virginia, there is a Santa Claus," wrote the editor.

a. April 12, 1996 is the final deadline for all applications.
b. The coach having bawled us out thoroughly, we left the locker room with his last harsh words ringing in our ears.
c. Good technique does not guarantee however, that the power you develop will be sufficient for Kyok Pa competition.
d. We all piled into Sadiq's car which we affectionately referred to as the Blue Goose.
e. Please make the check payable to David Kerr D.D.S., not David Kerr M.D.

1. Mr. Mundy was born on July 22, 1939 in Arkansas, where his family had lived for four generations.

2. It has been reported that the Republican who suggested Eisenhower as a presidential candidate meant Milton not Ike.
3. One substitute for CFC's has environmentalists concerned because it contains chlorine which is also damaging to the ozone layer.
4. We pulled into the first apartment complex we saw, and slowly patrolled the parking lots.
5. Eating raw limpets, I found out, is like trying to eat art gum erasers.
6. Cobbled streets, too narrow for two cars to pass, were lined with tiny houses leaning so close together they almost touched.
7. We wondered how our overweight grandmother could have been the slim bride in the picture, but we kept our wonderings to ourselves.
8. "The last flight" she said with a sigh "went out five minutes before I arrived at the airport."
9. The Rio Grande, the border between Texas and Mexico lay before us. It was a sluggish mud-filled meandering stream that gave off an odor akin to sewage.
10. Pittsburgh, Pennsylvania is the home of several fine colleges and universities.

33

Unnecessary commas

Many common misuses of the comma result from an incomplete understanding of the major comma rules presented in 32. In particular, writers frequently form misconceptions about rules 32a–32e, either extending the rules inappropriately or misinterpreting them. Such misconceptions can lead to the errors described in 33a–33e; rules 33f–33h list other common misuses of the comma.

33a Do not use a comma between compound elements that are not independent clauses.

Though a comma should be used before a coordinating conjunction joining independent clauses (see 32a), this rule should not be extended to other compound word groups.

▶ Jake still doesn't realize that his illness is serious/and that

he will have to alter his diet to improve.

And links two subordinate clauses, each beginning with *that*.

▶ The director led the cast members to their positions/and gave

an inspiring last-minute pep talk.

And links the two parts of a compound predicate: *led . . . and gave*.

33b Do not use a comma after a phrase that begins an inverted sentence.

Though a comma belongs after most introductory phrases (see 32b), it does not belong after phrases that begin an inverted sentence. In an inverted sentence, the subject follows the verb, and a phrase that ordinarily would follow the verb is moved to the beginning (see 58c).

▶ At the bottom of the Atlantic Ocean/lies a Japanese submarine

laden with gold.

The subject, *submarine*, follows the verb, *lies*.

33c Do not use a comma before the first or after the last item in a series.

Though commas are required between items in a series (32c), do not place them either before or after the whole series.

▶ Other causes of asthmatic attacks are/stress, change in

temperature, humidity, and cold air.

▶ Ironically, this job that appears so glamorous, carefree, and

easy/carries a high degree of responsibility.

33d Do not use a comma between cumulative adjectives, between an adjective and a noun, or between an adverb and an adjective.

Commas are required between coordinate adjectives (those that can be joined with *and*), but they do not belong between cumulative adjectives (those that cannot be joined with *and*). (For a full discussion, see 32d.)

▶ In the corner of the closet we found an old⁄maroon hatbox.

A comma should never be used to separate an adjective from the noun that follows it.

▶ It was a senseless, dangerous⁄mission.

Nor should a comma be used to separate an adverb from an adjective that follows it.

▶ The Hurst Home is unsuitable as a mental facility for severely⁄

disturbed youths.

33e Do not use commas to set off restrictive or mildly parenthetical elements.

Restrictive elements are modifiers or appositives that restrict the meaning of the nouns they follow. Because they are essential to the meaning of the sentence, they are not set off with commas. (For a full discussion of both restrictive and nonrestrictive elements, see 32e.)

▶ Drivers⁄who think they own the road⁄make cycling a

dangerous sport.

The modifier *who think they own the road* restricts the meaning of *Drivers* and is therefore essential to the meaning of the sentence. Putting commas around the *who* clause falsely suggests that all drivers think they own the road.

▶ Margaret Mead's book/*Coming of Age in Samoa*/ stirred up

considerable controversy when it was published.

Since Mead wrote more than one book, the appositive contains information essential to the meaning of the sentence.

Although commas should be used with distinctly parenthetical expressions (see 32f), do not use them to set off elements that are only mildly parenthetical.

▶ As long as patients are treated in a professional yet compassion-

ate manner, most/eventually/learn to deal with their illness.

33f Do not use a comma to set off a concluding adverb clause that is essential to the meaning of the sentence.

When adverb clauses introduce a sentence, they are nearly always followed by a comma (see 32b). When they conclude a sentence, however, they are not set off by commas if their content is essential to the meaning of the earlier part of the sentence. Adverb clauses beginning with *after, as soon as, before, because, if, since, unless, until,* and *when* are usually essential.

▶ Don't visit Paris at the height of the tourist season/unless you

have booked hotel reservations.

Without the *unless* clause, the meaning of the sentence would be broader than the writer intended.

When a concluding adverb clause is nonessential, it should be preceded by a comma. Clauses beginning with *although, even though, though,* and *whereas* are usually nonessential.

▶ The lecture seemed to last only a short time‸ although the clock

said it had gone on for more than an hour.

33g Do not use a comma to separate a verb from its subject or object.

A sentence should flow from subject to verb to object without unnecessary pauses. Commas may appear between these sentence elements only when a specific rule calls for them.

▶ Zoos large enough to give the animals freedom to roam/ are

becoming more popular.

▶ I explained to him/ that I was busy and would see him later.

In the first sentence, the comma should not separate the subject, *Zoos*, from the verb, *are becoming*. In the second sentence, the comma should not separate the verb, *explained*, from its object, the subordinate clause *that I was busy and would see him later*.

33h Avoid other common misuses of the comma.

Do not use a comma in the following situations.

AFTER A COORDINATING CONJUNCTION (*AND, BUT, OR, NOR, FOR, SO, YET*)

▶ Occasionally soap operas are performed live, but/ more often

they are taped.

AFTER *SUCH AS* OR *LIKE*

▶ Many shade-loving plants, such as/ begonias, impatiens, and

coleus, can add color to a shady garden.

BEFORE *THAN*

▶ Touring Crete was more thrilling for us/ than visiting the Greek

islands frequented by the jet set.

AFTER *ALTHOUGH*

▶ Although/the air was balmy, the water was too cold for

swimming.

BEFORE A PARENTHESIS

▶ At MCI Sylvia began at the bottom/(with only three and a half

walls and a swivel chair), but within five years she had been

promoted to supervisor.

TO SET OFF AN INDIRECT (REPORTED) QUOTATION

▶ Samuel Goldwyn once said/that a verbal contract isn't worth

the paper it's written on.

WITH A QUESTION MARK OR AN EXCLAMATION POINT

▶ "Why don't you try it?/" she coaxed. "You can't do any worse

than the rest of us."

EXERCISE 33–1

Delete commas where necessary in the following sentences. If a sentence is correct, write "correct" after it. Answers to lettered sentences
appear in the back of the book. Example:

Loretta Lynn has paved the way for artists such as/Reba

McEntire and Wynonna Judd.

a. We'd rather spend our money on blue-chip stocks, than speculate
   on porkbellies.
b. Being prepared for the worst, is one way to escape disappointment.
c. When he heard the groans, he opened the door, and ran out.
d. My father said, that he would move to California, if I would agree
   to transfer to UCLA.

e. I quickly accepted the fact that I was, literally, in third-class quarters.

1. He wore a thick, black, wool coat over army fatigues.
2. Often public figures, (Michael Jackson is a good example) go to great lengths to guard their private lives.
3. Male supremacy was assumed by my father, and accepted by my mother.
4. The kitchen was covered with black soot, that had been deposited by the wood-burning stove, which stood in the middle of the room.
5. Many abusive parents were themselves abused children, so they have no history of benevolent experiences, and lack appropriate healthy role models after which to pattern their behavior as parents.

34

The semicolon

The semicolon is used to connect major sentence elements of equal grammatical rank.

34a Use a semicolon between closely related independent clauses not joined by a coordinating conjunction.

When related independent clauses appear in one sentence, they are ordinarily linked with a comma and a coordinating conjunction (*and, but, or, nor, for, so, yet*). The coordinating conjunction signals the relation between the clauses. If the clauses are closely related and the relation is clear without a conjunction, they may be linked with a semicolon instead.

> Injustice is relatively easy to bear; what stings is justice.
> —H. L. Mencken

A semicolon must be used whenever a coordinating conjunction has been omitted between independent clauses. To use merely a comma creates a kind of run-on sentence known as a comma splice. (See 20.)

▶ Grandmother's basement had walls of Mississippi clay/; to me

it looked like a dungeon.

CAUTION: Do not overuse the semicolon as a means of revising run-on sentences. For other revision strategies, see 20a, 20c, and 20d.

34b Use a semicolon between independent clauses linked with a transitional expression.

Transitional expressions include conjunctive adverbs and transitional phrases.

CONJUNCTIVE ADVERBS
accordingly, also, anyway, besides, certainly, consequently, conversely, finally, furthermore, hence, however, incidentally, indeed, instead, likewise, meanwhile, moreover, nevertheless, next, nonetheless, otherwise, similarly, specifically, still, subsequently, then, therefore, thus

TRANSITIONAL PHRASES
after all, as a matter of fact, as a result, at any rate, at the same time, even so, for example, for instance, in addition, in conclusion, in fact, in other words, in the first place, on the contrary, on the other hand

When a transitional expression appears between independent clauses, it is preceded by a semicolon and usually followed by a comma.

▶ I learned all the rules and regulations/; however, I never really

learned to control the ball.

When a transitional expression appears in the middle or at the end of the second independent clause, the semicolon goes *between the clauses.*

▶ Most singers gain fame through hard work and dedication/;
 ^

  Evita, however, found other means.

Transitional expressions should not be confused with the coordinating conjunctions *and, but, or, nor, for, so,* and *yet,* which are preceded by a comma when they link independent clauses. (See 32a.)

34c Use a semicolon between items in a series containing internal punctuation.

▶ Classic science fiction sagas are *Star Trek,* with Mr. Spock and

  his large pointed ears/; *Battlestar Galactica,* with its Cylon
              ^

  Raiders/; and *Star Wars,* with Han Solo, Luke Skywalker, and
        ^

  Darth Vader.

Without the semicolons, the reader would have to sort out the major groupings, distinguishing between important and less important pauses according to the logic of the sentence. By inserting semicolons at the major breaks, the writer does this work for the reader.

34d Avoid common misuses of the semicolon.

Do not use a semicolon in the following situations.

BETWEEN A SUBORDINATE CLAUSE AND THE REST OF THE SENTENCE

▶ Unless you brush your teeth within ten or fifteen minutes after

  eating/, brushing does almost no good.
      ^

BETWEEN AN APPOSITIVE AND THE WORD IT REFERS TO

▶ Another delicious dish is the chef's special/, a roasted duck
                       ^

  rubbed with spices and stuffed with wild rice.

TO INTRODUCE A LIST

▶ Some of my favorite artists are featured on *Red, Hot, and Blue*:

the Neville Brothers, Sinead O'Connor, Kirsty MacColl, Annie

Lennox, and Neneh Cherry.

BETWEEN INDEPENDENT CLAUSES JOINED BY *AND, BUT, OR, NOR, FOR, SO,* OR *YET*

▶ Five of the applicants had worked with spreadsheets, but only

one was familiar with database management.

EXCEPTION: If at least one of the independent clauses contains internal punctuation, you may use a semicolon even though the clauses are joined with a coordinating conjunction.

> As a vehicle [the model T] was hard-working, commonplace, and heroic; and it often seemed to transmit those qualities to the person who rode in it.   —E. B. White

Although a comma would also be correct in this sentence, the semicolon is more effective, for it indicates the relative weights of the pauses.

Occasionally, a semicolon may be used to emphasize a sharp contrast or a firm distinction between clauses joined with a coordinating conjunction.

> We hate some persons because we do not know them; and we will not know them because we hate them.
>   —Charles Caleb Colton

EXERCISE 34–1

Edit the following sentences to correct errors in the use of the comma and the semicolon. If a sentence is correct, write "correct" after it. Answers to lettered sentences appear in the back of the book. Example:

> Love is blind; envy has its eyes wide open.

a. Many people believe that ferrets are vicious little rodents, in fact, ferrets are affectionate animals that tend to bite only out of fear.

b. America has been called a country of pragmatists; although the American devotion to ideals is legendary.

c. The first requirement is honesty, everything else follows.

d. I am not fond of opera, I must admit; however, that I was greatly moved by *Les Misérables*.

e. Deaf-REACH runs a group home, which prepares residents to live independently; a daytime activity center, where walk-in clients receive job training; and a community service center, which provides counseling and legal representation.

1. When Chao Neng joined the police force in 1993; he had no idea how hard it would be to bury a fellow officer.

2. Martin Luther King, Jr., had not intended to be a preacher, initially, he had planned to become a lawyer.

3. Severe, unremitting pain is a ravaging force; especially when the patient tries to hide it from others.

4. I entered this class feeling jittery and incapable, I leave feeling poised and confident.

5. Some educators believe that African American history should be taught in separate courses, others prefer to see it integrated into survey courses.

35

The colon

The colon is used primarily to call attention to the words that follow it.

35a Use a colon after an independent clause to direct attention to a list, an appositive, or a quotation.

A LIST
The daily routine should include at least the following: twenty knee bends, fifty sit-ups, fifteen leg lifts, and five minutes of running in place.

AN APPOSITIVE
My roommate is guilty of two of the seven deadly sins: gluttony and sloth.

A QUOTATION

Consider the words of John F. Kennedy: "Ask not what your country can do for you; ask what you can do for your country."

For other ways of introducing quotations, see 37f.

35b Use a colon between independent clauses if the second summarizes or explains the first.

Faith is like love: It cannot be forced.

NOTE: When an independent clause follows a colon, it may begin with a lowercase or a capital letter.

35c Use a colon after the salutation in a formal letter, to indicate hours and minutes, to show proportions, between a title and subtitle, and between city and publisher in bibliographic entries.

Dear Sir or Madam:

5:30 P.M. (or p.m.)

The ratio of women to men was 2:1.

The Glory of Hera: Greek Mythology and the Greek Family

Boston: Bedford, 1996

NOTE: In biblical references, a colon is ordinarily used between chapter and verse (Luke 2:14). The Modern Language Association recommends a period instead (Luke 2.14).

35d Avoid common misuses of the colon.

A colon must be preceded by a full independent clause. Therefore, avoid using it in the following situations.

BETWEEN A VERB AND ITS OBJECT OR COMPLEMENT

▶ Some important vitamins found in vegetables are⫽ vitamin A, thiamine, niacin, and vitamin C.

BETWEEN A PREPOSITION AND ITS OBJECT

▶ The areas to be painted consisted of/ three gable ends, trim work, sixteen windows, and a front and back porch.

AFTER *SUCH AS, INCLUDING,* OR *FOR EXAMPLE*

▶ The trees on our campus include many fine Japanese specimens such as/ black pines, ginkgos, and weeping cherries.

EXERCISE 35–1

Edit the following sentences to correct errors in the use of the comma, the semicolon, or the colon. If a sentence is correct, write "correct" after it. Answers to lettered sentences appear in the back of the book. Example:

> Smiling confidently, the young man stated his major goal in
>
> life/: to be secretary of agriculture before he was thirty.
>   ∧

a. The second and most memorable week of survival school consisted of five stages: orientation; long treks; POW camp; escape and evasion; and return to civilization.
b. Among the canceled classes were: calculus, physics, advanced biology, and English 101.
c. There are only three seasons here: winter, July, and August.
d. For example: Teddy Roosevelt once referred to the wolf as "the beast of waste and desolation."
e. In his introduction to Katharine White's book on gardening, E. B. White describes her writing process: "The editor in her fought the writer every inch of the way; the struggle was felt all through the house. She would write eight or ten words, then draw her gun and shoot them down."

1. The patient survived for one reason, the medics got to her in time.
2. While traveling through France, Fiona visited: the Loire Valley, Chartres, the Louvre, and the McDonald's stand at the foot of the Eiffel Tower.
3. Minds are like parachutes, they function only when open.
4. Historian Robert Kee looks to the past for the source of the political troubles in Ireland: "If blame is to be apportioned for today's

situation in Northern Ireland, it should be laid not at the door of men today but of history."

5. Robin sorts the crabs into three groups: males, females, and crabs about to molt.

36

The apostrophe

36a Use an apostrophe to indicate that a noun is possessive.

Possessive nouns usually indicate ownership, as in *Tim's hat* or *the lawyer's desk*. Frequently, however, ownership is only loosely implied: *the tree's roots, a day's work*. If you are not sure whether a noun is possessive, try turning it into an *of* phrase: *the roots of the tree, the work of a day*.

When to add -'s

1. If the noun does not end in *-s*, add *-'s*.

   Roy managed to climb out on the driver's side.

   Thank you for refunding the children's money.

2. If the noun is singular and ends in *-s*, add *-'s*.

   Lois's sister spent last year in India.

EXCEPTION: If pronunciation would be awkward with the added *-'s*, some writers use only the apostrophe. Either use is acceptable.

   Sophocles' plays are among my favorites.

When to add only an apostrophe

If the noun is plural and ends in *-s*, add only an apostrophe.

   Both diplomats' briefcases were stolen.

Joint possession

To show joint possession, use *-'s* or (*-s'*) with the last noun only; to show individual possession, make all nouns possessive.

> Have you seen Joyce and Greg's new camper?

> John's and Marie's expectations of marriage couldn't have been more different.

In the first sentence, Joyce and Greg jointly own one camper. In the second sentence, John and Marie individually have different expectations.

Compound nouns

If a noun is compound, use *-'s* (or *-s'*) with the last element.

> My father-in-law's sculpture won first place.

36b Use an apostrophe and *-s* to indicate that an indefinite pronoun is possessive.

Indefinite pronouns refer to no specific person or thing: *everyone, someone, no one, something.* (See 57b.)

> Someone's raincoat has been left behind.

> This diet will improve almost anyone's health.

36c Use an apostrophe to mark omissions in contractions and numbers.

In contractions the apostrophe takes the place of missing letters.

> It's a shame that Frank can't go on the tour.

It's stands for *it is, can't* for *cannot.*
> The apostrophe is also used to mark the omission of the first two digits of a year (the class of '95) or years (the '60s generation).

> We'll never forget the blizzard of '78.

36d Use an apostrophe and *-s* to pluralize numbers mentioned as numbers, letters mentioned as letters, words mentioned as words, and abbreviations.

Margarita skated nearly perfect figure 8's.

The bleachers in our section were marked with large red *J*'s.

We've heard enough *maybe*'s.

You must ask to see their I.D.'s.

Notice that the *-s* is not italicized when used with an italicized number, letter, or word.

EXCEPTION: An *-s* alone is often added to the years in a decade: *the 1980s.*

MLA NOTE: The Modern Language Association recommends no apostrophe in plurals of numbers and abbreviations: figure 8s, VCRs.

36e Avoid common misuses of the apostrophe.

Do not use an apostrophe in the following situations.

WITH NOUNS THAT ARE NOT POSSESSIVE

outpatients
▶ Some ~~outpatient's~~ are given special parking permits.
   ^

IN THE POSSESSIVE PRONOUNS *ITS*, *WHOSE*, *HIS*, *HERS*, *OURS*, *YOURS*, AND *THEIRS*

its
▶ Each area has ~~it's~~ own conference room.
   ^

It's means *it is*. The possessive pronoun *its* contains no apostrophe despite the fact that it is possessive.

EXERCISE 36–1

Edit the following sentences to correct errors in the use of the apostrophe. If a sentence is correct, write "correct" after it. Answers to lettered sentences appear in the back of the book. Example:

Jack's.
Marietta lived above the only bar in town, Smiling ~~Jacks.~~
   ^

a. In a democracy anyones vote counts as much as mine.
b. He received two A's, three B's, and a C.
c. The puppy's favorite activity was chasing it's tail.
d. After we bought J.J. the latest style pants and shirts, he decided that last years faded, ragged jeans were perfect for all occasions.
e. A crocodiles' life span is about thirteen years.

1. For a bus driver, complaints, fare disputes, and robberies are all part of a days work.
2. We cleared four years accumulation of trash out of the attic; its amazing how much junk can pile up.
3. Booties are placed on the sled dogs feet to protect them from sharp rocks and ice. [*more than one dog*]
4. Three teenage son's can devour about as much food as four full-grown field hands. The only difference is that they dont do half as much work.
5. Luck is an important element in a rock musicians career.

37

Quotation marks

37a Use quotation marks to enclose direct quotations.

Direct quotations of a person's words, whether spoken or written, must be in quotation marks.

> "A foolish consistency is the hobgoblin of little minds," wrote Ralph Waldo Emerson.

CAUTION: Do not use quotation marks around indirect quotations. An indirect quotation reports someone's ideas without using that person's exact words.

> Ralph Waldo Emerson believed that consistency for its own sake is the mark of a small mind.

NOTE: In dialogue, begin a new paragraph to mark a change in speaker.

> "Mom, his name is Willie, not William. A thousand times I've told you, it's *Willie*."

> "Willie is a derivative of William, Lester. Surely his birth certificate doesn't have Willie on it, and I like calling people by their proper names."
>
> "Yes, it does, ma'am. My mother named me Willie K. Mason."
>
> —Gloria Naylor

If a single speaker utters more than one paragraph, introduce each paragraph with quotation marks, but do not use closing quotation marks until the end of the speech.

37b Set off long quotations of prose or poetry by indenting.

When a quotation of prose runs to more than four typed lines in your paper, set it off by indenting one inch (ten spaces) from the left margin. Quotation marks are not required because the indented format tells readers that the quotation is taken word for word from a source. Long quotations are ordinarily introduced by a sentence ending with a colon.

```
After making an exhaustive study of the historical
record, James Horan evaluates Billy the Kid like
this:
              The portrait that emerges of [the Kid] from
         the thousands of pages of affidavits, re-
         ports, trial transcripts, his letters, and
         his testimony is neither the mythical Robin
         Hood nor the stereotyped adenoidal moron and
         pathological killer.  Rather Billy appears
         as a disturbed, lonely young man, honest,
         loyal to his friends, dedicated to his be-
         liefs, and betrayed by our institutions and
         the corrupt, ambitious, and compromising
         politicians of his time.  (158)
```

The one-inch (ten-space) indent and number in parentheses are handled according to the Modern Language Association style. (See page 359 and 55a.)

NOTE: When you quote two or more paragraphs from the source, indent the first line of each paragraph an additional three spaces.

When you quote more than three lines of a poem, set the quoted lines off from the text by indenting one inch (ten spaces) from the left margin. Use no quotation marks unless they appear in the poem itself. (To punctuate two or three lines of poetry, see 39e.)

```
Although many anthologizers "modernize" her punctua-
tion, Emily Dickinson relied heavily on dashes, using
them, perhaps, as a musical device. Here, for ex-
ample, is the original version of the opening stanza
from "The Snake":
               A narrow Fellow in the Grass
               Occasionally rides--
               You may have met Him--did you not
               His notice sudden is--
```

NOTE: The American Psychological Association has slightly different guidelines for setting off long quotations. (See 56a.)

37c Use single quotation marks to enclose a quotation within a quotation.

According to Paul Eliott, Eskimo hunters "chant an ancient magic song to the seal they are after: 'Beast of the sea! Come and place yourself before me in the early morning!' "

37d Use quotation marks around the titles of short works: newspaper and magazine articles, poems, short stories, songs, episodes of television and radio programs, and chapters or subdivisions of books.

Katherine Mansfield's "The Garden Party" provoked a lively discussion in our short-story class last night.

NOTE: Titles of books, plays, and films and names of magazines and newspapers are put in italics or underlined. (See 42a.)

37e Quotation marks may be used to set off words used as words.

Although words used as words are ordinarily underlined, to indicate italics (see 42d), quotation marks are also acceptable. Just be sure to follow consistent practice throughout a paper.

The words "flaunt" and "flout" are frequently confused.

The words *flaunt* and *flout* are frequently confused.

37f Use punctuation with quotation marks according to convention.

This section describes the conventions used by American publishers in placing various marks of punctuation inside or outside quotation marks. It also explains how to punctuate when introducing quoted material.

Periods and commas

Always place periods and commas inside quotation marks.

"This is a stick-up," said the well-dressed young couple. "We want all your money."

This rule applies to single quotation marks as well as double quotation marks. (See 37c.) It also applies to all uses of quotation marks: for quoted material, for titles of works, and for words used as words.

EXCEPTION: In the Modern Language Association's style of parenthetical in-text citations (see 55a), the period follows the citation in parentheses.

James M. McPherson acknowledges that the Whigs "were not averse to extending the blessings of American liberty, even to Mexicans and Indians" (48).

Colons and semicolons

Put colons and semicolons outside quotation marks.

Harold wrote, "I regret that I am unable to attend the fundraiser for AIDS research"; his letter, however, came with a substantial contribution.

Question marks and exclamation points

Put question marks and exclamation points inside quotation marks unless they apply to the whole sentence.

> Contrary to tradition, bedtime at my house is marked by "Mommy, can I tell you a story now?"

> Have you heard the old proverb "Do not climb the hill until you reach it"?

In the first sentence, the question mark applies only to the quoted question. In the second sentence, the question mark applies to the whole sentence.

NOTE: Modern Language Association parenthetical citations create a special problem. According to MLA, the question mark or exclamation point should appear before the quotation mark, and a period should follow the parenthetical citation.

> Rosie Thomas asks, "Is nothing in life ever straight and clear, the way children see it?" (77).

Introducing quoted material

After a word group introducing a quotation, choose a colon, a comma, or no punctuation at all, whichever is appropriate in context.

If a quotation is formally introduced, a colon is appropriate. A formal introduction is a full independent clause, not just an expression such as *he said* or *she remarked*.

> Morrow views personal ads in the classifieds as an art form: "The personal ad is like a haiku of self-celebration, a brief solo played on one's own horn."

If a quotation is introduced with an expression such as *he said* or *she remarked* — or if it is followed by such an expression — a comma is needed.

> Robert Frost said, "You can be a little ungrammatical if you come from the right part of the country."

> "You can be a little ungrammatical if you come from the right part of the country," Robert Frost said.

When a quotation is blended into the writer's own sentence, either a comma or no punctuation is appropriate, depending on the way in which the quotation fits into the sentence structure.

The future champion could, as he put it, "float like a butterfly and sting like a bee."

Charles Hudson noted that the prisoners escaped "by squeezing through a tiny window eighteen feet above the floor of their cell."

If a quotation appears at the beginning of a sentence, set it off with a comma unless the quotation ends with a question mark or an exclamation point.

"We shot them like dogs," boasted Davy Crockett, who was among Jackson's troops.

"What is it?" I asked, bracing myself.

If a quoted sentence is interrupted by explanatory words, use commas to set off the explanatory words.

"A great many people think they are thinking," wrote William James, "when they are merely rearranging their prejudices."

If two successive quoted sentences from the same source are interrupted by explanatory words, use a comma before the explanatory words and a period after them.

"I was a flop as a daily reporter," admitted E. B. White. "Every piece had to be a masterpiece—and before you knew it, Tuesday was Wednesday."

37g Avoid common misuses of quotation marks.

Do not use quotation marks to draw attention to familiar slang, to disown trite expressions, or to justify an attempt at humor.

▶ Between Thanksgiving and Super Bowl Sunday, many American

  wives become/football widows.❩

Do not use quotation marks around indirect quotations. (See also 37a.)

▶ After leaving the scene of the domestic quarrel, the officer said

  that/he was due for a coffee break.❩

Do not use quotation marks around the title of your own essay.

EXERCISE 37–1

Add or delete quotation marks as needed and make any other necessary changes in punctuation in the following sentences. If a sentence is correct, write "correct" after it. Answers to lettered sentences appear in the back of the book. Example:

> Bill Cosby once said, "I don't know the key to success, but the
> key to failure is trying to please everyone."

a. My commanding officer said, "If we wanted you to have children, we would have issued them to you."

b. As Emerson wrote in 1849, I hate quotations. Tell me what you know.

c. Andrew Marvell's most famous poem, To His Coy Mistress, is a tightly structured argument.

d. "Ladies and gentlemen," said the emcee, "I am happy to present our guest speaker."

e. Historians Segal and Stineback tell us that the English settlers considered these epidemics "the hand of God making room for His followers in the "New World"."

1. The dispatcher's voice cut through the still night air: "Scout 41, robbery in progress, alley rear of 58th and Blaine.

2. My skiing instructor promised us that "we would all be ready for the intermediate slope in one week."

3. Gloria Steinem once twisted an old proverb like this, "A woman without a man is like a fish without a bicycle."

4. Joan was a self-proclaimed "rabid Blue Jays fan"; she went to every home game and even flew to Atlanta for the World Series.

5. "Even when freshly washed and relieved of all obvious confections," says Fran Lebowitz, "children tend to be sticky."

38

End punctuation

38a The period

Use a period to end all sentences except direct questions or genuine exclamations. Also use periods in abbreviations according to convention.

To end sentences

Everyone knows that a period should be used to end most sentences. The only problems that arise concern the choice between a period and a question mark or between a period and an exclamation point.

If a sentence reports a question instead of asking it directly, it should end with a period, not a question mark.

▶ Celia asked whether the picnic would be canceled̸.
                                                  ʌ

If a sentence is not a genuine exclamation, it should end with a period, not an exclamation point.

▶ After years of working her way through school, Pat finally

graduated with high honors̸.
                          ʌ

In abbreviations

A period is conventionally used in abbreviations such as these:

Mr.	B.A.	B.C.	i.e.	A.M. (or a.m.)
Mrs.	M.A.	B.C.E.	e.g.	P.M. (or p.m.)
Ms.	Ph.D.	A.D.	etc.	
Dr.	R.N.	C.E.		

A period is not used with U.S. Postal Service abbreviations for states: MD, TX, CA.

Ordinarily a period is not used in abbreviations of organization names:

NATO	UNESCO	AFL-CIO	FCC
TVA	IRS	SEC	IBM
USA	NAACP	PUSH	FTC
(or U.S.A.)	UCLA	NBA	NIH

Usage varies, however. When in doubt, consult a dictionary, a style manual, or a publication by the agency in question. Even the yellow pages can help.

NOTE: If a sentence ends with a period marking an abbreviation, do not add a second period.

38b The question mark

Obviously a direct question should be followed by a question mark.

> What is the horsepower of a 747 engine?

If a polite request is written in the form of a question, it too is usually followed by a question mark, although usage varies.

> Would you please send me your catalog of lilies?

CAUTION: Do not use a question mark after an indirect question, one that is reported rather than asked directly. Use a period instead.

> ▶ He asked me who was teaching the mythology course̸.
>   ^

NOTE: Questions in a series may be followed by question marks even when they are not complete sentences.

> We wondered where Calamity had hidden this time. Under the sink? Behind the furnace? On top of the bookcase?

38c The exclamation point

Use an exclamation point after a word group or sentence that expresses exceptional feeling or deserves special emphasis.

> The medic shook me and kept yelling, "He's dead! He's dead! Can't you see that?"

CAUTION: Do not overuse the exclamation point.

> ▶ In the fisherman's memory the fish lives on, increasing in
>
> length and weight with each passing year, until at last it is big
>
> enough to shade a fishing boat̸.
>   ^
> This sentence doesn't need to be pumped up with an exclamation point. It is emphatic enough without it.

▶ Whenever I see Steffi lunging forward to put away an overhead

smash, it might as well be me̷, She does it just the way that I
                            ^

would!

The first exclamation point should be deleted so that the second
one will have more force.

EXERCISE 38–1

Add appropriate end punctuation in the following paragraph.

Although I am generally rational, I am superstitious I never walk
under ladders or put shoes on the table If I spill the salt, I go into
frenzied calisthenics picking up the grains and tossing them over my
left shoulder As a result of these curious activities, I've always wondered whether knowing the roots of superstitions would quell my
irrational responses Superstition has it, for example, that one should
never place a hat on the bed This superstition arises from a time
when head lice were quite common and placing a guest's hat on the
bed stood a good chance of spreading lice through the host's bed
Doesn't this make good sense And doesn't it stand to reason that if I
know that my guests don't have lice I shouldn't care where their hats
go Of course it does It is fair to ask, then, whether I have changed
my ways and place hats on beds Are you kidding I wouldn't put a hat
on a bed if my life depended on it

39

Other punctuation marks: the dash, parentheses, brackets, the ellipsis mark, the slash

39a The dash

When typing, use two hyphens to form a dash (--). Do not put
spaces before or after the dash. Dashes are used for the following purposes.

To set off parenthetical material that deserves emphasis

Everything that went wrong—from the peeping Tom at her
window to my head-on collision—was blamed on our move.

To set off appositives that contain commas

An appositive is a noun or noun phrase that renames a nearby noun. Ordinarily most appositives are set off with commas (32e), but when the appositive contains commas, a pair of dashes helps readers see the relative importance of all the pauses.

> In my hometown the basic needs of people — food, clothing, and shelter — are less costly than in Los Angeles.

To prepare for a list, a restatement, an amplification, or a dramatic shift in tone or thought

> Along the wall are the bulk liquids — sesame seed oil, honey, safflower oil, and that half-liquid "peanuts only" peanut butter.

> Consider the amount of sugar in the average person's diet — 104 pounds per year, 90 percent more than that consumed by our ancestors.

> Everywhere we looked there were little kids — a box of Cracker Jacks in one hand and mommy or daddy's sleeve in the other.

> Kiere took a few steps back, came running full speed, kicked a mighty kick — and missed the ball.

In the first two examples, the writer could also use a colon. (See 35a.) The colon is more formal than the dash, and not quite as dramatic.

CAUTION: Unless there is a specific reason for using the dash, avoid it. Unnecessary dashes create a choppy effect.

▶ Insisting that students use computers as instructional tools ⫻

  for information retrieval ⫻ makes good sense. Herding them ⫻

  sheeplike ⫻ into computer technology does not.

39b Parentheses

Use parentheses to enclose supplemental material, minor digressions, and afterthoughts.

> After taking her temperature, pulse, and blood pressure (routine vital signs), the nurse made Becky as comfortable as possible.

The weights James was first able to move (not lift, mind you) were measured in ounces.

Use parentheses to enclose letters or numbers labeling items in a series.

Regulations stipulated that only the following equipment could be used on the survival mission: (1) a knife, (2) thirty feet of parachute line, (3) a book of matches, (4) two ponchos, (5) an *E* tool, and (6) a signal flare.

CAUTION: Do not overuse parentheses.

Rough drafts are likely to contain more afterthoughts than necessary. As writers head into a sentence, they often think of additional details, occasionally working them in as best they can with parentheses. Usually such sentences should be revised so that the additional details no longer seem to be afterthoughts.

> Researchers have said that ~~ten million (estimates run as high as~~ *from ten to fifty million* ~~fifty million)~~ Americans have hypoglycemia.

39c Brackets

Use brackets to enclose any words or phrases that you have inserted into an otherwise word-for-word quotation.

Audubon reports that "if there are not enough young to balance deaths, the end of the species [California condor] is inevitable."

The sentence quoted from the *Audubon* article did not contain the words *California condor* (since the context made clear what species was meant), so the writer in this example needed to add the name in brackets.

The Latin word *sic* in brackets indicates that an error in a quoted sentence appears in the original source.

According to the review, k. d. lang's performance was brilliant, "exceding [*sic*] the expectations of even her most loyal fans."

Do not overuse *sic,* however, since calling attention to others' mistakes can appear snobbish. The preceding quotation, for example, might have been paraphrased instead: *According to*

*the review, even k. d. lang's most loyal fans were surprised by the
brilliance of her performance.*

39d The ellipsis mark

The ellipsis mark consists of three spaced periods. Use an ellipsis mark to indicate that you have deleted words from an otherwise word-for-word quotation.

> Reuben reports that "when the amount of cholesterol circulating in the blood rises over . . . 300 milligrams per 100, the chances of a heart attack increase dramatically."

If you delete a full sentence or more in the middle of a quoted passage, use a period before the three ellipsis dots.

> "Most of our efforts," writes Dave Erikson, "are directed toward saving the bald eagle's wintering habitat along the Mississippi River. . . . It's important that the wintering birds have a place to roost, where they can get out of the cold wind and be undisturbed by man."

CAUTION: Do not use the ellipsis mark at the beginning of a quotation; do not use it at the end of a quotation unless you have cut some words from the final sentence quoted. (See also 54c.)

In quoted poetry, use a full line of dots to indicate that you have dropped a line or more from the poem.

> Had we but world enough, and time,
> This coyness, lady, were no crime.
> . . . .
> But at my back I always hear
> Time's wingèd chariot hurrying near;   — Andrew Marvell

The ellipsis mark may also be used to indicate a hesitation or interruption in speech or to suggest unfinished thoughts.

> Before falling into a coma, the victim whispered, "It was a man with a tattoo on his. . . ."

39e The slash

Use the slash to separate two or three lines of poetry that have been run in to your text. Add a space both before and after the slash.

> In the opening lines of "Jordan," George Herbert pokes gentle fun at popular poems of his time: "Who says that fictions only and false hair / Become a verse? Is there in truth no beauty?"

More than three lines of poetry should be handled as an indented quotation. (See 37b.)

The slash may occasionally be used to separate paired terms such as *pass/fail* and *producer/director*. Do not use a space before or after the slash.

> Roger, the producer/director, announced a casting change.

Be sparing, however, in this use of the slash. In particular, avoid use of *and/or, he/she,* and *his/her*.

EXERCISE 39–1

Edit the following sentences to correct errors in punctuation, focusing especially on appropriate use of the dash, parentheses, brackets, ellipsis mark, and slash. If a sentence is correct, write "correct" after it. Answers to lettered sentences appear in the back of the book. Example:

> Social insects /—bees, for example /— are able to communicate
>   ^   ^
> complicated messages to their fellows.

a. We lived in Iowa (Davenport, to be specific) during the early years of our marriage.
b. Every night—after her jazzercise class—Elizaveta bragged about how invigorated she felt, but she always looked exhausted.
c. *Infoworld* reports that "customers without any particular aptitude for computers can easily learn to use it [the Bay Area Teleguide] through simple, three-step instructions located at the booth."
d. Every person there—from the youngest toddler to the oldest great-grandparent, was expected to sit through the three-hour sermon in respectful silence.
e. The class stood, faced the flag, placed hands over hearts, and raced through "I pledge allegiance—liberty and justice for all" in less than sixty seconds.

1. Of the three basic schools of detective fiction, the tea-and-crumpet, the hard-boiled detective, and the police procedural, I find the quaint, civilized quality of the tea-and-crumpet school the most appealing.

2. In *Lifeboat,* Alfred Hitchcock appears (some say without his knowledge) in a newspaper advertisement for weight loss.
3. There are three points of etiquette in poker: 1. always allow someone to cut the cards, 2. don't forget to ante up, and 3. never stack your chips.
4. When he was informed that fewer than 20 percent of the panelists scheduled for the 1986 PEN conference were women, Norman Mailer gave this explanation: "There are more men who are deeply interested in intellectual matters than women . . . [If we put more women on the panel] all we'd be doing is lowering the level of discussion."
5. The old Valentine verse we used to chant said it all: "Roses are red, / Violets are blue, / Sugar is sweet, / And so are you."

Mechanics

40

Abbreviations

40a Use standard abbreviations for titles immediately before and after proper names.

TITLES BEFORE PROPER NAMES	TITLES AFTER PROPER NAMES
Ms. Nancy Linehan	Thomas Hines, Jr.
Mrs. Edward Horn	Anita Lor, Ph.D.
Dr. Margaret Simmons	Robert Simkowski, M.D.
the Rev. John Stone	Margaret Chin, LL.D.

Do not abbreviate a title if it is not used with a proper name.

> *professor*
> ▶ My history ~~prof.~~ was an expert on America's use of the atomic
>   ^
> bomb in World War II.

Avoid redundant titles such as *Dr. Amy Day, M.D.* Choose one title or the other: *Dr. Amy Day* or *Amy Day, M.D.*

40b Use familiar abbreviations for the names of organizations, corporations, and countries.

Familiar abbreviations, often written without periods, are acceptable:

CIA	FBI	AFL-CIO
IBM	UPI	NEA
YMCA	CBS	USA (or U.S.A.)
NAACP	IRS	

While in Washington the schoolchildren toured the FBI.

NOTE: When using an unfamiliar abbreviation (such as CBE for Council of Biology Editors) throughout a paper, write the full name followed by the abbreviation in parentheses at the first mention of the name. Then use the abbreviation throughout the rest of the paper.

40c Use B.C., A.D., A.M., P.M., No., and $ only with specific dates, times, numbers, and amounts.

The abbreviation B.C. ("before Christ") follows a date, and A.D. ("*anno Domini*") precedes a date. Acceptable alternatives are B.C.E. ("before the common era") and C.E. ("common era").

40 B.C. (or B.C.E)	4:00 A.M. (or a.m.)	No. 12 (or no. 12)
A.D. 44 (or C.E.)	6:00 P.M. (or p.m.)	$150

Avoid using A.M., P.M., No., or $ when not accompanied by a specific figure.

> We set off for the lake early in the ~~a.m.~~ *morning.*

40d Be sparing in your use of Latin abbreviations.

Latin abbreviations are acceptable in footnotes and bibliographies and in informal writing for comments in parentheses.

cf. (Latin *confer*, "compare")
e.g. (Latin *exempli gratia*, "for example")
et al. (Latin *et alii*, "and others")
etc. (Latin *et cetera*, "and so forth")
i.e. (Latin *id est*, "that is")
N.B. (Latin *nota bene*, "note well")

In formal writing use the appropriate English phrases.

> Many obsolete laws remain on the books, ~~e.g.,~~ *for example,* a law in
>
> Vermont forbidding an unmarried man and woman to sit
>
> closer than six inches apart on a park bench.

40e Avoid inappropriate abbreviations.

In formal writing, abbreviations for the following are not commonly accepted: personal names, units of measurement, days of the week, holidays, months, courses of study, divisions of written works, states, and countries (except in addresses and except Washington, D.C.).

In company names, use abbreviated forms such as *Co., Inc.,* and & if they are part of the official name: *Temps & Co., Bogart Inc.* Do not use such abbreviations if they are not part of the official name: *Dunn Photographic Associates* (not *Dunn Photo. Assoc.*). When in doubt about a company's official name, consult a business card, company letterhead, or the yellow pages.

PERSONAL NAME   Charles (not Chas.)

UNITS OF MEASUREMENT   pound (not lb.)

DAYS OF THE WEEK   Monday (not Mon.)

HOLIDAYS   Christmas (not Xmas)

MONTHS   January, February (not Jan., Feb.)

COURSES OF STUDY   political science (not poli. sci.)

DIVISIONS OF WRITTEN WORKS   chapter, page (not ch., p.)

STATES AND COUNTRIES   Massachusetts (not MA or Mass.)

PARTS OF A BUSINESS NAME   Adams Lighting Company (not Adams Lighting Co.); Kim and Brothers (not Kim and Bros.)

▶ Eliza promised to buy me one ~~lb.~~ of Godiva chocolate for my
                                    pound
                    Friday.
birthday, which was last ~~Fri.~~

EXERCISE 40–1

Edit the following sentences to correct errors in abbreviations. If a sentence is correct, write "correct" after it. Answers to lettered sentences appear in the back of the book. Example:

      Christmas   *Friday.*
This year ~~Xmas~~ will fall on a ~~Fri.~~

a. Audrey Hepburn was a powerful spokesperson for UNICEF for many years.
b. Denzil spent all night studying for his psych. exam.
c. "Mahatma" Gandhi has inspired many modern leaders, including Martin Luther King, Jr.
d. The first discovery of America was definitely not in 1492 A.D.

e. Turning to p. 195, Marion realized that she had finally reached the end of ch. 22.

1. Many girls fall prey to a cult worship of great entertainers — e.g., in my mother's generation, girls worshiped the Beatles.
2. Three interns were selected to assist the chief surgeon, Dr. Enrique Derenzo, M.D., in the hospital's first heart-lung transplant.
3. Some historians think that the New Testament was completed by A.D. 100.
4. My soc. prof. spends most of his lecture time talking about political science.
5. Since its inception, the BBC has maintained a consistently high standard of radio and television broadcasting.

41

Numbers

41a Spell out numbers of one or two words or those that begin a sentence. Use figures for numbers that require more than two words to spell out.

▶ Now, some ~~8~~ *eight* years later, Muffin is still with us.

▶ I counted ~~one hundred seventy-six~~ *176* CD's on the shelf.

If a sentence begins with a number, spell out the number or rewrite the sentence.

▶ ~~150~~ *One hundred fifty* children in our program need expensive dental treatment.

Rewriting the sentence will also correct the error and may be less awkward if the number is long: *In our program 150 children need expensive dental treatment.*

EXCEPTIONS: In technical and some business writing, figures are preferred even when spellings would be brief, but usage varies.

When several numbers appear in the same passage, many writers prefer consistency to strict adherence to the rule.

When one number immediately follows another, spell out one and use figures for the other: three 100-meter events, 125 four-poster beds.

41b In general, use figures for dates, addresses, percentages, fractions, decimals, scores, statistics and other numerical results, exact amounts of money, divisions of books and plays, pages, identification numbers, and the time.

DATES   July 4, 1776, 56 B.C., A.D. 30

ADDRESSES   77 Latches Lane, 519 West 42nd Street

PERCENTAGES   55 percent (or 55%)

FRACTIONS, DECIMALS   ½, 0.047

SCORES   7 to 3, 21–18

STATISTICS   average age 37, average weight 180

SURVEYS   4 out of 5

EXACT AMOUNTS OF MONEY $105.37, $106,000

DIVISIONS OF BOOKS   volume 3, chapter 4, page 189

DIVISIONS OF PLAYS   act III, scene iii (or act 3, scene 3)

IDENTIFICATION NUMBERS   serial number 10988675

TIME OF DAY   4:00 P.M., 1:30 A.M.

$255,000
▶ Several doctors put up ~~two hundred fifty-five thousand dollars~~
  ^
for the construction of a golf course.

NOTE: When not using A.M. or P.M., write out the time in words (*four o'clock in the afternoon, twelve noon, seven in the morning*).

EXERCISE 41–1

Edit the following sentences to correct errors in the use of numbers. If a sentence is correct, write "correct" after it. Answers to lettered sentences appear in the back of the book. Example:

$3.06
By the end of the evening Ashanti had only ~~three dollars and~~
  ^
~~six cents~~ left.

a. We have ordered 4 azaleas, 3 rhododendrons, and 2 mountain laurels for the back area of the garden.
b. Venezuelan independence from Spain was declared on July 5, 1811.
c. The score was tied at 5–5 when the momentum shifted and carried the Standards to a decisive 12–5 win.
d. We ordered three four-door sedans for company executives.
e. The Vietnam Veterans Memorial in Washington, D.C., had fifty-eight thousand one hundred thirty-two names inscribed on it when it was dedicated in 1982.

1. One of my favorite scenes in Shakespeare is the property division scene in act I of *King Lear*.
2. The botany lecture will begin at precisely 3:30 P.M.
3. 90 of the firm's employees signed up for the insurance program.
4. After her 5th marriage ended in divorce, Melinda decided to give up her quest for the perfect husband.
5. With 6 students and 2 teachers, the class had a 3:1 student-teacher ratio.

42

Italics (underlining)

Italics, a slanting typeface used in printed material, can be produced by some word processing programs. In handwritten or typed papers, this typeface is indicated by <u>underlining</u>. Some instructors prefer underlining even if their students can produce italics.

42a Underline the titles of works according to convention.

Titles of the following works should be underlined or italicized:

TITLES OF BOOKS *The Great Gatsby, A Distant Mirror*

MAGAZINES *Time, Scientific American*

NEWSPAPERS the *St. Louis Post-Dispatch*

PAMPHLETS *Common Sense, Facts about Marijuana*

LONG POEMS   *The Waste Land, Paradise Lost*

PLAYS   *King Lear, A Raisin in the Sun*

FILMS   *Malcolm X, Pulp Fiction*

TELEVISION PROGRAMS   *Seinfeld, 60 Minutes*

RADIO PROGRAMS   *All Things Considered*

MUSICAL COMPOSITIONS   Gershwin's *Porgy and Bess*

CHOREOGRAPHIC WORKS   Twyla Tharp's *In the Upper Room*

WORKS OF VISUAL ART   Rodin's *The Thinker*

COMIC STRIPS   *Calvin and Hobbes*

SOFTWARE   *WordPerfect*

The titles of other works, such as short stories, essays, songs, and short poems, are enclosed in quotation marks. (See 37d.)

NOTE: Do not use underlining or italics when referring to the Bible, titles of books in the Bible (Genesis, not *Genesis*), or titles of legal documents (the Constitution, not the *Constitution*). Do not underline the title of your own paper.

42b Underline the names of spacecraft, aircraft, ships, and trains.

Challenger, Spirit of St. Louis, Queen Elizabeth II, Silver Streak

▶ The success of the <u>Sputnik</u> galvanized the U.S. space program.

42c Underline foreign words used in an English sentence.

▶ Although Joe's method seemed to be successful, I decided to

establish my own <u>modus operandi</u>.

EXCEPTION: Do not underline foreign words that have become part of the English language — "laissez-faire," "fait accompli," "habeus corpus," and "per diem," for example.

42d Underline words mentioned as words, letters mentioned as letters, and numbers mentioned as numbers.

▶ Tim assured us that the howling probably came from his

bloodhound, Hill Billy, but his <u>probably</u> stuck in our minds.

▶ Sarah called her father by his given name, Johnny, but she

was unable to pronounce <u>J</u>.

▶ A big <u>3</u> was painted on the door.

NOTE: Quotation marks may be used instead of underlining to set off words mentioned as words. (See 37e.)

42e Avoid excessive underlining for emphasis.

Underlining to emphasize words or ideas is distracting and should be used sparingly.

▶ Tennis is a sport that has become an ~~<u>addiction</u>~~.

EXERCISE 42–1

Edit the following sentences to correct errors in the use of italics. If a sentence is correct, write "correct" after it. Answers to lettered sentences appear in the back of the book. Example:

> <u>Leaves of Grass</u> by Walt Whitman was quite controversial when
>
> it was published a century ago.

a. Howard Hughes commissioned the Spruce Goose, a beautifully built but thoroughly impractical wooden aircraft.

b. Pulaski was so *exhausted* he could barely lift his foot the six inches to the elevator floor.

c. Even though it is almost always hot in Mexico in the summer, you can usually find a cool spot on one of the park benches in the town's zócalo.

d. Cinema audiences once gasped at hearing the word *damn* in *Gone with the Wind*.

e. "The City and the Pillar" was an early novel by Gore Vidal.

1. Bernard watched as Eileen stood transfixed in front of Vermeer's Head of a Young Girl.

2. The monastery walls were painted with scenes described in the book of Genesis.

3. I learned the Latin term ad infinitum from an old nursery rhyme about fleas: "Great fleas have little fleas upon their back to bite 'em, / Little fleas have lesser fleas and so on ad infinitum."

4. Redford and Newman in the movie "The Sting" were amateurs compared with the seventeen-year-old con artist who lives at our house.

5. I find it impossible to remember the second *l* in *llama*.

43

Spelling

You learned to spell from repeated experience with words in both reading and writing, but especially writing. Words have a look, a sound, and even a feel to them as the hand moves across the page. As you proofread, you can probably tell if a word doesn't look quite right. In such cases, the solution is obvious: Look up the word in the dictionary.

A word processor equipped with a spelling checker is a useful alternative to a dictionary, but only up to a point. A spelling checker will not tell you how to spell words not listed in its dictionary; nor will it help you catch words commonly confused, such as *accept* and *except,* or common typographical errors, such as *own* for *won*. You will still need to proofread, and for some words you may need to turn to the dictionary.

43a Become familiar with your dictionary.

A good desk dictionary—such as *The American Heritage Dictionary of the English Language, The Random House College Dictionary,* or *Merriam-Webster's Collegiate Dictionary* or *New World Dictionary of the American Language*—is an indispensable writer's aid.

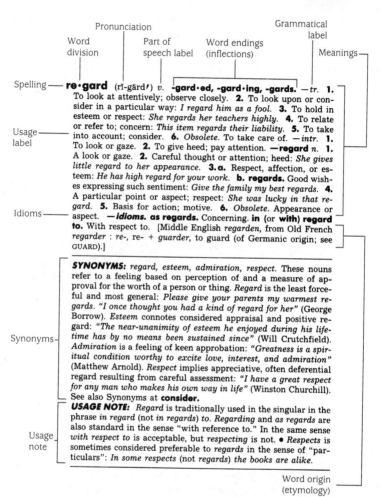

Pronunciation

Word division

Part of speech label

Word endings (inflections)

Grammatical label

Meanings

Spelling — **re·gard** (rĭ-gärd′) *v.* **-gard·ed, -gard·ing, -gards.** —*tr.* **1.** To look at attentively; observe closely. **2.** To look upon or consider in a particular way: *I regard him as a fool.* **3.** To hold in esteem or respect: *She regards her teachers highly.* **4.** To relate or refer to; concern: *This item regards their liability.* **5.** To take into account; consider. **6.** *Obsolete.* To take care of. —*intr.* **1.** To look or gaze. **2.** To give heed; pay attention. —**regard** *n.* **1.** A look or gaze. **2.** Careful thought or attention; heed: *She gives little regard to her appearance.* **3.a.** Respect, affection, or esteem: *He has high regard for your work.* **b. regards.** Good wishes expressing such sentiment: *Give the family my best regards.* **4.** A particular point or aspect; respect: *She was lucky in that regard.* **5.** Basis for action; motive. **6.** *Obsolete.* Appearance or aspect. —**idioms. as regards.** Concerning. **in** (or **with**) **regard to.** With respect to. [Middle English *regarden,* from Old French *regarder : re-,* re- + *guarder,* to guard (of Germanic origin; see GUARD).]

Usage label

Idioms

SYNONYMS: *regard, esteem, admiration, respect.* These nouns refer to a feeling based on perception of and a measure of approval for the worth of a person or thing. *Regard* is the least forceful and most general: *Please give your parents my warmest regards.* "*I once thought you had a kind of regard for her*" (George Borrow). *Esteem* connotes considered appraisal and positive regard: "*The near-unanimity of esteem he enjoyed during his lifetime has by no means been sustained since*" (Will Crutchfield). *Admiration* is a feeling of keen approbation: "*Greatness is a spiritual condition worthy to excite love, interest, and admiration*" (Matthew Arnold). *Respect* implies appreciative, often deferential regard resulting from careful assessment: "*I have a great respect for any man who makes his own way in life*" (Winston Churchill). See also Synonyms at **consider.**

Synonyms

USAGE NOTE: *Regard* is traditionally used in the singular in the phrase *in regard* (not *in regards*) *to. Regarding* and *as regards* are also standard in the sense "with reference to." In the same sense *with respect to* is acceptable, but *respecting* is not. ● *Respects* is sometimes considered preferable to *regards* in the sense of "particulars": *In some respects* (not *regards*) *the books are alike.*

Usage note

Word origin (etymology)

A sample dictionary entry, taken from *The American Heritage Dictionary,* appears above. Labels show where various kinds of information about a word can be found in that dictionary.

Spelling, word division, pronunciation

The main entry (*re·gard* in the sample entry) shows the correct spelling of the word. When there are two correct spellings of a word (as in *collectible, collectable*, for example), both are given, with the preferred spelling usually appearing first.

The main entry also shows how the word is divided into syllables. The dot between *re* and *gard* separates the word's two syllables. When a word is compound, the main entry shows how to write it: as one word (*crossroad*), as a hyphenated word (*cross-stitch*), or as two words (*cross section*).

The word's pronunciation is given just after the main entry. The accents indicate which syllables are stressed; the other marks are explained in the dictionary's pronunciation key.

Word endings and grammatical labels

When a word takes endings to indicate grammatical functions (called *inflections*), the endings are listed in boldface, as with *-garded, -garding,* and *-gards* in the sample entry.

Labels for the parts of speech and for other grammatical terms are abbreviated. The most commonly used abbreviations are these:

n.	noun	adj.	adjective
pl.	plural	adv.	adverb
sing.	singular	pron.	pronoun
v.	verb	prep.	preposition
tr.	transitive verb	conj.	conjunction
intr.	intransitive verb	interj.	interjection

Meanings, word origin, synonyms, and antonyms

Each meaning for the word is given a number. Occasionally a word's use is illustrated in a quoted sentence.

Sometimes a word can be used as more than one part of speech (*regard*, for instance, can be used as either a verb or a noun). In such a case, all the meanings for one part of speech are given before all the meanings for another, as in the sample entry. The entry also gives idiomatic uses of the word.

The origin of the word, called its *etymology,* appears in brackets after all the meanings (in some dictionaries it appears before the meanings).

Synonyms, words similar in meaning to the main entry, are frequently listed. In the sample entry, the dictionary draws distinctions in meaning among the various synonyms. Antonyms, which do not appear in the sample entry, are words having a meaning opposite from that of the main entry.

Usage

Usage labels indicate when, where, or under what conditions a particular meaning for a word is appropriately used. Common labels are *informal* (or *colloquial*), *slang, nonstandard, dialect, obsolete, archaic, poetic,* and *British.* In the sample entry, two meanings of *regard* are labeled *obsolete* because they are no longer in use.

Dictionaries sometimes include usage notes as well. In the sample entry, the dictionary offers advice on several uses of *regard* not specifically covered by the meanings. Such advice is based on the opinions of many experts and on actual usage in current magazines, newspapers, and books.

43b Discriminate between words that sound similar but have different meanings.

Words that sound alike or nearly alike but have different meanings and spellings are commonly confused. In fact, the following sets of words are so commonly confused that a good proofreader will double-check their every use.

affect (verb: "to exert an influence")
effect (verb: "to accomplish"; noun: "result")

its (possessive pronoun: "of or belonging to it")
it's (contraction for "it is")

loose (adjective: "free, not securely attached")
lose (verb: "to fail to keep, to be deprived of")

principal (adjective: "most important"; noun: "head of a school")
principle (noun: "a general or fundamental truth")

their (possessive pronoun: "belonging to them")
they're (contraction for "they are")
there (adverb: "that place or position")

who's (contraction for "who is")
whose (possessive form of "who")

your (possessive form of "you")
you're (contraction of "you are")

To check for correct use of these and other commonly confused words, consult the Glossary of Usage, which begins on page 451.

43c Become familiar with major spelling rules.

1. Use *i* before *e* except after *c* or when sounded like the letter *a*, as in *neighbor* and *weigh*.

i **BEFORE** *e*	relieve, believe, sieve, frieze
e **BEFORE** *i*	receive, deceive, sleigh, freight, eight
EXCEPTIONS	seize, either, weird, height, foreign, leisure

2. Generally, drop a final silent *-e* when adding a suffix that begins with a vowel. Keep the final *-e* if the suffix begins with a consonant.

desire, desiring; remove, removable

achieve, achievement; care, careful

Words such as *argument, truly,* and *changeable* are exceptions.

3. When adding *-s* or *-d* to words ending in *-y*, ordinarily change the *y* to *ie* when the *y* is preceded by a consonant but not when it is preceded by a vowel.

comedy, comedies; dry, dried

monkey, monkeys; play, played

With proper names ending in *y,* however, do not change the *y* to *i* even if it is preceded by a consonant: *Dougherty, the Doughertys.*

4. If a final consonant is preceded by a single vowel *and* the consonant ends a one-syllable word or a stressed syllable, double the consonant when adding a suffix beginning with a vowel.

bet, betting; commit, committed; occur, occurrence

5. Add *-s* to form the plural of most nouns; add *-es* to singular nouns ending in *-s, -sh, -ch,* and *-x.*

table, tables; paper, papers

church, churches; dish, dishes

Ordinarily add *-s* to nouns ending in *-o* when the *o* is preceded by a vowel. Add *-es* when it is preceded by a consonant.

radio, radios; video, videos

hero, heroes; tomato, tomatoes

To form the plural of a hyphenated compound word, add the *-s* to the chief word even if it does not appear at the end.

mother-in-law, mothers-in-law

NOTE: English words derived from other languages such as Latin or French sometimes form the plural as they would in their original language.

medium, media; criterion, criteria; chateau, chateaux

ESL NOTE: Spelling may vary slightly among English-speaking countries. This can prove particularly confusing for ESL students, who may have learned British or Canadian English. Following is a list of some common words spelled differently in American and British English. Consult a dictionary for others.

AMERICAN	BRITISH
canceled, traveled	cancelled, travelled
color, humor	colour, humour
judgment	judgement
check	cheque
realize, apologize	realise, apologise
defense	defence
anemia, anesthetic	anaemia, anaesthetic
theater, center	theatre, centre
fetus	foetus
mold, smolder	mould, smoulder
civilization	civilisation
connection, inflection	connexion, inflexion
licorice	liquorice

43d Be alert to the following commonly misspelled words.

absence	conscience	irresistible	rhythm
academic	conscientious	knowledge	roommate
accidentally	conscious	license	sandwich
accommodate	criticism	lightning	schedule
achievement	criticize	loneliness	seize
acknowledge	decision	maintenance	separate
acquaintance	definitely	maneuver	sergeant
acquire	descendant	marriage	siege
across	develop	mathematics	similar
address	dictionary	mischievous	sincerely
all right	disappear	necessary	sophomore
amateur	disastrous	noticeable	strictly
analyze	eighth	occasion	subtly
answer	eligible	occurred	succeed
apparently	embarrass	occurrence	surprise
appearance	emphasize	optimistic	thorough
arctic	entirely	pamphlet	tragedy
argument	environment	parallel	transferred
arithmetic	especially	particularly	tries
arrangement	exaggerated	pastime	truly
ascend	exhaust	permissible	unnecessarily
athlete	existence	perseverance	usually
athletics	extraordinary	phenomenon	vacuum
attendance	extremely	physically	vengeance
basically	familiar	picnicking	villain
beginning	fascinate	playwright	weird
believe	February	practically	whether
benefited	foreign	precede	writing
bureau	forty	preference	
business	fourth	preferred	
calendar	friend	prejudice	
candidate	government	prevalent	
cemetery	grammar	privilege	
changeable	guard	probably	
column	harass	proceed	
coming	height	professor	
commitment	humorous	pronunciation	
committed	incidentally	quiet	
committee	incredible	quite	
competitive	indispensable	quizzes	
conceivable	inevitable	receive	
conferred	intelligence	referred	
conqueror	irrelevant	restaurant	

44

The hyphen

44a Consult the dictionary to determine how to treat a compound word.

Most dictionaries will tell you whether to treat a compound word as a hyphenated compound (*water-repellent*), one word (*waterproof*), or two words (*water table*). If the compound word is not in the dictionary, treat it as two words.

▶ The prosecutor chose not to cross ⁻examine any witnesses.

▶ Grandma kept a small note book in her apron pocket.

▶ Alice walked through the looking/glass into a strange and

backward world.

44b Use a hyphen to connect two or more words functioning together as an adjective before a noun.

▶ Mrs. Douglas gave Toshiko a seashell and some newspaper ⁻

wrapped fish to take home to her mother.

▶ Priscilla Hobbes is not yet a well⁻known candidate.

Newspaper-wrapped and *well-known* are adjectives used before the nouns *fish* and *candidate*.

Generally, do not use a hyphen when such compounds follow the noun.

▶ After our television campaign, Priscilla Hobbes will be well/

known.

Do not use a hyphen to connect *-ly* adverbs to the words they modify.

▶ A slowly/moving truck tied up traffic.

NOTE: In a series, hyphens are suspended.

Do you prefer first-, second-, or third-class tickets?

44c Hyphenate the written form of fractions and of compound numbers from twenty-one to ninety-nine.

▶ One-fourth of my income goes to pay off the national debt.
   ^

44d Use a hyphen with the prefixes *all-*, *ex-* (meaning "former"), and *self-* and with the suffix *-elect.*

▶ The charity is funneling more money into self-help projects.
   ^

▶ Anne King is our club's president-elect.
   ^

44e A hyphen is used in some words to avoid ambiguity or to separate awkward double or triple letters.

Without the hyphen there would be no way to distinguish between words such as *re-creation* and *recreation.*

Bicycling in the country is my favorite recreation.

The film was praised for its astonishing re-creation of nineteenth-century London.

Hyphens are sometimes used to separate awkward double or triple letters in compound words (*anti-intellectual, cross-stitch*). Always check a dictionary for the standard form of the word.

44f **If a word must be divided at the end of a line, divide it correctly.**

1. Divide words between syllables.

▶ When I returned from my trip overseas, I didn't ~~reco-~~ *recog-*
nize ^
~~gnize~~ one face on the magazine covers.

2. Never divide one-syllable words.

▶ Christopher didn't have the courage or the ~~stren-~~
strength
~~gth~~ to open the door.
^

3. Never divide a word so that a single letter stands alone at the end of a line or fewer than three letters begin a line.

▶ She'll be sure to bring her brother with her when she comes ~~a-~~
again.
~~gain.~~

▶ As audience to *The Mousetrap,* Hamlet is actually a ~~watch-~~
watcher
~~er~~ watching watchers.
^

4. When dividing a compound word at the end of a line, either make the break between the words that form the compound or put the whole word on the next line.

▶ My five-year-old niece is determined to become a long-~~dis-~~
distance
~~tance~~ runner when she grows up.
^

EXERCISE 44–1

Edit the following sentences to correct errors in hyphenation. If a sentence is correct, write "correct" after it. Answers to lettered sentences appear in the back of the book. Example:

Zola's first readers were scandalized by his slice-of-life novels.
^ ^

a. Gold is the seventy-ninth element in the periodic table.
b. The quietly-purring cat cleaned first one paw and then the other before curling up under the stove.
c. The Moche were a pre-Columbian people who establish-ed a sophisticated culture in ancient Peru.
d. Your dog is well-known in our neighborhood.
e. Dmitri did fifty push-ups in two minutes and then collapsed.

1. We knew we were driving too fast when our tires skidded over the rain slick surface.
2. The Black Death reduced the population of some medieval villages by two thirds.
3. The flight attendant asked us to fasten our seat belts before lift-off.
4. One-quarter of the class signed up for the debate on U.S. foreign aid to Latin America.
5. Joan had been brought up to be independent and self reliant.

45

Capital letters

In addition to the following rules, you can use a good diction-ary to tell you when to use capital letters.

45a Capitalize proper nouns and words derived from them; do not capitalize common nouns.

Proper nouns are the names of specific persons, places, and things. All other nouns are common nouns. The following types of words are usually capitalized: names for the deity, religions, religious followers, sacred books; words of family relationship used as names; particular places; nationalities and their lan-guages, races, tribes; educational institutions, departments, degrees, particular courses; government departments, organiza-tions, political parties; and historical movements, periods, events, documents.

PROPER NOUNS	COMMON NOUNS
God (used as a name)	a god
Book of Jeremiah	a book
Uncle Pedro	my uncle

PROPER NOUNS	COMMON NOUNS
Father (used as a name)	my father
Lake Superior	a picturesque lake
the Capital Center	a center for advanced studies
the South	a southern state
Japan, a Japanese garden	an ornamental garden
University of Wisconsin	a good university
Geology 101	geology
Environmental Protection Agency	a federal agency
Phi Kappa Psi	a fraternity
a Democrat	an independent
the Enlightenment	the eighteenth century
the Declaration of Independence	a treaty

Months, holidays, and days of the week are treated as proper nouns; the seasons and numbers of the days of the month are not.

> Our academic year begins on a Tuesday in early September, right after Labor Day.

> My mother's birthday is in spring, on the fifth of May.

Names of school subjects are capitalized only if they are names of languages. Names of particular courses are capitalized.

> This semester Austin is taking only math and English.

> Professor Anderson offers Modern American Fiction 501 to graduate students.

CAUTION: Do not capitalize common nouns to make them seem important: *Our company is currently hiring computer programmers* (not *Company, Computer Programmers*).

45b Capitalize titles of persons when used as part of a proper name but usually not when used alone.

> Professor Margaret Barnes; Dr. Harold Stevens; John Scott Williams, Jr.; Anne Tilton, LL.D.

> District Attorney Marshall was reprimanded for badgering the witness.

The district attorney was elected for a two-year term.

Usage varies when the title of an important public figure is used alone: *The president* (or *President*) *vetoed the bill.*

45c Capitalize the first, last, and all major words in titles and subtitles of works such as books, articles, and songs.

In both titles and subtitles, major words such as nouns, pronouns, verbs, adjectives, and adverbs should be capitalized. Minor words such as articles, prepositions, and coordinating conjunctions are not capitalized unless they are the first or last word of a title or subtitle. Capitalize the second part of a hyphenated term in a title if it is a major word but not if it is a minor word.

> *The Country of the Pointed Firs*
>
> *The Impossible Theater: A Manifesto*
>
> *The F-Plan Diet*

Capitalize chapter titles and the titles of other major divisions of a work following the same guidelines used for titles of complete works.

> "Work and Play" in Santayana's *The Nature of Beauty*

45d Capitalize the first word of a sentence.

Obviously the first word of a sentence should be capitalized.

> When lightning struck the house, the chimney collapsed.

When a sentence appears within parentheses, capitalize its first word unless the parentheses appear within another sentence.

> Early detection of breast cancer significantly increases survival rates. (See table 2.)
>
> Early detection of breast cancer significantly increases survival rates (see table 2).

45e Capitalize the first word of a quoted sentence unless it is blended into the sentence that introduces it.

> In *Time* magazine Robert Hughes writes, "There are only about sixty Watteau paintings on whose authenticity all experts agree."

> Russell Baker has written that in our country "it is sport that is the opiate of the masses."

If a quoted sentence is interrupted by explanatory words, do not capitalize the first word after the interruption. (See 37f.)

> "If you wanted to go out," he said sharply, "you should have told me."

When quoting poetry, copy the poet's capitalization exactly. Many poets capitalize the first word of every line of poetry; a few poets dismiss capitalization altogether.

> When I consider everything that grows
> Holds in perfection but a little moment   — Shakespeare

> it was the week   that
> i felt the city's narrow breezes rush about
> me   — Don L. Lee

45f Do not capitalize the first word after a colon unless it begins an independent clause, in which case capitalization is optional.

> Most of the bar's patrons can be divided into two groups: the occasional after-work socializers and the nothing-to-go-home-to regulars.

> This we are forced to conclude: the [*or* The] federal government is needed to protect the rights of minorities.

45g Capitalize abbreviations for departments and agencies of government, other organizations, and corporations; capitalize trade names and the call letters of radio and television stations.

EPA, FBI, OPEC, IBM, Xerox, WCRB, KNBC-TV

EXERCISE 45-1

Edit the following sentences to correct errors in capitalization. If a sentence is correct, write "correct" after it. Answers to lettered sentences appear in the back of the book. Example:

On our trip to the West we visited the *g̶*rand *c̶*anyon and the
*g̶*reat *s̶*alt *d̶*esert.

a. District attorney Johnson was disgusted when the jurors turned in a verdict of not guilty after only one hour of deliberation.

b. My mother has begun to research the history of her cherokee ancestors in Georgia.

c. W. C. Fields's epitaph reads, "On the whole, I'd rather be in Philadelphia."

d. Refugees from central America are finding it more and more difficult to cross the rio Grande into the United States.

e. I want to take Environmental Biology 103, one other Biology course, and one English course.

1. "O Liberty," cried madame Roland from the scaffold, "What crimes are committed in thy name!"

2. The grunion is an unremarkable fish except for one curious habit: it comes ashore to spawn.

3. Does your Aunt still preach in local churches whenever she's asked?

4. Historians have described Robert E. Lee as the aristocratic south personified.

5. My brother is a Doctor and my sister-in-law is an Attorney.

Argument

In argumentative writing, you take a stand on a debatable issue. The issue being debated might be a matter of public policy: Should religious groups be allowed to meet on school property? What is the least dangerous way to dispose of nuclear waste? Should a state enact laws rationing medical care? On such questions, reasonable persons can disagree.

Reasonable men and women also disagree about many scholarly issues. Psychologists debate the validity of behaviorism; historians interpret the causes of the Civil War quite differently; biologists conduct genetic experiments to challenge the conclusions of other researchers.

46

Build a convincing case.

Your goal, in argumentative writing, is to change the way your readers think about a subject or to convince them to take an action that they might not otherwise be inclined to take. Do not assume that your audience already agrees with you; instead, envision skeptical readers who will make up their minds after listening to both sides of the debate. To have an impact on such readers, you will need to build a case convincing enough to stand up to the arguments put forward by your opponents (sometimes called *the opposition*).

46a Plan a strategy.

Although thinking critically about your topic is an important first step in all writing, it is especially important in argumentative writing. Planning a strategy for an argumentative essay is much like planning a debate for a speech class. A good way to begin is to list your arguments and the arguments of the opposition and then consider the likely impact of these arguments on your audience. If the arguments of the opposition look very powerful, you may want to rethink your position. By modifying your initial position—perhaps by claiming less or by proposing a less radical solution to a problem—you may have a greater chance of persuading readers to change their views.

Listing your arguments

Let's say that your tentative purpose (which may change as you think about your audience and the opposition) is to argue in favor of lowering the legal drinking age from twenty-one to eighteen. Here is a list of possible arguments in favor of this point of view.

> — Society treats eighteen-year-olds as mature for most purposes.
>> — They can vote.
>> — They can go away to college.
>> — At eighteen, men must register with Selective Service and be available for a possible draft.
> — Age is not necessarily an indication of maturity.
> — The current drinking age is unfair, since many older Americans were allowed to drink at eighteen.
> — An unrealistic drinking age is almost impossible to enforce, and it breeds disrespect for the law.
> — In European countries that allow eighteen-year-olds to drink, there is less irresponsible teenage drinking than in our country.

Listing the arguments of the opposition

The next step is to list the key arguments of the opposition. Here are some possible arguments *against* lowering the drinking age to eighteen.

> — Teenage drinking frequently leads to drunken driving, which in turn leads to many deaths.
> — Teenage drinking sometimes leads to date rape and gang violence.
> — Alcoholism is a serious problem in our society, and a delayed drinking age can help prevent it.
> — If the legal age were eighteen, many fifteen- and sixteen-year-olds would find a way to purchase alcohol illegally.

If possible, you should talk to someone who disagrees with your view or read some articles that are critical of your position. By familiarizing yourself with the views of the opposition, you can be reasonably sure you have not overlooked an important argument that might be used against you.

Considering your audience

Once you have listed the major arguments on both sides, think realistically about the impact they are likely to have on your intended audience. If your audience is the voting age population in the United States, for example, consider how you might assess some of the arguments of each side of the drinking age question.

Looking at your list, you would see that your audience, which includes many older Americans, might not be impressed by the suggestion that age is no sign of maturity or by the argument that because eighteen-year-olds are old enough to attend college they should be allowed to drink. You would decide to emphasize your other arguments instead. Americans who remember a time when young men were drafted, for example, might be persuaded that it is unfair to ask a man to die for his country but not allow him to drink. And anyone who has heard of Prohibition might be moved by the argument that an unrealistic drinking regulation can breed disrespect for the law.

As for the arguments of the opposition, clearly the first one on the list is the most powerful. Statistics show that drunken driving by teenagers causes much carnage on our highways and that teenagers themselves are frequently the victims. To have any hope of convincing your audience, you would need to take this argument very seriously; it would be almost impossible to argue successfully that reducing highway deaths is not important.

Rethinking your position

After exploring both sides of an argument, you may decide to modify your initial position. Maybe your first thoughts about the issue were oversimplified, too extreme, or mistaken in some other respect. Or maybe, after thinking more about your readers, you see little hope of persuading them of the truth or wisdom of your position.

If you were writing about the drinking age, for example, you might decide to modify your position in light of your audience. To have a better chance of convincing the audience, you could argue that eighteen-year-olds *in the military* should be allowed to drink. Or you could argue that eighteen-year-olds should be allowed to drink beer and wine, not hard alcohol. Or you could link your proposal to new tough laws against drunken driving.

46b Frame a thesis and state your major arguments.

A thesis is a sentence that expresses the main point of an essay. (See 2a.) In argumentative writing, your thesis should clearly state your position on the issue you have chosen to write about. Let's say your issue is the high insurance rates that most companies set for young male drivers. After thinking carefully about your own views, the arguments of the opposition, and your audience (the general public), you might state your position like this:

> Although young male drivers have a high accident rate, insurance companies should not be allowed to discriminate against anyone who has driven for the past two years without a traffic violation.

Notice that this is a debatable point, one about which reasonable persons can disagree. It is not merely a fact (for example, that companies do set higher rates for young males). Nor is it a statement of belief (for example, that differing rates are always unfair). Neither facts nor beliefs can be substantiated by reasons, so they cannot serve as a thesis for an argument.

Once you have framed a thesis, try to state your major arguments, preferably in sentence form. Together, your thesis and your arguments will give you a rough outline of your essay. Consider the following rough outline of an essay written by Julian L. Simon, a business professor at the University of Maryland. Simon argues for an easing of restrictions on immigration into the United States. His thesis frames the issue in economic terms, and his major arguments are economic reasons that support his thesis.

> Thesis: Despite claims that increased immigration would hurt the economy, the evidence strongly suggests that new immigrants strengthen the economy in a variety of ways.
>
> —Immigrants do not cause native unemployment, even among low-paid and minority groups.
> —Immigrants do not overuse welfare services.
> —Immigrants bring high-tech skills that the economy needs badly.

—Immigration is lower than it was in the peak years at the turn of the century.

—Natural resources and the environment are not at risk from immigration.

—Immigration reduces the social costs of the elderly, which can't be cut.

Some of the sentences in your rough outline might become topic sentences of paragraphs in your final essay. (See 5a.)

46c Draft an introduction that states your position without alienating readers.

In argumentative writing, your introduction should state your position on an issue in a clear thesis sentence (see 2a and 46b), and it should do this without needlessly alienating the audience whom you hope to convince. Where possible, try to establish common ground with readers who may not be in initial agreement with your views.

One student, who argued against allowing prayer in public schools, established common ground with readers who disagreed with her by explaining that she once shared their views. Her introduction ends with a clear thesis that states her current position on the issue.

> During most of my school years, the Lord's Prayer was a part of our opening exercises. I never gave it a second thought, and I never heard anyone complain about it. So when prayer in the schools became an issue in the courts, I was surprised to hear that anyone viewed it as a threat to individual rights or as a violation of the division between church and state. But now that I've thought about it, I would not like to see the practice of prayer in the schools reinstituted.

In her first draft, the student began the introduction like this: "I do not think prayer should be allowed in schools." This sentence clearly stated her position, but its blunt tone was likely to alienate readers who favor school prayer. The student wisely decided to establish common ground with her readers before stating her position. Notice that her new thesis statement, at the end of the introduction, is as clear as her original thesis but has a much more reasonable tone.

One way to establish common ground with readers who disagree with your position is to show that you share common values. If your subject is school prayer, for instance, you might show that even though you oppose allowing prayer in schools, you believe in the value of prayer. The writer of the following introduction successfully used this strategy.

> Although the Supreme Court has ruled against prayer in public schools on First Amendment grounds, many people still feel that prayers should be allowed. These people, most of whom hold strong religious beliefs, are well intentioned. What they fail to realize is that the Supreme Court decision, although it was made on legal grounds, makes good sense on religious grounds as well. Prayer is too important to be trusted to our public schools.

Like the writer of the other introduction about school prayer, this writer sounds reasonable. He states his position clearly and firmly in a thesis at the end of the paragraph, but because he takes into consideration the values of those who disagree with him, readers are likely to approach his essay with an open mind.

46d Support each argument with specific evidence.

When presenting the arguments for your position, you will of course need to back them up with evidence: facts, statistics, examples and illustrations, expert opinion, and so on. Depending on the issue you have chosen to write about, you may or may not need to do some reading to gather evidence. Some argumentative topics, such as whether class attendance should be required at your college or university, can be developed through personal experience and maybe questionnaires or interviews. Other debatable topics, such as the extent to which apes can learn language, require library research.

If any of your evidence is based on reading, you will need to document your sources. Documentation gives credit to your sources and shows readers how to track down the source in case they want to assess its credibility or explore the issue further. The style of documentation used in most English classes is described in 55; another style is described in 56. Always find out from your instructor which style he or she prefers.

Using facts and statistics

A fact is something that is known with certainty because it has been objectively verified: The capital of Wyoming is Cheyenne. Carbon has an atomic weight of 12. John F. Kennedy was assassinated on November 22, 1963. Statistics are collections of numerical facts: One-half of U.S. households currently own a VCR. North America holds only 4 percent of the world's proven oil reserves; together, Iraq, Kuwait, and Saudi Arabia own 44 percent.

Most arguments are supported at least to some extent by facts and statistics. For example, if you were arguing against mandatory class attendance, you might include facts about the attendance policies of professors in several disciplines; you could also report statistics on the views of students.

Karen Shaw, the student who wrote the MLA research essay on apes and language that is printed on pages 384–97, gathered facts and statistics from printed sources. When she included them in her essay, she documented them, as in the following example.

> After some experimentation, the chimpanzees succeeded 97 percent of the time (Marx 1333).

Shaw got this statistic from a journal article by Jean L. Marx. The parenthetical citation at the end of the sentence includes the last name of the author and the page number on which the information appears. (See 55 for more about documentation.)

Using examples and anecdotes

Examples and anecdotes (illustrative stories) alone rarely prove a point, but when used in combination with other forms of evidence, they flesh out an argument and bring it to life. In an essay arguing against mandatory class attendance, you might give examples of class sessions that were obviously a waste of time, maybe because the professor simply read from the textbook or because you were asked to play games that had nothing to do with the subject.

In her research essay, Karen Shaw used several examples from a variety of sources to show that apes are capable of using language creatively (see page 390).

Citing expert opinion

Although they are no substitute for careful reasoning of your own, the views of an expert can contribute to the force of your argument. You might interview an educational psychologist on learning styles, for example, to help support your argument that class attendance is not the only way to learn. Or, if you were arguing in favor of mandatory class attendance, you might interview a dean to learn about academic goals (such as increased tolerance for persons from other cultures) that can be accomplished only through class attendance.

When you rely on expert opinion, you must document your sources. You can summarize or paraphrase the expert's opinion or you can quote the expert's exact words. For important advice on appropriate use of written sources, see 53b.

46e Anticipate objections; refute opposing arguments.

Readers who already agree with you need no convincing, although a well-argued case for their own point of view is always welcome. But indifferent and skeptical readers may resist your arguments because they have minds of their own. To give up a position that seems reasonable, a reader has to see that there is an even more reasonable one. In addition to presenting your own case, therefore, you should review the chief arguments of the opposition and explain what you think is wrong with them.

There is no best place in an essay to deal with the opposition. Often it is useful to summarize the opposing position early in your essay. After stating your thesis but before developing your own arguments, you might have a paragraph beginning "Critics of this view argue that. . . ." But sometimes a better plan is to anticipate objections as you develop your case paragraph by paragraph. Wherever you decide to deal with opposing arguments, do your best to refute them. Show that those who oppose you are not as persuasive as they claim because their arguments are flawed or because your arguments to the contrary have greater weight.

As you refute opposing arguments, try to establish common ground with readers who are not in initial agreement with your views. If you can show that you share your readers' values, they may be able to switch to your position without giving up what they feel is important. For example, to persuade people opposed to shooting deer, a state wildlife commission would have to show that it too cares about preserving deer and does not want them to die needlessly. Having established these values in common, the commission might be able to persuade critics that a carefully controlled hunting season is good for the deer population because it prevents starvation caused by overpopulation. Likewise, if those opposed to hunting want to persuade the commission to ban the hunting season, they would need to show that the commission could achieve its goals by some other feasible means, such as expanding the deer preserve or increasing the food supply to support an increased herd.

People believe that intelligence and decency support their side of an argument. To change sides, they must continue to feel intelligent and decent. Otherwise they will persist in their opposition.

47

Avoid common mistakes in reasoning.

Certain errors in reasoning occur frequently enough to deserve special attention. In both your reading and your writing, you will want to be alert to common mistakes in inductive and deductive reasoning and to certain mistakes known as logical fallacies.

47a Use inductive reasoning with care.

When you reason inductively, you draw a conclusion from an array of facts. For example, you might conclude that a professor is friendly because he or she smiles frequently and talks to students after class or that fifty-five miles per hour is a safer speed limit than sixty-five miles per hour because there are fewer deaths per accident at that speed.

Inductive reasoning deals in probability, not certainty. For a conclusion based on inductive reasoning to be highly probable, the evidence must be sufficient, representative, and relevant. Consider, for example, how you would decide whether to trust the following conclusion, drawn from evidence gathered in a survey.

> **CONCLUSION** The majority of households in our city would subscribe to cable television if it were available.
>
> **EVIDENCE** In a recent survey, 356 of the 500 households questioned say they would subscribe to cable television.

Is the evidence sufficient? That depends. In a city of 10,000, the 500 households are a 5 percent sample, sufficient for the purposes of marketing research. But in a city of 2 million, the households would amount to one-fortieth of 1 percent of the population, an inadequate sample on which to base an important decision.

Is the evidence representative? Again, that depends. The cable company would trust the survey if it knew that the sample had been carefully constructed to reflect the age, sex, geographic distribution, and income of the city's population as a whole. If, however, the 500 households were concentrated in one wealthy neighborhood, the company would be wise to question the survey's conclusion.

Is the evidence relevant? The answer is a cautious yes. The survey question is directly linked to the conclusion. A question about the number of hours spent watching television, by contrast, would not be relevant, because it would not be about *subscribing* to *cable* television. In addition, a cautious interpreter of the evidence would want to know whether people who *say* they would subscribe tend to subscribe *in fact*. By looking at marketing research done in other cities, the cable television company could determine — through a new round of inductive reasoning — how many of the 356 households who say they would subscribe are likely in fact to subscribe.

47b Use deductive reasoning with care.

When you reason deductively, you draw a conclusion from two or more assertions (called premises).

> The police do not give speeding tickets to people driving less than five miles per hour over the limit. Sam is driving fifty-nine miles per hour in a fifty-five-mile-per-hour zone. Therefore, the police will not give Sam a speeding ticket.

The conclusion is true only if the premises are true. If the police sometimes give tickets for less than five-mile-per-hour violations or if the speedometer is inaccurate, Sam cannot safely conclude that he will avoid a ticket.

Deductive reasoning can often be structured in a three-step argument called a *syllogism*. The three steps are the major premise, the minor premise, and the conclusion:

1. Anything that increases radiation in the environment is dangerous to public health. (Major premise)
2. Nuclear reactors increase radiation in the environment. (Minor premise)
3. Therefore, nuclear reactors are dangerous to public health. (Conclusion)

The major premise is a generalization. The minor premise is a specific case. The conclusion follows from applying the generalization to the specific case.

Many deductive arguments do not state one of the premises but rather leave the reader to infer it. In the preceding example, the conclusion would still sound plausible without the major premise: *Nuclear reactors increase radiation in the environment; therefore, they are dangerous to public health.* A careful reader, however, will see the missing premise and will question the whole argument if the premise is debatable.

Deductive arguments break down if one of the premises is not true or if the conclusion does not logically follow from them. For example, consider this argument:

> The deer population in our state should be preserved. During hunting season hundreds of deer are killed. Therefore, the hunting season should be discontinued.

To challenge this argument, the state's wildlife commission might agree with both the major and minor premises but question whether the conclusion follows logically from them. True, the deer population should be preserved; true, deer are killed during hunting season. However, in an area where deer have no natural enemies, herds become too large for the forest vegetation to support them. The overpopulated herds strip the leaves and bark from the young trees, killing the trees before dying of starvation themselves. The commission might conclude, therefore, that a limited hunting season helps preserve a healthier and more stable population of deer.

47c Avoid logical fallacies.

Some errors in reasoning are so common that writers and readers call them by name: hasty generalization, non sequitur, false analogy, and so on. Such errors are known as *logical fallacies*.

Hasty generalization

A hasty generalization is a conclusion based on insufficient or unrepresentative evidence.

> Deaths from drug overdoses in Metropolis have doubled in the past three years. Therefore, more Americans than ever are dying from drug abuse.

Data from one city do not justify a conclusion about the whole United States.

Many hasty generalizations contain words like *all, every, always,* and *never,* when qualifiers such as *most, many, usually,* and *seldom* would be more accurate. Go over your writing carefully for such general statements and make sure that you have enough data to verify your position or that you qualify the statements.

A *stereotype* is a hasty generalization (usually derogatory) about a group. Examples: Women are bad bosses; politicians are corrupt; people without children are self-centered. Stereotyping is common because of our human tendency to perceive selectively. We tend to see what we want to see; that is, we notice evidence confirming our already formed opinions and fail to notice evidence to the contrary. For example, if you have concluded that politicians are corrupt, your stereotype will be confirmed by occasional news reports of legislators being indicted — even though every day the newspapers describe conscientious officials serving the public honestly and well. Generalizations about people must be based on numerous typical cases and not contradicted by many exceptions. And even conclusions that are generally valid — that Americans tend to place a high value on individual rights, for example—will have significant exceptions because what is generally true about groups of people will not be true of all individuals within those groups.

Non sequitur

A non sequitur (Latin for "does not follow") is a conclusion that does not follow logically from preceding statements or that is based on irrelevant data.

> Mary loves good food; therefore, she will be an excellent chef.

Mary's love of good food does not guarantee that she will be able to cook it well.

False analogy

An analogy points out a similarity between two things that are otherwise dissimilar. Analogies can be an effective means of illustrating a point (see 6b), but they are not proof. In a false analogy, a writer falsely assumes that because two things are alike in one respect, they must be alike in others.

> If we can put humans on the moon, we should be able to find a cure for the common cold.

Putting humans on the moon and finding a cure for the common cold are both scientific challenges, but the technical problems confronting medical researchers are quite different from those solved by space scientists.

Either . . . or *fallacy*

The *either . . . or* fallacy is the suggestion that only two alternatives exist when in fact there are more.

> Either learn how to operate a computer or you won't be able to get a decent job after college.

In fact, some occupations do not require knowledge of computers.

Faulty cause-and-effect reasoning

Careless thinkers often assume that because one event follows another, the first is the cause of the second. This common fallacy is known as *post hoc*, from the Latin *post hoc, ergo propter hoc*, meaning "after this, therefore because of this." Like a non sequitur, it is a leap to an unjustified conclusion.

> Since Governor Smith took office, unemployment of minorities in the state has decreased by 7 percent. Governor Smith should be applauded for reducing unemployment among minorities.

The writer must show that Governor Smith's policies are responsible for the decrease in unemployment; it is not enough to show merely that the decrease followed the governor's taking office.

Demonstrating the connection between causes and effects is rarely a simple matter. For example, to explain why an introductory chemistry course has a very high failure rate, you would begin by listing possible causes: inadequate preparation of students, poor teaching, large class size, unavailability of qualified tutors, and so on. Next you would need to investigate each possible cause by gathering statistical data. For example, to see whether inadequate preparation of students contributes to the high failure rate, you might do a statistical comparison of the math and science backgrounds of successful and failing students. Or to see whether large class size is a contributing cause, you might run a pilot program of small classes and then compare grades in the small classes with those in the larger ones. Only after thoroughly investigating all of the possible causes would you be able to weigh the relative impact of each cause and then suggest appropriate remedies.

Circular reasoning and begging the question

Suppose you go to see a doctor about a rash you suddenly developed. "I have a rash," you say to the doctor. "What is your diagnosis?" The doctor answers, "You have allergitis." When you ask, "What's that?" the doctor replies, "It's a rash." This is an example of circular reasoning: No real information has been introduced; by a trick of semantics you have wound up back where you started.

Like circular reasoning, begging the question is a way of ducking the issue. Instead of supporting the conclusion with evidence and logic, the writer simply restates the conclusion in different language.

> Faculty and administrators should not be permitted to come to student council meetings because student council meetings should be for students only.

The writer has given no reason for this position but has merely repeated the point.

Appeals to emotion

Many of the arguments we see in the media strive to win our sympathy rather than our intelligent agreement. A TV commercial suggesting that you will be thin and sexy if you drink a certain diet beverage is making a pitch to emotions. So is a political speech that recommends electing John D'Eau because he is a devoted husband and father who fought for his country in Vietnam.

The following passage illustrates several types of emotional appeals.

> This progressive proposal to build a large ski resort in the state park has been carefully researched by Fidelity, the largest bank in the state; furthermore, it is favored by a majority of the local merchants. The only opposition comes from narrow-minded, do-gooder environmentalists who care more about trees than they do about people; one of their leaders was actually arrested for disturbing the peace several years ago.

Words with strong positive or negative connotations, such as *progressive* and *do-gooders,* are examples of *biased language.* Attacking the persons who hold a belief (environmentalists) rather than refuting their argument is called *ad hominem,* a Latin term meaning "to the man." Associating a prestigious name (Fidelity) with the writer's side is called *transfer.* Claiming that an idea should be accepted because a large number of people are in favor (the majority of merchants) is called the *bandwagon appeal.* Bringing in irrelevant issues (the arrest) is a *red herring,* named after a trick used in fox hunts to mislead the dogs by dragging a smelly fish across the trail.

In examining your own and other people's writing for errors of logic, you will find that logical fallacies are frequently not so clear-cut that a casual reader can spot them immediately. Often they show up in combination. To recognize such fallacies in your own writing takes discipline, but you can do it if you train yourself to become a skeptical and demanding reader—the kind of person who measures all claims against the evidence.

EXERCISE 47–1

Explain what is illogical in the following brief arguments. It may be helpful to identify the logical fallacy or fallacies by name. Answers to lettered sentences appear in the back of the book.

a. All of my blind dates have been embarrassing disasters, so I know this one will be too.

b. If you're old enough to vote, you're old enough to drink. Therefore, the drinking age should be lowered to eighteen.

c. This country has been run too long by old, out-of-date, out-of-touch, entrenched politicians protecting the special interests that got them elected.

d. It was possible to feed a family of four on $70 a week before Governor Leroy took office and drove up food prices.

e. If you're not part of the solution, you're part of the problem.

1. Whenever I wash my car, it rains. I have discovered a way to end all droughts—get all the people to wash their cars.

2. Our current war on drugs has not worked. Either we should legalize drugs or we should turn the drug war over to our armed forces and let them fight it.

3. College professors tend to be sarcastic. Three of my five professors this semester make sarcastic remarks.

4. Although Ms. Bell's book on Joe DiMaggio was well researched, I doubt that an Australian historian can contribute much to our knowledge of an American baseball player.

5. Self-righteous nonsmoking fanatics have eroded our basic individual freedoms by railroading the passage of oppressive anti-smoking laws that interfere with our natural right to make our own decisions.

6. If professional sports teams didn't pay athletes such high salaries, we wouldn't have so many kids breaking their legs at hockey and basketball camps.

7. Ninety percent of the students oppose a tuition increase; therefore, the board of trustees should not pass the proposed increase.

8. If the president had learned the lesson of Vietnam, he would realize that sending U.S. troops into a foreign country can only end in disaster.

9. A mandatory ten-cent deposit on bottles and cans will eliminate litter because everyone I know will return the containers for the money rather than throw them away.

10. Soliciting money to save whales and baby seals is irresponsible when thousands of human beings can't afford food and shelter.

Research Guide

College research assignments are an opportunity for you to contribute to an intellectual inquiry or debate. Most college assignments ask you to pose a question worth exploring, to read widely in search of possible answers, to interpret what you read, to draw reasoned conclusions, and to support those conclusions with valid and well-documented evidence. Such assignments may at first seem overwhelming, but if you pose a question that intrigues you and approach it like a detective, with genuine curiosity, you will soon learn how rewarding doing research can be.

Setting realistic deadlines

Admittedly, the process takes time: time for researching and time for drafting, revising, and documenting the paper in the style recommended by your instructor (see 55 or 56). Before beginning a research project, you should set a realistic schedule of deadlines. For example, before she began researching the paper that appears on pages 384–97, Karen Shaw constructed the following schedule. She received her assignment on October 2, and the due date was November 2.

SCHEDULE	FINISHED BY
1. Take the college's library tour.	October 3
2. Choose a topic and plan a search strategy.	5
3. Compile a bibliography.	9
4. Read and take notes.	16
5. Decide on a tentative thesis and outline.	18
6. Draft the paper.	23
7. Visit the writing center to get help with ideas for revision.	25
8. Revise the paper.	26
9. Prepare a list of works cited.	27
10. Type and proofread the final draft.	30

Notice that Shaw built some extra time into her schedule to allow for unexpected delays. Although the due date for the paper was November 2, her schedule called for completing the paper by October 30.

48

Pose questions worth exploring.

Working within the guidelines of your assignment, jot down a few questions that seem worth researching. Here, for example, are some preliminary questions jotted down by students who were asked to write about a significant political or scholarly issue:

Should the use of lie detectors be banned?

What was Marcus Garvey's contribution to the fight for racial equality?

What are the hazards of fad diets?

Does investing in wind energy make economic sense?

Have gorillas and chimpanzees demonstrated significant language skills?

Why was amateur archaeologist Heinrich Schliemann such a controversial figure in his own time?

Which geological formations are the safest repositories for nuclear waste?

How can governments and zoos help preserve China's endangered giant panda?

If you have trouble coming up with a list of questions, you can browse through certain library references for ideas. For example, *Opposing Viewpoints Series* compiles recent articles on controversial social issues and current events, and *CQ Researcher* contains digests of recent articles and editorials on contemporary issues. You can discover other possible lines of inquiry by skimming through current magazines such as *Newsweek, Harper's, Science News,* and *Smithsonian* or by consulting specialized periodicals in your academic discipline. Scholarly controversies encountered in college courses are yet another potential source of ideas; ask your professors for suggestions.

Once you have come up with a list of possible questions, choose the question that intrigues you the most and do a bit of preliminary research to see where your line of inquiry might lead. If it seems to be leading to a dead end — maybe because you can't find a variety of sources on the subject or because the information is too technical for you to understand — turn to another question on your list, which may prove more promising.

Once you have settled on a question that looks promising, check to see if it is too broad, given the length of the paper you plan to write. If you suspect it is — and most writers' initial questions are — look for ways to narrow your focus as you begin researching.

Narrowing your focus

Even before you visit the library, you may be able to limit the scope of your investigation. For instance, if initially you asked "Should the use of lie detectors be banned?" you might restrict your inquiry to the use of lie detectors *in the military.* Or if at first you asked "What are the hazards of fad diets?" you might narrow your focus to the hazards of *liquid* diets.

Once inside the library, you can use reference tools to help narrow your topic. For example, by scanning encyclopedia articles, you can get a sense of your subject's natural subdivisions. For current topics you can check the headings and subheadings in periodical indexes such as the computerized *General Periodicals Ondisc* or *Academic Index.* One of these subheadings might help you restrict your topic even before you have read a single article.

As you begin reading books and articles and become more knowledgeable, you may be able to restrict your focus even further and at the same time decide what approach you will take in your paper — or even decide on a tentative main point. The main point of your paper, known as a *thesis,* will be an answer to the central question that you finally decide to pose. (See 52a.)

49

Follow a search strategy.

A search strategy is a systematic plan for tracking down source materials. To create a search strategy, you'll need to ask yourself two questions:

What kinds of source materials should I consult?

In what order should I consult them?

A good search strategy moves from sources that give you an overview of your subject to those that supply you with more specialized information. For a historical subject you might begin with general reference works such as encyclopedias and then move to books and finally to scholarly articles. For a current subject, you might begin with magazines of general interest and end with specialized articles in scholarly journals.

To research the topic of apes and language, Karen Shaw, whose paper appears on pages 384–97, decided to turn to magazines for an overview of her subject. Her librarian recommended *Periodical Abstracts Ondisc* as the fastest way to locate magazine articles on her topic. Working at a computer terminal, Shaw typed the keywords *apes* and *language* to call up abstracts of articles of possible interest. The abstracts helped Shaw decide which articles would give her an overview of her subject.

Once Shaw had located and read several magazine articles, she became intrigued by current research with pygmy chimpanzees at Yerkes Primate Center in Atlanta. At this point she realized that her search strategy should focus mainly on periodicals, since books would be too dated to supply her with information about such recent studies. Using *Periodical Abstracts Ondisc* again, Shaw located several articles about pygmy chimpanzees in magazines, newspapers, and scholarly journals.

Shaw didn't overlook books entirely, however, because she needed a historical overview of ape language studies. In particular, she was interested to learn about the scholarly battles that had been waged over the past twenty-five years, especially between two key researchers, Herbert Terrace and Francine Patterson. The computer catalog led Shaw to several books, including one by Terrace and one by Patterson. Shaw didn't have time to read the books cover to cover, so she used the table of contents and the index of each book to lead her to relevant chapters and pages: those that focused on the scholarly controversies surrounding the early years of the ape language studies.

Because Shaw had planned her search strategy carefully, most of her reading was relevant to her final approach to the topic. As you survey the possible sources of information listed on the following pages, try to develop an organized search strategy appropriate to your topic. Remember that if you run into problems, a reference librarian will be glad to help.

Reference works

Often you'll want to begin by reading background information in a general encyclopedia, a specialized encyclopedia, or a biographical reference. Later you may need to turn to other reference works such as atlases, almanacs, or unabridged dictionaries. Many college libraries provide handouts that list their reference works, sometimes organized by academic discipline.

Books

Your library may have a computer catalog, a card catalog, a microform catalog, or some combination of these. Most libraries now have computer catalogs that allow you to search for information about books and often other materials through a terminal or personal computer. A computer catalog is a database that contains bibliographic and location information about a library's books. It can be searched by subject, author, or title.

While computer catalogs vary from library to library, most are easy to use, and a reference librarian will be able to help you if you get stuck. Look for instructions on the computer terminal's menu display or look for a "help" key. To begin a search, you will usually respond to a direction such as "Type in an author's name" or "Enter your subject." The computer will then display either a list of books under that author's name or subject heading or a list of subcategories from which you can choose the one closest to your topic.

Searching by subject involves the use of keywords or subject headings. The keywords may be used alone, such as *chimpanzees* or *sign language*, or they can be combined.

If you began your search with the general subject heading *human animal communication*, you might see a screen like the one at the top of page 337. Notice that this list contains the overall subject category as well as four subcategories. If you selected the overall subject category, you would see a screen like the one at the bottom of page 337. This screen gives you a choice of a number of titles. If a title looks useful, you can call up a search screen that displays the complete record of the book (see the top of page 338). Usually you can command the

SUBJECT SEARCH: SCREEN 1

```
HU GUIDE: SUBJECT HEADING LIST          18 items retrieved by your search:
FIND SU HUMAN ANIMAL COMMUNICATION
-----------------------------------------------------------
 1 HUMAN ANIMAL COMMUNICATION
15 HUMAN ANIMAL COMMUNICATION --CONGRESSES
16 HUMAN ANIMAL COMMUNICATION --DATA PROCESSING
17 HUMAN ANIMAL COMMUNICATION --FOLKLORE
18 HUMAN ANIMAL COMMUNICATION --RESEARCH --CONGRESSES




-----------------------------------------------------------
OPTIONS: INDEX (or I 5 etc) to see list of items    HELP
                                                    START - search options
         REDO - edit search                         QUIT - exit database
COMMAND?
```

SUBJECT SEARCH: SCREEN 2

```
HU INDEX: LIST OF ITEMS RETRIEVED        18 items retrieved by your search:
FIND SU HUMAN ANIMAL COMMUNICATION
-----------------------------------------------------------
HUMAN ANIMAL COMMUNICATION
 1 adams task calling animals by name /hearne vicki 1946/ 1986 bks
 2 animals are equal an exploration of animal consciousn /hall rebec/ 1980 bks
 3 apes men and language /linden eugene/ 1976 bks
 4 aping language /wallman joel/ 1992 bks
 5 butterfly revelations /swanson henry f 1923/ 1979 bks
 6 communication between man and dolphin the possibilit /lilly john/ 1987 bks
 7 education of koko /patterson francine/ 1981 bks
 8 gavagai or the future history of the animal language /premack da/ 1986 bks
 9 hund und mensch eine semiotische analyse ihrer kommu /fleischer/ 1987 bks
10 language in primates perspectives and implications/ 1983 bks
11 nim /terrace herbert s 1936/ 1979 bks
12 silent partners the legacy of the ape language exper /linden eug/ 1986 bks
13 speaking of apes a critical anthology of two way com/ 1980 bks
14 teaching sign language to chimpanzees/ 1989 bks
----------------------------------- (CONTINUES) ---------
OPTIONS: DISPLAY 1 (or D 5 etc) to see a record    HELP
         GUIDE              MORE - next page        START - search options
         REDO - edit search                         QUIT - exit database
COMMAND?
```

SUBJECT SEARCH: SCREEN 3

```
HU LONG DISPLAY page 1 of 1        Item 7 of 18 retrieved by your search:
FIND SU HUMAN ANIMAL COMMUNICATION
--------------------------------- HU HOLLIS# AEK5177 /bks
       AUTHOR: Patterson, Francine.
        TITLE: The education of Koko / Francine Patterson and Eugene Linden.
      EDITION: 1st ed.
    PUB. INFO: New York : Holt, Rinehart and Winston, c1981.
  DESCRIPTION: xiv, 224 p. : ill. ; 24 cm.
        NOTES: Includes index.
               Bibliography: p. 215-216.

     SUBJECTS: *S1 Gorilla--Psychology.
               *S2 Human-animal communication.
               *S3 Sign language.
      AUTHORS: *A1 Patterson, Francine.
               *A2 Linden, Eugene.

     LOCATION: Gutman Education: QL737, P96 P37
- - --------------------------------------------------
OPTIONS: DISPLAY SHORT                       NEXT: next item      HELP
         LOCATION                            PREVIOUS - prev item INDEX
         HELP COMMANDS    TRACE *S1 (etc)    QUIT - exit database REDO
COMMAND?
```

computer to print out this record, which includes bibliographic information and the location of the book. You will need the bibliographic information — author, title, publisher, and the place and date of publication — if you decide to use the book in your paper (see 50b and 55b). In the sample record, the location of the book appears after the bibliographic information. It includes the building where the book may be found and the call number, the book's address on the shelf.

Periodicals

Periodicals are publications issued at regular intervals, such as magazines, newspapers, and scholarly or technical journals. To track down useful articles, consult a magazine index, a newspaper index, or one of the many specialized indexes to scholarly or technical journals.

Some periodical indexes are in print form; others are stored as CD-ROM (compact disc–read-only memory) databases that can be accessed and read at a computer terminal. You search for articles in the CD-ROM database just as you look for books in the library's computer catalog, by typing the author, title, or subject keywords. Bibliographic records appear on the screen; sometimes an abstract or even the full text of an article can be printed.

Most libraries provide a list of the periodicals they own. This list tells you the form in which the periodical has been preserved: on microfilm, on microfiche, in bound volumes, or in unbound files. It also tells you which years and volumes of the periodical the library owns. In some libraries, all of this information appears on the screen of a computer index.

Other library sources

A library's holdings are not limited to reference works, books, and periodicals. Your library may have pamphlets, usually located in a large file cabinet known as a *vertical file*, or rare

COMPUTER INDEX RECORD WITH ABSTRACT

SilverPlatter 3.1   Journal Articles (1/74-12/86)

Journal Articles (1/74-12/86) usage is subject to the terms and conditions of the Subscription and License Agreement and the applicable Copyright and intellectual property protection as dictated by the appropriate laws of your country and/or by International Convention.

9 of 15

TI: Can an ape create a sentence?
AU: Terrace,-H.-S.;Petitto,-L.A.;Sanders,-R.J.;Bever,-T.G.
IN: Columbia U
JN: Science; 1979 Nov Vol 206(4421)891-902
AB: Recent demonstrations that chimpanzees and gorillas can communicate with humans via arbitrary "words" raise the issue of whether the ability to create and understand sentences is uniquely human. To answer this question, more than 19,000 multisign utterances of an infant chimpanzee (Nim) were analyzed for syntactic and semantic regularities. Lexical regularities were observed in the case of 2-sign combinations: particular signs (e.g. more) tended to occur in a particular position. These regularities could not be attributed to memorization or to position habits, suggesting that they were structurally constrained. That conclusion, however, was invalidated by videotape analyses, which showed that most of Nim's utterances were prompted by his teacher's prior utterance and that Nim interrupted his teachers to a much larger extent than a child interrupts an adult's speech. Signed utterances of other apes (as shown on films) showed similar nonhuman patterns of discourse. (PsycLIT Database Copyright 1981 American Psychological Assn, all rights reserved)
AN: 65-00553

©1986-1995 American Psychological Association.
©1986-1995 SilverPlatter International N.V.

and unpublished manuscripts in a special collection. Holdings might also include records, tapes, and compact discs; films, filmstrips, videos, and interactive videodiscs; drawings, paintings, engravings, and slides.

If your research topic is especially complex or unusual, you may need other resources than those your library offers. In such cases, talk to a librarian about interlibrary loan, a process in which one library borrows materials from another. This procedure can take several weeks for books, but magazine articles are commonly sent by fax in less than a week.

Sources beyond the library

For some topics, you may want to look beyond the library for information. Many organizations, both public and private, willingly mail literature in response to a phone call or a letter. The *Encyclopedia of Associations* lists organizations by their special interests, such as environment or family planning, and provides titles of their publications. Consider also the possibility of learning more about your subject through interviews or experiments that you conduct yourself.

The Internet

The Internet is a computer network through which users can communicate with other users and access material such as journal articles, newsletters, and books. Because of its scope and accessibility, the Internet can help you in several ways that the library can't. In the early stages of a research project, when you are trying to come up with an idea for a paper or to narrow a broad idea into a workable topic, you can get advice and insights from others interested in your topic by participating in "discussion groups." The Internet can also provide access to documents too new or obscure to be included in a library collection.

To use the Internet you need a computer with a modem and an Internet address (which your library may have or which you can procure on your own). Libraries and academic computing centers often offer classes on Internet use. You might also consult one of the many current books on Internet resources. The annual *Directory of Electronic Journals, Newsletters, and Academic Discussion Lists,* published by the Association of Research Libraries, lists specific Internet resources by discipline.

Although the Internet can be a rich source of information, it has limitations. Because anyone with a computer and a modem can publish and communicate on the Internet, some material may be outdated, limited in scope, frivolous, or of questionable authority. You will need to apply your critical reading skills to any material you find on the Internet. (See 50 for more advice on reading critically.)

50

Read critically.

When you read in search of answers to a research question, you must read critically. Critical readers do not just process information; they assess what they read. With their research questions in mind, they seek the truth. And this often means questioning an author's expertise or objectivity, looking for possible flaws in an author's reasoning, and weighing the evidence of one author against evidence presented by others.

You can exercise your critical intelligence at two points: when selecting sources and when doing the actual reading.

50a Read selectively.

As you consult the library's catalog and its periodical indexes, take down bibliographic information only for sources that seem promising (see page 343 for the exact information to take down). Be alert for clues that indicate whether a book or article is worth tracking down. Many of the CD-ROM indexes for magazines and newspapers provide abstracts—brief summaries of articles—that can help you choose which ones to use. Here are some questions to guide you as you make your choices.

> **DECIDING WHETHER TO TRACK DOWN A SOURCE**
> —How relevant to your research question is the work's title?
> —How recent is the source? For current topics, some books or articles may be outdated.

— How long is the source? A very short article may be too general to be helpful.
— Is the source available in your library?

Once you have tracked down a source, preview it quickly to see how much of your attention, if any, it is worth. Techniques for previewing a book and an article are a bit different.

PREVIEWING A BOOK
— Glance through the table of contents, keeping your research question in mind.
— Skim the preface in search of a statement of the author's purposes.
— Using the index, look up a few words related to your research question.
— If a chapter seems useful, read its opening and closing paragraphs and skim any headings.
— Consider the author's style, level, and tone. Does the style invite further reading? Is the level appropriate (neither above nor below your ability to comprehend)? Does the tone suggest a balanced approach?
— If the author's credentials are given on the cover or dust jacket, how relevant are they to the book and your research question?

PREVIEWING AN ARTICLE
— For magazine and journal articles, look for a statement of purpose in the opening paragraphs; look for a possible summary in the closing paragraph.
— For newspaper articles, focus on the headline and the opening sentences, known as the *lead*.
— Skim any headings and take a look at any charts, graphs, diagrams, or illustrations that might indicate the article's focus and scope.

50b Maintain a working bibliography.

Keep a record of any sources that you decide to consult. You will need this record, called a *working bibliography*, when you compile the list of works cited that will appear at the end of your paper. (See pages 396–97 for an example.) Your list of works cited will almost certainly be shorter than your working bibliography, since it will include only the sources that you actually cite in your paper.

You may record bibliographic information about sources in a notebook or on separate 3" × 5" cards. The advantage of 3" × 5" cards is that you can easily arrange them in alphabetical order when you type the list of works cited. (If you have used a computer catalog or index that prints bibliographic information, you can use the printouts as your working bibliography.) For books, you will need the following bibliographic information:

Call number

All authors; any editors or translators

Title and subtitle

Edition (if not the first)

Publishing information: city, publishing company, date

For periodical articles you need this information:

All authors of the article

Title and subtitle of the article

Title of the magazine, journal, or newspaper

Volume and issue numbers, if relevant

Date and page numbers

NOTE: For the exact bibliographic form to be used in the final paper, see 55b.

SAMPLE BIBLIOGRAPHY CARD FOR A BOOK

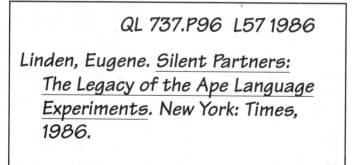

QL 737.P96 L57 1986

*Linden, Eugene. Silent Partners:
    The Legacy of the Ape Language
    Experiments. New York: Times,
    1986.*

SAMPLE BIBLIOGRAPHY CARD FOR A PERIODICAL

> *Lewin, Roger. "Look Who's Talking Now." New Scientist 29 Apr. 1991: 49–52.*

50C Read with a critical eye.

When you read critically, you are not necessarily judging an author's work harshly; you are simply examining its assumptions, assessing its evidence, and weighing its conclusions.

Distinguishing between primary and secondary sources

As you begin assessing the evidence in a text, consider whether you are reading a primary or a secondary source. Primary sources are original documents such as speeches, diaries, novels, legislative bills, laboratory studies, field research reports, or eyewitness accounts. Secondary sources are commentaries on primary sources.

A primary source for Karen Shaw, whose research paper appears beginning on page 384, was an article by Patricia Marks Greenfield and E. Sue Savage-Rumbaugh reporting experiments with the pygmy chimpanzee Kanzi. Shaw also consulted Flora Davis's book *Eloquent Animals*, a secondary source that reports on the studies of several researchers.

Although a primary source is not necessarily more reliable than a secondary source, it has the advantage of being a first-hand account. Naturally, you can better evaluate what a secondary source says if you have first read the primary source and are familiar with it.

Being alert for signs of bias

As you are no doubt aware, some publishers are more objective than others. If you were exploring the conspiracy theories surrounding the Kennedy assassination, for example, you wouldn't look to a supermarket tabloid such as the *National Enquirer* for answers. You would rely instead on newspapers and magazines with a national reputation for fair and objective reporting.

Like publishers, some authors are more objective than others. Few authors are altogether objective, of course, since they are human beings with their own life experiences, values, and beliefs. But if you have reason to believe that an author is particularly biased, you will want to assess his or her arguments with special care.

Here are some questions to ask yourself as you look for possible signs of bias in an author or a publisher.

— Do the author and publisher have reputations for accurate and balanced reporting?
— Does the author or publisher have political leanings or religious views that could affect objectivity?
— Is the author or publisher associated with a special-interest group, such as the National Rifle Association, that tends to see only one side of an issue?
— How fairly does the author treat those with opposing views?
— Does the author's language show signs of bias? (See 47.)

Assessing the author's argument

In nearly all subjects worth writing about, there is some element of argument, so don't be surprised to encounter experts who disagree. When you encounter areas of disagreement, you will want to read your sources' arguments with special care, testing them with your own critical intelligence. Questions such as the following can help you weigh the strengths and weaknesses of each author's argument.

— What is the author's central claim or thesis?
— How does the author support this claim — with relevant and sufficient evidence or with just a few anecdotes or emotional examples?
— Are statistics accurate? Have they been used fairly? (It is possible to "lie" with statistics by using them selectively or by omitting mathematical details.)

—Are any of the author's assumptions questionable?
—Does the author consider opposing arguments and refute them persuasively? (See 46e.)

51

Take notes without plagiarizing.

51a As you read, take notes systematically.

Taking systematic notes as you read will help you remember later, as you are drafting your paper, just which words and phrases belong to your sources and which are your own. This is a crucial matter, for if any language from your sources finds its way into your final draft without quotation marks and proper documentation, you will be guilty of plagiarism, a serious academic offense. (See 53.)

Many researchers use the note card system for taking notes. If you decide to use note cards, purchase a large stack of 3" × 5" or 4" × 6" cards. Write one note on each card so you can shuffle and reshuffle the cards in different orders later as you experiment with the organization of your paper. Put the last name of the author of your source in the upper right corner of the card, and put a subject label in the upper left corner. If you have read enough to form a preliminary outline, use the subdivisions of the outline as subject headings on your cards.

Not every researcher uses note cards. For short research projects, some writers prefer to photocopy important material and underline or highlight key ideas, sometimes color coding the highlighted passages to reflect subdivisions of the topic. In the margins they may write personal comments or cross-references to other sources. Photocopying has the obvious advantage of saving time and labor. For extensive research projects, however, the technique is of limited value since there is no way of physically sorting the highlighted passages into separate batches of information.

A second alternative to note cards, the use of computer software, overcomes this disadvantage. With the appropriate software, you can type notes as you read, coding them to reflect the divisions of your outline. You can then print the notes in sorted batches. For example, Karen Shaw might have printed one batch of notes on the apes' sign language vocabularies, another on their creative uses of language, another on their mastery of grammar, and so on.

Although software programs can be time savers, their advantages should not be oversold. Any style of note taking demands that you read carefully, analyze what you read, and record information with care.

51b As you take notes, avoid unintentional plagiarism.

You will discover that it is amazingly easy to borrow too much language from a source as you take notes. Do not allow this to happen. You are guilty of the academic offense known as plagiarism if you half-copy the author's sentences — either by mixing the author's phrases with your own without using quotation marks or by plugging your synonyms into the author's sentence structure. (For examples of this kind of plagiarism, see 53.)

To prevent unintentional borrowing, resist the temptation to look at the source as you take notes — except when you are quoting. Keep the source close by so you can check for accuracy, but don't try to put ideas in your own words with the source's sentences in front of you. You should also follow this advice while drafting your paper.

There are four kinds of note taking: summarizing, paraphrasing, quoting, and writing personal comments. When you summarize, paraphrase, or quote, be sure to include exact page references, since you will need the page numbers later if you use the information in your paper.

Notes that summarize

Summarizing is the best kind of preliminary note taking because it is the fastest. A summary condenses information, perhaps reducing a chapter to a short paragraph or a paragraph to a single sentence. A summary should be written in your own words; if you use phrases from the source, put them in quotation marks.

Here is a passage from an original source read by Karen Shaw in researching her essay on apes and language. Following the passage is Shaw's note card summarizing it.

ORIGINAL SOURCE
Public and scientific interest in the question of apes' ability to use language first soared some 15 years ago when Washoe, a chimpanzee raised like a human child by R. Allen Gardner and Beatrix T. Gardner of the University of Nevada, learned to make hand signs for many words and even seemed to be making short sentences.

Since then researchers have taught many chimpanzees and a few gorillas and orangutans to "talk" using the sign language of deaf humans, plastic chips or, like Kanzi, keyboard symbols. Washoe, Sarah, a chimpanzee trained by David Premack of the University of Pennsylvania, and Koko, a gorilla trained by the psychologist Francine Patterson, became media stars.

—Eckholm, "Pygmy," p. B7

SUMMARY

> *Types of languages*
> *Eckholm, "Pygmy"*
> The ape experiments began in the 1970s with Washoe, who learned sign language. In later experiments some apes learned to communicate using plastic chips or symbols on a keyboard. (p. B7)

Notes that paraphrase

Like a summary, a paraphrase is written in your own words; but whereas a summary reports significant information in fewer words than the source, a paraphrase retells the information in roughly the same number of words. If you retain occa-

PARAPHRASE

Washoe   *Eckholm, "Pygmy"*

A chimpanzee named Washoe, trained in the early '70s by U. of Nevada professors R. Allen and Beatrix T. Gardner, learned words in the sign language of the deaf and may even have created short sentences. (p. B7)

---

sional choice phrases from the source, use quotation marks so you'll know later which phrases are your own.

As you read the note card at the top of this page, which paraphrases the first paragraph of Shaw's original source (see page 348), notice that the language is significantly different from that in the original. Working with this note card, Shaw was in no danger of unintentional plagiarism.

Notes that quote

A quotation consists of the exact words from a source. In your notes, put all quoted material in quotation marks; do not trust yourself to remember later which words, phrases, and passages you have quoted and which are your own. When you quote, be sure to copy the words of your source exactly, including punctuation and capitalization.

Quotations should be reserved for special purposes: to use a writer's especially vivid or expressive wording, to allow an expert to explain a complex matter clearly, or to let critics of an opinion object in their own words. If you find yourself quoting a great deal in your notes, you are probably wasting time, because your final essay should not contain excessive quotations. (See 54.)

At the top of page 350 is an example of a note card with a quotation from Shaw's original source (page 348).

QUOTATION

> *Washoe   Eckholm, "Pygmy"*
>
> *Washoe, trained by R. Allen and Beatrix T. Gardner, "learned to make hand signs for many words and even seemed to be making short sentences." (p. B7)*

Personal notes

At unexpected moments in your reading, you will experience the lucky accidents typical of the creative process: flashes of insight, connections with other reading, sharp questions, a more restricted topic, ways to set up the arguments of two

PERSONAL COMMENT

> *Types of training*
>
> *Washoe (and I think Koko) were raised almost like children, not in a laboratory setting. Does the setting affect the apes' performance? What about scientific objectivity?*

opposing positions, a vivid scenario. Write these inspirations down before you forget them. An example of such a personal note appears at the bottom of page 350.

52

Sketch a preliminary plan.

A look through your notes will probably suggest many ways to focus and organize your material. Before you begin writing, you should decide on a tentative thesis and construct a preliminary outline or you will flounder among the possibilities. Remain flexible, however, because you may need to revise your approach later. Writing about a subject is a way of learning about it; as you write, your understanding of your subject will almost certainly deepen.

52a Form a tentative thesis.

A thesis is a sentence asserting the main point of your essay (see 2a). If you are writing on a clearly argumentative topic, such as some aspect of the problem of nuclear waste, your thesis should state your informed opinion: that seabed disposal is not as safe as has been claimed, for example, or that because of politics and economics certain states have become dumping grounds for nuclear waste. You should avoid writing a paper that reports information for no apparent purpose. Few instructors want to read a paper that simply lists and describes the methods for disposing of nuclear waste. Most instructors want their students to take a stand.

Even if your subject is not so obviously controversial as nuclear waste, you can still assert a thesis. Nearly all subjects worth writing about contain some element of controversy; that is why scholars so often engage in polite — and sometimes not so polite — arguments.

In researching the topic of apes and language, Karen Shaw, whose paper appears on pages 384–97, encountered a number of scholarly arguments. Some early researchers, such as

Herbert Terrace, discounted the linguistic abilities of gorillas and chimpanzees, arguing that the apes were being cued by their trainers and that they could not form even simple sentences. Other early researchers, such as Francine Patterson, insisted that the apes used language spontaneously (without being cued) and suggested that apes could form primitive sentences. After looking at the evidence, Shaw reached a conclusion: Patterson was right in insisting that the apes had used language spontaneously; Terrace was right in claiming that the apes' ability to form a sentence had not been proved in the early studies. More recent studies, however, convinced Shaw that pygmy chimpanzees may well have the ability to understand and create sentences. Shaw's thesis articulates her assessment of the evidence:

> The great apes resemble humans in language abilities more than researchers once believed, and evidence is mounting that pygmy chimpanzees can understand and perhaps even create sentences.

52b Construct a preliminary outline.

Before committing yourself to a detailed outline, experiment with alternatives. Shuffle and reshuffle your note cards or rearrange your computer notes to get a feeling for the possibilities. After some experimenting, Karen Shaw sorted her notes into three large batches: early ape language studies, recent studies, and the philosophical implications of the ape language research. Then she drafted the following simple outline.

Thesis: The great apes resemble humans in language abilities more than researchers once believed, and evidence is mounting that pygmy chimpanzees can understand and perhaps even create sentences.

I. Early ape language studies showed that apes could acquire significant language skills but failed to prove they could create sentences.

II. Recent research demonstrates that pygmy chimpanzees can understand and perhaps even create sentences.

III. Evidence suggests that linguistic abilities in humans and apes are part of a continuum.

It is a good idea to keep your preliminary outline simple, as Shaw did, since a simple outline is easier to adjust as you gain new insights about your topic while writing the paper. As she drafted each of the three parts of her paper, Shaw sorted her information into smaller batches, which became the basis for her final outline (see pages 385–86).

53

Cite sources; avoid plagiarism.

In a research paper, you will be drawing on the work of other writers, and you must document their contributions by citing your sources. In research writing, sources are cited for two reasons: to alert readers to the sources of your information and to give credit to the writers from whom you have borrowed words and ideas. To borrow another writer's language or ideas without proper acknowledgment is a form of dishonesty known as plagiarism.

53a Use a consistent system for citing sources, such as the MLA style of in-text citations. (See 55 for important details.)

Citations are required when you quote from a source, when you summarize or paraphrase a source, and when you borrow facts and ideas from a source (except for common knowledge). (See also 53b.)

The various academic disciplines use their own editorial styles for citing sources. Most English instructors prefer the Modern Language Association's system of in-text citations. Here, very briefly, is how an MLA in-text citation usually works:

1. The source is introduced by a signal phrase that names its author.
2. The source is followed by a page number in parentheses.
3. At the end of the paper, a list of works cited (arranged alphabetically according to the authors' last names) gives complete publishing information about the source.

SAMPLE IN-TEXT CITATION

According to Eugene Linden, some psychologists have adopted the oddly unscientific attitude that "the idea of the language capacity of apes is so preposterous that it should not be investigated at all" (11).

SAMPLE ENTRY IN THE LIST OF WORKS CITED

Linden, Eugene. Silent Partners: The Legacy of the Ape Language Experiments. New York: Times, 1986.

Handling an MLA citation is not always this simple. When the author is not named in a signal phrase, for example, the parentheses must include the author's last name along with the page number. For a detailed discussion of this and other variations, see 55a.

If your instructor has asked you to use the APA style of in-text citation, consult 56a and 56b. For a list of style manuals used in a variety of disciplines, see 56d.

53b Avoid plagiarism.

Your research paper is a collaboration between you and your sources. To be fair and ethical, you must acknowledge your debt to the writers of these sources. If you don't, you are guilty of plagiarism, a serious academic offense.

Three different acts are considered plagiarism: (1) failing to cite quotations and borrowed ideas, (2) failing to enclose borrowed language in quotation marks, and (3) failing to put summaries and paraphrases in your own words.

Citing quotations and borrowed ideas

You must of course cite all direct quotations. You must also document any ideas borrowed from a source: paraphrases of sentences, summaries of paragraphs or chapters, statistics and little-known facts, and tables, graphs, or diagrams.

The only exception is common knowledge — information that your readers could find in any number of general sources because it is commonly known. For example, the current population of the United States is common knowledge in such fields as sociology and economics; Freud's theory of the unconscious is common knowledge in the field of psychology.

As a rule, when you have seen certain information repeatedly in your reading, you don't need to document it. However, when information has appeared in only one or two sources or when it is controversial, you should document it. If a topic is new to you and you are not sure what is considered common knowledge or what is a matter of controversy, ask someone with expertise. When in doubt, cite the source.

Enclosing borrowed language in quotation marks

To indicate that you are using a source's exact phrases or sentences, you must enclose them in quotation marks unless they have been set off from the text by indenting. (See 54b.) To omit the quotation marks is to claim — falsely — that the language is your own. Such an omission is plagiarism even if you have cited the source.

ORIGINAL SOURCE
No animal has done more to renew interest in animal intelligence than a beguiling, bilingual bonobo named Kanzi, who has the grammatical abilities of a 2½-year-old child and a taste for movies about cavemen.   — Eugene Linden, "Animals," p. 57

PLAGIARISM
According to Eugene Linden, no animal has done more to renew interest in animal intelligence than a beguiling, bilingual bonobo named Kanzi, who has the grammatical abilities of a 2-1/2-year-old child and a taste for movies about cavemen (57).

BORROWED LANGUAGE IN QUOTATION MARKS
According to Eugene Linden, "No animal has done more to renew interest in animal intelligence than a beguiling, bilingual bonobo named Kanzi, who has the grammatical abilities of a 2-1/2-year-old child and a taste for movies about cavemen" (57).

Putting summaries and paraphrases in your own words

When you summarize or paraphrase, it is not enough to name the source; you must restate the source's meaning using your own language. (See also 51.) You are guilty of plagiarism if you half-copy the author's sentences — either by mixing the author's well-chosen phrases without using quotation marks or by plugging your own synonyms into the author's sentence structure. The following paraphrases are plagiarized — even though the source is cited — because their language is too close to that of the original source.

ORIGINAL VERSION
If the existence of a signing ape was unsettling for linguists, it was also startling news for animal behaviorists.
— Davis, *Eloquent Animals,* p. 26

UNACCEPTABLE BORROWING OF PHRASES
The existence of a signing ape unsettled linguists and startled animal behaviorists (Davis 26).

UNACCEPTABLE BORROWING OF STRUCTURE
If the presence of a sign-language-using chimp was disturbing for scientists studying language, it was also surprising to scientists studying animal behavior (Davis 26).

To avoid plagiarizing an author's language, resist the temptation to look at the source while you are summarizing or paraphrasing. Close the book, write from memory, and then open the book to check for accuracy. This technique prevents you from being captivated by the words on the page.

ACCEPTABLE PARAPHRASES
When they learned of an ape's ability to use sign language, both linguists and animal behaviorists were taken by surprise (Davis 26).

According to Flora Davis, linguists and animal behaviorists were unprepared for the news that a

```
chimp could communicate with its trainers through
sign language (26).
```

54

Integrate quotations as smoothly as possible.

If you include too many quotations in a research essay, readers form the impression that you cannot think for yourself. Use quotations only when a source is particularly clear or expressive or when it is important to let the debaters of an issue explain their positions in their own words. Except for this infrequent need for quotations, use your own words to summarize or paraphrase your sources and explain your own ideas.

When you choose to use quotations, make sure that they are integrated smoothly into the text of your paper. Readers should be able to move from your own words to the words you quote without feeling a jolt.

54a Use signal phrases.

Avoid dropping quotations into the text without warning; instead, provide clear signal phrases, usually including the author's name, to prepare readers for the quotation.

DROPPED QUOTATION

```
Although the bald eagle is still listed as an
endangered species, its ever-increasing population
is very encouraging.   "The bald eagle seems to
have stabilized its population, at the very least,
almost everywhere" (Sheppard 96).
```

QUOTATION WITH SIGNAL PHRASE

```
Although the bald eagle is still listed as an
endangered species, its ever-increasing population
```

is very encouraging. According to ornithologist
Jay Sheppard, "The bald eagle seems to have stabi-
lized its population, at the very least, almost
everywhere" (96).

To avoid monotony, try to vary your signal phrases. The
following models suggest a range of possibilities.

In the words of researcher Herbert Terrace, ". . ."
As Flora Davis has noted, ". . ."
The Gardners, Washoe's trainers, point out that ". . ."
". . . ," claims linguist Noam Chomsky.
Psychologist H. S. Terrace offers an odd argument for this
view: ". . ."
Terrace answers these objections with the following analy-
sis: ". . ."

When your signal phrase includes a verb, choose one that
is appropriate in the context. Is your source arguing a point,
making an observation, reporting a fact, drawing a conclusion,
refuting an argument, or stating a belief? By choosing an
appropriate verb, such as one on the following list, you can
make your source's stance clear.

acknowledges	comments	endorses	reasons
adds	compares	grants	refutes
admits	confirms	illustrates	rejects
agrees	contends	implies	reports
argues	declares	insists	responds
asserts	denies	notes	suggests
believes	disputes	observes	thinks
claims	emphasizes	points out	writes

It is not always necessary to quote full sentences from a
source. At times you may wish to borrow only a phrase or to
weave part of a source's sentence into your own sentence
structure.

Bruce Bower reports that Kanzi practices "simple
grammatical ordering rules," such as putting
actions before objects (140).

> Perhaps the best summation of the current state of
> ape language studies comes from biologist Robert
> Seyfarth, who writes that the line separating
> humans from other animals "remains hazily drawn,
> somewhere between the word and the sentence" (18).

54b Set off long quotations.

When you quote more than four typed lines of prose or more than three lines of poetry, set off the quotation by indenting it one inch (or ten spaces) from the left margin. Use the normal right margin and do not single-space.

Long quotations should be introduced by an informative sentence, usually followed by a colon. Quotation marks are unnecessary because the indented format tells readers that the words are taken directly from the source.

> Desmond describes how Washoe tried signing to the
> other apes when the Gardners returned her to an
> ape colony in Oklahoma:
>
>> One particularly memorable day, a snake
>> spread terror through the castaways on
>> the ape island, and all but one fled in
>> panic. This male sat absorbed, staring
>> intently at the serpent. Then Washoe
>> was seen running over signing to him
>> "come, hurry up." (42)

Notice that at the end of an indented quotation the parenthetical citation goes outside the final period.

54c Use the ellipsis mark and brackets to indicate changes you make in a quotation.

Two useful marks of punctuation, the ellipsis mark and brackets, allow you to keep quoted material to a minimum and integrate it smoothly into your text.

The ellipsis mark

To condense a quoted passage, you can use the ellipsis mark (three periods, with spaces between) to indicate that you have omitted words. What remains must be grammatically complete.

```
In a recent New York Times article, Erik Eckholm
reports that "a 4-year-old pygmy chimpanzee . . .
has demonstrated what scientists say are the most
human-like linguistic skills ever documented in
another animal" (A1).
```

The writer has omitted the words *at a research center near Atlanta*, which appeared in the original.

When you want to omit a full sentence or more, use a period before the three ellipsis dots.

```
According to Wade, the horse Clever Hans seemed
to be counting "by tapping out numbers with his
hoof. . . . Clever Hans owes his celebrity to his
master's innocence. Von Osten sincerely believed
he had taught Hans to solve arithmetical problems"
(1349).
```

Ordinarily, do not use an ellipsis mark at the beginning or at the end of a quotation. Your readers will understand that the quoted material is taken from a longer passage. The only exception occurs when you have omitted words at the end of a final quoted sentence.

Obviously you should not use an ellipsis mark to distort the meaning of your source.

Brackets

Brackets (square parentheses) allow you to insert words of your own into quoted material, perhaps to explain a confusing reference or to keep a sentence grammatical in your context.

```
Robert Seyfarth reports that "Premack [a scientist
at the University of Pennsylvania] taught a seven-
year-old chimpanzee, Sarah, that the word for
'apple' was a small, plastic triangle" (13).
```

2	3	4
245/120	246/119	247/118
9	10	11
252/113	253/112	254/111
16	17	18
259/106	260/105	261/104
23	30	24	25
266/99	273/92	267/98	268/97

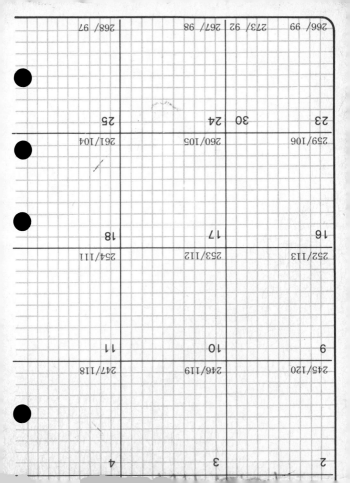

8	9	10	11
220/145	221/144	222/143	223/142
15	16	17	18
227/138	228/137	229/136	230/135
22	23	24	25
234/131	235/130	236/129	237/128
29	30	31	
241/124	242/123	243/122	

Most computers have bracket keys. If you are using a typewriter that has no brackets, you can simply ink them in by hand.

55

MLA documentation

In academic research papers and in any other writing that borrows information from sources, the borrowed information — quotations, summaries, paraphrases, and any facts or ideas that are not common knowledge — must be clearly documented. (See also 53.)

The various academic disciplines use their own editorial styles for citing sources and for listing the works that have been cited. The style described in this section is that of the Modern Language Association (MLA), contained in the *MLA Handbook for Writers of Research Papers* (4th ed., 1995), which recommends that citations be given in the text of the paper rather than in footnotes or endnotes. If your instructor prefers the American Psychological Association (APA) style of in-text citation, see 56, where you will also find a list of style manuals.

55a MLA in-text citations

The Modern Language Association's in-text citations are made with a combination of signal phrases and parenthetical references. A signal phrase indicates that something drawn from a source (such as a quotation, summary, or paraphrase) is about to be used; usually the signal phrase includes the author's name. The parenthetical reference includes at least a page number.

Citations in parentheses should be as concise as possible but complete enough so that readers can find the source in the list of works cited at the end of the paper, where sources are listed alphabetically by the authors' last names. The following models illustrate the form for the MLA style of citation.

Directory to the MLA system

55a: MLA in-text citations

55b: MLA list of works cited

BOOKS

ARTICLES IN PERIODICALS

Directory to the MLA system (*continued*)

CD-ROMS AND ONLINE DATABASES

OTHER SOURCES

NOTE: For a sample research paper documented with the MLA system, see pages 384–97.

AUTHOR NAMED IN A SIGNAL PHRASE Ordinarily, you should introduce the material being cited with a signal phrase that includes the author's name. In addition to preparing readers for the source, the signal phrase allows you to keep the parenthetical citation brief.

> Flora Davis reports that a chimp at the Yerkes
> Primate Research Center "has combined words into
> new sentences that she was never taught" (67).

The signal phrase — "Flora Davis reports" — provides the name of the author; the parenthetical citation gives the page number where the quoted sentence may be found. By looking up the author's last name in the list of works cited, readers will find complete information about the work's title, publisher, and date of publication.

Notice that the period follows the parenthetical citation. For the MLA technique for handling quotations that end in a question mark or exclamation point, see 37f.

AUTHOR NOT NAMED IN A SIGNAL PHRASE   If the signal phrase does not include the author's name (or if there is no signal phrase), the author's last name must appear in parentheses along with the page number.

```
Although the baby chimp lived only a few hours,

Washoe signed to it before it died (Davis 42).
```

TWO OR MORE WORKS BY THE SAME AUTHOR   If your list of works cited includes two or more works by the same author, include the title of the work either in the signal phrase or in abbreviated form in the parenthetical reference.

```
In Eloquent Animals, Flora Davis reports that a

chimp at the Yerkes Primate Research Center "has

combined words into sentences that she was never

taught" (67).
```

```
Flora Davis reports that a chimp at the Yerkes

Primate Research Center "has combined words into

sentences that she was never taught" (Eloquent 67).
```

The title of a book should be underlined, as in the examples just given. The title of an article from a periodical should be put in quotation marks instead.

In the rare case when both the author and a short title must be given in parentheses, the citation should appear as follows:

```
Although the baby chimpanzee lived only for a few

hours, Washoe signed to it before it died (Davis,

Eloquent 42).
```

TWO OR THREE AUTHORS   If your source has two or three authors, name them in the signal phrase or include them in the parenthetical reference.

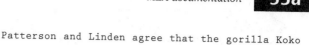

```
Patterson and Linden agree that the gorilla Koko

acquired language more slowly than a normal

speaking child (89).
```

FOUR OR MORE AUTHORS   If your source has four or more authors, include only the first author's name followed by "et al." (Latin for "and others") in the signal phrase or in the parenthetical reference.

```
The study was extended for two years, and only

after results were duplicated on both coasts did

the authors publish their results (Doe et al.

137).
```

CORPORATE AUTHOR   Name the corporate author in the signal phrase or parentheses.

```
The Internal Revenue Service warns businesses that

deductions for "lavish and extravagant entertain-

ment" are not allowed (43).
```

UNKNOWN AUTHOR   If the author is not given, either use the complete title in a signal phrase or use a short form of the title in the parentheses.

```
The UFO reported by the crew of a Japan Air Lines

flight remains a mystery.  Radar tapes did not

confirm the presence of another craft ("Strange

Encounter" 26).
```

AUTHORS WITH THE SAME LAST NAME   If your list of works cited includes works by two or more authors with the same last name, include the first name of the author you are citing in the signal phrase or parenthetical reference.

```
Both Lucy and Koko have been reported to lie

(Adrian Desmond 201).
```

A MULTIVOLUME WORK   If your paper cites more than one volume of a multivolume work, you must indicate in the parentheses which volume you are referring to.

```
Terman's studies of gifted children reveal a pattern

of accelerated language acquisition (2: 279).
```

If your paper cites only one volume of a multivolume work, you will include the volume number in the list of works cited at the end of the paper and will not need to include it in the parentheses.

A NOVEL, A PLAY, OR A POEM In citing literary sources, include information that will enable readers to find the passage in various editions of the work. For a novel, put the page number first and then, if possible, indicate the part or chapter in which the passage can be found.

```
Fitzgerald's narrator captures Gatsby in a moment

of isolation: "A sudden emptiness seemed to flow

now from the windows and the great doors, endowing

with complete isolation the figure of the host"

(56; ch. 3).
```

For a verse play, list the act, scene, and line numbers. Use arabic numerals unless your instructor prefers roman numerals.

```
In his famous advice to the players, Hamlet

defines the purpose of theater, "whose end, both

at the first and now, was and is, to hold, as

'twere, the mirror up to nature" (3.2.21-23).
```

For a poem, cite the part (if there are a number of parts) and the line numbers.

```
When Homer's Odysseus came to the hall of Circe,

he found his men "mild / in her soft spell, fed

on her drug of evil" (10.209-11).
```

A WORK IN AN ANTHOLOGY Put the name of the author of the work (not the editor of the anthology) in the signal phrase or in the parentheses.

```
At the end of Kate Chopin's "The Story of an

Hour," Mrs. Mallard drops dead upon learning that

her husband is alive. In the final irony of the
```

```
story, doctors report that she has died of a "joy
that kills" (25).
```

AN INDIRECT SOURCE   When a writer's or speaker's quoted words appear in a source written by someone else, begin the citation with the abbreviation "qtd. in."

```
"We only used seven signs in his presence," says
Fouts. "All of his signs were learned from the
other chimps at the laboratory" (qtd. in Toner 24).
```

AN ENTIRE WORK   To cite an entire work, use the author's name in a signal phrase or a parenthetical reference.

```
Patterson and Linden provide convincing evidence for
the speech-making abilities of nonhuman primates.
```

TWO OR MORE WORKS   You may want to cite more than one source to document a particular point. Separate the citations with a semicolon.

```
With intensive training, the apes in this study
learned over 200 signs or signals (Desmond 229;
Linden 173).
```

Multiple citations can be distracting to readers, however, so the technique should not be overused. If you want to alert readers to several sources that discuss a particular topic, consider using a bibliographic note instead (see 55c).

A WORK WITHOUT PAGE NUMBERS   You may omit the page number if a work has no page numbers or if a work is only one page long or is organized alphabetically (as with encyclopedias). Some electronic sources use paragraph numbers instead of page numbers. For such sources, use the abbreviation "par." or "pars." in the parentheses: (Smith, par. 4).

55b MLA list of works cited

A list of works cited, which appears at the end of your paper, gives full publishing information for each of the sources you have cited in the paper. Start on a new page and title your list

"Works Cited." Then list in alphabetical order all the sources that you have cited in the paper. Unless your instructor asks for them, sources not actually cited in the paper should not be given in this list, even if you have read them.

Alphabetize the list by the last names of the authors (or editors); if a work has no author or editor, alphabetize by the first word of the title other than *a, an,* or *the.*

Do not indent the first line of each entry in the list of works cited but indent any additional lines five spaces or one-half inch. This technique highlights the names by which the list has been alphabetized. (For a sample list of works cited, see pages 396–97.)

The following models illustrate the forms that the Modern Language Association (MLA) recommends for the works cited entries.

Books

BASIC FORMAT FOR A BOOK   For most books, arrange the information into three units, each followed by a period and one space: (1) the author's name, last name first; (2) the title and sub-title, underlined; and (3) the place of publication, the publisher, and the date.

```
Tompkins, Jane. West of Everything: The Inner Life
     of Westerns. New York: Oxford UP, 1992.
```

The information is taken from the title page and the copyright page. You may use a short form of the publisher's name as long as it is easily identifiable; omit terms such as *Press, Inc.,* and *Co.* except when naming university presses (Harvard UP, for example). If several copyright dates are given, use the most recent one.

TWO OR THREE AUTHORS   Name the authors in the order in which they are presented on the title page; reverse the name of only the first author.

```
Rico, Barbara, and Sandra Mano. American Mosaic:
     Multicultural Readings in Context. Boston:
     Houghton, 1991.
```

The names of three authors are separated by commas.

Bentley, Nicolas, Michael Slater, and Nina Burgis.
The Dickens Index. New York: Oxford UP, 1990.

FOUR OR MORE AUTHORS Cite only the first author, name reversed, followed by "et al." (Latin for "and others").

Medhurst, Martin J., et al. Cold War Rhetoric:
Strategy, Metaphor, and Ideology. New York:
Greenwood, 1990.

EDITORS After the name or names, use the abbreviation "ed." for editor or "eds." for "editors."

Anaya, Rodolfo, and Francisco Lomeli, eds. Aztlán:
Essays on the Chicano Homeland. Albuquerque:
Academia-El Norte, 1989.

AUTHOR WITH AN EDITOR Begin with the author and title, followed by "Ed." and the name of the editor. Use "Ed." (for "edited by") for one or more editors.

Franklin, Benjamin. The Autobiography and Other
Writings. Ed. Kenneth Silverman. New York:
Penguin, 1986.

TRANSLATION List the entry under the name of the author, not the translator. After the title, write "Trans." (for "Translated by") and the name of the translator.

Eco, Umberto. Foucault's Pendulum. Trans. William
Weaver. San Diego: Harcourt, 1989.

CORPORATE AUTHOR List the entry under the name of the corporate author, even if it is also the name of the publisher.

Fidelity Investments. Mutual Brokerage Services
Handbook. Boston: Fidelity Investments, 1993.

UNKNOWN AUTHOR Begin with the title. Alphabetize the entry by the first word of the title other than *a, an,* or *the.*

The Times Atlas of the World. 9th ed. New York:
Times, 1992.

TWO OR MORE WORKS BY THE SAME AUTHOR If your list of works cited includes two or more works by the same author, use the author's name only for the first entry. For subsequent entries use three hyphens followed by a period. The three hyphens must stand for exactly the same name or names as in the preceding entry. List the titles in alphabetical order.

> Gordon, Mary. <u>Good Boys and Dead Girls and Other</u>
> <u>Essays</u>. New York: Viking, 1991.
>
> ---. <u>The Other Side</u>. New York: Viking, 1989.

EDITION OTHER THAN THE FIRST Include the number of the edition after the title.

> Lindemann, Erika. <u>A Rhetoric for Writing Teachers</u>.
> 2nd ed. New York: Oxford UP, 1987.

MULTIVOLUME WORK Include the number of volumes before the city and publisher, using the abbreviation "vols."

> <u>Mark Twain: Collected Tales, Sketches, Speeches,</u>
> <u>and Essays</u>. 2 vols. New York: Library of
> America, 1992.

If your paper cites only one of the volumes, write the volume number before the city and publisher and write the total number of volumes in the work after the date.

> <u>Mark Twain: Collected Tales, Sketches, Speeches,</u>
> <u>and Essays</u>. Vol. 2. New York: Library of
> America, 1992. 2 vols.

ENCYCLOPEDIA OR DICTIONARY List the author of the entry (if any), the entry heading or title, the title of the encyclopedia or dictionary, the edition number (if any), and the date of the edition.

> "Croatia." <u>The New Encyclopaedia Britannica:</u>
> <u>Micropaedia</u>. 1991.

Volume and page numbers are not necessary because the entries are arranged alphabetically and therefore are easy to locate.

If a reference work is not well known, provide full publishing information as well.

WORK IN AN ANTHOLOGY Begin with the author and title of the selection; then give the title and the editor of the anthology. After the publishing information, give the page numbers on which the selection appears.

```
Synge, J. M. "On an Anniversary." The New Oxford
     Book of Irish Verse. Ed. Thomas Kinsella.
     Oxford: Oxford UP, 1986. 318.
```

If an anthology gives original publishing information for a selection, you may cite that information first. Follow with "Rpt. in," the title, editor, and publishing information for the anthology, and the page numbers on which the selection appears.

```
Rodriguez, Richard. "Late Victorians." Harper's
     Oct. 1990: 57-66. Rpt. in The Best American
     Essays 1991. Ed. Joyce Carol Oates. New York:
     Ticknor, 1991. 119-34.
```

TWO OR MORE WORKS FROM THE SAME ANTHOLOGY If you wish, you may cross-reference two or more works from the same anthology. Provide a separate entry for the anthology with complete publication information.

```
Kinsella, Thomas, ed. The New Oxford Book of Irish
     Verse.  Oxford: Oxford UP, 1986.
```

Then list an entry for each selection from the anthology by author and title of the selection with a cross-reference to the anthology. The cross-reference should include the last name of the editor of the anthology and the page numbers in the anthology on which the selection appears.

```
Colum, Padraic. "An Old Woman of the Roads."
     Kinsella 321-22.
Synge, J. M. "On an Anniversary." Kinsella 318.
```

FOREWORD, INTRODUCTION, PREFACE, OR AFTERWORD If in your paper you quote from one of these elements, begin with the name of the writer of that element. Then identify the element being cited, followed by the title of the book, the author, and the editor, if any. After the publishing information, give the page numbers on which the foreword, introduction, preface, or afterword appears.

```
Murray, Charles. Foreword. Unfinished Business: A
     Civil Rights Strategy for America's Third
     Century. By Clint Bolick. San Francisco:
     Pacific Research Inst. for Public Policy,
     1990. ix-xiii.
```

BOOK WITH A TITLE WITHIN ITS TITLE   If the book title contains a title normally underlined, neither underline the internal title nor place it in quotation marks.

```
Abbott, Keith. Downstream from Trout Fishing in
     America: A memoir of Richard Brautigan.
     Santa Barbara: Capra, 1989.
```

If the title within the title is normally enclosed within quotation marks, retain the quotation marks and underline the entire title.

```
Faulkner, Dewey R. Twentieth Century Interpre-
     tations of "The Pardoner's Tale." Englewood
     Cliffs: Spectrum-Prentice, 1973.
```

BOOK IN A SERIES   Before the publishing information, cite the series name followed by the series number, if any.

```
Laughlin, Robert M. Of Cabbages and Kings: Tales
     from Zinacantán. Smithsonian Contributions to
     Anthropology 23. Washington: Smithsonian,
     1977.
```

REPUBLISHED BOOK   After the title of the book, cite the original publication date followed by the current publishing information. If the republished book contains new material, such as an introduction or afterword, include that information after the original date.

```
McClintock, Walter. Old Indian Trails. 1926.
     Foreword William Least Heat Moon. Boston:
     Houghton, 1992.
```

PUBLISHER'S IMPRINT   If a book was published by an imprint of a publishing company, cite the name of the imprint followed by a hyphen and the publisher's name. An imprint name usually precedes the publisher's name on the title page.

```
Oates, Joyce Carol. (Woman) Writer: Occasions and
     Opportunities. New York: Abrahams-Dutton,
     1988.
```

Articles in periodicals

ARTICLE IN A MONTHLY MAGAZINE   In addition to the author, the title of the article, and the title of the magazine, list the month and year and the page numbers on which the article appears. Abbreviate the names of months except May, June, and July.

```
Lukacs, John. "The End of the Twentieth Century."
     Harper's Jan. 1993: 39-58.
```

If the article had appeared on pages 39–40 and 60–62, you would write "39 + " (not "39–62").

ARTICLE IN A WEEKLY MAGAZINE   Handle articles in weekly (or biweekly) magazines as you do those for monthly magazines, but give the exact date of the issue, not just the month and year.

```
Weil, Andrew. "The New Politics of Coca." New
     Yorker 15 May 1995: 70-80.
```

ARTICLE IN A JOURNAL PAGINATED BY VOLUME   Many professional journals continue page numbers throughout the year instead of beginning each issue with page 1; at the end of the year, all of the issues are collected in a volume. Interested readers need only the volume number, the year, and the page numbers to find a particular article.

Segal, Gabriel. "Seeing What Is Not There."

Philosophical Review 98 (1989): 189-214.

ARTICLE IN A JOURNAL PAGINATED BY ISSUE If each issue of the journal begins with page 1, you need to indicate the number of the issue. Simply place a period after the number of the volume, followed by the number of the issue.

Johnson, G. J. "A Distinctiveness Model of Serial

Learning." Psychological Review 98.2 (1991):

204-17.

ARTICLE IN A DAILY NEWSPAPER Begin with the author, if there is one, followed by the title of the article. Next give the name of the newspaper, the date, the section letter or number, and the page number.

Sun, Lena H. "Chinese Feel the Strain of a New

Society." Washington Post 13 June 1993: A1+.

If the section is marked with a number rather than a letter, handle the entry as follows:

Greenhouse, Linda. "Justices Plan to Delve Anew

into Race and Voting Rights." New York Times

11 July 1993, sec. 1: 1+.

If an edition of the newspaper is specified on the masthead, name the edition after the date and before the page reference: eastern ed., late ed., natl. ed., and so on.

UNSIGNED ARTICLE IN A NEWSPAPER OR MAGAZINE Use the same form that you would for an article in a newspaper or a weekly or monthly magazine, but begin with the article title.

"Radiation in Russia." U.S. News & World Report 9

Aug. 1993: 40-42.

EDITORIAL IN A NEWSPAPER Cite an editorial as you would an article with an unknown author, adding the word "Editorial" after the title.

"Limits on Democracy." Editorial. Boston Globe 23

May 1995: 18.

LETTER TO THE EDITOR Cite the writer's name, followed by the word "Letter" and the publishing information for the newspaper or magazine in which the letter appears.

```
Benston, Graham. Letter. Opera Now May 1993: 12.
```

BOOK OR FILM REVIEW Cite first the reviewer's name and the title of the review, if any, followed by the words "Rev. of" and the title and author or director of the work. Add the publishing information for the publication in which the review appears.

```
Shetley, Vernon. "The Changing Light." Rev. of
        A Scattering of Salts, by James Merrill. New
        Republic 5 June 1995: 38.

Holden, Stephen. "A Union of Convenience across a
        Cultural Divide." Rev. of The Wedding
        Banquet, dir. Ang Lee. With Winston Chao, May
        Chin, and Mitchell Lichtenstein. Goldwyn,
        1993. New York Times 4 Aug. 1993: C18.
```

CD-ROMs and online databases

Research material is available in electronic form on CD-ROM (compact disc) from vendors such as SilverPlatter and UMI-Proquest and online from computer services or networks such as Dialog, Nexis, and the Internet. In citations for electronic sources, you give the same publishing information as for other sources and in addition give pertinent information about the electronic source. You may find that some of the information about an electronic source, such as the name of the vendor, is not available. If so, you may omit this information.

CD-ROM ISSUED PERIODICALLY CD-ROM databases that are produced periodically (monthly or quarterly, for example) may contain previously published material, such as journal or newspaper articles, or material that has not been previously published, such as reports. In either case, cite such material as you would a printed source, followed by the title of the database (underlined), the medium (CD-ROM), the name of the company producing the CD-ROM, and the date of the electronic publication.

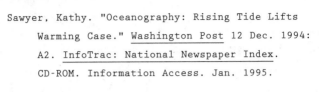
```
Sawyer, Kathy. "Oceanography: Rising Tide Lifts
        Warming Case." Washington Post 12 Dec. 1994:
        A2. InfoTrac: National Newspaper Index.
        CD-ROM. Information Access. Jan. 1995.

Gauch, Patricia Lee. "A Quest for the Heart of
        Fantasy." New Advocate 7.3 (1994): 159-67.
        ERIC. CD-ROM. SilverPlatter. Dec. 1994.
```

CD-ROM ISSUED IN A SINGLE EDITION Some works on CD-ROM, such as dictionaries and encyclopedias, are released in single editions that are not updated periodically. Treat such sources as you would a book, but give the medium (CD-ROM) before the publishing information.

```
The Oxford English Dictionary. 1st ed. CD-ROM.
        Oxford: Oxford UP, 1987.

"O'Keeffe, Georgia." The 1995 Grolier Multimedia
        Encyclopedia. CD-ROM. Danbury: Grolier, 1995.
```

ONLINE MATERIAL FROM A COMPUTER SERVICE Computer services such as Dialog, CompuServe, America Online, and Nexis provide a variety of databases that may be revised continually or periodically. For material from such a source, cite the publication information given in the source, the title of the database (underlined), the medium (Online), and the name of the computer service. In addition, because it is often not possible to determine when material has been entered or updated in the service's database, give the date on which you accessed the material.

```
Bass, Alison. "Women Just as Spatial as Men."
        Boston Globe 22 Feb. 1993, 3rd ed.: 25.
        Boston Globe-File 631. Online. Dialog. 6 Feb.
        1995.

Mann, Charles C., and Mark L. Plummer. "Empowering
        Species." Atlantic Monthly Feb. 1995.
```

```
Atlantic Monthly Online. Online. America
    Online. 16 Feb. 1995.
```

ONLINE MATERIAL FROM A COMPUTER NETWORK A computer network such as the Internet provides access to material such as journal articles, newsletters, and even entire books. For such material, cite whatever publication information is given in the electronic source, using the format for citing a journal article or book. Give the number of pages or paragraphs, followed by "p." (or "pp.") or "par." (or "pars."); if neither is specified, use "n. pag." for "no pagination." In addition, give the title of the database (underlined), the medium (Online), the computer network, and the date you accessed the material. If your instructor wants you to specify the electronic address of the source, place it after the word "Available" at the end of your citation.

```
Spetalnick, Terrie. "Privacy in the Electronic
    Community." EDUCOM Review 28.3 (1993): n.
    pag. Online. Internet. 7 Feb. 1995.
    Available: gopher.cic.net.

Wells, H. G. The War of the Worlds. 1898. Online.
    U. of Minnesota Lib. Internet. 5 Feb. 1995.
    Available: gopher.micro.umn.edu.
```

Other sources

GOVERNMENT PUBLICATION Treat the government agency as the author, giving the name of the government followed by the name of the agency.

```
United States. Natl. Endowment for the Humanities.
    Study Grants for College and University
    Teachers. Washington: GPO, 1993.
```

PAMPHLET Cite a pamphlet as you would a book.

```
United States. Dept. of the Interior. Natl. Park
    Service. Ford's Theatre and the House Where
    Lincoln Died. Washington: GPO, 1989.
```

PUBLISHED DISSERTATION   Cite a published dissertation as you would a book, but after the title add the word "Diss.," the institution name, and the year the dissertation was written.

```
Healey, Robert F. Eleusinian Sacrifices in the
     Athenian Law Code. Diss. Harvard U, 1961. New
     York: Garland, 1990.
```

UNPUBLISHED DISSERTATION   Begin with the author's name, followed by the dissertation title in quotation marks, the word "Diss.," the name of the institution, and the year the dissertation was written.

```
Fedorko, Kathy Anne. "Edith Wharton's Haunted
     House: The Gothic in Her Fiction." Diss.
     Rutgers U, 1987.
```

ABSTRACT OF A DISSERTATION   Give the author's name, the dissertation title in quotation marks, and the abbreviation *DA* or *DAI* (for *Dissertation Abstracts* or *Dissertation Abstracts International*) followed by the volume number, date, and page number. Add the name of the institution at the end.

```
Berkman, Anne Elizabeth. "The Quest for
     Authenticity: The Novels of Toni Morrison."
     DAI 48 (1988): 2059A. Columbia U.
```

PUBLISHED PROCEEDINGS OF A CONFERENCE   Cite published conference proceedings as you would a book, adding information about the conference after the title.

```
Howell, Benita J., ed. Cultural Heritage
     Conservation in the American South. Proc. of
     Southern Anthropology Society. Tampa, 1988.
     Athens: U of Georgia P, 1990.
```

WORK OF ART   Cite the artist's name, followed by the title of the artwork, usually underlined, and the institution and city in which the artwork can be found.

```
Cassatt, Mary. At the Opera. Museum of Fine Arts,
     Boston.
```

MUSICAL COMPOSITION Cite the composer's name, followed by the title of the work. Underline the title of an opera, a ballet, or a composition identified by name, but do not underline or use quotation marks around a composition identified by number or form.

Copland, Aaron. <u>Appalachian Spring</u>.

Shostakovich, Dmitri. Quartet no. 1 in C, op. 49.

PERSONAL LETTER To cite a letter you have received, begin with the writer's name and add the phrase "Letter to the author," followed by the date. For a letter received via electronic mail, use the designation "E-mail."

Cipriani, Karen. Letter to the author. 25 Apr. 1993.

Gray, William A. E-mail to the author. 26 Jan. 1995.

LECTURE OR PUBLIC ADDRESS Cite the speaker's name, followed by the title of the lecture (if any) in quotation marks, the organization sponsoring the lecture, the location, and date.

Quinn, Karen. "John Singleton Copley's <u>Watson and the Shark</u>." Museum of Fine Arts. Boston, 1 July 1993.

PERSONAL INTERVIEW To cite an interview that you conducted, begin with the name of the person interviewed. Then write "Personal interview," followed by the date of the interview.

Harrison, Patricia. Personal interview. 19 Feb. 1993.

PUBLISHED INTERVIEW Name the person interviewed, followed by the word "Interview" and the publication in which the interview was printed. If the interview has a title, put it in quotation marks after the interviewee's name and do not use the word "Interview."

Ehrenreich, Barbara. Interview. <u>The Progressive</u>. Feb. 1995: 34-38.

RADIO OR TELEVISION INTERVIEW Name the person interviewed, followed by the word "Interview." Then give the title of the program, underlined, and identifying information about the broadcast.

> Miller, Sue. Interview. <u>The Connection</u>. WBUR,
>
> Boston. 8 May 1995.

FILM OR VIDEOTAPE   Begin with the title. For a film, cite the director and the names of the lead actors or narrator; for a videotape, give the word "Videotape" followed by the director and the names of the lead actors or narrator. End with the distributor and year and any other pertinent information, such as running time.

> <u>Much Ado about Nothing</u>. Dir. Kenneth Branagh. With
>
> Emma Thompson, Kenneth Branagh, Denzel
>
> Washington, Michael Keaton, and Keanu Reeves.
>
> Goldwyn, 1993.

> <u>Through the Wire</u>. Videotape. Dir. Nina Rosenblum.
>
> Narr. Susan Sarandon. Fox/Lorber Home Video,
>
> 1990. 77 min.

RADIO OR TELEVISION PROGRAM   List the information about the program in this order: the title of the program, underlined; the writer ("By"), director ("Dir."), narrator ("Narr."), producer ("Prod."), or main actors ("With"), if relevant; the network; the local station on which you heard or saw the program, followed by the city; and the date the program was broadcast.

If a television episode or radio segment has a title, the order is as follows: episode or segment title in quotation marks; writer, director, narrator, and so on; title of the program, underlined; network; local station and city; and the date the program was broadcast.

> <u>Be-Bop City</u>. With Michael Anderson. WBGO, Newark.
>
> 23 May 1995.

> "This Old Pyramid." With Mark Lehner and Roger
>
> Hopkins. <u>Nova</u>. PBS. WGBH, Boston. 4 Aug.
>
> 1993.

LIVE PERFORMANCE OF A PLAY   Begin with the title of the play, followed by the author. Then include specific information about the live performance: the director, the major actors, the theater company and its location, and the date of the performance.

> The Sisters Rosensweig. By Wendy Wasserstein.
>> Dir. Daniel Sullivan. With Jane Alexander,
>> Christine Estabrook, and Madeline Kahn.
>> Barrymore, New York. 11 July 1993.

RECORD, TAPE, OR CD   Begin with the composer (or author, if the recording is spoken), followed by the title of the piece. Next list pertinent artists (for instance, the conductor, the pianist, or the reader). End with the company label, the catalog number, and the date.

> Verdi, Giuseppe. Falstaff. With Tito Gobbi, Elisabeth
>> Schwarzkopf, Nan Merriman, and Fedora Barbieri.
>> Cond. Herbert von Karajan. Philharmonica Orch.
>> and Chorus. EMI, 7 49668 2, 1988.

CARTOON   Begin with the cartoonist's name, the title of the cartoon (if it has one) in quotation marks, the word "Cartoon," and the publishing information for the publication in which the cartoon appears.

> Chast, Roz. "Are You All Right?" Cartoon. New
>> Yorker 5 July 1993: 65.

MAP OR CHART   Cite a map or chart as you would a book with an unknown author. Underline the title and add the word "Map" or "Chart" following the title.

> Spain/Portugal. Map. Paris: Michelin, 1992.

COMPUTER SOFTWARE   Begin with the author of the program (if known), the title of the program, underlined, and the words "Computer software." Then name the distributor and the year of publication. At the end of the entry you may add other pertinent information, such as the computer for which the program is designed or the form of the program.

<u>TriplePlayPlus! Spanish</u>. Computer software.
        Syracuse Language Systems, 1995. PC-DOS,
        Microsoft Windows 3.1, 386SX, CD-ROM.

55c Content and bibliographic notes (optional)

Content and bibliographic notes are optional; do not include them unless you have a legitimate need for them. Content notes provide additional information that would interrupt the flow of the paper yet is important enough to include. Bibliographic notes refer readers to sources that contain information about the topic at hand; sometimes they comment on the sources.

Such notes may be either footnotes, which appear at the foot of the page, or endnotes, which appear at the end of the paper, just before the list of works cited. For either style, notes are numbered consecutively throughout the paper. The text of the paper contains a superscript numeral that corresponds to the number of the note.

Content note

TEXT

In spite of claims made for the apes, however, some researchers have questioned whether the apes really learn signs or whether they merely imitate or respond to the cues of their trainers.[1]

NOTE

[1] The most famous example of cuing involves a horse named Clever Hans. The horse's owner sincerely thought that Clever Hans could solve mathematical problems, tapping out the answers with his foot. In fact, the horse was responding to the involuntary jerks of the owner's head at the point when the correct number of taps had been reached.

Bibliographic note

TEXT

The apes' achievements cannot be explained away as the simple results of conditioning or unconscious cuing by trainers.[1]

NOTE

[1] For a discussion of the cuing of animals, see Wade 1349-51.

55d Sample research paper: MLA style

On the following pages is a research paper written by Karen Shaw, a student in a college composition class. Shaw's paper is documented with the MLA style of in-text citations and list of works cited. Annotations in the margins of the paper draw your attention to features of special interest.

In preparing her final manuscript, Shaw consulted the MLA guidelines in 4b of this book. Shaw included a separate title page because her instructor requested one.

Title centered
about one-third
down the page.

Between the Word and the Sentence:

Apes and Language

Writer's name
centered near
middle of page.

Karen Shaw

Name and
section number
of the course,
professor's
name, and date
are centered
near bottom of
page.

English 101, Section 30

Dr. Robert Barshay

2 November 1995

Outline pages
numbered with
small roman
numerals.

Outline

Thesis: The great apes resemble humans in language abilities more than researchers
once believed, and evidence is mounting
that pygmy chimpanzees can understand
and perhaps even create sentences.

Outline begins
with thesis and
uses standard
format.

I. Early ape language studies showed that
apes could acquire significant language
skills, but researchers failed to prove
that apes could create sentences.

A. Apes acquired impressive vocabularies
in sign language and in artificial
languages.

B. Despite charges that they were
responding to cues, apes were using
language spontaneously.

1. They performed well in experiments
that eliminated the possibility of
cuing.

2. They learned signs and symbols from
each other and initiated conversa-
tions on their own.

C. Apes were using language creatively.

1. They invented creative names.

2. They may even have lied and joked.

Sentences are
parallel and
simple.

D. There was once little evidence that
apes could order symbols grammatically
to form sentences.

      1. The apes' sequences of signs were often confusing and repetitious.

      2. Evidence of meaningful sequences was inconclusive.

II. Recent research with Kanzi demonstrates that pygmy chimpanzees can understand and perhaps even create grammatical patterns.

  A. Kanzi can understand grammatically complex spoken English.

  B. Kanzi has picked up simple grammatical patterns from his caretakers.

  C. Kanzi appears to have developed his own patterns.

III. Evidence suggests that linguistic abilities in humans and apes are part of a continuum.

  A. The skeptics tend to apply a double standard: one for very young human children, another for apes.

  B. In our human ancestors, the ability to communicate in language must have preceded language itself.

Shaw 1

Between the Word and the Sentence:
Apes and Language

One afternoon, Koko the gorilla, who was
often bored with language lessons, stubbornly
and repeatedly signaled "red" in American Sign
Language when asked the color of a white
towel. She did this even though she had identified the color white many times before. At
last the gorilla plucked a bit of red lint
from the towel and showed it to her trainer
(Patterson and Linden 80-81). At Yerkes
Primate Center, chimpanzees Sherman and
Austin, who had been taught symbols for foods
and tools, were put in separate rooms. To
obtain food in different containers, one chimp
had to ask the other for a tool, such as a
wrench, by projecting symbols onto a screen
using a computer. After some experimentation,
the chimpanzees succeeded 97 percent of the
time (Marx 1333). These and hundreds of similar scenes played out over the last twenty-
five years demonstrate that the great apes
(gorillas, orangutans, and chimpanzees) resemble humans in language abilities far more than
researchers once thought. And evidence is
mounting, despite opposition from some linguists and psychologists, that the most intelligent of the apes--pygmy chimpanzees--can
understand and perhaps even create sentences.

Title centered and double-spaced.

Citation with author's name and page number in parentheses.

Thesis states writer's conclusions about the ape language experiments.

Shaw 2

Although apes lack the vocal ability to produce human sounds, they have acquired vocabularies in American Sign Language (Ameslan) and in artificial languages. Vocabularies ranging from 100 to 200 signs or symbols have been reported for the gorillas Koko and Michael; for the orangutan Chantek; and for numerous chimpanzees, including Washoe, Nim, Lana, Sherman, Austin, and Kanzi.

The apes' acquisition of these vocabularies is not in dispute, but some researchers have questioned whether the apes are truly learning the signs and symbols. These critics suggest that the apes may be merely imitating their trainers or responding to cues. Psychologist H. S. Terrace, the chief trainer of a chimp named Nim, is one of the most formidable of the skeptics because he was once a believer. Ultimately Terrace concluded that in many cases "the teacher's signs had prompted Nim's signs" (75). Terrace argued that cuing had also played a large role in Beatrix T. Gardner's training of Washoe.

While it is possible that in these early studies many of the apes' signs were in response to cues, Terrace and other critics failed to prove that all of them were. Even as early as 1979, psychologists R. Allen and Beatrix T. Gardner were performing double-

Author named in signal phrase; page number in parentheses at end of quotation.

The writer interprets the evidence; she doesn't just report it.

Shaw 3

blind experiments that prevented any possibility
of cuing (Sebeok and Umiker-Sebeok 81-82). When
Terrace criticized these experiments, he failed
to mention the double-blind technique.

Perhaps the most convincing evidence that the
apes have not been simply responding to cues is
that they have used signs or symbols spontaneously
among themselves. Francine Patterson's gorillas
Koko and Michael sign to one another, with Michael
occasionally using signs that he could have learned
only from Koko. "Even more intriguing," write
Patterson and Linden, "is his variation of the
tickle sign depending on whom he is conversing
with" (176).

The most dramatic instances of spontaneous
signing have involved Washoe. In 1976, she had a
baby, and although the baby chimp lived only a
few hours, Washoe signed to it before it died
(Davis 42). Later, another baby chimpanzee
placed in Washoe's care mastered more than 50
signs in Ameslan without help from humans
(Toner). When the Gardners returned Washoe to an
ape colony in Oklahoma, she desperately signaled
to humans from whom she was separated by a moat,
and from the start she signaled to other apes.
Adrian Desmond vividly describes Washoe's efforts
to converse:

> Frustrated by lack of conversation-
> alists, she [Washoe] even tried

For variety, the signal phrase is placed between parts of the quotations.

The writer supports her point with examples from a variety of sources.

No page number needed for Toner because the article is one page long.

Brackets indicate words not in original source.

talking to dogs. . . . One particularly memorable day, a snake spread
terror through . . . the ape island,
and all but one fled in panic. Then
Washoe was seen running over signing
to him "come, hurry up." (42)

In addition to learning signs and using
them spontaneously, apes have used language
creatively. Koko has signed "finger bracelet"
to describe a ring and "bottle match" for a
cigarette lighter (Patterson and Linden 146).
The Gardners' Lucy is reported to have called
an onion "cry fruit" and a radish "cry hurt
food" (Desmond 40). And the pygmy chimpanzee
Kanzi has punched symbols for "campfire" and
"TV" to ask to see Quest for Fire, a film
about early primates discovering fire
(Eckholm, "Kanzi" C3).

Apes who invent creative names are not
simply learning by rote. They are adapting
language for their own purposes. And those
purposes, it turns out, may even include lying
and joking. In a recent personal interview,
Professor Esther Robbins, who worked with
Francine Patterson's gorilla Michael for seven
months, pointed out how difficult it is to
verify such uses of language quantitatively.
What counts as language is "a very gray area,"
she says. "But you know that animal, and

Ellipsis dots
indicate words
deleted from
original source.

Quotation
longer than
four lines is
indented 1"
(or ten spaces);
quotation
marks are
omitted; no
period used
after citation.

Citation
includes short
title because
two works by
Eckholm
appear in list
of works cited.

Use of personal
interview as
source.

Shaw 5

there is very definitely communication, even
lying and joking."

Although the great apes have demonstrated
significant language skills, one central question remains: Can they be taught to use that
uniquely human language tool we call grammar, to
learn the difference, for instance, between "ape
bite human" and "human bite ape"? In other
words, can an ape create a sentence?

A clear transi-
tion prepares
readers for
next major
point.

Apes have used multisign sequences, but
until recently there was little convincing evidence that the combinations displayed a grasp of
grammar. Many of the sequences seemed confusing
and repetitious, such as Nim's longest sequence:
"give orange me give eat orange me eat orange
give me eat orange give me you" (Terrace et al.
895). Currently, however, E. Sue Savage-
Rumbaugh's studies on the pygmy chimpanzee Kanzi
are making even the skeptics take notice. Young
Kanzi had played in the lab while his mother was
being tutored in a language of symbols, and when
he was two and a half, his mother was sent away
for breeding. "To the scientists' amazement,"
writes Erik Eckholm, "he had been learning symbols out of the corner of his eye. He hit the
symbol for apple, then proved he knew what he
was saying by picking an apple from an assort-
ment of foods" ("Kanzi" C1).

Citation of a
work with
four or more
authors.

Short title
needed
because two
works by
Eckholm
appear in list
of works cited.

Impressed by Kanzi's ability to pick up

language without explicit training, Savage-
Rumbaugh decided to replace rote learning with
"a more naturalistic approach": Kanzi would
learn language much the way human children do
(Lewin 50). Consequently, Kanzi's linguistic
development has taken place not in a laboratory
but in a fifty-five-acre forest, which he roams
in the company of his caretakers. During games
of tag and hide-and-seek and other childhood
activities, Kanzi communicates with his caregivers on a computerized keyboard equipped with
a voice synthesizer. A word is spoken each time
Kanzi touches a symbol on the board.

　　　　Evidence of Kanzi's linguistic progress was
published in 1991, when Kanzi was ten. The
results show that he can understand grammatically complex spoken English and he seems to be
developing a primitive grammar. In their studies of Kanzi and his half sister Mulika, Savage-
Rumbaugh and members of her team have taken
great care to avoid cuing. Lewin reports that
spoken instructions to Kanzi were "delivered by
someone out of his sight" and that the other team
members "could not hear the instructions and so
could not cue Kanzi, even unconsciously" (51).
When Kanzi correctly responded to sentences like
"Can you put the raisins in the bowl?" his caretakers made the instructions more difficult.
For example, in response to the question "Can

Citation
appears after
quotation
mark and
before period.

you go to the colony room and get the telephone?"
Kanzi brought back the telephone even though
there were other objects in the room.

Most surprising is Kanzi's apparent grasp of
grammar. The first grammatical rule that Kanzi
began to display was to put action before object
(as in "hide peanut" and "grab Kanzi"), a pattern
probably picked up from his caregivers. In 1985,
Eckholm reported that Kanzi's "two and three word
statements are often made without prompting, sys-
tematically add useful information and represent
his own creative responses to novel situations"
("Pygmy" B7). In the first month of study,
Kanzi showed no understanding of grammatical
ordering, but gradually he began to pick it up.
Patricia Marks Greenfield and E. Sue Savage-
Rumbaugh point out that this developmental trend
"was also found for human children at the two-
word stage" (559).

At times Kanzi deviated from the grammar of
his keepers and began to develop his own patterns, an ability that may be more impressive
than picking up rules from keepers. Without
prompting, Kanzi began to combine gestures and
symbols, usually pointing to the symbol first.
For example, Ann Gibbons reports that when Kanzi
wanted to visit the lab's dog, "he would point
to the symbol for dog, then make a gesture for
'go'" (1561). Perhaps even more significant is

Clear topic
sentences, like
this one, used
throughout
paper.

Citation of a
work with two
authors.

Shaw 8

the pattern that Kanzi developed on his own in
combining various symbols. According to Gibbons,
"When he gave an order combining two symbols
for action--such as 'chase' and 'hide'--it was
important to him that the first action--'chase'--be
done first" (1561). Kanzi's consistency in combining symbols suggests that he has at least a
rudimentary grasp of grammar.

Smooth transi-
tion links sec-
ond and third
parts of paper
(parts II and III
of outline).

Quotation set
off from text
is clearly
introduced.

If Kanzi and other pygmy chimpanzees continue
to develop grammatical patterns, the implications
for the study of human evolution could be profound.
Anthropologist Richard Leakey and coauthor Roger
Lewin pose the issue like this:

> Is spoken language merely an extension
> and enhancement of cognitive capaci-
> ties to be found among our ape rela-
> tives? Or is spoken language a
> unique human characteristic completely
> separate from any cognitive abilities
> in apes? (240)

In quotations
set off from
text, final
punctuation
mark goes
before paren-
theses.

Leakey and Lewin believe that there is a
continuity in linguistic ability between apes
and humans. Linguist Noam Chomsky believes the
opposite. Chomsky describes the entire ape
language field as gripped by "sentimental confusion" and dismisses the studies on Kanzi with a
flippant analogy: "To maintain that Kanzi has
language ability is like saying a man can fly
because he can jump in the air" (qtd. in Booth).
This is certainly strong language from a man

Citation of
indirect source
(words quoted
in another
source).

Shaw 9

who, in the words of Ann Gibbons, has not even
"seen the new data--and doesn't care to" (1562).

Skeptics such as Chomsky seem to be applying a double standard when they compare apes'
linguistic abilities to those of young human
children. As Savage-Rumbaugh puts it, "When
children make up novel words it is called lexical
innovation, but when chimpanzees do the same
thing it is called ambiguous" (qtd. in Lewin 51).
The double standard issue is unlikely to be
resolved any time soon, however, because the
methodologies used in studies of human children
are different from--and possibly less rigorous
than--those used in the ape language studies.

Certainly no one expects any chimpanzee to
perform linguistically far beyond the level of a
very young human child. After all, a chimpanzee's
brain is only one-third the size of our own.
But the brains of the ancestors of Homo sapiens
at some point were of similar size. Surely it
makes more sense that an animal with whom we
share 99 percent of our genetic makeup would at
least have the inklings in its brain of the
ability to communicate in language. And surely
the ability to communicate in language in our
human ancestors came before language itself.
Maybe I am "sentimental," to use Chomsky's word,
but when I read about Kanzi's achievements, it
is difficult not to believe that there is some
commonality of abilities.

The writer
addresses
opposing
arguments.

No citation
needed for
"common
knowledge."

The writer ends
with her own
stand on the
controversy.

List of works
cited begins
on separate
page.

Heading, cen-
tered, 1" from
top of page.

List alpha-
betized by
authors' last
names.

First line of
entry is at left
margin; sub-
sequent lines
indent 1/2" (or
five spaces).

Works Cited

Booth, William. "Monkeying with Language: Is Chimp Using Words or Merely Aping Handlers?" Washington Post 29 Oct. 1990: A3.

Davis, Flora. Eloquent Animals: A Study in Animal Communication. New York: Coward, 1978.

Desmond, Adrian. The Ape's Reflexion. New York: Wade-Dial, 1979.

Eckholm, Erik. "Kanzi the Chimp: A Life in Science." New York Times 25 June 1985, local ed.: C1+.

---. "Pygmy Chimp Readily Learns Language Skill." New York Times 24 June 1985, local ed.: A1+.

Gibbons, Ann. "Déjà Vu All Over Again: Chimp-Language Wars." Science 251 (1991): 1561-62.

Greenfield, Patricia Marks, and E. Sue Savage-Rumbaugh. "Grammatical Combination in Pan paniscus: Processes of Learning and Invention in the Evolution and Development of Language." "Language" and Intelligence in Monkeys and Apes: Comparative Developmental Perspectives. Ed. Sue Taylor Parker and Kathleen Rita Gibson. Cambridge: Cambridge UP, 1990. 540-78.

Leakey, Richard, and Roger Lewin. Origins Reconsidered: In Search of What Makes Us Human. New York: Doubleday, 1992.

Lewin, Roger. "Look Who's Talking Now." New
    Scientist 29 Apr. 1991: 49-52.

Marx, Jean L. "Ape-Language Controversy Flares
    Up." Science 207 (1980): 1330-33.

Patterson, Francine, and Eugene Linden. The
    Education of Koko. New York: Holt, 1981.

Robbins, Esther. Personal interview. 17 Oct. 1995.

Sebeok, Thomas A., and Jean Umiker-Sebeok.
    "Performing Animals: Secrets of the Trade."
    Psychology Today Nov. 1979: 78-91.

Terrace, H. S. "How Nim Chimpsky Changed My
    Mind." Psychology Today Nov. 1979: 65-76.

Terrace, H. S., et al. "Can an Ape Create a
    Sentence?" Science 206 (1979): 891-902.

Toner, Mike. "Loulis, the Talking Chimp."
    National Wildlife Feb.-Mar. 1986: 24.

Double-spacing
used through-
out.

56

APA and other styles

In the social sciences, you will usually be asked to use the American Psychological Association (APA) style of in-text citations. These citations refer readers to a list of references at the end of the paper. The following models are consistent with advice given in the *Publication Manual of the American Psychological Association* (4th ed., 1994).

If you have been asked to use a style other than MLA or APA, see 56d.

56a APA in-text citations

The APA's in-text citations provide at least the author's last name and the date of publication. For direct quotations, a page number is given as well.

NOTE: In the models that follow, notice that APA style requires the use of the past tense or present perfect tense in signal phrases introducing material that has been cited: *Smith reported, Smith has argued.* (See 28a.)

BASIC FORMAT FOR A QUOTATION Ordinarily, introduce the quotation with a signal phrase that includes the author's last name followed by the date of publication in parentheses. Put the page number (preceded by "p.") in parentheses at the end of the quotation.

```
As Davis (1978) reported, "If the existence of a
signing ape was unsettling for linguists, it was also
startling news for animal behaviorists" (p. 26).
```

When the author's name does not appear in the signal phrase, place the author's last name, the date, and the page number in parentheses at the end of the quotation. Use commas between items in the parentheses: (Davis, 1978, p. 26).

Directory to the APA system

NOTE: For a sample APA research paper, see pages 408–17.

BASIC FORMAT FOR A SUMMARY OR A PARAPHRASE   For a summary or a paraphrase, include the author's last name and the date either in a signal phrase or in parentheses at the end.

```
According to Davis (1978), when they learned of an
ape's ability to use sign language, both linguists
and animal behaviorists were taken by surprise.
```

```
When they learned of an ape's ability to use sign
language, both linguists and animal behaviorists
were taken by surprise (Davis, 1978).
```

NOTE: A page number is not required, but you should provide one if it would help your readers find a specific page in a long work.

A WORK WITH TWO AUTHORS   Name both authors in the signal phrase or parentheses each time you cite the work. In the parentheses, use "&" between the authors' names; in the signal phrase, use "and."

```
Patterson and Linden (1981) agreed that the
gorilla Koko acquired language more slowly than
a normal speaking child.
```

```
Koko acquired language more slowly than a normal
speaking child (Patterson & Linden, 1981).
```

A WORK WITH THREE TO FIVE AUTHORS   Identify all authors in the signal phrase or the parentheses the first time you cite the source.

```
The study noted a fluctuating divorce rate in
Middletown from the 1920s to the 1970s (Caplow,
Bahr, Chadwick, Hill, & Williamson, 1982).
```

In subsequent citations, use the first author's name followed by "et al." in either the signal phrase or the parentheses.

```
While the incidence of wife abuse may not be
higher than in the past, the researchers found
```

```
that women are more willing to report it (Caplow
et al., 1982).
```

A WORK WITH SIX OR MORE AUTHORS Use only the first author's name followed by "et al." in all citations.

```
Communes in the 1960s functioned like extended
families, with child-rearing responsibilities
shared by all adult members (Berger et al., 1971).
```

UNKNOWN AUTHOR If the author is not given, either use the complete title in a signal phrase or use the first two or three words of the title in the parenthetical citation.

```
The UFO reported by the crew of a Japan Air Lines
flight remains a mystery.  Radar tapes did not
confirm the presence of another craft ("Strange
Encounter," 1987).
```

If "Anonymous" is specified as the author, treat it as if it were a real name: (Anonymous, 1987). In the list of references, also use the name Anonymous as author.

CORPORATE AUTHOR If the author is a government agency or other corporate organization with a long and cumbersome name, spell out the name the first time you use it in a citation, followed by an abbreviation in brackets. In later citations, simply use the abbreviation.

```
FIRST CITATION:   (National Institute of Mental Health
                  [NIMH], 1995).

LATER CITATIONS:  (NIMH, 1995).
```

TWO OR MORE WORKS IN THE SAME PARENTHESES When your parenthetical citation names two or more works, put them in the same order that they appear in the list of references, separated by semicolons: (Berger et al., 1971; Smith, 1995).

AUTHORS WITH THE SAME LAST NAME To avoid confusion, use initials with the last names if your list of references contains two or more authors with the same last name.

```
Research by J. A. Smith (1994) revealed that. . . .
```

PERSONAL COMMUNICATION Unpublished personal communications should be cited by initials, last name, and precise date.

```
L. Smith (personal communication, October 12,
1995) predicted that government funding of this
type of research will end soon.
```

Do not include personal communications in your list of references.

56b APA references (bibliographic list)

In APA style, the alphabetical list of works cited is entitled "References." The general principles are as follows.

1. Invert *all* authors' names and use initials instead of first names. With two or more authors, use an ampersand (&) rather than the word "and." Separate the names with commas.
2. Use all authors' names; do not use "et al."
3. Place the date of publication in parentheses immediately after the last author's name.
4. Underline titles and subtitles of books; capitalize only the first word of the title and subtitle (as well as all proper nouns).
5. Do not place titles of articles in quotation marks, and capitalize only the first word of the title and subtitle (and all proper nouns). Capitalize names of periodicals as you would capitalize them ordinarily (see 45c). Underline the volume number of periodicals.
6. Use the abbreviation "p." (or "pp." for plural) before page numbers of newspaper articles and works in anthologies, but do not use it before page numbers of articles appearing in magazines and scholarly journals.
7. You may use a short form of the publisher's name as long as it is easily identifiable.
8. Alphabetize your list by the last name of the author (or editor); if there is no author or editor, alphabetize by the first word of the title other than *a, an,* or *the.*
9. Unless your instructor suggests otherwise, do not indent the first line of an entry but indent any additional lines

one-half inch (or five spaces). This technique, known as a "hanging indent," is used for final copy: student papers and actual journal articles. (For manuscripts submitted to journals, APA requires paragraph-style indents that are then converted to hanging indents.)

Books

BASIC FORMAT FOR A BOOK

Schaller, G. B. (1993). <u>The last panda.</u> Chicago: University of Chicago Press.

TWO OR MORE AUTHORS

Eggan, P. D., & Kauchall, D. (1992). <u>Educational psychology: Classroom connections.</u> New York: Merrill.

Caplow, T., Bahr, H. M., Chadwick, B. A., Hill, R., & Williamson, M. H. (1982). <u>Middletown families: Fifty years of change and continuity.</u> Minneapolis: University of Minnesota Press.

CORPORATE AUTHOR When the author is an organization, the publisher is often the same organization. In such a case, give the publisher's name as "Author."

Fidelity Investments. (1993). <u>Fidelity Brokerage Services handbook.</u> Boston: Author.

UNKNOWN AUTHOR

<u>The Times atlas of the world</u> (9th ed.). (1992). New York: Times Books.

EDITORS

Fox, R. W., & Lears, T. J. J. (Eds.). (1993). <u>The power of culture: Critical essays in American history.</u> Chicago: University of Chicago Press.

TRANSLATION

Miller, A. (1990). The untouched key: Tracing
    childhood trauma in creativity and destruc-
    tiveness (H. & H. Hannum, Trans.). New York:
    Doubleday. (Original work published 1988)

EDITION OTHER THAN THE FIRST

Cavanaugh, J. C. (1993). Adult development and
    aging (2nd ed.). Pacific Grove, CA:
    Brooks/Cole.

WORK IN AN ANTHOLOGY

Ochs, E., & Schieffelin, B. (1984). Language
    acquisition and socialization: Three develop-
    mental stories. In R. Schweder & R. Levine
    (Eds.), Culture theory: Essays in mind, self,
    and emotion (pp. 276-320). New York:
    Cambridge University Press.

A MULTIVOLUME WORK Include the number of volumes
before the city and publisher, using the abbreviation "Vols."

Wiener, P. (Ed.). (1973). Dictionary of the history
    of ideas (Vols. 1-4). New York: Scribner's.

If your paper cites only one of the volumes, include the volume
number before the city and publisher.

Wiener, P. (Ed.). (1973). Dictionary of the history
    of ideas (Vol. 2). New York: Scribner's.

TWO OR MORE WORKS BY THE SAME AUTHOR Use the author's
name for first and subsequent entries. Arrange the entries by
date, the earliest first.

Davis, F. (1973). Inside intuition: What we know
    about nonverbal communication. New York:
    McGraw-Hill.

Davis, F. (1978). Eloquent animals: A study in
    animal communication. New York: Coward,
    McCann & Geoghegan.

Articles in periodicals

ARTICLE IN A JOURNAL PAGINATED BY VOLUME

Block, N. (1992). Begging the question: Against
    phenomenal consciousness. Behavioral and
    Brain Sciences, 15, 205-206.

ARTICLE IN A JOURNAL PAGINATED BY ISSUE

Searle, J. (1990). Is the brain a digital
    computer? Proceedings of the American
    Philosophical Association, 64(3),
    21-37.

ARTICLE IN A MAGAZINE

Jamison, K. R. (1995, February). Manic-depressive
    illness and creativity. Scientific American,
    272, 62-67.

ARTICLE IN A DAILY NEWSPAPER

McGrory, B. (1995, May 23). Pathways to college.
    The Boston Globe, pp. 1, 12-13.

UNSIGNED ARTICLE IN A MAGAZINE OR NEWSPAPER Begin with
the title of the article and alphabetize the entry by the first
word of the title other than *a, an,* or *the.*

EMFs on the brain. (1995, January 21). Science
    News, 141, 44.

LETTER TO THE EDITOR

Fuller, K. S. (1993). The issue of ivory [Letter
    to the editor]. Audubon, 95(4), 12.

REVIEW

Blaut, J. M. (1993). [Review of the book Global
    capitalism: Theories of societal development].
    Science and Society, 57(1), 106-107.

TWO OR MORE WORKS BY THE SAME AUTHOR IN THE SAME YEAR
Cite the works according to the usual style, and arrange them
alphabetically by title. Add lowercase letters beginning with
"a," "b," and so on within the parentheses immediately following the year.

Eckholm, Erik. (1985a, June 25). Kanzi the chimp:
    A life in science. The New York Times, pp.
    C1, C3.

Eckholm, Erik. (1985b, June 24). Pygmy chimp
    readily learns language skill. The New York
    Times, pp. A1, B7.

Other sources

MATERIAL FROM AN INFORMATION SERVICE OR A DATABASE   Cite
the material as you would any other material, including all
publishing information. At the end of the citation add the name
of the service (such as ERIC) and the number the service
assigns to the material.

Horn, P. (1989). The Victorian governess. History
    of Education, 18, 333-344. (ERIC Document
    Reproduction Service No. EJ 401 533)

DISSERTATION ABSTRACT

Pellman, J. L. (1988). Community integration: Its
    influence on the stress of widowhood
    (Doctoral dissertation, University of
    Missouri, 1988). Dissertation Abstracts
    International, 49, 2367.

GOVERNMENT DOCUMENT

U.S. Bureau of the Census. (1989). <u>Statistical abstract of the United States</u> (109th ed.). Washington, DC: U.S. Government Printing Office.

PROCEEDINGS OF A CONFERENCE

Waterhouse, L. H. (1982). Maternal speech patterns and differential development. In C. E. Johnson & C. L. Thew (Eds.), <u>Proceedings of the Second Annual International Study of Child Language</u> (pp. 442-454). Washington, DC: University Press of America.

COMPUTER PROGRAM

<u>Notebuilder</u> [Computer software]. (1993). Palo Alto, CA: Pro/Tem.

VIDEOTAPE

National Geographic Society (Producer). (1987). <u>In the shadow of Vesuvius</u> [Videotape]. Washington, DC: National Geographic Society.

56c Sample research paper: APA style

On the following pages is a research paper written by Karen Shaw, a student in a psychology class. Shaw's assignment was to write a "review of the literature" paper documented with the APA style of citations and references. Shaw received permission from her instructor to review the literature written by psychologists studying the linguistic abilities of apes, a topic she had previously investigated in an English class (see pages 384–97). Shaw's two papers are quite different both in the approach and in their styles of documentation.

In preparing her final manuscript, Shaw followed the APA guidelines in 4b of this book. She did not include an abstract because her instructor did not require one.

Short title and
page number
for student
papers.

                 Apes and Language   1

Full title,
writer's name,
name and
section number
of the course,
instructor's
name, and date,
all centered and
double-spaced.

                 Apes and Language:

            A Review of the Literature

                  Karen Shaw

           Psychology 110, Section 2

              Professor Verdi

               April 4, 1996

Full title, centered.

Apes and Language:

A Review of the Literature

Over the past twenty-five years, researchers have demonstrated that the great apes (chimpanzees, gorillas, and orangutans) resemble humans in language abilities more than had been thought possible. Just how far that resemblance extends, however, has been a matter of some controversy. Researchers agree that the apes have acquired fairly large vocabularies in American Sign Language and in artificial languages, but they have drawn quite different conclusions in addressing the following questions:

1. How spontaneously have apes used language?

2. How creatively have apes used language?

3. Can apes create sentences?

4. What are the implications of the ape language studies?

This review of the literature on apes and language focuses on these four questions.

How Spontaneously Have Apes Used Language?

In an influential article, Terrace, Petitto, Sanders, and Bever (1979) argued that the apes in language experiments were not using language spontaneously, that they were merely imitating their trainers, responding to conscious

The writer sets up her organization in the introduction.

Headings, centered, help readers follow the organization.

A signal phrase names all four authors and gives date in parentheses.

or unconscious cues. Terrace and his colleagues at
Columbia University had trained a chimpanzee, Nim,
in American Sign Language, so their skepticism
about the apes' abilities received much attention.
In fact, funding for ape language research was
sharply reduced following publication of their 1979
article "Can an Ape Create a Sentence?"

In retrospect, the conclusions of Terrace et
al. seem to have been premature. Although some of
the early ape language studies had not been rigor-
ously controlled to eliminate cuing, even as early
as 1979 R. A. Gardner and B. T. Gardner were conducting double-blind experiments that prevented any
possibility of cuing (Sebeok & Umiker-Sebeok,
1979). Since 1979, researchers have diligently
guarded against cuing. For example, Lewin (1991)
reported that instructions for pygmy chimpanzee
Kanzi were "delivered by someone out of his sight,"
with other team members wearing earphones so that
they "could not hear the instructions and so could
not cue Kanzi, even unconsciously" (p. 51).

There is considerable evidence that apes
have signed to one another spontaneously, without
trainers present. Like many of the apes studied,
gorillas Koko and Michael have been observed
signing to one another (Patterson & Linden,
1981). At Central Washington University the baby
chimpanzee Loulis, placed in the care of an

Because the
authors of the
work are not
named in the
signal phrase,
their names
appear in
parentheses,
along with the
date.

For quota-
tions, a page
number pre-
ceded by "p."
appears in
parentheses.

An ampersand
links the
names of two
authors in
parentheses.

older, signing chimpanzee, mastered more than fifty signs in American Sign Language without help from humans. "We only used seven signs in his presence," said psychologist Roger Fouts. "All of his signs were learned from the other chimps in the laboratory" (Toner, 1986, p. 24).

The extent to which chimpanzees spontaneously use language may depend on their training. Terrace trained Nim using the behaviorist technique of operant conditioning, so it is not surprising that many of Nim's signs were cued. Many other researchers have used a conversational approach that parallels the process by which human children acquire language. In an experimental study, O'Sullivan and Yeager (1989) contrasted the two techniques, using Terrace's Nim as their subject. They found that Nim's use of language was significantly more spontaneous under conversational conditions.

How Creatively Have Apes Used Language?

There is considerable evidence that apes have invented creative names. One of the earliest and most controversial examples involved the Gardners' chimpanzee Washoe. Washoe, who knew the signs for "water" and "bird," once signed "water bird" when in the presence of a swan. Terrace et al. (1979) suggested that there was "no basis for concluding that Washoe was characterizing the swan as a 'bird

The word *and* links the names of two authors in the signal phrase

When this article was first cited, all four authors were named. In subsequent citations of a work with three to five authors, "et al." is used after the first author's name.

Research Guide

that inhabits water.' " Washoe may simply
have been "identifying correctly a body of
water and a bird, in that order" (p. 895).

Other examples are not so easily
explained away. The pygmy chimpanzee Kanzi
has requested particular films by combining
symbols in a creative way. For instance, to
ask for Quest for Fire, a film about early
primates discovering fire, Kanzi began to use
symbols for "campfire" and "TV" (Eckholm,
1985). And the gorilla Koko has a long list
of creative names to her credit: "elephant
baby" to describe a Pinocchio doll, "finger
bracelet" to describe a ring, "bottle match"
to describe a cigarette lighter, and so on
(Patterson & Linden, 1981, p. 146). If
Terrace's analysis of the "water bird" example
were applied to the examples just mentioned,
it would not hold. Surely Koko did not first
see an elephant and then a baby before signing
"elephant baby"--or a bottle and a match
before signing "bottle match."

Can Apes Create Sentences?

The early ape language studies offered
little proof that apes could combine symbols
into grammatically ordered sentences. Apes
strung together various signs, but the
sequences were often random and repetitious.
Nim's series of sixteen signs is a case in

The writer
interprets the
evidence; she
doesn't just
report it.

Apes and Language   6

point: "give orange me give eat orange me eat
orange give me eat orange give me you"
(Terrace et al., 1979, p. 895). The Gardners
were impressed by Washoe's multisign
sequences, seeing in them the beginnings of
some grasp of grammar, but their findings have
been disputed. In one frequently cited film
sequence, Washoe's teacher placed a baby doll
in a cup. Washoe signed "baby in baby in my
drink," a series of signs that seemed to make
grammatical sense. Terrace et al. noted, however, that Washoe had previously been drilled
in similar patterns and that the teacher had
pointed to the objects.

Recent studies with pygmy chimpanzees at
the Yerkes Primate Center in Atlanta are
breaking new ground. Kanzi, a pygmy chimpanzee trained by E. S. Savage-Rumbaugh, seems
to understand simple grammatical rules about
lexigram order. For instance, Kanzi learned
that in two-word utterances action precedes
object, an ordering also used by human children at the two-word stage. In a major new
article reporting on their research,
Greenfield and Savage-Rumbaugh (1990) wrote
that Kanzi rarely "repeated himself or formed
combinations that were semantically unrelated"
(p. 556).

More important, Kanzi began on his own to

The writer
draws atten-
tion to an
important
article.

create certain patterns that may not exist in
English but can be found among deaf children
and in other human languages. For example,
Kanzi used his own rules when combining action
symbols. Lexigrams that involved an invitation
to play, such as "chase," would appear first;
lexigrams that indicated what was to be done
during play ("hide") would appear second.
Kanzi also created his own rules when combining
gestures and lexigrams. He would use the lexigram first and then gesture, a practice often
followed by young deaf children (Greenfield &
Savage-Rumbaugh, 1990, p. 560).

> The writer gives a page number for this summary because the article is long.

What Are the Implications of the Ape
Language Studies?

Kanzi's linguistic abilities are so impressive that they may help us understand how humans
came to acquire language. Pointing out that 99%
of our genetic material is held in common with
the chimpanzees, Greenfield and Savage-Rumbaugh
(1990) have suggested that something of the "evo-
lutionary root of human language" can be found in
the "linguistic abilities of the great apes"
(p. 540). Noting that apes' brains are similar
to those of our human ancestors, Leakey and Lewin
(1992) argued that in ape brains "the cognitive
foundations on which human language could be
built are already present" (p. 244).

The suggestion that there is a continuity in

Apes and Language   8

the linguistic abilities of apes and humans has
created much controversy. Linguist Noam Chomsky
has strongly asserted that language is a unique
human characteristic (Booth, 1990). Terrace
has continued to be skeptical of the claims
made for the apes, as have Petitto and Bever,
coauthors of the 1979 article that caused such
skepticism earlier (Gibbons, 1991). However,
according to Lewin (1991), "Many psychologists
are extremely impressed with Kanzi and the
implications of the observations" (p. 52).

The writer presents a balanced view of the philosophical controversy.

    Although the ape language studies con-
tinue to generate controversy, researchers
have shown over the past twenty-five years
that the gap between the linguistic abilities
of apes and humans is far less dramatic than
was once believed.

The tone of the conclusion is objective.

Apes and Language   9

References

Booth, W. (1990, October 29). Monkeying with
        language: Is chimp using words or merely
        aping handlers? The Washington Post, p. A3.
Eckholm, E. (1985, June 25). Kanzi the chimp: A
        life in science. The New York Times, pp.
        C1, C3.
Gibbons, A. (1991). Déjà vu all over again:
        Chimp-language wars. Science, 251, 1561-
        1562.
Greenfield, P. M., & Savage-Rumbaugh, E. S.
        (1990). Grammatical combination in Pan
        paniscus: Processes of learning and inven-
        tion in the evolution and development of
        language. In S. T. Parker & K. R. Gibson
        (Eds.), "Language" and intelligence in
        monkeys and apes: Comparative developmen-
        tal perspectives (pp. 540-578). Cambridge:
        Cambridge University Press.
Leakey, R., & Lewin, R. (1992). Origins recon-
        sidered: In search of what makes us human.
        New York: Doubleday.
Lewin, R. (1991, April 29). Look who's talking
        now. New Scientist, 130, 49-52.
O'Sullivan, C., & Yeager, C. P. (1989). Communi-
        cative context and linguistic competence:
        The effect of social setting on a chim-
        panzee's conversational skill. In R. A.
        Gardner, B. T. Gardner, & T. E. Van

List of refer-
ences appears
on a separate
page.

Heading is
centered.

List is alpha-
betized by
authors' last
names.

In student
papers the
first line of an
entry is at left
margin; subse-
quent lines
indent 1/2" (or
five spaces).
(See pp.
402–03.)

Double-
spacing used
throughout

Cantfort (Eds.), Teaching sign language to chimpanzees (pp. 269-279). Albany: SUNY Press.

Patterson, F., & Linden, E. (1981). The education of Koko. New York: Holt, Rinehart & Winston.

Sebeok, T. A., & Umiker-Sebeok, J. (1979, November). Performing animals: Secrets of the trade. Psychology Today, 13, 78-91.

Terrace, H. S., Petitto, L. A., Sanders, R. J., & Bever, T. G. (1979). Can an ape create a sentence? Science, 206, 891-902.

Toner, M. (1986, February-March). Loulis, the talking chimp. National Wildlife, 24, 24.

56d List of style manuals

Rules for Writers describes two commonly used systems of documentation: MLA in-text citations, used in English and the humanities (see 55) and APA in-text citations, used in psychology and the social sciences (see 56 a–c). Following is a list of style manuals used in a variety of disciplines.

BIOLOGY

Council of Biology Editors. *Scientific Style and Format: The CBE Manual for Authors, Editors, and Publishers.* 6th ed. New York: Cambridge UP, 1994.

CHEMISTRY

Dodd, Janet S., ed. *The ACS Style Guide: A Manual for Authors and Editors.* Washington: American Chemical Soc., 1986.

ENGLISH AND THE HUMANITIES (SEE 55.)

Gibaldi, Joseph. *MLA Handbook for Writers of Research Papers.* 4th ed. New York: Modern Language Assn. of America, 1995.

University of Chicago Press. *The Chicago Manual of Style.* 14th ed. Chicago: U of Chicago P, 1993.

GEOLOGY

Cochran, Wendell, Peter Fenner, and Mary Hills, eds. *Geowriting: A Guide to Writing, Editing, and Printing in Earth Science.* Alexandria, VA: American Geological Inst., 1984.

GOVERNMENT DOCUMENTS

Garner, Diane L. *The Complete Guide to Citing Government Information Resources: A Manual for Writers and Librarians.* Rev. ed. Bethesda: Congressional Information Service, 1993.

United States Government Printing Office. *Manual of Style.* Washington: GPO, 1988.

JOURNALISM

Associated Press Staff. *Associated Press Stylebook and Libel Manual.* Reading, MA: Addison, 1992.

LAW

The Bluebook: A Uniform System of Citation. Comp. editors of *Columbia Law Review* et al. 15th ed. Cambridge: Harvard Law Review, 1991.

LINGUISTICS

Linguistic Society of America. "LSA Style Sheet." Published annually in the December issue of the *LSA Bulletin*.

MATHEMATICS

American Mathematical Society. *A Manual for Authors of Mathematical Papers*. Rev. ed. Providence: AMS, 1990.

MEDICINE

Iverson, Cheryl, et al. *American Medical Association Manual of Style*. 8th ed. Baltimore: Williams and Wilkins, 1989.

MUSIC

Holoman, D. Kern, ed. *Writing about Music: A Style Sheet from the Editors of* 19th-Century Music. Berkeley: U of California P, 1988.

PHYSICS

American Institute of Physics. *AIP Style Manual*. 4th ed. New York: AIP, 1990.

PSYCHOLOGY AND THE SOCIAL SCIENCES (SEE 56a~c.)

American Psychological Association. *Publication Manual of the American Psychological Association*. 4th ed. Washington: APA, 1994.

SCIENCE AND TECHNICAL WRITING

Rubens, Philip, ed. *Science and Technical Writing: A Manual of Style*. New York: Holt, 1992.

The Basics

57

Parts of speech

Traditional grammar recognizes eight parts of speech: noun, pronoun, verb, adjective, adverb, preposition, conjunction, and interjection. Many words can function as more than one part of speech. For example, depending on its use in a sentence, the word *paint* can be a noun (*The paint is wet*) or a verb (*Please paint the ceiling next*).

57a Nouns

A noun is the name of a person, place, thing, or idea. Nouns are often but not always signaled by an article (*a, an, the*).

> The *cat* in *gloves* catches no *mice*.

Nouns sometimes function as adjectives modifying other nouns. Because of their dual function, nouns used in this manner may be called *noun/adjectives*.

> You can't make a *silk* purse out of a *sow's* ear.

Nouns are classified for a variety of purposes. When capitalization is the issue, we speak of *proper* versus *common nouns* (see 45a). If the problem is one of word choice, we may speak of *concrete* versus *abstract nouns* (see 18b). The distinction between *count nouns* and *noncount nouns* is useful primarily for nonnative speakers of English (see 30a, 30b). The term *collective noun* refers to a set of nouns that may cause problems with subject-verb or pronoun-antecedent agreement (see 21e and 22b).

EXERCISE 57–1

Underline the nouns (and noun/adjectives) in the following sentences. Answers to lettered sentences appear in the back of the book. Example:

> Idle hands are the devil's workshop.

a. Clothe an idea in words, and it loses its freedom of movement.
—Egon Freidell

b. Pride is at the bottom of all great mistakes.   —John Ruskin

c. The trouble with being in the rat race is that even if you win, you're still a rat.   —Lily Tomlin

d. The ultimate censorship is the flick of the dial.
—Tom Smothers

e. Figures won't lie, but liars will figure.   —Anonymous

1. Conservatism is the worship of dead revolutions.
—Clinton Rossiter

2. Luck is a matter of preparation meeting opportunity.
—Oprah Winfrey

3. Problems are only opportunities in work clothes.
—Henry Kaiser

4. A woman must have money and a room of her own.
—Virginia Woolf

5. Prejudice is the child of ignorance.   —William Hazlitt

57b Pronouns

A pronoun is a word used in place of a noun. Usually the pronoun substitutes for a specific noun, known as its *antecedent*.

When the *wheel* squeaks, *it* is greased.

Although most pronouns function as substitutes for nouns, some can function as adjectives modifying nouns.

This hanging will surely be a lesson to me.

Because they have the form of a pronoun and the function of an adjective, such pronouns may be called *pronoun/adjectives*.

Pronouns are classified as personal, possessive, intensive and reflexive, relative, interrogative, demonstrative, indefinite, and reciprocal. Most of the pronouns in English are listed in this section.

PERSONAL PRONOUNS Personal pronouns refer to specific persons or things. They always function as noun equivalents.

SINGULAR   I, me, you, she, her, he, him, it

PLURAL   we, us, you, they, them

POSSESSIVE PRONOUNS Possessive pronouns indicate ownership.

SINGULAR my, mine, your, yours, her, hers, his, its

PLURAL our, ours, your, yours, their, theirs

Some of these possessive pronouns function as adjectives modifying nouns: *my, your, his, her, its, our, their.*

INTENSIVE AND REFLEXIVE PRONOUNS Intensive pronouns emphasize a noun or another pronoun (The senator *herself* met us at the door). Reflexive pronouns, which have the same form as intensive pronouns, name a receiver of an action identical with the doer of the action (Paula cut *herself*).

SINGULAR myself, yourself, himself, herself, itself

PLURAL ourselves, yourselves, themselves

RELATIVE PRONOUNS Relative pronouns introduce subordinate clauses functioning as adjectives (The man *who robbed us* was never caught). In addition to introducing the clause, the relative pronoun, in this case *who,* points back to a noun or pronoun that the clause modifies (*man*). (See 59b.)

who, whom, whose, which, that

INTERROGATIVE PRONOUNS Interrogative pronouns introduce questions (*Who* is expected to win the election?).

who, whom, whose, which, what

DEMONSTRATIVE PRONOUNS Demonstrative pronouns identify or point to nouns. Frequently they function as adjectives (*This* chair is my favorite), but they may also function as noun equivalents (*This* is my favorite chair).

this, that, these, those

INDEFINITE PRONOUNS Indefinite pronouns refer to nonspecific persons or things. Most are always singular (*everyone, each*); some are always plural (*both, many*); a few may be singular or plural (see 21d). Most indefinite pronouns function as noun equivalents (*Something* is burning), but some can also function as adjectives (*All* campers must check in at the lodge).

all	anything	everyone	nobody	several
another	both	everything	none	some
any	each	few	no one	somebody
anybody	either	many	nothing	someone
anyone	everybody	neither	one	something

RECIPROCAL PRONOUNS Reciprocal pronouns refer to individual parts of a plural antecedent (By turns, we helped *each other* through college).

each other, one another

NOTE: Pronouns cause a variety of problems for writers. See Pronoun-antecedent agreement (22), Pronoun reference (23), Distinguishing between pronouns such as *I* and *me* (24), and Distinguishing between *who* and *whom* (25).

EXERCISE 57–2

Underline the pronouns (and pronoun/adjectives) in the following sentences. Answers to lettered sentences appear in the back of the book. Example:

Beware of persons <u>who</u> are praised by <u>everyone</u>.

a. Every society honors its live conformists and its dead trouble-makers.   — Mignon McLaughlin
b. Watch the faces of those who bow low.   — Polish proverb
c. I have written some poetry that I myself don't understand.
                                                — Carl Sandburg
d. I am firm. You are obstinate. He is a pig-headed fool.
                                                —Katherine Whitehorn
e. I must govern the clock, not be governed by it.   — Golda Meir

1. Doctors can bury their mistakes, but architects can only advise their clients to plant vines.   — Frank Lloyd Wright
2. Nothing is interesting if you are not interested.
                                                — Helen MacInness
3. We will never have friends if we expect to find them without fault.   — Thomas Fuller
4. The gods help those who help themselves.   — Aesop
5. You never find yourself until you face the truth.   — Pearl Bailey

57c Verbs

The verb of a sentence usually expresses action (*jump, think*) or being (*is, become*). It is composed of a main verb possibly preceded by one or more helping verbs:

MV

The best fish *swim* near the bottom.

HV   MV

A marriage *is* not *built* in a day.

HV   HV   MV

Even God *has been defended* with nonsense.

Notice that words can intervene between the helping and the main verb (*is* not *built*).

Helping verbs

There are twenty-three helping verbs in English: forms of *have, do,* and *be,* which may also function as main verbs; and nine modals, which function only as helping verbs. The forms of *have, do,* and *be* change form to indicate tense; the nine modals do not.

FORMS OF *HAVE, DO,* AND *BE*

have, has, had

do, does, did

be, am, is, are, was, were, being, been

MODALS

can, could, may, might, must, shall, should, will, would

The phrase *ought to* is often classified as a modal as well.

Main verbs

The main verb of a sentence is always the kind of word that would change form if put into these test sentences:

BASE FORM	Usually I (*walk, ride*).
PAST TENSE	Yesterday I (*walked, rode*).
PAST PARTICIPLE	I have (*walked, ridden*) many times before.

PRESENT PARTICIPLE   I am (*walking, riding*) right now.

-*S* FORM   Usually he/she/it (*walks, rides*).

If a word doesn't change form when slipped into these test sentences, you can be certain that it is not a main verb. For example, the noun *revolution,* though it may seem to suggest an action, can never function as a main verb. Just try to make it behave like one (*Today I revolution . . . Yesterday I revolutioned . . .*) and you'll see why.

When both the past-tense and the past-participle forms of a verb end in *-ed,* the verb is regular (*walked, walked*). Otherwise, the verb is irregular (*rode, ridden*). (See 27a.)

The verb *be* is highly irregular, having eight forms instead of the usual five: the base form *be;* the present-tense forms *am, is,* and *are;* the past-tense forms *was* and *were;* the present participle *being;* and the past participle *been.*

Helping verbs combine with the various forms of main verbs to create tenses. For a survey of tenses, see 28a.

NOTE: Some verbs are followed by words that look like prepositions but are so closely associated with the verb that they are a part of its meaning. These words are known as *particles.* Common verb-particle combinations include *bring up, call off, drop off, give in, look up, run into,* and *take off.*

> A lot of parents *pack up* their troubles and *send* them *off* to camp.
>   —Raymond Duncan

NOTE: Verbs cause many problems for writers. See Subject-verb agreement (21), Standard English verb forms (27), Verb tense, mood, and voice (28), and ESL problems with verbs (29).

EXERCISE 57–3

Underline the verbs in the following sentences, including helping verbs and particles. If a verb is part of a contraction (such as *is* in *isn't* or *would* in *I'd*), underline only the letters that represent the verb. Answers to lettered sentences appear in the back of the book. Example:

> A full cup must be carried steadily.

a. Great persons have not commonly been great scholars.
                                              —Oliver Wendell Holmes, Sr.

b. Without the spice of guilt, can sin be fully savored?
—Alexander Chase

c. One arrow does not bring down two birds.   —Turkish proverb

d. If love is the answer, could you please rephrase the question?
—Lily Tomlin

e. Don't scald your tongue in other people's broth.
—English proverb

1. Do not needlessly endanger your lives until I give you the signal.
—Dwight D. Eisenhower

2. The road to ruin is always kept in good repair.   —Anonymous

3. Love your neighbor, but don't pull down the hedge.
—Swiss proverb

4. I'd rather have roses on my table than diamonds around my neck.
—Emma Goldman

5. He is a fine friend. He stabs you in the front.
—Leonard Louis Levinson

57d Adjectives

An adjective is a word used to modify, or describe, a noun or pronoun. An adjective usually answers one of these questions: Which one? What kind of? How many?

the *lame* elephant [Which elephant?]

rare valuable old stamps [What kind of stamps?]

sixteen candles [How many candles?]

Adjectives usually precede the words they modify. However, they may also follow linking verbs, in which case they describe the subject. (See 58b.)

Good medicine always tastes *bitter*.

Articles, sometimes classified as adjectives, are used to mark nouns. There are only three: the definite article *the* and the indefinite articles *a* and *an*.

A country can be judged by *the* quality of its proverbs.

NOTE: Writers sometimes misuse adjectives (see 26b). Speakers of English as a second language may have trouble placing adjectives correctly (see 31d); they may also encounter problems with articles (see 30).

57e Adverbs

An adverb is a word used to modify, or qualify, a verb (or verbal), an adjective, or another adverb. It usually answers one of these questions: When? Where? How? Why? Under what conditions? To what degree?

> Pull *gently* at a weak rope. [Pull how?]
>
> Read the best books *first*. [Read when?]

Adverbs modifying adjectives or other adverbs usually intensify or limit the intensity of the word they modify.

> Be *extremely* good, and you will be *very* lonesome.

The negators *not* and *never* are classified as adverbs.

NOTE: Writers sometimes misuse adverbs (see 26a). Speakers of English as a second language may have trouble placing adverbs correctly (see 31d).

EXERCISE 57–4

Underline the adjectives and circle the adverbs in the following sentences. If a word is a pronoun in form but an adjective in function, treat it as an adjective. Also treat the articles *a, an,* and *the* as adjectives. Answers to lettered sentences appear in the back of the book. Example:

> A wild goose (never) laid a tame egg.

a. General notions are generally wrong.
— Lady Mary Wortley Montagu
b. The American public is wonderfully tolerant. — Anonymous
c. Gardening is not a rational act. — Margaret Atwood
d. Hope is a very thin diet. — Thomas Shadwell
e. Sleep faster. We need the pillows. — Yiddish proverb

1. I'd rather be strongly wrong than weakly right.
— Tallulah Bankhead
2. Their civil discussions were not interesting, and their interesting discussions were not civil. — Lisa Alther
3. Money will buy a pretty good dog, but it will not buy the wag of its tail. — Josh Billings

4. A little sincerity is a dangerous thing, and a great deal of it is absolutely fatal. — Oscar Wilde
5. An old quarrel can be easily revived. — Italian proverb

57f Prepositions

A preposition is a word placed before a noun or pronoun to form a phrase modifying another word in the sentence. The prepositional phrase nearly always functions as an adjective or as an adverb. (See 59a.)

The road *to hell* is usually paved *with good intentions.*

To hell functions as an adjective, modifying the noun *road; with good intentions* functions as an adverb, modifying the verb *is paved.*

There are a limited number of prepositions in English. The most common ones are included in the following list.

about	beyond	next	through
above	but	of	throughout
across	by	off	till
after	concerning	on	to
against	considering	onto	toward
along	despite	opposite	under
among	down	out	underneath
around	during	outside	unlike
as	except	over	until
at	for	past	unto
before	from	plus	up
behind	in	regarding	upon
below	inside	respecting	with
beside	into	round	within
besides	like	since	without
between	near	than	

Some prepositions are more than one word long. *Along with, as well as, in addition to,* and *next to* are common examples.

NOTE: Except for certain idiomatic uses (see 18d), prepositions cause few problems for native speakers of English. For second language speakers, however, prepositions can cause considerable difficulty (see 29d and 31f).

57g Conjunctions

Conjunctions join words, phrases, or clauses, and they indicate the relation between the elements joined.

COORDINATING CONJUNCTIONS A coordinating conjunction is used to connect grammatically equal elements. The coordinating conjunctions are *and, but, or, nor, for, so,* and *yet.*

Poverty is the parent of revolution *and* crime.

Admire a little ship, *but* put your cargo in a big one.

In the first sentence, *and* connects two nouns; in the second, *but* connects two independent clauses.

CORRELATIVE CONJUNCTIONS Correlative conjunctions come in pairs: *either . . . or; neither . . . nor; not only . . . but also; whether . . . or; both . . . and.* Like coordinating conjunctions, they connect grammatically equal elements.

Either Jack Sprat *or* his wife could eat no fat.

SUBORDINATING CONJUNCTIONS A subordinating conjunction introduces a subordinate clause and indicates its relation to the rest of the sentence. (See 59b.) The most common subordinating conjunctions are *after, although, as, as if, because, before, even though, if, in order that, rather than, since, so that, than, that, though, unless, until, when, where, whether,* and *while.*

If you want service, serve yourself.

CONJUNCTIVE ADVERBS A conjunctive adverb may be used with a semicolon to connect independent clauses; it usually serves as a transition between the clauses. The most common conjunctive adverbs are *consequently, finally, furthermore, however, moreover, nevertheless, similarly, then, therefore,* and *thus.* (See page 264 for a more complete list.)

When we want to murder a tiger, we call it sport; *however,* when the tiger wants to murder us, we call it ferocity.

NOTE: The ability to distinguish between conjunctive adverbs and coordinating conjunctions will help you avoid comma splices and make punctuation decisions (see 20, 32a, and 34b). The ability to recognize subordinating conjunctions will help you avoid sentence fragments (see 19).

57h Interjections

An interjection is a word used to express surprise or emotion (*Oh! Hey! Wow!*).

58

Sentence patterns

Most English sentences flow from subject to verb to any objects or complements. The vast majority of sentences conform to one of these five patterns:

    subject / verb / subject complement

    subject / verb / direct object

    subject / verb / indirect object / direct object

    subject / verb / direct object / object complement

    subject / verb

Adverbial modifiers (single words, phrases, or clauses) may be added to any of these patterns, and they may appear nearly anywhere — at the beginning, the middle, or the end.

    Predicate is the grammatical term given to the verb plus its objects, complements, and adverbial modifiers.

58a Subjects

The subject of a sentence names who or what the sentence is about. The *complete subject* is usually composed of a *simple subject,* always a noun or pronoun, plus any words or word groups modifying the simple subject. To find the complete subject, ask Who? or What?, insert the verb, and finish the question. The answer is the complete subject.

```
 ┌── COMPLETE SUBJECT ──┐
```
The purity of a revolution usually lasts about two weeks.

Who or what lasts about two weeks? *The purity of a revolution.*

```
 ┌──────── COMPLETE SUBJECT ────────┐
```
Historical books that contain no lies are extremely tedious.

Who or what are extremely tedious? *Historical books that contain no lies.*

```
       COMPLETE SUBJECT
        ┌──────┐
```
In every country the sun rises in the morning.

Who or what rises in the morning? *The sun.* Notice that *In every country the sun* is not a sensible answer to the question. *In every country* is a prepositional phrase modifying the verb *rises.* Since sentences frequently open with such modifiers, it is not safe to assume that the subject must always appear first in a sentence.

To find the simple subject, strip away all modifiers in the complete subject. This includes single-word modifiers such as *the* and *historical,* phrases such as *of a revolution,* and subordinate clauses such as *that contain no lies.*

```
  ┌─ SS ─┐
```
The purity of a revolution usually lasts about two weeks.

```
  ┌─ SS ─┐
```
Historical books that contain no lies are extremely tedious.

```
        ┌SS┐
```
In every country *the sun* rises in the morning.

A sentence may have a compound subject containing two or more simple subjects joined with a coordinating conjunction such as *and, but,* or *or.*

```
  ┌── SS ──┐      ┌── SS ──┐
```
Much industry and little conscience make us rich.

Occasionally a verb's subject is understood but not present in the sentence. In imperative sentences, which give advice or commands, the subject is understood to be *you.*

[*You*] Hitch your wagon to a star.

Although the subject ordinarily comes before the verb, occasionally it does not. When a sentence begins with *There is* or *There are* (or *There was* or *There were*), the subject follows the verb. The word *There* is an expletive in such constructions, an empty word serving merely to get the sentence started.

┌── SS ──┐
There is *no substitute for victory*.

Occasionally a writer will invert a sentence for effect.

┌─SS─┐
Happy is *the nation that has no history*.

Happy is an adjective, so it cannot be the subject. Turn this sentence around and its structure becomes obvious: *The nation that has no history is happy*.

In questions, the subject frequently appears in an unusual position, sandwiched between parts of the verb.

┌SS┐
Do *married men* make the best husbands?

Turn the question into a statement, and the words will appear in their usual order: *Married men do make the best husbands*. (*Do make* is the verb.)

NOTE: The ability to recognize the subject of a sentence will help you edit for a variety of problems such as Sentence fragments (19), Subject-verb agreement (21), and Distinguishing between pronouns such as *I* and *me* (24). If English is not your native language, see also 31a and 31b.

EXERCISE 58–1

In the following sentences, underline the complete subject and write *ss* above the simple subject(s). If the subject is an understood *you*, insert it in parentheses. Answers to lettered sentences appear in the back of the book. Example:

   ss   *ss*
Fools and their money are soon parted.

a. A spoiled child never loves its mother. — Sir Henry Taylor
b. To some lawyers, all facts are created equal.

                           — Felix Frankfurter

c. Speak softly and carry a big stick. —Theodore Roosevelt
d. There is nothing permanent except change. —Heraclitus
e. The only difference between a rut and a grave is their dimensions. —Ellen Glasgow

1. The secret of being a bore is to tell everything. —Voltaire
2. Don't be humble. You're not that great. —Golda Meir
3. In every country dogs bite. —English proverb
4. The wind and the waves are always on the side of the ablest navigators. —Anonymous
5. There are no signposts in the sea. —Vita Sackville-West

58b Verbs, objects, and complements

Section 57c explains how to find the verb of a sentence, which consists of a main verb possibly preceded by one or more helping verbs. A sentence's verb is classified as linking, transitive, or intransitive, depending on the kinds of objects or complements the verb can (or cannot) take.

Linking verbs and subject complements

Linking verbs take subject complements, words or word groups that complete the meaning of the subject by either renaming it or describing it.

$$\overbrace{\text{The quarrels of friends}}^{\text{S}} \overbrace{\text{are}}^{\text{V}} \overbrace{\text{the opportunities of foes.}}^{\text{SC}}$$

$$\overbrace{\text{Love}}^{\text{S}} \overbrace{\text{is}}^{\text{V}} \overbrace{\text{blind.}}^{\text{SC}}$$

When the simple subject complement renames the subject, it is a noun or pronoun, such as *opportunities;* when it describes the subject, it is an adjective, such as *blind.*

Linking verbs are usually a form of *be: be, am, is, are, was, were, being, been.* Verbs such as *appear, become, feel, grow, look, make, prove, remain, seem, smell, sound,* and *taste* are linking when they are followed by a word group that names or describes the subject.

Transitive verbs and direct objects

A transitive verb takes a direct object, a word or word group that names a receiver of the action.

```
 ┌──── S ────┐ ┌─V─┐ ┌──────── DO ──────────┐
```
The little snake studies the ways of the big serpent.

In such sentences, the subject and verb alone will seem incomplete. Once we have read "The little snake studies," for example, we want to know the rest: The little snake studies what? The answer to the question What? (or Whom?) is the complete direct object: *the ways of the big serpent.* The simple direct object is always a noun or pronoun, in this case *ways.* To find it, simply strip away all modifiers.

Transitive verbs usually appear in the active voice, with the subject doing the action and a direct object receiving the action. Active-voice sentences can be transformed into the passive voice, with the subject receiving the action instead. See 58c.

Transitive verbs, indirect objects, and direct objects

The direct object of a transitive verb is sometimes preceded by an indirect object, a noun or pronoun telling to whom or for whom the action of the sentence is done.

```
 S    V   IO ┌─DO─┐   S┌──V──┐ IO ┌──DO─┐
```
You show me a hero, and I will write you a tragedy.

The simple indirect object is always a noun or pronoun. To test for an indirect object, insert the word *to* or *for* before the word or word group in question. If the sentence makes sense, the word or word group is an indirect object.

You show [to] me a hero, and I will write [for] you a tragedy.

An indirect object may be turned into a prepositional phrase using *to* or *for: You show a hero to me, and I will write a tragedy for you.*

Only certain transitive verbs take indirect objects. Common examples are *give, ask, bring, find, get, hand, lend, offer, pay, pour, promise, read, send, show, teach, tell, throw,* and *write.*

Transitive verbs, direct objects, and object complements

The direct object of a transitive verb is sometimes followed by an object complement, a word or word group that completes the direct object's meaning by renaming or describing it.

```
  ┌─S─┐     ┌V┐┌─DO─┐┌───────OC───────┐
```
People now call a spade an agricultural implement.

```
  ┌─S─┐┌─V─┐┌────DO────┐┌OC┐
```
Love makes all hard hearts gentle.

When the object complement renames the direct object, it is a noun or pronoun (such as *implement*). When it describes the direct object, it is an adjective (such as *gentle*).

Intransitive verbs

Intransitive verbs take no objects or complements. Their pattern is always subject/verb.

```
   S    V
```
Money talks.

```
  ┌────S────┐    ┌V┐
```
Revolutions never go backward.

Nothing receives the actions of talking and going in these sentences, so the verbs are intransitive. Notice that such verbs may or may not be followed by adverbial modifiers. In the second sentence, *backward* is an adverb modifying *go*.

NOTE: The dictionary will tell you whether a verb is transitive or intransitive. Some verbs have both transitive and intransitive functions.

> **TRANSITIVE**   Sandra flew her Cessna over the canyon.

> **INTRANSITIVE**   A bald eagle flew overhead.

In the first example, *flew* has a direct object that receives the action: *her Cessna*. In the second example, the verb is followed by an adverb (*overhead*), not by a direct object.

EXERCISE 58–2

Label the subject complements, direct objects, indirect objects, and object complements in the following sentences. If an object or complement consists of more than one word, bracket and label all of it. Answers to lettered sentences appear in the back of the book. Example:

```
              DO ┌──OC──┐
```
All work and no play make Jack a dull boy.

a. The best mind-altering drug is truth.   —Lily Tomlin
b. No one tests the depth of a river with both feet.
        —West African proverb
c. All looks yellow to a jaundiced eye.   —Alexander Pope
d. Luck never made a man [or a woman] wise.
        —Seneca the Younger
e. You show me a capitalist and I will show you a bloodsucker.
        —Malcolm X

1. Accomplishments have no color.   —Leontyne Price
2. Gardening is an exercise in optimism.   —Marina Schinz
3. The mob has many heads but no brains.   —Thomas Fuller
4. I never promised you a rose garden.   —Hannah Green
5. Moral indignation is jealousy with a halo.   —H. G. Wells

58c Pattern variations

Although most sentences follow one of the five patterns listed at the beginning of this section, variations of these patterns commonly occur in questions, commands, sentences with delayed subjects, and passive transformations.

Questions and commands

Questions are sometimes patterned in normal word order, with the subject preceding the verb.

  S ——V——
  Who will take the first step?

Just as frequently, however, the pattern of a question is inverted, with the subject appearing between the helping and main verbs or after the verb.

  HV S MV
  Will you take the first step?

  V ——— S———
  Why is the first step so difficult?

In commands, the subject of the sentence is an understood *you.*

  [*You*] Keep your mouth shut and your eyes open.

Sentences with delayed subjects

Writers sometimes choose to delay the subject of a sentence to achieve a special effect such as suspense or humor.

$$\overset{\text{V}}{} \overset{\text{S}}{\rule{2cm}{0pt}}$$

Behind the phony tinsel of Hollywood lies the real tinsel.

The subject of the sentence is also delayed in sentences opening with the expletives *There* or *It*. When used as expletives, the words *There* and *It* have no strict grammatical function; they serve merely to get the sentence started.

$$\overset{\text{V}}{} \overset{\text{S}}{\rule{4cm}{0pt}}$$

There are many paths to the top of the mountain.

$$\overset{\text{V}}{} \overset{\text{S}}{\rule{3cm}{0pt}}$$

It is not good to wake a sleeping lion.

The subject in the second example is an infinitive phrase. (See 59c.)

Passive transformations

Transitive verbs, those that can take direct objects, usually appear in the active voice. In the active voice, the subject does the action and a direct object receives the action.

$$\overset{\text{S}}{} \overset{\text{V}}{} \overset{\text{DO}}{\rule{2cm}{0pt}}$$

ACTIVE   The early *bird* sometimes *catches the early worm.*

Sentences in the active voice may be transformed into the passive voice, with the subject receiving the action instead.

$$\overset{\text{S}}{\rule{2cm}{0pt}} \overset{\text{HV}}{} \overset{\text{MV}}{}$$

PASSIVE   *The early worm is* sometimes *caught* by the early bird.

What was once the direct object (*the early worm*) has become the subject in the passive-voice transformation, and the original subject appears in a prepositional phrase beginning with *by*. The *by* phrase is frequently omitted in passive-voice constructions.

PASSIVE   The early worm is sometimes caught.

Verbs in the passive voice can be identified by their form alone. The main verb is always a past participle, such as *caught* (see 57c), preceded by a form of *be* (*be, am, is, are, was, were, being, been*): *is caught.* Sometimes adverbs intervene (*is sometimes caught*).

NOTE: Writers sometimes use the passive voice when the active voice would be more appropriate (see 14a). For a review of the uses of the active and the passive voice, see 28c.

59

Subordinate word groups

Subordinate word groups include prepositional phrases, subordinate clauses, verbal phrases, appositives, and absolutes. Not all of these word groups are subordinate in quite the same way. Some are subordinate because they are modifiers; others function as noun equivalents, not as modifiers.

59a Prepositional phrases

A prepositional phrase begins with a preposition such as *at, by, for, from, in, of, on, to,* or *with* (see 57f) and usually ends with a noun or noun equivalent: *on the table, for him, with great fanfare.* The noun or noun equivalent is known as the *object of the preposition.*

Prepositional phrases function either as adjectives modifying a noun or pronoun or as adverbs modifying a verb, an adjective, or another adverb. When functioning as an adjective, a prepositional phrase nearly always appears immediately following the noun or pronoun it modifies.

Variety is the spice *of life*.

Adjective phrases usually answer one or both of the questions Which one? and What kind of? If we ask Which spice? or What kind of spice? we get a sensible answer: the spice *of life*.

Adverbial prepositional phrases that modify the verb can appear nearly anywhere in a sentence.

Do not judge a tree *by its bark.*

Tyranny will *in time* lead to revolution.

To the ant, a few drops of rain are a flood.

Adverbial word groups usually answer one of these questions: When? Where? How? Why? Under what conditions? To what degree?

> Do not judge a tree *how? By its bark.*
>
> Tyranny will lead to revolution *when? In time.*
>
> A few drops of rain are a flood *under what conditions? To the ant.*

In questions and subordinate clauses, a preposition may appear after its object.

> *What* are you afraid *of?*
>
> We avoided the clerk *whom* John had warned us *about.*

NOTE: The ability to recognize the object of a preposition will help you distinguish between pronouns such as *I* and *me* (see 24).

EXERCISE 59–1

Underline the prepositional phrases in the following sentences. Be prepared to explain the function of each phrase. Answers to lettered sentences appear in the back of the book. Example:

> You can stroke people with words. *(Adverbial phrase*
>
> *modifying can stroke)*

a. Laughter is a tranquilizer with no side effects.
    —Arnold Glasgow
b. Any mother could perform the job of several air traffic controllers with ease.   —Lisa Alther
c. She wears her morals like a loose garment.   —Langston Hughes

d. You can tell the ideals of a nation by its advertising.

        —Norman Douglas

   e. In prosperity, no altar smokes.   —Italian proverb

1. We know that the road to freedom has always been stalked by death.   —Angela Davis
2. A society of sheep produces a government of wolves.

        —Bertrand de Jouvenal
3. Some people feel with their heads and think with their hearts.

        —G. C. Lichtenberg
4. In love and war, all is fair.   —Francis Edward Smedley
5. On their side, the workers had only the Constitution. The other side had bayonets.   —Mother Jones

59b Subordinate clauses

Subordinate clauses are patterned like sentences, having subjects and verbs and sometimes objects or complements. But they function within sentences as adjectives, adverbs, or nouns. Subordinate clauses cannot stand alone as complete sentences.

A subordinate clause usually begins with a subordinating conjunction or a relative pronoun.

SUBORDINATING CONJUNCTIONS

after	before	rather than	though	where
although	even though	since	unless	whether
as	if	so that	until	while
as if	how	than	when	why
because	in order that	that		

RELATIVE PRONOUNS

that	who	whom	whose	which

Adjective clauses

Adjective clauses modify nouns or pronouns, usually answering the question Which one? or What kind of? They begin with a relative pronoun (*who, whom, whose, which,* or *that*) or a relative adverb (*when* or *where*), marking them as grammatically subordinate.

The arrow *that has left the bow* never returns.

Relatives are persons *who live too near and visit too often.*

In addition to introducing the clause, the relative pronoun or adverb points back to the noun that the clause modifies.

The fur *that warms a monarch* once warmed a bear.

Relative pronouns are sometimes "understood."

> The things [*that*] we know best are the things [*that*] we haven't been taught.

Occasionally an adjective clause is introduced by a relative adverb, usually *when, where,* or *why.*

Home is the place *where you slip in the tub and break your neck.*

The parts of an adjective clause are often arranged as in sentences (subject / verb/object or complement).

>   **S   V DO**
> We often forgive the people *who bore us.*

Frequently, however, the object or complement appears first, violating the normal order of subject/verb/object.

>   **DO   S V**
> We rarely forgive those *whom we bore.*

NOTE: For punctuation of adjective clauses, see 32e and 33e. If English is not your native language, see 31c for a common problem with adjective clauses.

Adverb clauses

Adverb clauses modify verbs, adjectives, or other adverbs, usually answering one of these questions: When? Where? Why? How? Under what conditions? To what degree? They begin with a subordinating conjunction (*after, although, as, as if, because, before, even though, if, in order that, rather than, since, so that, than, that, though, unless, until, when, where, whether, while*).

When the well is dry, we know the worth of water.

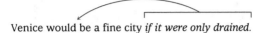

Venice would be a fine city *if it were only drained.*

Noun clauses

Noun clauses function as subjects, objects, or complements. They usually begin with one of the following words: *how, that, which, who, whoever, whom, whomever, what, whatever, when, where, whether, whose, why.*

— S —
Whoever gossips to you will gossip of you.

— DO —
We never forget *that we buried the hatchet.*

As with adjective clauses, the parts of a noun clause may appear out of their normal order (subject/verb/object).

DO S V
Talent is *what you possess.*

The parts of a noun clause may also appear in their normal order.

S V DO
Genius is *what possesses you.*

EXERCISE 59–2

Underline the subordinate clauses in the following sentences. Be prepared to explain the function of each clause. Answers to lettered sentences appear in the back of the book. Example:

Dig a well <u>before you are thirsty</u>. *(Adverb clause modifying Dig)*

a. It is hard to fight an enemy who has outposts in your head.
—Sally Kempton
b. An idea that is not dangerous is unworthy to be called an idea at all. —Elbert Hubbard
c. When I am an old woman, I shall wear purple. —Jenny Joseph
d. Dreams say what they mean, but they don't say it in daytime language. —Gail Godwin
e. A fraud is not perfect unless it is practiced on clever persons.
—Arab proverb

1. What history teaches us is that we have never learned anything
   from it.   —Georg Wilhelm Hegel
2. When a dog is drowning, everyone offers him a drink.
                                                    —George Herbert
3. Whoever named it necking was a poor judge of anatomy.
                                                    —Groucho Marx
4. Science commits suicide when it adopts a creed.
                                                    —T. H. Huxley
5. He gave her a look that you could have poured on a waffle.
                                                    —Ring Lardner

59C Verbal phrases

A verbal is a verb form that does not function as the verb of a
clause. Verbals include infinitives (the word *to* plus the base
form of the verb), present participles (the *-ing* form of the verb),
and past participles (the verb form usually ending in *-d, -ed, -n,
-en,* or *-t*). (See 27a and 57c.)

Verbals can take objects, complements, and modifiers to
form verbal phrases. These phrases are classified as participial,
gerund, and infinitive.

Participial phrases

Participial phrases always function as adjectives. Their verbals
are either present participles or past participles.

Being a philosopher, I have a problem for every solution.

Truth *kept in the dark* will never save the world.

Gerund phrases

Gerund phrases always function as nouns: usually as subjects,
subject complements, direct objects, or objects of the preposition. Their verbals are present participles.

Justifying a fault doubles it.

Kleptomaniacs can't help *helping themselves*.

Infinitive phrases

Infinitive phrases, usually constructed around *to* plus the base form of the verb (*to call, to drink*), can function as adjectives, adverbs, or nouns. When functioning as a noun, an infinitive phrase usually plays the role of subject, subject complement, or direct object.

We do not have the right *to abandon the poor*.

He cut off his nose *to spite his face*.

To side with truth is noble.

NOTE: In some constructions, the infinitive is unmarked; in other words, the *to* does not appear: *No one can make you [to] feel inferior without your consent*. (See 29c.)

EXERCISE 59–3

Underline the verbal phrases in the following sentences. Be prepared to explain the function of each phrase. Answers to lettered sentences appear in the back of the book. Example:

Do you want to be a writer? Then write. *(Infinitive phrase used*

as direct object of Do want)

a. The best substitute for experience is being sixteen.
— Raymond Duncan
b. Fate tried to conceal him by naming him Smith.
— Oliver Wendell Holmes, Jr.
c. Scandal is gossip made tedious by morality.   — Oscar Wilde
d. Being weak, foxes are distinguished by superior tact.
— Anonymous
e. For years I wanted to be older, and now I am.
— Margaret Atwood

1. The thing generally raised on city land is taxes.
— C. D. Warner
2. Do not use a hatchet to remove a fly from your friend's forehead.
— Chinese proverb

3. He has the gall of a shoplifter returning an item for a refund.
                                              — W. I. E. Gates
4. I don't deserve any credit for turning the other cheek as my
    tongue is always in it.   — Flannery O'Connor
5. Concealing a disease is no way to cure it.   — Ethiopian proverb

59d Appositive phrases

Though strictly speaking they are not subordinate word
groups, appositive phrases function somewhat as adjectives
do, to describe nouns or pronouns. Instead of modifying nouns
or pronouns, however, appositive phrases rename them. In
form they are nouns or noun equivalents.

Appositives are said to be "in apposition" to the nouns or
pronouns they rename.

> Politicians, *acrobats at heart,* can sit on a fence and yet keep
> both ears to the ground.

Acrobats at heart is in apposition to the noun *politicians.*

59e Absolute phrases

An absolute phrase modifies a whole clause or sentence, not
just one word, and it may appear nearly anywhere in the sentence. It consists of a noun or noun equivalent usually followed
by a participial phrase.

> *His words dipped in honey,* the senator mesmerized the crowd.

60

Sentence types

Sentences are classified in two ways: according to their structure (simple, compound, complex, and compound-complex)
and according to their purpose (declarative, imperative, interrogative, and exclamatory).

60a Sentence structures

Depending on the number and types of clauses they contain, sentences are classified as simple, compound, complex, or compound-complex.

Clauses come in two varieties: independent and subordinate. An independent clause is a full sentence pattern that does not function within another sentence pattern: It contains a subject and verb plus any objects, complements, and modifiers of that verb, and it either stands alone or could stand alone. A subordinate clause is a full sentence pattern that functions within a sentence as an adjective, an adverb, or a noun but that cannot stand alone as a complete sentence. (See 59b.)

Simple sentences

A simple sentence is one independent clause with no subordinate clauses.

┌─────────── INDEPENDENT CLAUSE ───────────┐
Without music, life would be a mistake.

This sentence contains a subject (*life*), a verb (*would be*), a complement (*a mistake*), and an adverbial modifier (*Without music*).

A simple sentence may contain compound elements—a compound subject, verb, or object, for example—but it does not contain more than one full sentence pattern. The following sentence is simple because its two verbs (*enters* and *spreads*) share a subject (*Evil*).

┌─────────── INDEPENDENT CLAUSE ───────────┐
Evil enters like a needle and spreads like an oak.

Compound sentences

A compound sentence is composed of two or more independent clauses with no subordinate clauses. The independent clauses are usually joined with a comma and a coordinating conjunction (*and, but, or, nor, for, so, yet*) or with a semicolon. (See 8.)

┌─ INDEPENDENT CLAUSE ─┐   ┌── INDEPENDENT CLAUSE ──┐
One arrow is easily broken, but you can't break a bundle of ten.

┌─────── INDEPENDENT CLAUSE ───────┐┌INDEPENDENT──
We are born brave, trusting, and greedy; most of us have

─CLAUSE────────┐
remained greedy.

Complex sentences

A complex sentence is composed of one independent clause
with one or more subordinate clauses. (See 59b.)

           SUBORDINATE
         ┌─── CLAUSE ───┐
ADJECTIVE   They that sow in tears shall reap in joy.

           SUBORDINATE
         ┌───CLAUSE───┐
ADVERB   If you scatter thorns, don't go barefoot.

        ┌────── SUBORDINATE CLAUSE──────┐
NOUN   What the scientists have in their briefcases is
        terrifying.

Compound-complex sentences

A compound-complex sentence contains at least two independent clauses and at least one subordinate clause. The following
sentence contains two full sentence patterns that can stand
alone.

┌INDEPENDENT CLAUSE┐ ┌── INDEPENDENT CLAUSE──┐
Tell me what you eat, and I will tell you what you are.

And each independent clause contains a subordinate clause,
making the sentence both compound and complex.

┌───── IND CL ────┐   ┌─────── IND CL───────┐
     ┌── SUB CL ──┐   ┌─ SUB CL ──┐
Tell me what you eat, and I will tell you what you are.

60b Sentence purposes

Writers use declarative sentences to make statements, imperative sentences to issue requests or commands, interrogative
sentences to ask questions, and exclamatory sentences to
make exclamations.

DECLARATIVE	The echo always has the last word.
IMPERATIVE	Love your neighbor.
INTERROGATIVE	Are second thoughts always wisest?
EXCLAMATORY	I want to wash the flag, not burn it!

EXERCISE 60–1

Identify the following sentences as simple, compound, complex, or compound-complex. Be prepared to identify the subordinate clauses and classify them according to their function: adjective, adverb, or noun. (See 59b.) Answers to lettered sentences appear in the back of the book. Example:

The frog in the well knows nothing of the ocean. *simple*

a. A primitive artist is an amateur whose work sells.
— Grandma Moses

b. My folks didn't come over on the Mayflower; they were there to meet the boat.   — Will Rogers

c. No pessimist ever discovered the secrets of the stars, or sailed to an uncharted land, or opened a new heaven to the human spirit.
— Helen Keller

d. If you don't go to other people's funerals, they won't go to yours.
— Clarence Day

e. Tell us your phobias, and we will tell you what you are afraid of.
— Robert Benchley

1. Seek simplicity and distrust it.   — Alfred North Whitehead

2. Those who write clearly have readers; those who write obscurely have commentators.   — Albert Camus

3. The children are always the chief victims of social chaos.
— Agnes Meyer

4. Morality cannot be legislated, but behavior can be regulated.
— Martin Luther King, Jr.

5. When an elephant is in trouble, even a frog will kick him.
— Hindu proverb

Glossary of Usage

This glossary includes words commonly confused (such as *accept* and *except*), words commonly misused (such as *hopefully*), and words that are nonstandard (such as *hisself*). It also lists colloquialisms and jargon. Colloquialisms are expressions that may be appropriate in informal speech but are inappropriate in formal writing. Jargon is needlessly technical or pretentious language that is inappropriate in most contexts.

If an item is not listed here, consult the index. For irregular verbs (such as *sing, sang, sung*), see 27a. For idiomatic use of prepositions (such as *angry at* and *angry with),* see 18d.

a, an Use *an* before a vowel sound, *a* before a consonant sound: *an apple, a peach.* Problems sometimes arise with words beginning with *h.* If the *h* is silent, the word begins with a vowel sound, so use *an: an hour, an heir, an honest senator, an honorable deed.* If the *h* is pronounced, the word begins with a consonant sound, so use *a: a hospital, a hymn, a historian, a hotel.* When an abbreviation or acronym begins with a vowel sound, use *an: an EKG, an MRI, an AIDS patient.*

accept, except *Accept* is a verb meaning "to receive." *Except* is usually a preposition meaning "excluding." *I will accept all the packages except that one. Except* is also a verb meaning "to exclude." *Please except that item from the list.*

adapt, adopt *Adapt* means "to adjust or become accustomed"; it is usually followed by *to. Adopt* means "to take as one's own." *Our family adopted a Vietnamese orphan, who quickly adapted to his new surroundings.*

adverse, averse *Adverse* means "unfavorable." *Averse* means "opposed" or "reluctant"; it is usually followed by *to. I am averse to your proposal because it could have an adverse impact on the economy.*

advice, advise   *Advice* is a noun, *advise* a verb. *We advise you to follow John's advice.*

affect, effect   *Affect* is usually a verb meaning "to influence." *Effect* is usually a noun meaning "result." *The drug did not affect the disease, and it had several adverse side effects. Effect* can also be a verb meaning "to bring about." *Only the president can effect such a dramatic change.*

aggravate   *Aggravate* means "to make worse or more troublesome." *Overgrazing aggravated the soil erosion.* In formal writing, avoid the colloquial use of *aggravate* meaning "to annoy or irritate." *Her babbling annoyed* [not *aggravated*] *me.*

agree to, agree with   *Agree to* means "to give consent." *Agree with* means "to be in accord" or "to come to an understanding." *He agrees with me about the need for change, but he won't agree to my plan.*

ain't   *Ain't* is nonstandard. Use *am not, are not* (*aren't*), or *is not* (*isn't*). *I am not* [not *ain't*] *going home for spring break.*

all ready, already   *All ready* means "completely prepared." *Already* means "previously." *Susan was all ready for the concert, but her friends had already left.*

all right   *All right* is written as two words. *Alright* is nonstandard.

all together, altogether   *All together* means "everyone gathered." *Altogether* means "entirely." *We were not altogether certain that we could bring the family all together for the reunion.*

allude   To *allude* to something is to make an indirect reference to it. Do not use *allude* to mean "to refer directly." *In his lecture the professor referred* [not *alluded*] *to several pre-Socratic philosophers.*

allusion, illusion   An *allusion* is an indirect reference. An *illusion* is a misconception or false impression. *Did you catch my allusion to Shakespeare? Mirrors give the room an illusion of depth.*

a lot   *A lot* is two words. Do not write *alot. We have had a lot of rain this spring.* See also *lots, lots of.*

among, between   See *between, among.*

amongst   In American English, *among* is preferred.

amoral, immoral   *Amoral* means "neither moral nor immoral"; it also means "not caring about moral judgments." *Immoral* means "morally wrong." *Until recently, most business courses were taught from an amoral perspective. Murder is immoral.*

amount, number   Use *amount* with quantities that cannot be counted; use *number* with those that can. *This recipe calls for a large amount of sugar. We have a large number of toads in our garden.*

an   See *a, an.*

and etc.   *Et cetera* (*etc.*) means "and so forth"; therefore, *and etc.* is redundant. See also *etc.*

and/or   Avoid the awkward construction *and/or* except in technical or legal documents.

angry at, angry with   To write that one is *angry at* another person is nonstandard. Use *angry with* instead.

ante-, anti-   The prefix *ante-* means "earlier" or "in front of"; the prefix *anti-* means "against" or "opposed to." *William Lloyd Garrison was one of the leaders of the antislavery movement during the antebellum period.* *Anti-* should be used with a hyphen when it is followed by a capital letter or a word beginning with *i*.

anxious   *Anxious* means "worried" or "apprehensive." In formal writing, avoid using *anxious* to mean "eager." *We are eager* [not *anxious*] *to see your new house.*

anybody, anyone   *Anybody* and *anyone* are singular. (See 21d and 22a.)

anymore   Reserve the adverb *anymore* for negative contexts, where it means "any longer." *Moviegoers are rarely shocked anymore by profanity.* Do not use *anymore* in positive contexts. Use *now* or *nowadays* instead. *Interest rates are so low nowadays* [not *anymore*] *that more people can afford to buy homes.*

anyone   See *anybody, anyone.*

anyone, any one   *Anyone,* an indefinite pronoun, means "any person at all." *Any one,* the pronoun *one* preceded by the adjective *any,* refers to a particular person or thing in a group. *Anyone from Chicago may choose any one of the games on display.*

anyplace   *Anyplace* is informal for *anywhere.* Avoid *anyplace* in formal writing.

anyways, anywheres   *Anyways* and *anywheres* are nonstandard. Use *anyway* and *anywhere.*

as   *As* is sometimes used to mean "because." But do not use it if there is any chance of ambiguity. *We canceled the picnic because* [not *as*] *it began raining. As* here could mean "because" or "when."

as, like   See *like, as.*

as to   *As to* is jargon for *about. He inquired about* [not *as to*] *the job.*

averse   See *adverse, averse.*

awful   The adjective *awful* means "awe-inspiring." Colloquially it is used to mean "terrible" or "bad." The adverb *awfully* is sometimes used in conversation as an intensifier meaning "very." In formal writing, avoid these colloquial uses. *I was very* [not *awfully*] *upset last night. Susan had a terrible* [not *an awful*] *time calming her nerves.*

awhile, a while   *Awhile* is an adverb; it can modify a verb, but it cannot be the object of a preposition such as *for.* The two-word form *a while* is a noun preceded by an article and therefore can be the object of a preposition. *Stay awhile. Stay for a while.*

bad, badly   *Bad* is an adjective, *badly* an adverb. (See 26a and 26b.) *They felt bad about being early and ruining the surprise. Her arm hurt badly after she slid headfirst into second base.*

being as, being that   *Being as* and *being that* are nonstandard expressions. Write *because* or *since* instead. *Because* [not *Being as*] *I slept late, I had to skip breakfast.*

beside, besides   *Beside* is a preposition meaning "at the side of" or "next to." *Annie Oakley slept with her gun beside her bed. Besides* is a preposition meaning "except" or "in addition to." *No one besides Terrie can have that ice cream. Besides* is also an adverb meaning "in addition." *I'm not hungry; besides, I don't like ice cream.*

between, among   Ordinarily, use *among* with three or more entities, *between* with two. *The prize was divided among several contestants. You have a choice between carrots and beans.*

bring, take   Use *bring* when an object is being transported toward you, *take* when it is being moved away. *Please bring me a glass of water. Please take these flowers to Mr. Scott.*

burst, bursted; bust, busted   *Burst* is an irregular verb meaning "to come open or fly apart suddenly or violently." Its principal parts are *burst, burst, burst.* The past-tense form *bursted* is nonstandard. *Bust* and *busted* are slang for *burst* and, along with *bursted,* should not be used in formal writing.

can, may   The distinction between *can* and *may* is fading, but many careful writers still observe it in formal writing. *Can* is traditionally reserved for ability, *may* for permission. *Can you ski down the advanced slope without falling? May I help you?*

capital, capitol   *Capital* refers to a city, *capitol* to a building where lawmakers meet. *Capital* also refers to wealth or resources. *The capitol has undergone extensive renovations. The residents of the state capital protested the development plans.*

censor, censure   *Censor* means "to remove or suppress material considered objectionable." *Censure* means "to criticize severely." *The library's new policy of censoring controversial books has been censured by the media.*

cite, site   *Cite* means "to quote as an authority or example." *Site* is usually a noun meaning "a particular place." *He cited the zoning law in his argument against the proposed site of the gas station.*

climactic, climatic   *Climactic* is derived from *climax,* the point of greatest intensity in a series or progression of events. *Climatic* is derived from *climate* and refers to meteorological conditions. *The climactic period in the dinosaurs' reign was reached just before severe climatic conditions brought on an ice age.*

coarse, course   *Coarse* means "crude" or "rough in texture." *The coarse weave of the wall hanging gave it a three-dimensional quality.*

Course usually refers to a path, a playing field, or a unit of study; the expression *of course* means "certainly." *I plan to take a course in car repair this summer. Of course, you are welcome to join me.*

compare to, compare with　　*Compare to* means "to represent as similar." *She compared him to a wild stallion. Compare with* means "to examine the ways in which two things are similar." *The study compared the language ability of apes with that of dolphins.*

complement, compliment　　*Complement* is a verb meaning "to go with or complete" or a noun meaning "something that completes." *Compliment* as a verb means "to flatter"; as a noun it means "flattering remark." *Her skill at rushing the net complements his skill at volleying. Mother's flower arrangements receive many compliments.*

conscience, conscious　　*Conscience* is a noun meaning "moral principles." *Conscious* is an adjective meaning "aware or alert." *Let your conscience be your guide. Were you conscious of his love for you?*

contact　　Although the use of *contact* to mean "to get in touch with" is common in speech, it is not appropriate in formal writing. If possible, use a precise verb such as *write* or *telephone. We will telephone* [not *contact*] *you soon.*

continual, continuous　　*Continual* means "repeated regularly and frequently." *She grew weary of the continual telephone calls. Continuous* means "extended or prolonged without interruption." *The broken siren made a continuous wail.*

could care less　　*Could care less* is a nonstandard expression. Write *couldn't care less* instead. *He couldn't* [not *could*] *care less about his psychology final.*

could of　　*Could of* is nonstandard for *could have. We could have* [not *could of*] *had steak for dinner if we had been hungry.*

council, counsel　　A *council* is a deliberative body, and a *councilor* is a member of such a body. *Counsel* usually means "advice" and can also mean "lawyer"; *counselor* is one who gives advice or guidance. *The councilors met to draft the council's position paper. The pastor offered wise counsel to the troubled teenager.*

criteria　　*Criteria* is the plural of *criterion*, which means "a standard or rule or test on which a judgment or decision can be based." *The only criterion for the scholarship is ability.*

data　　*Data* is a plural noun technically meaning "facts or propositions." But *data* is increasingly being accepted as a singular noun. *The new data suggest* [or *suggests*] *that our theory is correct.* (The singular *datum* is rarely used.)

different from, different than　　Ordinarily, write *different from. Your sense of style is different from Jim's.* However, *different than* is acceptable to avoid an awkward construction. *Please let me know if your plans are different than* [to avoid *from what*] *they were six weeks ago.*

disinterested, uninterested   *Disinterested* means "impartial, objective"; *uninterested* means "not interested." *We sought the advice of a disinterested counselor to help us solve our problem. He was uninterested in anyone's opinion but his own.*

don't   *Don't* is the contraction for *do not. I don't want any. Don't* should not be used as the contraction for *does not*, which is *doesn't. He doesn't* [not *don't*] *want any.* (See 27c.)

double negative   Standard English allows two negatives only if a positive meaning is intended. *The runners were not unhappy with their performance.* Double negatives used to emphasize negation are nonstandard. *Jack doesn't have to answer to anybody* [not *nobody*].

due to   *Due to* is an adjective phrase and should not be used as a preposition meaning "because of." *The trip was canceled because of* [not *due to*] *lack of interest. Due to* is acceptable as a subject complement and usually follows a form of the verb *be. His success was due to hard work.*

each   *Each* is singular. (See 21d and 22a.)

effect   See *affect, effect.*

e.g.   In formal writing, replace the Latin abbreviation *e.g.* with its English equivalent: *for example* or *for instance.*

either   *Either* is singular. (See 21d and 22a.) (For *either . . . or* constructions, see 21c and 22d.)

elicit, illicit   *Elicit* is a verb meaning "to bring out" or "to evoke." *Illicit* is an adjective meaning "unlawful." *The reporter was unable to elicit any information from the police about illicit drug traffic.*

emigrate from, immigrate to   *Emigrate* means "to leave one country or region to settle in another." *In 1900, my grandfather emigrated from Russia to escape the religious pogroms. Immigrate* means "to enter another country and reside there." *Many Mexicans immigrate to the United States to find work.*

eminent, imminent   *Eminent* means "outstanding" or "distinguished." *We met an eminent professor of Greek history. Imminent* means "about to happen." *The announcement is imminent.*

enthused   Many people object to the use of *enthused* as an adjective. Use *enthusiastic* instead. *The children were enthusiastic* [not *enthused*] *about going to the circus.*

-ess   Many people find the *-ess* suffix demeaning. Write *poet*, not *poetess; Jew*, not *Jewess; author*, not *authoress.*

etc.   Avoid ending a list with *etc.* It is more emphatic to end with an example, and in most contexts readers will understand that the list is not exhaustive. When you don't wish to end with an example, *and so on* is more graceful than *etc.* See also *and etc.*

eventually, ultimately   Often used interchangeably, *eventually* is the better choice to mean "at an unspecified time in the future" and *ulti-*

mately is better to mean "the furthest possible extent or greatest extreme." *He knew that eventually he would complete his degree. The existentialist considered suicide the ultimately rational act.*

everybody, everyone   *Everybody* and *everyone* are singular. (See 21d and 22a.)

everyone, every one   *Everyone* is an indefinite pronoun. *Every one,* the pronoun *one* preceded by the adjective *every,* means "each individual or thing in a particular group." *Every one* is usually followed by *of. Everyone wanted to go. Every one of the missing books was found.*

except   See *accept, except.*

expect   Avoid the colloquial use of *expect* meaning "to believe, think, or suppose." *I think* [not *expect*] *it will rain tonight.*

explicit, implicit   *Explicit* means "expressed directly" or "clearly defined"; *implicit* means "implied, unstated." *I gave him explicit instructions not to go swimming. My mother's silence indicated her implicit approval.*

farther, further   *Farther* usually describes distances. *Further* usually suggests quantity or degree. *Chicago is farther from Miami than I thought. You extended the curfew further than you should have.*

female, male   The terms *female* and *male* are jargon when used to refer to specific people. *Two women* [not *females*] *and one man* [not *male*] *applied for the position.*

fewer, less   *Fewer* refers to items that can be counted; *less* refers to general amounts. *Fewer people are living in the city. Please put less sugar in my tea.*

finalize   *Finalize* is jargon meaning "to make final or complete." Use ordinary English instead. *The architect prepared final drawings* [not *finalized the drawings*].

firstly   *Firstly* sounds pretentious, and it leads to the ungainly series *firstly, secondly, thirdly, fourthly,* and so on. Write *first, second, third* instead.

further   See *farther, further.*

get   *Get* has many colloquial uses. In writing, avoid using *get* to mean the following: "to evoke an emotional response" (*That music always gets to me*); "to annoy" (*After a while his sulking got to me*); "to take revenge on" (*I got back at him by leaving the room*); "to become" (*He got sick*); "to start or begin" (*Let's get going*). Avoid using *have got to* in place of *must. I must* [not *have got to*] *finish this paper tonight.*

good, well   *Good* is an adjective, *well* an adverb. (See 26.) *He hasn't felt good about his game since he sprained his wrist last season. She performed well on the uneven parallel bars.*

hanged, hung   *Hanged* is the past-tense and past-participle form of the verb *hang* meaning "to execute." *The prisoner was hanged at dawn. Hung* is the past-tense and past-participle form of the verb *hang* meaning "to fasten or suspend." *The stockings were hung by the chimney with care.*

hardly Avoid expressions such as *can't hardly* and *not hardly,* which are considered double negatives. *I can* [not *can't*] *hardly describe my elation at getting the job.*

has got, have got *Got* is unnecessary and awkward in such constructions. It should be dropped. *We have* [not *have got*] *three days to prepare for the opening.*

he At one time *he* was commonly used to mean "he or she." Today such usage is inappropriate. (See 17f and 22a for alternative constructions.)

he/she, his/her In formal writing, use *he or she* or *his or her.* For alternatives to these wordy constructions, see 17f and 22a.

hisself *Hisself* is nonstandard. Use *himself.*

hopefully *Hopefully* means "in a hopeful manner." *We looked hopefully to the future.* Do not use *hopefully* in constructions such as the following: *Hopefully, your daughter will recover soon.* Indicate who is doing the hoping: *I hope that your daughter will recover soon.*

hung See *hanged, hung.*

i.e. In formal writing, replace the Latin abbreviation *i.e.* with its English equivalent: *that is.*

if, whether Use *if* to express a condition and *whether* to express alternatives. *If you go on a trip, whether it be to Nebraska or New Jersey, remember to bring traveler's checks.*

illusion See *allusion, illusion.*

imminent See *eminent, imminent.*

immoral See *amoral, immoral.*

implement *Implement* is a pretentious way of saying "do," "carry out," or "accomplish." Use ordinary language instead. *We carried out* [not *implemented*] *the director's orders with some reluctance.*

imply, infer *Imply* means "to suggest or state indirectly"; *infer* means "to draw a conclusion." *John implied that he knew all about computers, but the interviewer inferred that John was inexperienced.*

in, into *In* indicates location or condition; *into* indicates movement or a change in condition. *They found the lost letters in a box after moving into the house.*

individual *Individual* is a pretentious substitute for *person.* *We invited several persons* [not *individuals*] *from the audience to participate in the experiment.*

ingenious, ingenuous *Ingenious* means "clever." *Sarah's solution to the problem was ingenious. Ingenuous* means "naive" or "frank." *For a successful manager, Ed is surprisingly ingenuous.*

in regards to *In regards to* confuses two different phrases: *in regard to* and *as regards*. Use one or the other. *In regard to* [or *As regards*] *the contract, ignore the first clause.*

irregardless *Irregardless* is nonstandard. Use *regardless*.

is when, is where These mixed constructions are often incorrectly used in definitions. *A run-off election is a second election held to break a tie* [not *is when a second election breaks a tie*]. (See 11c.)

it is *It is* is nonstandard when used to mean "there is." *There is* [not *It is*] *a fly in my soup.*

its, it's *Its* is a possessive pronoun; *it's* is a contraction for *it is*. (See 36c and 36e.) *The dog licked its wound whenever its owner walked into the room. It's a perfect day to walk the twenty-mile trail.*

kind(s) *Kind* is singular and should be treated as such. Don't write *These kind of chairs are rare*. Write instead *This kind of chair is rare. Kinds* is plural and should be used only when you mean more than one kind. *These kinds of chairs are rare.*

kind of, sort of Avoid using *kind of* or *sort of* to mean "somewhat." *The movie was somewhat* [not *kind of*] *boring*. Do not put *a* after either phrase. *That kind of* [not *kind of a*] *salesclerk annoys me.*

lead, led *Lead* is a noun referring to a metal. *Led* is the past tense of the verb *lead. He led me to the treasure.*

learn, teach *Learn* means "to gain knowledge"; *teach* means "to impart knowledge." *I must teach* [not *learn*] *my sister to read.*

leave, let *Leave* means "to exit." Avoid using it with the nonstandard meaning "to permit." *Let* [not *Leave*] *me help you with the dishes.*

less See *fewer, less.*

let, leave See *leave, let.*

liable *Liable* means "obligated" or "responsible." Do not use it to mean "likely." *You're likely* [not *liable*] *to trip if you don't tie your shoelaces.*

lie, lay *Lie* is an intransitive verb meaning "to recline or rest on a surface." Its principal parts are *lie, lay, lain. Lay* is a transitive verb meaning "to put or place." Its principal parts are *lay, laid, laid.* (See 27b.)

like, as *Like* is a preposition, not a subordinating conjunction. It can be followed only by a noun or a noun phrase. *As* is a subordinating conjunction that introduces a subordinate clause. In casual speech you may say *She looks like she hasn't slept* or *You don't know her like I do.* But in formal writing, use *as. She looks as if she hasn't slept. You don't know her as I do.* (See prepositions and subordinating conjunctions, 57f and 57g.)

loose, lose *Loose* is an adjective meaning "not securely fastened." *Lose* is a verb meaning "to misplace" or "to not win." *Did you lose your only loose pair of work pants?*

lots, lots of *Lots* and *lots of* are colloquial substitutes for *many*, *much*, or *a lot*. Avoid using them in formal writing.

male, female See *female, male*.

mankind Avoid *mankind* whenever possible. It offends many readers because it excludes women. Use *humanity, humans, the human race*, or *humankind* instead.

may See *can, may*.

maybe, may be *Maybe* is an adverb meaning "possibly." *May be* is a verb phrase. *Maybe the sun will shine tomorrow. Tomorrow may be a brighter day.*

may of, might of *May of* and *might of* are nonstandard for *may have* and *might have. We may have* [not *may of*] *had too many cookies.*

media, medium *Media* is the plural of *medium. Of all the media that cover the Olympics, television is the medium that best captures the spectacle of the events.*

most *Most* is colloquial when used to mean "almost" and should be avoided. *Almost* [not *Most*] *everyone went to the parade.*

must of *Must of* is nonstandard for *must have*.

myself *Myself* is a reflexive or intensive pronoun. Reflexive: *I cut myself*. Intensive: *I will drive you myself*. Do not use *myself* in place of *I* or *me. He gave the flowers to Joan and me* [not *myself*]. (See also 24.)

neither *Neither* is singular. (See 21d and 22a.) For *neither . . . nor* constructions, see 21c and 22d.

none *None* is usually singular. (See 21d.)

nowheres *Nowheres* is nonstandard for *nowhere*.

number See *amount, number*.

of Use the verb *have*, not the preposition *of*, after the verbs *could, should, would, may, might*, and *must. They must have* [not *of*] *left early.*

off of *Off* is sufficient. Omit *of. The ball rolled off* [not *off of*] *the table.*

OK, O.K., okay All three spellings are acceptable when used consistently, but in formal speech and writing avoid these colloquial expressions for consent or approval.

parameters *Parameter* is a mathematical term that has become jargon for "fixed limit," "boundary," or "guideline." Use ordinary English instead. *The task force was asked to work within certain guidelines* [not *parameters*].

passed, past *Passed* is the past tense of the verb *pass. Mother passed me another slice of cake. Past* usually means "belonging to a former time" or "beyond a time or place." *Our past president spoke until past midnight. The hotel is just past the next intersection.*

percent, per cent, percentage *Percent* (also spelled *per cent*) is always used with a specific number. *Percentage* is used with a descriptive term such as *large* or *small*, not with a specific number. *The candidate won 80 percent of the primary vote. Only a small percentage of registered voters turned out for the election.*

phenomena   *Phenomena* is the plural of *phenomenon*, which means "an observable occurrence or fact." *Strange phenomena occur at all hours of the night in that house, but last night's phenomenon was the strangest of all.*

plus   *Plus* should not be used to join independent clauses. *This raincoat is dirty; moreover* [not *plus*], *it has a hole in it.*

precede, proceed   *Precede* means "to come before." *Proceed* means "to go forward." *As we proceeded up the mountain path, we noticed fresh tracks in the mud, evidence that a group of hikers had preceded us.*

prejudice, prejudiced   *Prejudice* is a noun; *prejudiced* is an adjective. *Prejudice against Mexicans was common in our border town, but my family wasn't prejudiced.*

principal, principle   *Principal* is a noun meaning "the head of a school or organization" or "a sum of money." It is also an adjective meaning "most important." *Principle* is a noun meaning "a basic truth or law." *The principal expelled her for three principal reasons. We believe in the principle of equal justice for all.*

proceed, precede   See *precede, proceed.*

quote, quotation   *Quote* is a verb; *quotation* is a noun. Avoid using *quote* as a shortened form of *quotation. Her quotations* [not *quotes*] *from Shakespeare intrigued us.*

raise, rise   *Raise* is a transitive verb meaning "to move or cause to move upward." It takes a direct object. *I raised the shades. Rise* is an intransitive verb meaning "to go up." It does not take a direct object. *Heat rises.*

real, really   *Real* is an adjective; *really* is an adverb. *Real* is sometimes used informally as an adverb, but avoid this use in formal writing. *She was really* [not *real*] *angry.* (See 26a.)

reason is because   Use *that* instead of *because. The reason I'm late is that* [not *because*] *my car broke down.* (See 11c.)

reason why   The expression *reason why* is redundant. *The reason* [not *The reason why*] *Jones lost the election is clear.*

relation, relationship   *Relation* describes a connection between things. *Relationship* describes a connection between people. *There is a relation between poverty and infant mortality. Our business relationship has cooled over the years.*

respectfully, respectively   *Respectfully* means "showing or marked by respect." *Respectively* means "each in the order given." *He respectfully submitted his opinion to the judge. John, Tom, and Larry were a butcher, a baker, and a lawyer, respectively.*

set, sit   *Set* is a transitive verb meaning "to put" or "to place." Its principal parts are *set, set, set. Sit* is an intransitive verb meaning "to be seated." Its principal parts are *sit, sat, sat. She set the dough in a warm corner of the kitchen. The cat sat in the warmest part of the room.*

shall, will   *Shall* was once used as the helping verb with *I* or *we: I shall, we shall, you will, he/she/it will, they will.* Today, however, *will* is generally accepted even when the subject is *I* or *we.* The word *shall* occurs primarily in polite questions (*Shall I find you a pillow?*) and in legalistic sentences suggesting duty or obligation (*The applicant shall file form 1080 by December 31.*).

should of   *Should of* is nonstandard for *should have. They should have* [not *should of*] *been home an hour ago.*

since   Do not use *since* to mean "because" if there is any chance of ambiguity. *Since we won the game, we have been celebrating with a pitcher of beer. Since* here could mean "because" or "from the time that."

sit   See *set, sit.*

site, cite   See *cite, site.*

somebody, someone   *Somebody* and *someone* are singular. (See 21d and 22a.)

something   *Something* is singular. (See 21d.)

sometime, some time, sometimes   *Sometime* is an adverb meaning "at an indefinite or unstated time." *Some time* is the adjective *some* modifying the noun *time* and is spelled as two words to mean "a period of time." *Sometimes* is an adverb meaning "at times, now and then." *I'll see you sometime soon. I haven't lived there for some time. Sometimes I run into him at the library.*

suppose to   Write *supposed to.*

sure and   *Sure and* is nonstandard for *sure to. We were all taught to be sure to* [not *and*] *look both ways before crossing a street.*

take   See *bring, take.*

than, then   *Than* is a conjunction used in comparisons; *then* is an adverb denoting time. *That pizza is more than I can eat. Tom laughed, and then we recognized him.*

that   See *that, which* or *who, which, that.*

that, which   Many writers reserve *that* for restrictive clauses, *which* for nonrestrictive clauses. (See 32e.)

theirselves   *Theirselves* is nonstandard for *themselves. The two people were able to push the Volkswagen out of the way themselves* [not *theirselves*].

them   The use of *them* in place of *those* is nonstandard. *Please send those* [not *them*] *flowers to the patient in room 220.*

there, their, they're   *There* is an adverb specifying place; it is also an expletive. Adverb: *Sylvia is lying there unconscious.* Expletive: *There are two plums left. Their* is a possessive pronoun. *Fred and Jane finally washed their car. They're* is a contraction of *they are. They're later than usual today.*

they   The use of *they* to indicate possession is nonstandard. Use *their* instead. *Cindy and Sam decided to sell their* [not *they*] *1975 Corvette.*

this kind   See *kind(s)*.

to, too, two   *To* is a preposition; *too* is an adverb; *two* is a number. *Too many of your shots slice to the left, but the last two were right on the mark.*

toward, towards   *Toward* and *towards* are generally interchangeable, although *toward* is preferred in American English.

try and   *Try and* is nonstandard for *try to. The teacher asked us all to try to* [not *and*] *write an original haiku.*

ultimately, eventually   See *eventually, ultimately*.

unique   Avoid expressions such as *most unique, more straight, less perfect, very round.* Something either is unique or it isn't. It is illogical to suggest degrees of uniqueness. (See 26c.)

usage   The noun *usage* should not be substituted for *use* when the meaning intended is "employment of." *The use* [not *usage*] *of computers dramatically increased the company's profits.*

use to   Write *used to*.

utilize   *Utilize* means "to make use of." It often sounds pretentious; in most cases, *use* is sufficient. *I used* [not *utilized*] *the best workers to get the job done fast.*

wait for, wait on   *Wait for* means "to be in readiness for" or "await." *Wait on* means "to serve." *We're only waiting for* [not *waiting on*] *Ruth to take us to the game.*

ways   *Ways* is colloquial when used to mean "distance." *The city is a long way* [not *ways*] *from here.*

weather, whether   The noun *weather* refers to the state of the atmosphere. *Whether* is a conjunction referring to a choice between alternatives. *We wondered whether the weather would clear up in time for our picnic.*

well, good   See *good, well*.

where   Do not use *where* in place of *that. I heard that* [not *where*] *the crime rate is increasing.*

which   See *that, which* and *who, which, that*.

while   Avoid using *while* to mean "although" or "whereas" if there is any chance of ambiguity. *Although* [not *While*] *Gloria lost money in the* *slot machine, Tom won it at roulette.* Here *While* could mean either "although" or "at the same time that."

who, which, that Do not use *which* to refer to persons. Use *who* instead. *That,* though generally used to refer to things, may be used to refer to a group or class of people. *Fans wondered how an old man who* [not *that* or *which*] *walked with a limp could play football. The team that scores the most points in this game will win the tournament.*

who, whom *Who* is used for subjects and subject complements; *whom* is used for objects. (See 25.)

who's, whose *Who's* is a contraction of *who is; whose* is a possessive pronoun. *Who's ready for more popcorn? Whose coat is this?* (See 36c and 36e.)

will See *shall, will.*

would of *Would of* is nonstandard for *would have. She would have* [not *would of*] *had a chance to play if she had arrived on time.*

you In formal writing, avoid *you* in an indefinite sense meaning "anyone." (See 23d.) *Any spectator* [not *You*] *could tell by the way John caught the ball that his throw would be too late.*

your, you're *Your* is a possessive pronoun; *you're* is a contraction of *you are. Is that your new motorcycle? You're on the list of finalists.* (See 36c and 36e.)

Answers to Lettered Exercises

EXERCISE 8–1, page 96

Possible revisions:

a. My grandfather, who has dramatic mood swings, was diagnosed as manic-depressive.
b. The losing team was made up of superstars who acted as isolated individuals on the court.
c. Thurmont, meaning "gateway to the mountains," is minutes from the Blue Ridge Mountains and the historic town of Catoctin.
d. The aides help the younger children with their weakest subjects, reading and math.
e. My first sky dive, from an altitude of 12,500 feet, was the most frightening experience of my life.

EXERCISE 8–2, page 98

Possible revisions:

a. During a routine morning at the clinic, an infant in cardiac arrest arrived by ambulance.
b. My 1969 Camaro, an original SS396, is no longer street legal.
c. When I presented the idea of job sharing to my supervisors, to my surprise they were delighted with the idea.
d. Although outsiders have forced changes on them, native Hawaiians try to preserve their ancestors' sacred customs.
e. Sophia's country kitchen, formerly a lean-to porch, overlooks a field where horses and cattle graze among old tombstones.

EXERCISE 9–1, page 102

Possible revisions:

a. The system has capabilities such as communicating with other computers, processing records, and performing mathematical functions.
b. The personnel officer told me that I would answer the phone, welcome visitors, distribute mail, and do some typing.
c. Nolan helped by cutting the grass, trimming shrubs, mulching flowerbeds, and raking leaves.
d. How ideal it seems to raise a family here in Winnebago instead of in the air-polluted suburbs.
e. Michiko told the judge that she had been pulled out of a line of fast-moving traffic and that she had a perfect driving record.

EXERCISE 10–1, page 106

Possible revisions:

a. Dip the paintbrush into the paint remover and spread a thick coat on a small section of the door.
b. Christopher's attention span is longer than his sister's.
c. SETI (the Search for Extraterrestrial Intelligence) has excited and will continue to excite interest among space buffs.
d. Samantha got along better with the chimpanzees than with Albert. [or . . . than Albert did.]
e. We were glad to see that Yellowstone National Park was recovering from the devastating forest fire.

EXERCISE 11–1, page 109

Possible revisions:

a. My instant reaction was anger and disappointment.
b. I brought a problem into the house that my mother wasn't sure how to handle.
c. It is through the misery of others that old Harvey has become rich.
d. A cloverleaf allows traffic on limited-access freeways to change direction.
e. Bowman established the format that future football card companies would emulate for years to come.

EXERCISE 12–1, page 113

Possible revisions:

a. He wanted to buy only three roses, not a dozen.
b. Within the next few years, orthodontists will be using as standard practice the technique Kurtz developed.
c. Celia received a flier from a Japanese nun about a workshop on making a kimono.
d. Jurors are encouraged to sift through the evidence carefully and thoroughly.
e. Each state would set into motion a program of recycling all reusable products.

EXERCISE 12–2, page 116

Possible revisions:

a. Reaching the heart, the surgeon performed a bypass on the severely blocked arteries.
b. When I was nestled in the cockpit, the pounding of the engine was muffled only slightly by my helmet.
c. While we dined at night, the lights along the Baja coastline created a romantic atmosphere perfect for our first anniversary.
d. While my sister was still a beginner at tennis, the coaches recruited her to train for the Olympics.
e. After Marcus Garvey returned to Jamaica, his "Back to Africa" movement slowly died.

EXERCISE 13–1, page 120

Possible revisions:

a. The young man who burglarized our house was sentenced to probation for one year, a small price to pay for robbing us of our personal possessions as well as our trust in other human beings.
b. After the count of three, Mikah and I placed the injured woman on the scoop stretcher. Then I took her vital signs.

c. Ministers often have a hard time because they have to please so many different people.
d. We drove for eight hours until we reached the South Dakota Badlands. We could hardly believe the eeriness of the landscape at dusk.
e. The question is whether ferrets bred in captivity have the instinct to prey on prairie dogs or whether this is a learned skill.

EXERCISE 14-1, page 123

Possible revisions:

a. Her letter acknowledged the students' participation in the literacy program.
b. Ahmed, the producer, manages the entire operation.
c. Emphatic and active; no change.
d. Players were fighting on both sides of the rink.
e. Emphatic and active; no change.

EXERCISE 16-1, page 131

Possible revisions:

a. The drawing room in the west wing is said to be haunted.
b. Dr. Santini has seen problems like yours many times.
c. Bloom's race for the governorship is futile.
d. New fares must be reported to our transportation offices in Chicago, Peoria, and Springfield.
e. In the heart of Beijing lies the Forbidden City, an imperial palace built during the Ming dynasty.

EXERCISE 17-1, page 134

Possible revisions:

a. It is a widely held myth that middle-aged people can't change.
b. The former owner of the used car assured Kyle that the mileage had not been turned back.
c. In 1985 I bought a house in need of repair.
d. When Sal was laid off from his high-paying factory job, he learned what it was like to be poor.
e. Passengers should try to complete the customs declaration form before leaving the plane.

EXERCISE 17-3, page 140

Possible revisions:

a. Asha Purpura is the defense attorney appointed by the court. Al Jones has been assigned to work with her on the case.
b. A young graduate who is careful about investments can accumulate a significant sum in a relatively short period.
c. An elementary school teacher should understand the concept of nurturing if he or she intends to be a success.
d. Because Dr. Brown and Dr. Coombs were the senior professors in the department, they served as co-chairpersons of the promotion committee.
e. If we do not stop polluting our environment, we will perish.

EXERCISE 18-2, page 143

Possible revisions:

a. Many of us are not persistent enough to make a change for the better.
b. It is sometimes difficult to hear in church because the acoustics are so terrible.

c. Liu Kwan began his career as a lawyer, but now he is a real estate mogul.
d. When Robert Frost died at age eighty-eight, he left a legacy of poems that will make him immortal.
e. This patient is kept in isolation to prevent her from catching our germs.

EXERCISE 18–3, page 144

a. Queen Anne was so angry with Sarah Churchill that she refused to see her again.
b. Correct
c. Try to come up with the rough outline, and Marika will fill in the details.
d. For the frightened refugees, the dangerous trek across the mountains was preferable to life in a war zone.
e. The parade moved off the street and onto the beach.

EXERCISE 18–4, page 146

Possible revisions:

a. Juanita told Kyle that keeping secrets would be dangerous.
b. The president thought that the scientists were using science as a means of furthering their political goals.
c. Ours was a long courtship; we waited ten years before finally deciding to marry.
d. We ironed out the wrinkles in our relationship.
e. Sasha told us that he wasn't willing to take the chance.

EXERCISE 19–1, page 155

Possible revisions:

a. As I stood in front of the microwave, I recalled my grandmother bending over her old black stove and remembered what she taught me: that any food can have soul if you love the people you are cooking for.
b. After only one date with Tomás, I came to a conclusion: With his English and my Spanish we were destined never to communicate.
c. Correct
d. We need to stop believing myths about drinking—that strong black coffee will sober you up, for example, or that a cold shower will straighten you out.
e. As we walked up the path, we came upon the gun batteries, large gray concrete structures covered with ivy and weeds.

EXERCISE 20–1, page 161

Possible revisions:

a. The city had one public swimming pool that stayed packed with children all summer long.
b. The building is being renovated, so at times we have no heat, water, or electricity.
c. Why should we pay taxes to support public transportation? We prefer to save energy dollars by carpooling.
d. Suddenly there was a loud silence; the shelling had stopped.
e. Martin looked out the window in astonishment: He had never seen snow before.

EXERCISE 20–2, page 162

Possible revisions:

a. Because the trail up Mount Finegold was declared impassable, we decided to return to our hotel a day early.
b. Correct

c. The instructor never talked to the class; she just assigned busywork and sat at her desk reading the newspaper.
d. Researchers studying the fertility of Texas land tortoises X-rayed all the female tortoises to see how many eggs they had.
e. The suburbs seemed cold; they lacked the warmth and excitement of our Italian neighborhood.

EXERCISE 21–1, page 172

a. Subject: friendship and support; verb: have
b. Subject: rings; verb: are
c. Subject: Each; verb: was
d. Subject: source; verb: is
e. Subject: signs or traces; verb: were

EXERCISE 21–2, page 173

a. High concentrations of carbon monoxide result in headaches, dizziness, unconsciousness, and even death.
b. Correct
c. Correct
d. Crystal chandeliers, polished floors, and a new oil painting have transformed Sandra's apartment.
e. Either Gertrude or Alice takes the dog out for its nightly walk.

EXERCISE 22–1, page 177

Possible revisions:

a. I can be standing in front of a Xerox machine, with parts scattered around my feet, and someone will ask me for permission to make a copy.
b. Correct
c. The instructor has asked everyone to bring his or her own tools to carpentry class.
d. An eighteenth-century architect was also a classical scholar who was often at the forefront of archeological research.
e. On the first day of class, Mr. Bhatti asked each of us why we wanted to stop smoking.

EXERCISE 23–1, page 182

Possible revisions:

a. The detective photographed the body after removing the bloodstained shawl.
b. In Professor Jamal's class, students are lucky to earn a C.
c. Please be patient with the elderly residents who have difficulty moving through the cafeteria line.
d. The Comanche braves lived violent lives; they gained respect for their skill as warriors.
e. All students can secure parking permits from the campus police office, which is open from 8 A.M. until 8 P.M.

EXERCISE 24–1, page 188

a. My Ethiopian neighbor was puzzled by the dedication of us joggers.
b. Correct
c. Sue's husband is ten years older than she [*or* . . . than she is].
d. Everyone laughed whenever Sandra described how her brother and she had seen the Loch Ness monster and fed it sandwiches.
e. Correct

EXERCISE 25–1, page 191

a. In his first production of *Hamlet,* whom did Laurence Olivier replace?
b. Correct
c. Correct
d. Some group leaders cannot handle the pressure; they give whoever makes the most noise most of their attention.
e. One of the women whom Martinez hired became the most successful lawyer in the agency.

EXERCISE 26–1, page 196

a. When Tina began breathing normally, we could relax.
b. All of us on the team felt bad about our performance.
c. Tim's friends cheered and clapped very loudly when he made it to the bottom of the beginners' slope.
d. Correct
e. Last Christmas was the most wonderful day of my life.

EXERCISE 27–1, page 201

a. Noticing that my roommate was shivering and looking pale, I rang for the nurse.
b. When I get the urge to exercise, I lie down until it passes.
c. Grandmother had driven our new jeep to the sunrise church service on Savage Mountain, so we were left with the station wagon.
d. I just heard on the news that Claudia Brandolini has broken the world record for the high jump.
e. In her junior year, Cindy ran the 440-yard dash in 51.1 seconds.

EXERCISE 27–2, page 207

a. Correct
b. The museum visitors were not supposed to touch the exhibits.
c. Our church has all the latest technology, even a closed-circuit television.
d. We often don't know whether he is angry or just joking.
e. All four children play one or two instruments.

EXERCISE 28–1, page 214

a. Correct
b. Watson and Crick discovered the mechanism that controls inheritance in all life: the workings of the DNA molecule.
c. In 1941 Hitler decided to kill the Jews. But Himmler and his SS were three years ahead of him; they had had mass murder in mind since 1938.
d. Toni could be an excellent student if she weren't so distracted by problems at home.
e. My sister Deanna was outside playing with the new puppies that had been born only a few weeks earlier.

EXERCISE 28–2, page 216

Possible revisions:

a. Fra Angelico painted each monk's cell.
b. Scientists use carbon dating to determine the approximate age of an object.
c. As the patient undressed, we saw scars on his back, stomach, and thighs. We suspected child abuse.
d. We noted right away that the taxi driver had been exposed to Americans because he knew all the latest slang.
e. The painter patched and sanded the holes, primed the walls, and painted the ceiling.

EXERCISE 29–1, page 222

a. We will make this a better country.
b. There is nothing in the world that TV has not touched on.
c. Did you understand my question?
d. A hard wind was blowing while we were climbing the mountain.
e. The child's innocent world has been taken away from him.

EXERCISE 29–2, page 224

Possible revisions:

a. He would have won the election if he had gone to the inner city to campaign.
b. If Martin Luther King, Jr., were alive today, he would be appalled by the violence in our inner cities.
c. Whenever my uncle comes to visit, he brings me a present.
d. We will lose our largest client unless we update our computer system.
e. If Verena wins a fellowship, she will go to graduate school.

EXERCISE 29–3, page 226

Possible sentences:

a. I enjoy riding my motorcycle.
b. Will you help Samantha study for the test?
c. The team hopes to work hard and win the championship.
d. Ricardo and his brothers miss surfing during the winter.
e. The babysitter let Roger stay up until midnight.

EXERCISE 31–1, page 236

a. The roses they brought home cost three dollars each.
b. There are two grocery stores on Elm Street.
c. The prime minister is the most popular leader in my country.
d. Pavel hasn't heard from the cousin he wrote to last month.
e. The king, who had served since the age of sixteen, was an old man when he died.

EXERCISE 31–2, page 239

a. an attractive young Vietnamese woman
b. a dedicated Catholic priest
c. her old blue wool sweater
d. Joe's delicious Scandinavian bread
e. many beautiful antique bird cages

EXERCISE 31–3, page 240

a. Having to listen to everyone's complaints was irritating.
b. The noise in the hall was distracting to me.
c. Correct
d. The violence in recent movies is often disgusting.
e. Correct

EXERCISE 31–4, page 241

Possible revisions:

a. We spent seven days in June at the beach, and it rained every day.
b. Correct
c. Usually she met with her patients in the afternoon, but on that day she stayed at home to take care of her son.

d. The clock is hanging on the wall in the dining room.
e. In Germany it is difficult for foreigners to become citizens even if they've lived in the country for a long time.

EXERCISE 32–1, page 246

a. Correct
b. The man at the next table complained loudly, and the waiter stomped off in disgust.
c. Instead of eating half a cake or two dozen cookies, I now grab a banana or an orange.
d. Nursing is physically and mentally demanding, yet the pay is low.
e. Uncle Sven's dulcimers disappeared as soon as he put them up for sale, but he always kept one for himself.

EXERCISE 32–2, page 248

a. She wore a black silk cape, a rhinestone collar, satin gloves, and high tops.
b. There is no need to prune, weed, fertilize, or repot your air fern.
c. City Café is noted for its spicy vegetarian dishes and its friendly, efficient service.
d. Juan walked through the room with casual, elegant grace.
e. Correct

EXERCISE 32–3, page 251

a. B. B. King and Lucille, his customized black Gibson, have electrified audiences all over the world.
b. The Scott Pack, which is a twenty-five-pound steel bottle of air, is designed to be worn on a firefighter's back.
c. Correct
d. Shakespeare's tragedy *King Lear* was given a splendid performance by the actor Laurence Olivier.
e. Correct

EXERCISE 32–4, page 256

a. April 12, 1996, is the final deadline for all applications.
b. The coach having bawled us out thoroughly, we left the locker room with his last, harsh words ringing in our ears.
c. Good technique does not guarantee, however, that the power you develop will be sufficient for Kyok Pa competition.
d. We all piled into Sadiq's car, which we affectionately referred to as the Blue Goose.
e. Please make the check payable to David Kerr, D.D.S., not David Kerr, M.D.

EXERCISE 33–1, page 262

a. We'd rather spend our money on blue-chip stocks than speculate on pork-bellies.
b. Being prepared for the worst is one way to escape disappointment.
c. When he heard the groans, he opened the door and ran out.
d. My father said that he would move to California if I would agree to transfer to UCLA.
e. I quickly accepted the fact that I was literally in third-class quarters.

EXERCISE 34–1, page 266

a. Many people believe that ferrets are vicious little rodents; in fact, ferrets are affectionate animals that tend to bite only out of fear.

b. America has been called a country of pragmatists, although the American devotion to ideals is legendary.
c. The first requirement is honesty; everything else follows.
d. I am not fond of opera; I must admit, however, that I was greatly moved by *Les Misérables*.
e. Correct

EXERCISE 35–1, page 269

a. The second and most memorable week of survival school consisted of five stages: orientation, long treks, POW camp, escape and evasion, and return to civilization.
b. Among the canceled classes were calculus, physics, advanced biology, and English 101.
c. Correct
d. For example, Teddy Roosevelt once referred to the wolf as "the beast of waste and desolation."
e. Correct

EXERCISE 36–1, page 272

a. In a democracy anyone's vote counts as much as mine.
b. Correct
c. The puppy's favorite activity was chasing its tail.
d. After we bought J.J. the latest style pants and shirts, he decided that last year's faded, ragged jeans were perfect for all occasions.
e. A crocodile's life span is about thirteen years.

EXERCISE 37–1, page 279

a. Correct
b. As Emerson wrote in 1849, "I hate quotations. Tell me what you know."
c. Andrew Marvell's most famous poem, "To His Coy Mistress," is a tightly structured argument.
d. Correct
e. Historians Segal and Stineback tell us that the English settlers considered these epidemics "the hand of God making room for His followers in the 'New World.' "

EXERCISE 39–1, page 286

a. We lived in Davenport, Iowa, during the early years of our marriage.
b. Every night after her jazzercise class, Elizaveta bragged about how invigorated she felt, but she always looked exhausted.
c. Correct
d. Every person there—from the youngest toddler to the oldest great-grandparent—was expected to sit through the three-hour sermon in respectful silence.
e. The class stood, faced the flag, placed hands over hearts, and raced through "I pledge allegiance . . . liberty and justice for all" in less than sixty seconds.

EXERCISE 40–1, page 292

a. Correct
b. Denzil spent all night studying for his psychology exam.
c. Correct
d. The first discovery of America was definitely not in A.D. 1492.
e. Turning to page 195, Marion realized that she had finally reached the end of chapter 22.

EXERCISE 41–1, page 294

a. We have ordered four azaleas, three rhododendrons, and two mountain laurels for the back area of the garden.
b. Correct
c. Correct
d. We ordered three 4-door sedans for company executives.
e. The Vietnam Veterans Memorial in Washington, D.C., had 58,132 names inscribed on it when it was dedicated in 1982.

EXERCISE 42–1, page 297

a. Howard Hughes commissioned the *Spruce Goose,* a beautifully built but thoroughly impractical wooden aircraft.
b. Pulaski was so exhausted he could barely lift his foot the six inches to the elevator floor.
c. Even though it is almost always hot in Mexico in the summer, you can usually find a cool spot on one of the park benches in the town's *zócalo.*
d. Correct
e. *The City and the Pillar* was an early novel by Gore Vidal.

EXERCISE 44–1, page 307

a. Correct
b. The quietly purring cat cleaned first one paw and then the other before curling up under the stove.
c. The Moche were a pre-Columbian people who established a sophisticated culture in ancient Peru.
d. Your dog is well known in our neighborhood.
e. Correct

EXERCISE 45–1, page 312

a. District Attorney Johnson was disgusted when the jurors turned in a verdict of not guilty after only one hour of deliberation.
b. My mother has begun to research the history of her Cherokee ancestors in North Carolina.
c. Correct
d. Refugees from Central America are finding it more and more difficult to cross the Rio Grande into the United States.
e. I want to take Environmental Biology 103, one other biology course, and one English course.

EXERCISE 47–1, page 329

a. hasty generalization; b. false analogy; c. emotional appeal; d. faulty cause-and-effect reasoning; e. *either . . . or* fallacy

EXERCISE 57–1, page 422

a. idea, words, freedom, movement; b. Pride, bottom, mistakes; c. trouble, rat (noun/adjective), race, rat; d. censorship, flick, dial; e. Figures, liars

EXERCISE 57–2, page 425

a. Every (pronoun/adjective), its (pronoun/adjective), its (pronoun/adjective); b. those, who; c. I, some (pronoun/adjective), that, I, myself; d. I, You, He; e. I, it

EXERCISE 57–3, page 427

a. have been; b. can be savored; c. does bring down; d. is, could rephrase; e. Do scald

EXERCISE 57-4, page 429

a. Adjectives: General, wrong; adverb: generally; b. Adjectives: The (article), American, tolerant; adverb: wonderfully; c. Adjectives: a (article), rational; adverb: not; d. Adjectives: a (article), thin; adverb: very; e. Adjective: the (article); adverb: faster

EXERCISE 58-1, page 434

a. Complete subject: A spoiled child; simple subject: child; b. Complete subject: all facts; simple subject: facts; c. Complete subject: (You); d. Complete subject: nothing except change; simple subject: nothing; e. Complete subject: The only difference between a rut and a grave; simple subject: difference

EXERCISE 58-2, page 437

a. Subject complement: truth; b. Direct object: the depth of a river; c. Subject complement: yellow; d. Direct object: a man [or a woman]; object complement: wise; e. Indirect objects: me, you; direct objects: a capitalist, a bloodsucker

EXERCISE 59-1, page 441

a. with no side effects (adjective phrase modifying *tranquilizer*); b. of several air traffic controllers (adjective phrase modifying *job*), with ease (adverbial phrase modifying *could perform*); c. like a loose garment (adverbial phrase modifying *wears*); d. of a nation (adjective phrase modifying *ideals*), by its advertising (adverbial phrase modifying *can tell*); e. In prosperity (adverbial phrase modifying *smokes*)

EXERCISE 59-2, page 444

a. who has outposts in your head (adjective clause modifying *enemy*); b. that is not dangerous (adjective clause modifying *idea*); c. When I am an old woman (adverb clause modifying *shall wear*); d. what they mean (noun clause used as the direct object of *say*); e. unless it is practiced on clever persons (adverb clause modifying *is*)

EXERCISE 59-3, page 446

a. being sixteen (gerund phrase used as subject complement); b. to conceal him (infinitive phrase used as direct object of *tried*), naming him Smith (gerund phrase used as object of the preposition *by*); c. made tedious by morality (participial phrase modifying *gossip*); d. Being weak (participial phrase modifying *foxes*); e. to be older (infinitive phrase used as direct object of *wanted*)

EXERCISE 60-1, page 450

a. complex; whose work sells (adjective clause); b. compound; c. simple; d. complex; If you don't go to other people's funerals (adverb clause); e. compound-complex; what you are afraid of (noun clause)

(continued from page iv)

Bruce Catton, from "Grant and Lee: A Study in Contrasts," *The American Story*, Earl Schenck Miers, editor. © 1956 by Broadcast Music, Inc. Reprinted by permission of the U.S. Capitol Historical Society.

Barnaby Conrad III, from " 'Train of Kings, the King of Trains' Is Back on Track," *Smithsonian*, December 1983. Reprinted by permission of *Smithsonian*.

Earl Conrad, from *Harriet Tubman*. Reprinted by permission of Paul S. Erikson, Publisher.

James Underwood Crockett, Oliver E. Allen, and the Editors of Time-Life Books, from *The Time-Life Encyclopedia of Gardening, Wildflower Gardening*. © 1977 Time-Life Books, Inc. Reprinted by permission of Time-Life Books, Inc.

Emily Dickinson, from "The Snake." Reprinted by permission of the publishers and the Trustees of Amherst College from *The Poems of Emily Dickinson*, Thomas H. Johnson, Ed. Cambridge, Mass.: The Belknap Press of Harvard University Press. Copyright 1951, 1955, 1979, 1983 by the President and Fellows of Harvard College.

Erik Eckholm, from "Pygmy Chimp Readily Learns Language Skill," *The New York Times*. Copyright © 1985 by The New York Times Company. Reprinted by permission.

Jane Goodall, from *In the Shadow of Man*. Copyright © 1971 by Hugo and Jane van Lawick-Goodall. Reprinted by permission of Houghton Mifflin Company.

Ellen Goodman, from "Bad Samaritans." © 1984 The Boston Globe Newspaper Co./Washington Post Writers Group. Reprinted with permission.

Stephen Jay Gould, from "Were Dinosaurs Dumb?" *The Panda's Thumb: More Reflections on Natural History*. Copyright © 1980 by Stephen Jay Gould. Reprinted by permission of W. W. Norton & Company, Inc.

Hillary Hauser, from "Exploring a Sunken Realm in Australia," *National Geographic*, January 1984. Reprinted by permission of the National Geographic Society.

Richard Hofstadter, from *America at 1750: A Social Portrait*. Copyright © 1971 by Beatrice K. Hofstadter, executrix of the estate of Richard Hofstadter. Reprinted by permission of Alfred A. Knopf, Inc.

Phillip Kopper, "How to Open an Oyster." Copyright © 1979 by Phillip Kopper. Reprinted by permission of Times Books, a division of Quadrangle/The New York Times Book Co., Inc., from *The Wild Edge: Life and Love of the Great American Beaches* by Phillip Kopper.

William Least Heat Moon, from *Blue Highways*. Copyright © 1982 by William Least Heat Moon. Reprinted by permission of Little, Brown and Company.

Margaret Mead, from "New Superstitions for Old," *A Way of Seeing*. Reprinted by permission of William Morrow & Company, Inc.

Gloria Naylor, from *Linden Hills*. Copyright © 1985 by Gloria Naylor. Used by permission of Viking Penguin, a division of Penguin Books USA, Inc.

Chet Raymo, from "Curious Stuff, Water and Ice," *The Boston Globe*, January 27, 1986. Reprinted by permission of the author.

Paul Reps, from "The Moon Cannot Be Stolen," *Zen Flesh, Zen Bones*. Reprinted by permission of Charles E. Tuttle Co., Inc. of Tokyo, Japan.

Anne Rudloe and Jack Rudloe, from "Electric Warfare: The Fish That Kill with Thunderbolts," *Smithsonian*, August 1993. © Anne Rudloe and Jack Rudloe.

Julian Simon, "Immigration for a Stronger America." *The Washington Post*, September 1, 1990. Copyright © *The Washington Post*.

Lewis Thomas, from "On Societies as Organisms." Copyright © 1971 by The Massachusetts Medical Society, from *The Lives of a Cell* by Lewis Thomas. Reprinted by permission of Viking Penguin, a division of Penguin Books USA, Inc.

Margaret Visser, from *Much Depends on Dinner*. Copyright © 1986 by Margaret Visser. Reprinted by permission of Grove/Atlantic, Inc. in the United States and McClelland & Stewart, Inc. in Canada.

Olivia Vlahos, from *Human Beginnings*. Published by Viking Penguin, Inc. Reprinted by permission of the author.

Index

Special Help for ESL Students

Boldface numbers refer to sections of the book.

abbr	faulty abbreviation **40**		**p**	punctuation
ad	adverb or adjective **26**		⸜	comma **32**
add	add needed word **10**		**no ,**	no comma **33**
agr	agreement **21, 22**		**;**	semicolon **34**
appr	inappropriate language **17**		**:**	colon **35**
art	article **30**		⸜	apostrophe **36**
awk	awkward		**" "**	quotation marks **37**
cap	capital letter **45**		**. ? !**	period, question mark, exclamation point **38**
case	case **24, 25**			
cliché	cliché **18e**		**— ( )**	dash, parentheses,
coh	coherence **7**		**[ ] ...**	brackets, ellipsis mark,
coord	coordination **8b**		**/**	slash **39**
cs	comma splice **20**		**par. ¶**	new paragraph **6d**
dev	inadequate development **2, 6**		**pass**	ineffective passive **14a, 28c**
dm	dangling modifier **12e**		**proof**	proofreading problem **3c**
-ed	*-ed* ending **27d**		**ref**	pronoun reference **23**
emph	emphasis **14**		**run-on**	run-on sentence **20**
ESL	English as a second language **29–31**		***-s***	*-s* ending on verb **21, 27c**
exact	inexact language **18**		**sexist**	sexist language **17f, 22a**
frag	sentence fragment **19**		**shift**	distracting shift **13**
fs	fused sentence **20**		**sl**	slang **17d**
hyph	hyphen **44**		**sp**	misspelled word **43**
idiom	idioms **18d**		**sub**	subordination **8**
irreg	irregular verb **27a–b**		**s-v**	subject-verb agreement **21, 27c**
ital	italics (underlining) **42**		**t**	verb tense **28a**
jarg	jargon **17a**		**trans**	transition needed **7e**
lc	use lowercase letter **45**		**usage**	see Glossary of Usage
mix	mixed construction **11**		**v**	voice **14a, 28c**
mm	misplaced modifier **12a–d**		**var**	sentence variety **8, 15**
mood	mood **28b**		**vb**	problem with verb **27–29**
ms	manuscript form **4b**		**w**	wordy **16**
nonst	nonstandard usage **17d, 27**		**//**	faulty parallelism
num	numbers **41**		**∧**	insert
om	omitted word **10, 30, 31a**		**x**	obvious error
			#	insert space
			⌒	close up space

Detailed Menu

Answers to Exercises

Diana Hacker

RULES FOR WRITERS

Process

Paragraphs

Clarity

Grammar

Punctuation

Mechanics

Argument

Research

Basics

THIRD EDITION

Answers to
Numbered Exercises

Diana Hacker

RULES FOR
WRITERS

Third Edition

Bedford Books of St. Martin's Press ≈ Boston

For information, write: St. Martin's Press, Inc.
175 Fifth Avenue, New York, NY 10010

Editorial Offices: Bedford Books *of* St. Martin's Press
75 Arlington Street, Boston, MA 02116

ISBN: 0–312–13812–1

Answers to Numbered Exercises

EXERCISE 5–1, page 68

Topic sentence: A recent plan of the mayor's threatens to destroy one of the oldest and most successfully integrated neighborhoods in our city, replacing it with luxury condominiums and a shopping mall.

Eliminate the following sentences: The mayor has hired the best urban planners and architects in the country to design and build three large skyscrapers along with parking facilities for the area. One woman has even moved to the city from California to work on the project.

EXERCISE 7–1, page 86

1. Once children have learned to read, they go beyond their textbooks and explore the popular books written just for them.
    2. In order to see how these books portray men and women, I decided to visit the St. Peter Public Library.
        3. One book I found, *The Very Worst Thing,* tells of the adventures of a little boy on his first day in a new school.
            4. He arrives at school wearing the new sweater his mother has knit for him and is greeted by his teacher, Miss Pruce, and his male principal.
            4. At recess, the girls jump rope and toss a ball back and forth while the boys choose football teams and establish a tree house club.
            4. For show-and-tell that day, Henry, his new friend, brings a snake and some mice; Alice shows her foreign dolls; and Elizabeth demonstrates how to make fudge with Rice Krispies.
        3. In another book, *Come Back, Amelia Bedelia,* Amelia is fired from her job of baking for Mrs. Rogers, so she tries to find work as a beautician, a seamstress, a file clerk, and an office girl for a doctor.

    4. After trying all of these jobs unsuccessfully, she goes back to Mrs. Rogers and gets back her old job by making cream puffs.

  3. The rest of the books I looked at contained similar sex-role stereotypes.

    4. Boys wear jeans and T-shirts, set up lemonade stands, and play broomball, while girls wear dresses, play dress-up, and jump rope.

    4. Men are businessmen, soldiers, veterinarians, and truck drivers.

    4. Women are housewives, teachers, and witches who make love potions for girls wanting husbands.

EXERCISE 8–1, page 96

Possible revisions:

1. Bay Street, located in the heart of downtown Nassau, houses the Straw Market.
2. Noticing that the sky was glowing orange and red, I bent down to crawl into the bunker.
3. Our waitress, who was costumed in a kimono, had painted her face white and arranged her hair in an upswept lacquered beehive.
4. Cocaine is an addictive drug that can seriously harm you both physically and mentally, if death doesn't get you first.
5. These particles, known as "stealth liposomes," can hide in the body for a long time without detection.
6. At the airport I was met by my host mother, Madame Nicole Kimmel, a very excitable woman who knew absolutely no English.
7. He walked up to the pitcher's mound, dug his toe into the ground, and swung his arm around backward and forward. Then he threw the ball and struck the batter out.
8. The Chesapeake and Ohio Canal, a 184-mile waterway constructed in the 1800s, was a major source of transportation for goods during the Civil War era.
9. The lift chairs were going around so fast that they were bumping the skiers into their seats.
10. The first football card set, released by the Goudey Gum Company in 1933, featured only three football players: Red Grange, Bronko Nagurski, and Knute Rockne.

EXERCISE 8–2, page 98

Possible revisions:

1. My grandfather, who was born eighty-six years ago in Puerto Rico, raised his daughters the old-fashioned way.
2. As I was losing consciousness, my will to live kicked in.
3. Louis's team, which worked with the foreign mission, built new churches and restored those damaged by hurricanes.
4. When the rotor hit, it gouged a hole about an eighth of an inch deep in my helmet.
5. Although our family owned a Jeep, a pickup truck, and a sports car, Sarah felt that we lacked decent transportation.

EXERCISE 9–1, page 102

Possible revisions:

1. The summer of our engagement, we saw a few plays, attended family outings, and went to a few parties.
2. At the arts and crafts table, the children make potholders and key rings, weave baskets, paint, and assemble model cars.
3. The examiners observed us to see if we could stomach the grotesque accidents and knew how to cope with them.
4. During basic training, I was told not only what to do but also what to think.
5. Activities on Wednesday afternoons include fishing trips, dance lessons, and computer training.
6. Bill finds it harder to be fair to himself than to others.
7. More plants fail from improper watering than from any other cause.
8. Your adviser familiarizes you with the school and explains how to select classes appropriate for your curriculum.
9. To administer the poison, the tribe's sorcerers put it in their victims' food, throw it into their huts, or drop it into their mouths or nostrils while they sleep.
10. The babysitter was expected to feed two children, entertain them, take phone messages, and do some cleaning in the kitchen.

EXERCISE 10–1, page 106

Possible revisions:

1. Their starting salaries are higher than those of other professionals with more seniority.
2. In my opinion, her dependence on tranquilizers is no healthier than the alcoholic's dependence on alcohol or the addict's addiction to drugs.
3. Jupiter is larger than any other planet in our solar system.
4. Darryl was both gratified by and apprehensive about his scholarship to UCLA.
5. It was obvious that the students liked the new teacher more than they liked the principal. [*or* . . . than the principal did.]

EXERCISE 11–1, page 109

Possible revisions:

1. The number and strength of drinks, the amount of time that has passed since the last drink, and one's body weight determine the concentration of alcohol in the blood.
2. Pushing the button for the insert mode opens the computer's memory.
3. The Eskimos were forced to eat their dogs because the caribou, on which they depended for food, migrated out of reach.
4. The shelter George stayed in required the men to leave at nine in the morning and take their belongings with them.
5. As a precaution, dentists now wear surgical gloves to prevent contact with the patients' blood and saliva.

EXERCISE 12-1, page 113

Possible revisions:

1. After ten hours of grilling by the police, the orderly confessed that he had given a lethal injection to the patient.
2. Several recent studies have encouraged heart patients to watch their cholesterol levels more carefully.
3. He promised at her deathbed never to remarry.
4. The recordings were all done at Electric Ladyland, the studio of the late Jimi Hendrix.
5. The old Marlboro ads depicted a man on horseback smoking a cigarette.

EXERCISE 12-2, page 116

Possible revisions:

1. Exhausted from battling the tide and the undertow, the swimmer spotted a welcome respite—the beach!
2. When investigating burglaries and thefts, I found it easy to sympathize with the victims because I had been a victim myself.
3. When I was a child growing up in Nigeria, my mother taught me to treat all elders with respect.
4. When I was twelve, my social studies teacher entered me in a public speaking contest.
5. Although it was too expensive for her budget, Juanita bought the lavender skirt.

EXERCISE 13-1, page 120

Possible revisions:

1. The polygraph examiner will ask if you have ever stolen goods on the job, if you have ever taken drugs, and if you have ever killed or threatened to kill anyone.
2. A single parent often has only his or her ingenuity to rely on. *Or* Single parents often have only their ingenuity to rely on.
3. As I was pulling in the decoys, I could see and hear the geese heading back to the bay.
4. Rescue workers put water on her face and lifted her head gently onto a pillow. Finally, she opened her eyes.
5. With a little self-discipline and a desire to improve yourself, you too can enjoy the benefits of running.

EXERCISE 14-1, page 124

Possible revisions:

1. Just as the police closed in, the terrorists fired two shots from the roof of the hotel.
2. Julia passed the bar exam on her first attempt.
3. Emphatic and active; no change.
4. Truckers use C.B.'s to find parts, equipment, food, lodging, and anything else they need.
5. Fireworks exploded all around us.

EXERCISE 15–1, page 127

Possible revision:

After spending thirty years of my life on a tobacco farm, I cannot understand why people smoke. The whole process of raising tobacco involves deadly chemicals. Before the tobacco seed is ever planted, the ground is treated for mold and chemically fertilized. Once the seed is planted and begins to grow, the bed is treated with weed killer. The plant is then transferred to the field. After about two months, it is sprayed with poison to kill worms, and as the harvest approaches, it is sprayed once more with a chemical to retard the growth of suckers. When the tobacco is harvested, it is hung in a barn to dry. These barns are havens for birds, which defecate all over the leaves. After drying, the leaves are divided by color, and no feces are removed. They are then sold to the tobacco companies. What the tobacco companies do after they receive the tobacco I do not know. I do not need to know. They cannot remove what I know is in the leaf and on the leaf, and I don't want any of it to pass through my mouth.

EXERCISE 16–1, page 132

Possible revisions:

1. Seeing the barrels, the driver slammed on his brakes.
2. Data sets are used to communicate with other computers.
3. New Harmony, Indiana, was founded as a utopian community.
4. Martin Luther King, Jr., set a high standard for future leaders.
5. The price of driving while intoxicated can be extremely high.

EXERCISE 17–1, page 134

Possible revision:

1. Because factory orders and profits are down, we will not be increasing our staff over the next fiscal year.
2. As I approached the jail where my brother was being held, several inmates shouted lewd remarks.
3. The nurse said that the patient died because the surgeon had made a mistake.
4. When we returned from our evening walk, we were horrified to see that our house was on fire.
5. The important fact is that the company is losing money.

EXERCISE 17–2, page 138

Possible revision:

The graduation speaker disappointed us. He should have discussed the options and challenges facing the graduating class. Instead, he rebuked us for being lazy and pampered. He did make some good points, however. Our professors have certainly spoiled us by not holding fast to deadlines, by dismissing assignments when the class complained, by ignoring our tardiness, and by handing out too many unearned C's. Still, we resented this speech as the final word from the college administration. It should have been the orientation speech when we started college.

EXERCISE 17–3, page 140

Possible revisions:

1. I have been trained to doubt automobile mechanics, even those with excellent reputations.
2. A newly elected president must wait several months before inauguration.
3. In the recent gubernatorial race, Lena Weiss, a defense lawyer, easily defeated Harvey Tower, an architect.
4. In my hometown, the mayor has led the fight for a fair share of federal funds for new schools.
5. As partners in a successful real estate firm, John Crockett and Sarah Cooke have been an effective sales team; he is particularly skillful at arranging attractive mortgage packages; she is especially successful at telemarketing.

EXERCISE 18–1, page 141

Possible answers:

1. decay (verb): decompose, disintegrate, break up, corrode, rot, putrify, fester, molder
2. difficult (adjective): hard, tough, rigorous, formidable, arduous, tricky, demanding, complex
3. hurry (verb): rush, accelerate, bustle, speed up, scamper, scramble, quicken, hasten, dash, dart
4. pleasure (noun): enjoyment, contentment, euphoria, gratification, satisfaction, relish, gusto, fun, entertainment, amusement
5. secret (adjective): concealed, covert, cryptic, hidden, arcane, clandestine, undercover, furtive, stealthy, mysterious, unknown
6. talent (noun): ability, genius, skill, faculty, flair, gift, power, forte

EXERCISE 18–2, page 143

Possible revisions:

1. Waste, misuse of government money, security and health violations, and even pilfering have become major problems at the FBI.
2. Trifle, a popular English dessert, contains a mélange of ingredients that do not always appeal to American tastes.
3. Grand Isle State Park is bordered on three sides by water.
4. Frequently I cannot do my work because the music blaring from my son's room distracts me.
5. Tom Jones is an illegitimate child who grows up under the care of Squire Western.

EXERCISE 18–3, page 145

1. Be sure to report on the danger of releasing genetically engineered bacteria into the atmosphere.
2. Why do you assume that embezzling bank assets is so different from robbing the bank?
3. Most of the class agreed with Sylvia's view that nuclear proliferation is potentially a very dangerous problem.
4. What type of wedding are you planning?
5. Andrea intends to join the Peace Corps after graduation.

EXERCISE 18–4, page 147

Possible revisions:

1. I could read him plainly; he was very embarrassed.
2. Tears were rolling [*or* streaming] down the child's face.
3. High school is a place of volatile emotions.
4. There are too many managers here at corporate headquarters.
5. Once she had warmed up to it, Helen burned through the assignment.

EXERCISE 19–1, page 156

Possible revisions:

1. Sitting at a sidewalk café near the Sorbonne, I could pass as a French student as long as I kept my mouth shut.
2. Mother loved to play all our favorite games: canasta, Monopoly, hide-and-seek, and even kick the can.
3. Correct
4. I had pushed these fears into one of those quiet places in my mind, hoping they would stay there asleep.
5. To give my family a comfortable, secure home life is my most important goal.
6. If a woman from the desert tribe showed anger toward her husband, she was whipped in front of the whole village and shunned by the rest of the women.
7. A tornado is a violent whirling wind that produces a funnel-shaped cloud and moves over land in a slim path of destruction.
8. With machetes, the explorers cut their way through the tall grasses to the edge of the canyon, where they began to lay out their tapes for the survey.
9. In my three years of driving, I have never had an accident—not one wreck, not one fender-bender, not even a little dent.
10. The pilots ejected from the burning plane, landing in the water not far from the ship. Immediately they popped their flares and life vests.

EXERCISE 20–1, page 162

Possible revisions:

1. For the first time in her adult life, Lucia had time to waste; she could spend a whole day curled up with a good book.
2. Be sure to take your credit card, because Disney has a way of making you want to spend money.
3. The next time an event is canceled because of bad weather, don't blame the meteorologist. Blame nature.
4. While we were walking down Grover Avenue, Gary told us about his Aunt Elsinia, an extraordinary woman.
5. The president of Algeria was standing next to the podium waiting to be introduced.
6. On most days I had only enough money for bus fare; lunch was a luxury I could not afford.
7. There was one major reason for John's wealth: His grandfather had been a multimillionaire.
8. The neighborhood was ruled by gangs. What kind of environment was this for my four-year-old daughter?
9. Of the many geysers in Yellowstone National Park, the most famous is Old Faithful, which sometimes reaches 150 feet in height.
10. Wind power for the home, a supplementary source of energy, can be combined with electricity, gas, or solar energy.

EXERCISE 20-2, page 163

Possible revisions:

1. Are you able to endure boredom, isolation, and potential violence? Then the army may well be the adventure for you.
2. Jet funny cars are powered by the kind of jet engines that are used on fighter aircraft and helicopters.
3. If one of the dogs should happen to fall through the ice, it would be cut loose from the team and left to its fate. The sled drivers could not endanger the rest of the team for just one dog.
4. The volunteers worked hard to restore calm and search for survivors after the bombing; as a matter of fact, many of them did not sleep for the first three days of the emergency.
5. Correct
6. After days of struggling with her dilemma, Rosa came to a decision: She would sacrifice herself for her people and her cause.
7. The Carrier Air Wing Eight, called CAG-8, is made up of ten squadrons, each with its own mission and role.
8. We didn't trust her because she had lied before.
9. I pushed open the first door with my back. Turning to open the second door, I encountered a young woman in a wheelchair holding it open for me.
10. If you want to lose weight and keep if off, consider this advice: Don't try to take it off faster than you put it on.

EXERCISE 21-1, page 173

1. Subject: professor nor assistants; verb: were.
2. Subject: Quilts; verb: command.
3. Subject: pool, courts, and courts; verb: were.
4. Subject: device; verb: is.
5. Subject: gate and wall; verb: make.
6. Subject: dangers; verb: are.
7. Subject: cartoon and rhymes; verb: were.
8. Subject: supplies; verb: were.
9. Subject: slaughter; verb: has.
10. Subject: bag and sword; verb: were.

EXERCISE 21-2, page 174

1. Small pieces of fermented bread were placed around the edge of the platter.
2. Correct
3. Correct
4. Nearly everyone on the panel favors the arms control agreement.
5. Every year a number of kokanee salmon, not native to the region, are introduced into Flathead Lake.
6. Correct
7. Correct
8. At MGM Studios at Disney World, the wonders of moviemaking come alive.
9. SEACON is the only one of our war games that emphasizes scientific and technical issues.
10. The key program of Alcoholics Anonymous is the twelve steps to recovery.

EXERCISE 22–1, page 178

Possible revisions:

1. Drivers who refuse to take a blood or breath test will have their licenses suspended for six months.
2. Why should we care about the timber wolf? One answer is that it has proved beneficial to humans by killing off weakened prey.
3. No one should be forced to sacrifice his or her prized possession — life — for someone else.
4. Seven qualified Hispanic agents applied, all hoping for a career move that would let them use their language and cultural training on more than just translations and drug deals; the job went to a non-Hispanic who was taking a crash course in Spanish.
5. Anyone who notices any suspicious activity should report it to the police.
6. The crowd grew until it filled not only the plaza but also the surrounding streets.
7. David lent his motorcycle to someone who allowed a friend to use it.
8. Correct
9. Good teachers are patient with their students, and they usually maintain an even temper.
10. A graduate student needs to be willing to take on a sizable debt unless he or she has a wealthy family.

EXERCISE 23–1, page 182

Possible revisions:

1. Many people believe that the polygraph test is highly reliable if conducted by a licensed examiner.
2. Because of his outspoken attitude toward fascism, Paul Robeson was labeled a Communist.
3. The encyclopedia states that male moths can smell female moths from several miles away.
4. Be sure to visit Istanbul's bazaar, where vendors sell everything from Persian rugs to electronic calculators.
5. If you have a sweet tooth, you can visit the confectioner's shop, where candy is still made as it was a hundred years ago.

EXERCISE 24–1, page 188

1. Correct
2. A professional counselor advised the division chief that Marco, Fidelia, and I should be allowed to apply for the opening.
3. Because of last night's fire, we are fed up with his drinking and smoking.
4. The student ethics board gave Marlo and me the opportunity to defend ourselves against the instructor's false charges.
5. During the testimony, the witness pointed directly at the defendant and announced that the thief was he.

EXERCISE 25-1, page 191

1. When medicine is scarce and expensive, physicians must give it to whoever has the best chance to survive.
2. Correct
3. They will become business partners with whoever is willing to contribute to the company's coffers.
4. The only interstate travelers who get pulled over for speeding are the ones who cannot afford a radar detector.
5. The elderly woman whom I was asked to take care of was a clever, delightful companion.

EXERCISE 26-1, page 196

1. When answering the phone, you should speak clearly and courteously.
2. In the early 1970s, chances for survival of the bald eagle looked really slim.
3. After checking to see how badly I had been hurt, my sister dialed 911.
4. Professor Brown's public praise of my performance on the exam made me feel a little strange.
5. The hall closet is so filled with ski equipment that the door will hardly close.

EXERCISE 27-1, page 202

1. How many times have you sworn to yourself, "I'll diet tomorrow, after one more piece of cheesecake"?
2. The burglar must have gone immediately upstairs, grabbed what looked good, and taken off.
3. In just a week the ground had frozen, and the first winter storm had left over a foot of snow.
4. Correct
5. Larry claimed that he had drunk a bad soda, but Esther suspected the truth.

EXERCISE 27-2, page 207

1. The bald eagle feeds mostly on carrion, such as the carcasses of deer or the bodies of dead salmon.
2. We were asked to sign a contract committing ourselves to not smoking for forty-eight hours.
3. The training for security checkpoint screeners, which takes place in an empty airplane hangar, consists of watching out-of-date videos.
4. Does he have enough energy to hold down two jobs while going to night school?
5. How would you feel if a loved one had been a victim of a crime like this?

EXERCISE 28-1, page 215

1. Our neighbor stood at the door looking so pale and ashen that we thought he had just seen a ghost.
2. Correct
3. Correct
4. Don Quixote, in Cervantes' novel, is an idealist ill suited for life in the real world.
5. When the doctor said "It's a girl," I was stunned. For nine months I had dreamed about playing baseball with my son.

EXERCISE 28–2, page 217

Possible revisions:

1. My mother invited all of my friends to the party.
2. The dog showed no loyalty at all to his owner, who had mistreated him.
3. We can conclude that a college education provides a significant economic advantage.
4. The settlers ruthlessly stripped the land of timber before they realized the consequences of their actions.
5. The assistant manager explained home equity loans to me.

EXERCISE 29–1, page 222

1. Children are exposed at an early age to certain aspects of adult life.
2. We've spent too much money this month, especially on things we don't really need.
3. Have you found your wallet yet?
4. I have eaten Thai food only once before.
5. It would have helped to know the cost before the work began.

EXERCISE 29–2, page 224

1. If it were not raining, we could go fishing.
2. If Lee had followed the doctor's orders, he would have recovered from his operation by now.
3. You would have met my cousin if you had come to the party last night.
4. Whenever I wash my car, it rains.
5. Our daughter would have drowned if Officer Blake hadn't risked his life to save her.

EXERCISE 29–3, page 227

1. Pollen makes me sneeze.
2. The club president asked us to work three hours at the rummage sale. *Or* The club president asked to speak to us about the next fundraiser.
3. Next summer we plan to visit six countries in Europe.
4. Waverly intends to study sports management and to get a job in major league baseball.
5. Please stop running in the halls. *Or* Please stop to buy milk on your way home from school.

EXERCISE 30–1, page 233

The Moon Cannot Be Stolen

Ryokan, who was a Zen master, lived a simple life in a little hut at the foot of a mountain. One evening a thief visited the hut only to discover there was nothing in it to steal.

Ryokan returned and caught him. "You may have come a long way to visit me," he told the prowler, "and you should not return empty-handed. Please take my clothes as a gift." The thief was bewildered. He took Ryokan's clothes and slunk away. Ryokan sat naked, watching the moon. "Poor fellow," he mused, "I wish I could give him this beautiful moon."

EXERCISE 31–1, page 237

1. Henri and Nicole are good friends.
2. It is important to study the grammar of English.
3. The neighbor we trusted was a thief.
4. I don't use the subway because I am afraid.
5. Archaeologists have excavated the city where the old Persian kings are buried.

EXERCISE 31–2, page 239

1. two large round marble tables
2. several tiny yellow tulips
3. a classic sports car
4. a small square brick courtyard
5. several charming Italian restaurants

EXERCISE 31–3, page 241

1. Megan worked on her art project for eight hours but still she was not satisfied.
2. That blackout was the most frightening experience I've ever had.
3. Correct
4. Three weeks after his promotion, he decided that being the boss was boring.
5. The exhibit on the La Brea tar pits was fascinating.

EXERCISE 31–4, page 242

1. Correct
2. Only the adults in the family were allowed to sit at the dining room table; the children ate in another room.
3. If the train is on time it will arrive at six o'clock in the morning.
4. She licked the stamp, stuck it on the envelope, put the envelope in her pocket, and walked to the nearest mailbox.
5. The mailbox was at the intersection of Laidlaw Avenue and Williams Street.

EXERCISE 32–1, page 246

1. When the runaway race car hit, the gas tank exploded.
2. Correct
3. Lighting the area like a second moon, the helicopter circled the scene.
4. While one of the robbers tied Laureen to a chair and gagged her with an apron, the other emptied the contents of the safe into a knapsack.
5. Correct

EXERCISE 32–2, page 248

1. My brother and I found a dead garter snake, picked it up, and placed it on Miss Eunice's doorstep.
2. For breakfast the children ordered cornflakes, English muffins with peanut butter, and cherry Cokes.

3. Patients with severe, irreversible brain damage should not be put on life support machines.
4. Correct
5. Anne Frank and thousands like her were forced to hide in attics, cellars, and secret rooms in an effort to save their lives.

EXERCISE 32-3, page 251

1. I had the pleasure of talking to a woman who had just returned from India, where she had lived for ten years.
2. The Irish students knew by heart the exploits of Cuchulain, a legendary Irish warrior, but they knew nothing about Freud or Marx or any religion but their own.
3. Correct
4. Correct
5. Going on an archaeological dig, which has always been an ambition of mine, seems out of the question this year.

EXERCISE 32-4, page 256

1. Mr. Mundy was born on July 22, 1939, in Arkansas, where his family had lived for four generations.
2. It has been reported that the Republican who suggested Eisenhower as a presidential candidate meant Milton, not Ike.
3. One substitute for CFC's has environmentalists concerned because it contains chlorine, which is also damaging to the ozone layer.
4. We pulled into the first apartment complex we saw and slowly patrolled the parking lots.
5. Correct
6. Cobbled streets too narrow for two cars to pass were lined with tiny houses leaning so close together they almost touched.
7. Correct
8. "The last flight," she said with a sigh, "went out five minutes before I arrived at the airport."
9. The Rio Grande, the border between Texas and Mexico, lay before us. It was a sluggish, mud-filled, meandering stream that gave off an odor akin to sewage.
10. Pittsburgh, Pennsylvania, is the home of several fine colleges and universities.

EXERCISE 33-1, page 263

1. He wore a thick black wool coat over army fatigues.
2. Often public figures (Michael Jackson is a good example) go to great lengths to guard their private lives.
3. Male supremacy was assumed by my father and accepted by my mother.
4. The kitchen was covered with black soot that had been deposited by the wood-burning stove, which stood in the middle of the room.
5. Many abusive parents were themselves abused children, so they have no history of benevolent experiences and lack appropriate healthy role models after which to pattern their behavior as parents.

EXERCISE 34–1, page 267

1. When Chao Neng joined the police force in 1993, he had no idea how hard it would be to bury a fellow officer.
2. Martin Luther King, Jr., had not intended to be a preacher; initially, he had planned to become a lawyer.
3. Severe, unremitting pain is a ravaging force, especially when the patient tries to hide it from others.
4. I entered this class feeling jittery and incapable; I leave feeling poised and confident.
5. Some educators believe that African American history should be taught in separate courses; others prefer to see it integrated into survey courses.

EXERCISE 35–1, page 269

1. The patient survived for one reason: The medics got to her in time.
2. While traveling through France, Fiona visited the Loire Valley, Chartres, the Louvre, and the McDonald's stand at the foot of the Eiffel Tower.
3. Minds are like parachutes: They function only when open. *Or* Minds are like parachutes; they function only when open.
4. Correct
5. Correct

EXERCISE 36–1, page 273

1. For a bus driver, complaints, fare disputes, and robberies are all part of a day's work.
2. We cleared four years' accumulation of trash out of the attic; it's amazing how much junk can pile up.
3. Booties are placed on the sled dogs' feet to protect them from sharp rocks and ice.
4. Three teenage sons can devour about as much food as four full-grown field hands. The only difference is that they don't do half as much work.
5. Luck is an important element in a rock musician's career.

EXERCISE 37–1, page 279

1. The dispatcher's voice cut through the still night air: "Scout 41, robbery in progress, alley rear of 58th and Blaine."
2. My skiing instructor promised us that we would all be ready for the intermediate slope in one week.
3. Gloria Steinem once twisted an old proverb like this: "A woman without a man is like a fish without a bicycle."
4. Joan was a self-proclaimed rabid Blue Jays fan; she went to every home game and even flew to Atlanta for the World Series.
5. Correct

EXERCISE 38–1, page 282

Although I am generally rational, I am superstitious. I never walk under ladders or put shoes on the table. If I spill the salt, I go into frenzied calisthenics picking up the grains and tossing them over my left shoulder. As a result of these curious activities, I've always wondered whether knowing the roots of superstitions would quell my irrational responses. Superstition has it, for example, that one should never place a hat on the bed. This superstition arises from a time when head lice were quite common and placing a guest's hat on the bed stood a good chance of spreading lice through the host's bed. Doesn't this make good sense? And doesn't it stand to reason that if I know that my guests don't have lice I shouldn't care where their hats go? Of course it does. It is fair to ask, then, whether I have changed my ways and place hats on beds. Are you kidding? I wouldn't put a hat on a bed if my life depended on it!

EXERCISE 39–1, page 286

1. Of the three basic schools of detective fiction—the tea-and-crumpet, the hard-boiled detective, and the police procedural—I find the quaint, civilized quality of the tea-and-crumpet school the most appealing.
2. Correct
3. There are three points of etiquette in poker: (1) always allow someone to cut the cards, (2) don't forget to ante up, and (3) never stack your chips.
4. When he was informed that fewer than 20 percent of the panelists scheduled for the 1986 PEN conference were women, Norman Mailer gave this explanation: "There are more men who are deeply interested in intellectual matters than women. . . . [If we put more women on the panel] all we'd be doing is lowering the level of discussion."
5. Correct

EXERCISE 40–1, page 293

1. Many girls fall prey to a cult worship of great entertainers—for example, in my mother's generation, girls worshiped the Beatles.
2. Three interns were selected to assist the chief surgeon, Dr. Enrique Derenzo, in the hospital's first heart-lung transplant.
3. Correct
4. My sociology professor spends most of his lecture time talking about political science.
5. Correct

EXERCISE 41–1, page 295

1. Correct
2. Correct
3. Ninety of the firm's employees signed up for the insurance program.
4. After her fifth marriage ended in divorce, Melinda decided to give up her quest for the perfect husband.
5. With six students and two teachers, the class had a 3:1 student-teacher ratio.

EXERCISE 42–1, page 298

1. Bernard watched as Eileen stood transfixed in front of Vermeer's *Head of a Young Girl.*
2. Correct
3. I learned the Latin term *ad infinitum* from an old nursery rhyme about fleas: "Great fleas have little fleas upon their back to bite 'em,/Little fleas have lesser fleas and so on *ad infinitum.*"
4. Redford and Newman in the movie *The Sting* were amateurs compared with the seventeen-year-old con artist who lives at our house.
5. Correct

EXERCISE 44-1, page 308

1. We knew we were driving too fast when our tires skidded over the rain-slick surface.
2. The Black Death reduced the population of some medieval villages by two-thirds.
3. The flight attendant asked us to fasten our seat belts before liftoff.
4. Correct
5. Joan had been brought up to be independent and self-reliant.

EXERCISE 45-1, page 312

1. "O Liberty," cried Madame Roland from the scaffold, "what crimes are committed in thy name!"
2. Correct [*or* It]
3. Does your aunt still preach in local churches whenever she's asked?
4. Historians have described Robert E. Lee as the aristocratic South personified.
5. My brother is a doctor and my sister-in-law is an attorney.

EXERCISE 47-1, page 329

1. faulty cause-and-effect reasoning (*post hoc*)
2. *either . . . or* fallacy
3. hasty generalization
4. emotional appeal (*ad hominem*)
5. emotional appeal
6. faulty cause-and-effect reasoning
7. non sequitur
8. false analogy
9. hasty generalization
10. non sequitur

EXERCISE 57-1, page 422

1. Conservatism, worship, revolutions
2. Luck, matter, preparation, opportunity
3. Problems, opportunities, work (noun/adjective), clothes
4. woman, money, room
5. Prejudice, child, ignorance

EXERCISE 57-2, page 425

1. their (pronoun/adjective), their (pronoun/adjective)
2. Nothing, you
3. We, we, them
4. those, who, themselves
5. You, yourself, you

EXERCISE 57-3, page 427

1. Do endanger, give
2. is kept
3. Love, do pull down
4. I'd have
5. is, stabs

EXERCISE 57–4, page 429

1. Adjectives: wrong, right; adverbs: rather, strongly, weakly
2. Adjectives: Their (pronoun/adjective), civil, interesting, their (pronoun/adjective), interesting, civil; adverbs: not, not
3. Adjectives: a (article), good, the (article), its (pronoun/adjective); adverbs: pretty, not
4. Adjectives: A (article), little, a (article), dangerous, a (article), great, fatal; adverb: absolutely
5. Adjectives: An (article), old; adverb: easily

EXERCISE 58–1, page 434

1. Complete subject: The secret of being a bore; simple subject: secret
2. Complete subjects: (You), You
3. Complete subject: dogs
4. Complete subject: The wind and the waves; simple subjects: wind, waves
5. Complete subject: no signposts; simple subject: signposts

EXERCISE 58–2, page 437

1. Direct object: no color
2. Subject complement: an exercise in optimism
3. Direct object: many heads but no brains
4. Indirect object: you; direct object: a rose garden
5. Subject complement: jealousy with a halo

EXERCISE 59–1, page 441

1. to freedom (adjective phrase modifying *road*), by death (adverbial phrase modifying *has been stalked*)
2. of sheep (adjective phrase modifying *society*), of wolves (adjective phrase modifying *government*)
3. with their heads (adverbial phrase modifying *feel*), with their hearts (adverbial phrase modifying *think*)
4. In love and war (adverbial phrase modifying *is*)
5. On their side (adverbial phrase modifying *had*)

EXERCISE 59–2, page 444

1. What history teaches us (noun clause used as the subject of the sentence), that we have never learned anything from it (noun clause used as subject complement)
2. When a dog is drowning (adverbial clause modifying *offers*)
3. Whoever named it necking (noun clause used as the subject of the sentence)
4. when it adopts a creed (adverbial clause modifying *commits*)
5. that you could have poured on a waffle (adjective clause modifying *look*)

EXERCISE 59-3, page 446

1. generally raised on city land (participial phrase modifying *thing*)
2. to remove a fly from your friend's forehead (infinitive phrase modifying *Do use*)
3. returning an item for a refund (participial phrase modifying *shoplifter*)
4. turning the other cheek (gerund phrase used as object of the preposition *for*)
5. Concealing a disease (gerund phrase used as subject of the sentence), to cure it (infinitive phrase modifying *way*)

EXERCISE 60-1, page 450

1. simple
2. compound-complex; who write clearly, who write obscurely (adjective clauses)
3. simple
4. compound
5. complex; When an elephant is in trouble (adverb clause)